D1171353

# IGNORANCE

# IGNORANCE

## A GLOBAL HISTORY

PETER BURKE

YALE UNIVERSITY PRESS
NEW HAVEN AND LONDON

For information about this and other Yale University Press publications, please contact:
U.S. Office:    sales.press@yale.edu    yalebooks.com
Europe Office:    sales@yaleup.co.uk    yalebooks.co.uk

Set in Adobe Garamond Pro by IDSUK (DataConnection) Ltd
Printed in Great Britain by TJ Books, Padstow, Cornwall

Library of Congress Control Number: 2022946471

ISBN 978-0-300-26595-8

A catalogue record for this book is available from the British Library.

10 9 8 7 6 5 4 3 2 1

For the teachers of the world, heroes and heroines of the everyday attempts to remedy ignorance

*Education isn't expensive. What is expensive is ignorance*
Leonel Brizola

*Can there be a wider field . . . than a treatise on ignorance?*
Petrarch

# CONTENTS

# CONTENTS

# PLATES

1. *Intelletto umano liberato dai lacci dell'ignoranza*, by Luca Giordano, 1685. Sailko / CC BY 3.0.
2. *Trionfo sull'ignoranza*, by Sebastiano Ricci, 1706–7. Sailko/ CC BY 3.0.
3. 'Ignorance and Mercury': an allegory of virtue and vice (upper half), by the School of Andrea Mantegna, fifteenth century. Harvard Art Museums/Fogg Museum, transfer from the Fine Arts Department, Harvard University; © Photo President and Fellows of Harvard College.
4. Paolo Sarpi, by an unknown artist, *c.* 1607. Bodleian Library LP 85; © Bodleian Libraries, University of Oxford.
5. Montaigne, by Thomas de Leu, 1052–5. National Gallery of Victoria, Melbourne. Everard Studley Miller Bequest, 1961.
6. Frontispiece to Mary Astell, 'A serious proposal to the ladies: for the advancement of their true and greatest interest, by a lover of her sex'. London: Printed for R. Wilkin at the King's Head in St Paul's Church-Yard, 1694. Kn83 694a, Beinecke Rare Book and Manuscript Library, Yale University.
7. Mary Wollstonecraft, by John Opie, *c.* 1797. © National Portrait Gallery, London.
8. Mary Ritter Beard, photographer unknown, 24 July 1914/15. Women of Protest: Photographs from the Records of the National

Woman's Party, Manuscript Division, Library of Congress, Washington, D.C.

9. Frontispiece to *The English Physician* by Nicholas Culpeper, 1652. Wellcome Collection.

10. Florence Nightingale, by C.A. Tomkins, after J. Butterworth, 30 June 1855. Wellcome Collection.

11. John Snow, photographer unknown, nineteenth century. The National Library of Medicine.

12. Rosalind Franklin, photographer unknown. Heritage Image Partnership Ltd / Alamy Stock Photo.

13. Chernobyl power station.

14. Charles Minard's 1869 chart showing the number of men in Napoleon's 1812 Russian campaign army, their movements, as well as the temperature they encountered on the return path.

15. Carl von Clausewitz, by F. Michelis, 1830. Private collection / Bridgeman Images.

16. A.D. 1498. The Discovery Of America, in *An Historical Atlas; In A Series Of Maps Of The World As Known At Different Periods; Constructed Upon An Uniform Scale, And Coloured According To The Political Changes Of Each Period: Accompanied By A Narrative Of The Leading Events Exhibited In The Maps: Forming Together A General View Of Universal History, From The Creation To A.D. 1828*, by Edward Quin, London, 1828. David Rumsey Map Collection, David Rumsey Map Center, Stanford Libraries.

17. 'The South Sea Scheme', by William Hogarth, 1722. Met Museum, Harris Brisbane Dick Fund, 1932.

18. Crowds of people gather outside the New York Stock Exchange following the Crash, New York, 1929. Photograph by Pacific & Atlantic Photos, Inc., 1929. New York World-Telegram and the Sun Newspaper Photograph Collection, Library of Congress Prints and Photographs Division Washington, D.C., LC-USZ62-123429.

19. Woodrow Wilson, by Harris & Ewing, *c.* 1919. Library of Congress Prints and Photographs Division Washington, D.C., LC-USZC2-6247.

20. Activists project flames and commentary on the side of the Trump International Hotel in protest at President Donald Trump's response to science and climate change in the face of devastating wild fires burning throughout the United States on 21 October 2020 in Washington, D.C. Jemal Countess / Stringer / Getty Images.

# PREFACE AND ACKNOWLEDGEMENTS

Ignorance, defined as an absence of knowledge, may not sound like a topic at all – a friend of mine imagined that a book on the subject would contain nothing but blank pages. Nonetheless, the subject is evoking increasing interest, stimulated by spectacular examples of the ignorance of presidents Trump and Bolsonaro, to say nothing of other governments.[1]

In fact, the multidisciplinary enterprise known as 'ignorance studies' has been gathering force in the last thirty years, as chapter four will explain, even though historians were rarely involved in it until quite recently. It seems time for an overview of the role of ignorance (including active ignoring) in the past. I have come to believe that this role has been underrated, leading to misunderstanding, misjudgement and other kinds of mistake, often with disastrous consequences. The point is particularly obvious at a moment when the responses of governments to climate change are too little and too late, but as I hope to show, both the kinds of ignorance and the kinds of disaster that follow them are many and various.

I have written this book for two kinds of people. In the first place, for general readers. Since every individual is a unique combination of knowledge and ignorance, or as I prefer to say, knowledges and ignorances, the topic is surely of general interest. In the second place, I have written for other scholars – not only workers in my own field but also practitioners in all the disciplines where ignorance is now studied. I hope and expect that this attempt to present a 'big picture' of what has been and what might be done will encourage some younger scholars to enter what is not yet a 'field' – and, of course to criticize, qualify and refine my provisional conclusions.

A future history of ignorance might be organized in traditional fashion as a narrative that is organized century by century. Such a narrative would depend on the identification of general trends that were common to different fields. If this book encourages future studies of this kind, I shall be more than happy. At the moment, given current ignorance of the history of ignorance, it is more realistic to organize a general study as a series of essays on particular topics.

What follows concentrates, like my earlier studies of knowledge, on the West in the last five hundred years, despite offering a number of examples from Asia and Africa. Such a concentration is open to criticism on two opposite grounds. On one side, for not taking into account the rest of the world and earlier centuries. On the other, for going beyond the limits of my own research on Europe from 1500 to 1800.

I hope to persuade readers that in this situation, as in many other conflicts, there is a case for compromise. My reason for saying little or nothing about earlier periods and many parts of the globe is a simple one. 'Ignorance, Madam, pure ignorance,' as Dr Johnson once explained to a lady who pointed out a mistake in one of his books. On the other hand, I firmly believe that comparisons and contrasts between early modern Europe and the late modern world offer insights. I have been fortified in this belief by the example of Françoise Waquet, who has published several books on knowledge, each of them concerned with the last five hundred years.[2]

The long view reveals that practices often taken to be recent, such as leaking and disinformation, actually go back for centuries. It also calls attention to gradual, almost imperceptible changes in what was not known which do not respect the division between 'early modern' (before 1800) and 'late modern'. Each chapter of this book will therefore discuss examples from both sides of that divide.

The overview presented here is best seen as a prologue to a future history, a reconnaissance of a terrain in which many spaces are blank.

The idea of a map of the unknown may seem to be a contradiction. All the same, like some colleagues in history and the social sciences, I believe it to be a viable project. Critics may call the attempt 'premature'. I would reply that a reconnaissance of this kind is particularly useful at the beginning of interest in the history of ignorance. Looking to the future, I hope to encourage and orient potential authors of future studies by offering hypotheses for them to test and encouraging them to place their research within a bigger picture. The deep digging of the specialist and the bird's-eye view of the generalist each stimulate and depend on the other.

As in the case of my earlier books, friends and colleagues have been a great help, diminishing my ignorance of ignorance(s) by their general advice, commenting on drafts, suggesting gaps to be filled and references to follow up. Warmest thanks to Richard Drayton, Tim Harris, Julian Hoppit, Joe McDermott, Alan Macfarlane, Juan Maiguashca, David Maxwell, Anne Ploin, James Raven, David Reynolds, Jake Soll, Kajsa Weber, Iro Zoumbopoulos and Ghil'ad Zuckermann. I am particularly grateful to Geoffrey Lloyd for sharing his expertise on ancient Greece and China, and also to two anonymous reviewers for their constructive comments. Special thanks also to Cao Yijing for suggesting that I choose ignorance as the topic of the Gombrich Lectures, originally scheduled for 2002 but not yet delivered; to Lukas Verburgt, fellow worker in the 'field' of ignorance, for our many exchanges on the subject, as well as for reading the whole text in draft; and, once again, to my wife Maria Lúcia for references as well as for her acute comments on the draft.

# PART I

# IGNORANCE IN SOCIETY

# 1

# WHAT IS IGNORANCE?

Ignorance is a social creation, like knowledge

Michael Smithson

The project of writing a history of ignorance sounds almost as odd as Flaubert's wish to write a book about nothing, *un livre sur rien*, 'a book dependent on nothing external . . . a book which would have almost no subject, or at least in which the subject would be almost invisible', in other words an attempt at pure form.[1] Appropriately enough, Flaubert wrote nothing about nothing. In contrast, much has been written about ignorance, mainly negative. There is a long tradition of denouncing ignorance for different motives and reasons.

## DENOUNCING IGNORANCE

Arabic speakers talk of the pre-Islamic period as the 'Age of Ignorance' (*al-Jahiliyya*). During the Renaissance, the humanists viewed what they were the first to call the 'Middle Ages' as an age of darkness. In the seventeenth century, Lord Clarendon, the historian of the English Civil War, described the Fathers of the Church as 'great Lights which appeared in very dark Times', 'Times of so much Barbarity and Ignorance'.[2] During the Enlightenment, ignorance was presented as a support for 'despotism', 'fanaticism' and 'superstition', all of which would be swept away in an age of knowledge and reason. George Washington, for instance, declared that 'the foundation of our empire was not laid in the gloomy age of Ignorance and Superstition'.[3]

Views of this kind continued to be current much later. For example, the term *al-Jahiliyya* was applied to more recent periods by radical Muslims such as the Egyptian intellectual Sayyid Qutb, targeting the United States in particular.[4] Ignorance was one of the 'five giants' that the liberal politician William Beveridge promised to slay (along with Poverty, Disease, Squalor and Idleness). Beveridge's report served as the foundation of the British Welfare State by the Labour government of 1945.[5]

More recently, in the USA, Charles Simic has written that 'Widespread ignorance bordering on idiocy is our new national goal', while Robert Proctor, a historian of science, has declared our own time to be a 'golden age of ignorance'.[6] Although we are well aware that we know much that earlier generations did not, we are much less conscious of what they knew that we do not. Examples of this loss of knowledge – to be discussed later – range from familiarity with the Greek and Roman classics to the everyday knowledge of natural history.

In the past, a major reason for the ignorance of individuals was the fact that too little information was circulating in their society. Some knowledge was what the historian Martin Mulsow calls 'precarious', recorded only in manuscript and hidden away because the authorities in both church and state rejected it.[7] Today, paradoxically enough, abundance has become a problem, known as 'information overload'. Individuals experience a 'deluge' of information and are often unable to select what they want or need, a condition that is also known as 'filter failure'. In consequence, our so-called 'information age' 'enables the spread of ignorance just as much as the spread of knowledge'.[8]

## PRAISING IGNORANCE

Responding to the tradition of denouncing ignorance we find a counter-tradition: a relatively small number of thinkers and writers who have dared to suggest that enthusiasm for knowledge ('epistemophilia') has its dangers while ignorance is bliss, or at least possesses a few advantages. Some of these writers, in Renaissance Italy in particular, were playful, praising ignorance along with baldness, figs, flies, sausages and thistles in order to show off their ingenuity and their rhetorical skills by reviving the classical tradition of the mock-encomium.

More seriously, a long tradition, from Augustine onwards, has criticized 'vain' curiosity, implying that a certain kind of ignorance is a wiser option. Early modern clergy, whether Catholic or Protestant, were generally hostile to curiosity, 'treating it as a sin, usually venial but sometimes mortal'.[9] It has been presented as mortal in the legend of Faust, which has inspired plays, operas and novels.[10] When Kant used the phrase 'Dare to Know' (*Sapere Aude*) as the motto of the Enlightenment, he was reacting against the biblical recommendation, 'Do not wish to know higher things, but fear them' (*Noli altum sapere sed time*), paraphrased by the poet Alexander Pope as 'presume not God to scan'.[11]

Some secular arguments complemented the religious ones. Michel de Montaigne suggested that ignorance was a better recipe for happiness than curiosity. The philosopher-naturalist Henry Thoreau wished to found a Society for the Diffusion of Useful Ignorance as a complementary opposite to the already-existing Society for the Diffusion of Useful Knowledge.[12] In his *Studies of Nature* (1784), Bernardin de Saint-Pierre, novelist and botanist, praised ignorance because it stimulated the imagination.[13] Swimming against the stream of histories published during the Enlightenment, the French feminist Olympe de Gouges argued in *Le Bonheur primitif* (1789) that 'the first men' were happy because they were ignorant, while in her time 'man has extended his knowledge too far'.[14]

In the case of the law, Justice has often been represented from the Renaissance onwards as blindfolded, symbolizing ignorance in the sense of open-mindedness and lack of prejudice.[15] In accordance with this view, juries may be isolated in order to keep them away from information that might bias their verdict. Discussions of what is called 'virtuous ignorance' are becoming increasingly frequent. The philosopher John Rawls argued in favour of what he called 'the veil of ignorance', a blindness to race, class, nation or gender that helps us to see individuals as morally equal beings.[16]

'Virtuous' ignorance is a term that has been used to describe the renunciation of research on nuclear weapons, for instance, or at least the making public of the results. Other positive features of different kinds of ignorance have been emphasized by sociologists and anthropologists, writing about their various 'social functions' or 'regimes'. Priests, for instance, are bound to keep the secrets of the confessional, while doctors swear to respect the privacy of their patients. Democracy is protected by the secrecy of ballots. Anonymity allows examiners to mark papers without prejudice and participants in peer review to say exactly what they think about the work of their colleagues. Secret negotiations allow governments to make concessions to the other side that would be impossible in the glare of publicity. Information produces not only benefits but also hazards.[17]

By the end of the nineteenth century, ignorance was recommended as an answer to the increasingly acute problem of 'too much to know'. For example, the American neurologist George Beard claimed that 'ignorance is power as well as joy', a remedy for 'nervousness'.[18] Ignorance has been treated as a 'resource' or a 'factor in success' by writers on business and management.

Anthony Tjan, for instance, recommends 'embracing one's ignorance', since entrepreneurs who are 'unaware of their constraints and external realities' are likely to 'generate ideas freely'. Later and more cautiously, he explained that 'The key is recognizing the critical moments in a company's trajectory when a clean-sheet approach is a net positive'. The phrase 'creative ignorance' implies a recognition that too much knowledge may inhibit innovation, not only in business but in other domains as well.[19] The phrase 'creative ignorance' was coined by a writer in the *New Yorker* to refer to what prevented Beardsley Ruml, director of a major research foundation, 'from seeing the No Thoroughfare, Keep Off the Grass, Don't Trespass, and Dead End Street signs in the world of ideas', warnings that acted as obstacles to the interdisciplinarity that he favoured. At a more practical level, Henry Ford is said to have remarked that 'I am looking for a lot of people who have an infinite capacity to not know what can't be done'.[20]

The claim that ignorance has its uses leads to insights, at least if we are careful to ask, Useful for whom? Nevertheless, the examples discussed in this book suggest that the negative consequences of ignorance generally outweigh the positive ones – hence the dedication of this book to the teachers who have tried to remedy the ignorance of their pupils. The desire not to know (or for other people not to know) whatever threatens or embarrasses us, whether at an individual level or the level of an organization, is an understandable one, but its consequences are often negative, at least for other people. Ignoring or denying awkward facts will be a recurrent theme of this book.

## WHAT IS IGNORANCE?

In the long debate for and against ignorance, different positions obviously depend on what their holders have meant by the term. The traditional definition is a simple one, the absence or 'deprivation' of knowledge.[21] Such an absence or deprivation is often invisible to the ignorant individual or group, a form of blindness that has massive consequences, including the disasters that will be discussed in part two.

The traditional definition is sometimes criticized as too broad, requiring distinctions. In English, for instance, 'ignorance' is sometimes distinguished from 'nescience' and both from 'non-knowledge'. There is also 'unknowing', a term that looks as if it was coined yesterday, but goes back to the anonymous fourteenth-century author of a treatise on mysticism.[22] Similar distinctions exist in other languages. Germans, for instance, speak and write of *Unwissen* and *Nicht-Wissen*. For example, the sociologist Georg Simmel discussed what he called 'the everyday normality of non-knowledge' (*Nicht-Wissen*).[23] Unfortunately, different authors use these terms in different ways.[24]

What is generally agreed, on the other hand, is the need to distinguish between 'known unknowns', such as the structure of DNA before its discovery in 1953, and 'unknown unknowns' as in the case of Columbus discovering America while looking for the 'Indies'. Although this distinction was made earlier by engineers and psychologists, it is often attributed to the former US secretary of defense, Donald Rumsfeld.

At a press conference about preparations for the invasion of Iraq Rumsfeld was asked for evidence of Saddam Hussein's weapons of mass destruction and replied as follows:

> Reports that say that something hasn't happened are always interesting to me, because as we know, there are known knowns; there are things we know we know. We also know there are known unknowns; that is to say we know there are some things we do not know. But there are also unknown unknowns—the ones we don't know we don't know. And if one looks throughout the history of our country and other free countries, it is the latter category that tend to be the difficult ones.[25]

Irrespective of its use by Rumsfeld to avoid an awkward question, the distinction between known knowns, known unknowns and unknown unknowns remains a useful one.

## THE PSYCHOLOGY OF IGNORANCE

What about 'unknown knowns'? This phrase, which seems appropriate for discussing what is normally described as 'tacit knowledge', has been employed in a rather different sense by the philosopher Slavoj Žižek, who pointed out that Rumsfeld 'forgot to add . . . the crucial fourth term: "the unknown knowns" . . . the Freudian unconscious, "the knowledge which doesn't know itself", as Lacan used to say', including Rumsfeld's own knowledge of the tortures at Abu Ghraib.[26]

Freud was interested in other kinds of unconscious ignorance. In his famous discussion of the interpretation of dreams, he asked whether or not dreamers know what their dreams mean, concluding that 'it is quite possible, and indeed highly probable, that the dreamer *does* know what his dream means: *only he does not know that he knows it.*'[27] More generally, Freud was interested in what his patients did not want to know about themselves. Not wanting to know will be a recurrent theme in this book.

A particular interest in ignorance was shown by the unorthodox Freudian Jacques Lacan. He described psychoanalysts as the people who don't know what psychoanalysis is (and know that they don't know this), as opposed to the people who think they know but don't. Lacan regarded ignorance as a passion, like love and hate, suggesting that some patients move from resisting self-knowledge to developing a passion for it.[28]

## THE SOCIOLOGY OF IGNORANCE

'If there is a sociology of knowledge, then there should also be a sociology of ignorance.'[29] Such a sociology might begin with the question, Who does not know What? It is worth remembering that 'we are all ignorant, just about different things', as the American humorist Mark Twain remarked in one of his numerous epigrams on this subject. For example, there are about six thousand languages spoken in the world today, and even polyglots are ignorant of 99.9 per cent of them. Again, the spread of the Coronavirus was predicted by epidemiologists who had discovered the danger of the transfer of different diseases from wild animals to humans. On the other hand, governments either did not know or did not want to know about this prediction, so they were caught unprepared.

Many disasters, some of which will be discussed in later chapters, have occurred because those who knew could not act while those who acted did not know. The destruction of the World Trade Center in 2001 offers a dramatic example of failure in communication. Agents in the security services already suspected certain individuals of planning a terrorist attack, but their warnings were lost among the many messages sent to upper levels in Washington in a striking example of 'information overload'. As the national security adviser Condoleezza Rice admitted later, 'There was a lot of chatter in the system.'[30]

## VARIETIES OF IGNORANCE

Discussions of ignorance need to distinguish between its many varieties, 'ignorances' in the plural, in parallel to 'knowledges'.[31] One famous distinction contrasts knowing how to do something from knowing that something is the case, 'knowing how' from 'knowing that'.[32] The consequences of particular lacks of knowhow will be discussed on many occasions below. Another distinction is well known in French, German and other languages:

the contrast between *savoir* and *connaître*, *wissen* and *kennen*, where the terms *connaître* and *kennen* refer to knowledge gained from personal acquaintance – knowing one's London, for instance, as opposed to knowing that a city called London exists. Each form of knowledge has a form of ignorance as its complementary opposite.

A British sociologist who specializes on ignorance, Linsey McGoey, has complained that when she began research on the subject early in the present century, she found an 'impoverished language' to describe unknowns.[33] This is hardly the case today, when glut rather than scarcity is the problem. Many new varieties have been labelled and an elaborate taxonomy created, using a variety of adjectives from 'active' to 'wilful' (the glossary at the end of this book lists two more than Heinz's 57 varieties but makes no claim to be complete). Indeed, there are considerably more adjectives than the varieties they describe, a kind of re-invention of the wheel resulting from academic specialization, since individuals in one discipline are often ignorant of discoveries in another.

Some distinctions are useful and will be employed in what follows. An obvious example contrasts ignorance of the existence of something from ignorance of its explanation. Epidemics and earthquakes have long been known, but no one knew what caused them until relatively recently. 'Sanctioned' ignorance, a coinage of the philosopher-critic Gayatri Chakravorty Spivak, refers to a situation in which one group, such as Western intellectuals, feels entitled to remain ignorant of other cultures while expecting individuals from other cultures to know about them.[34]

Ignorance (like knowledge) is sometimes feigned, a theme developed in chapter eight. Governments may deny genocide while knowing about the massacres that they have either ordered or permitted. For a long time, ordinary Sicilians pretended to know nothing about the Mafia. In Victorian England, ladies might show their modesty by claiming to be ignorant of sexual practices, just as gentlemen might feign ignorance of the world of trade. Female modesty might also require false claims to lack other kinds of knowledge, of Latin, for instance, politics or the natural sciences (apart from botany). Hence the narrator of Jane Austen's *Northanger Abbey* remarks that a woman, 'if she have the misfortune of knowing any thing [*sic*], should conceal it as well as she can'.[35]

Another useful distinction is between conscious and unconscious ignorance, where the term 'unconscious' is used to mean 'unaware' rather than in the Freudian sense discussed earlier. The term 'deep' ignorance has been employed to refer to a lack of awareness of certain questions, including a lack of the concepts necessary for posing these questions.[36] The French historian Lucien Febvre made a similar point nearly eighty years earlier, pointing to some 'missing words' in sixteenth-century French. According to Febvre, this lack inhibited the development of philosophy at that time and so made it impossible to be an atheist.[37]

Another example of deep ignorance is the common lack of awareness of alternative modes of thought to one's own. Circularity is central here. A mode of thought persists because it is taken for granted, taken to be natural, whether at the micro-level of what Thomas Kuhn has called a scientific 'paradigm' or at the macro-level of a complete belief system. When we attempt to criticize our own norms, the limits of self-criticism become apparent.[38]

Historians have often treated individuals and groups in the past as 'credulous', in other words as incapable of criticizing their beliefs. In so doing they ignore the lack of access by these individuals and groups to alternative belief systems. In a closed system, it is difficult to keep an open mind.[39] It is difficult if not impossible to challenge it without some awareness of alternatives, which usually comes about as the result of encounters between individuals from different cultures, widening the horizon of expectations for both sides.[40]

The ostrich with its head in the sand is a famous symbol of not wanting to know or wanting not to know, also described as voluntary, wilful or resolute ignorance.[41] The idea may be extended to include deliberate omissions or silences. For example, the Haitian historian Michel-Rolph Trouillot distinguished four moments in the production of knowledge of the past in which individuals choose between communicating particular items of information and keeping silent about them. The four moments are those of producing documents, storing them in archives, retrieving the information and making use of it in a written history.[42]

For an example of the opposite quality, involuntary ignorance, we might turn to Catholic theology. Medieval theologians such as Thomas Aquinas used the phrase 'invincible ignorance' to refer to pagans (Aristotle, for instance), who were unaware of the existence of Christianity and so could not be blamed for their failure to accept it. On the other hand, if they were aware, they would be guilty of 'culpable' ignorance.

Culpable ignorance may be individual or collective. Social historians are particularly concerned with the latter, with 'white ignorance', for example, a phrase coined by the Jamaican philosopher Charles W. Mills to refer to the prejudices underlying racism. Collective ignorance supports the rule of one group over another by encouraging them to accept their situation as natural. The ignorance of the dominant keeps them from questioning their privileges, while the ignorance of the dominated has often kept them from rebellion. Hence the efforts of those in power, as Diderot remarked, 'to keep the people in a state of ignorance and stupidity'.[43]

What is now known as 'selective' ignorance was noted a century ago by the biographer Lytton Strachey in his customary teasing manner, claiming that 'ignorance is the first requisite of the historian, ignorance which simplifies and clarifies, which selects and omits'.[44] Selection may be unconscious, a form of inattention, as an informal experiment shows. If we watch a film with the sound turned off, we notice gestures and facial expressions of the actors that we normally ignore.

In similar fashion, different kinds of traveller notice different features of the same place because their 'gazes' differ according to their gender or profession. The reliability of observations by travellers, their knowledge or ignorance of the places that they have visited, is an old problem, but one that has only recently been viewed from the angle of gender, suggesting that female travellers notice different things from their male counterparts.[45] The prominence of domestic settings in female travelogues has been described as a different mode of 'constituting knowledge'.[46]

What women have seen and chosen to record tells us something important about what men chose to ignore or were simply unable to see. A famous example from the eighteenth century is the description of a bathhouse for women in Edirne (Adrianople), by the English traveller Lady Mary Wortley Montagu, since, as she remarked, ''Tis no less than Death for a Man to be found in one of these places'.[47] The multiplicity of gazes – imperial, ethnographic, medical, mercantile, missionary and so on – suggests that we should speak not only of 'teaching the eye to see' but also of its opposite, 'teaching the eye not to see'. Both insight and blindness are embodied in the habitus of particular professions.

In research, looking for one thing leads to inattention to others. A recent example comes from the doctors who were focusing on detecting Covid and for this reason, missed signs of other dangerous diseases.[48] Selective ignorance includes what the American sociologist Robert K. Merton called 'specified' ignorance, in other words a conscious turning away from knowledge on one topic in order to concentrate on another: choosing to raise certain questions, adopt certain methods or operate with certain paradigms.[49] In each case, a positive choice has some negative effects, excluding certain kinds of knowledge, whether deliberately or as an unintended consequence. In the case of twentieth-century historians, for instance, their shifts of interest from political to economic, social and cultural history each involved exclusions as well as inclusions, generational shifts in what was known or not known about the past.

Ignorance may also be described as either active or passive. 'Passive ignorance' refers to the absence of knowledge, including the failure to mobilize it for the purpose of action. The term 'active' ignorance, in the sense of resistance to new knowledge or ideas, was coined by the Austrian philosopher Karl Popper and employed to describe the opposition of some physicists to the disturbing views of Albert Einstein.[50] It may be extended to the habit of 'ignoring' whatever we do not want to know, often with serious consequences.

Think, for instance, of the history of British settlers in North America, Australia and New Zealand, who attempted to ignore the existence of the peoples who were already living in these regions, or at least the claims that these groups might have to the territory. The settlers treated the land as if it was empty or owned by no one (below, chapter eight). In similar fashion, the Balfour Declaration of 1917, which made Palestine the 'national home' for the Jewish people, ignored the Arabs who were already there, thus creating problems that remain unsolved more than a century later. Lord Curzon's question, 'What is to become of the people of the country?', remains unanswered.[51]

The phrase 'active ignorance' may also refer to what we think we know. As Will Rogers, an American humorist in the tradition of Mark Twain, used to say, 'Ignorance lies not in the things you don't know, but in the things you know that ain't so' (a remark that is also attributed to Twain himself).[52]

Phrases such as the 'production' or 'fabrication' of ignorance are particularly applicable here, together with the adjective 'strategic' ignorance. I must admit that I am not entirely happy with references to the 'production' of ignorance in cases where no knowledge preceded it. I prefer to use the old term 'obfuscation', or to speak of producing 'confusion' or 'doubt', or of maintaining ignorance, or creating obstacles to knowledge (the equivalent of the physical obstacles discussed in chapter five). At the price of sacrificing attention-grabbing phrases, it makes for more clarity to remain close to ordinary language wherever possible, describing attempts to deceive the public for political or economic reasons as simple 'lies'. I do, though, heartily agree that it has long been and still remains an all-too-common practice to cover up much that the public ought to know. This practice is also described as 'disinformation' or, euphemistically, as 'active measures', while the study of these measures has been christened 'agnotology'.[53]

The ignorance of other people is a source of power for those who are 'in the know', in domains such as politics, business and crime. A study of Marseilles in the French Revolution has argued that 'control of the definition of ignorance' by elites had major political implications, signifying what the author called 'the ability to brand others as ignorant and thereby disqualify them from a voice in the affairs of the city'.[54] The claim that men keep women ignorant in order to dominate them will be discussed in the following chapter.

## IGNORANCE AND ITS NEIGHBOURS

So far the discussion has concentrated on three major topics: not knowing something, not wanting to know something, and not wanting other people to know something. However, it is surely impossible to write a history of these topics without introducing concepts that are connected with them. Error, for instance, is the result of ignorance but also brings its own consequences, sometimes tragic, as the chapters on war and business will show.

To solve the problem of representing ignorance in art, some painters assimilated it to blindness or to folly. In the fifteenth century, the painter Andrea Mantegna, for example, showed ignorance as a naked woman without eyes. In the sixteenth century, in his dictionary of images, Cesare Ripa suggested representing ignorance and its dangers as a woman blindfold and walking in a field of thorns, or alternatively as a boy, also blindfold, riding an ass. In the eighteenth century, the Venetian artist Sebastiano Ricci personified ignorance as a man with ass's ears, once again illustrating the common assimilation of ignorance to stupidity.[55]

Today, the idea of ignorance is often employed as an intellectual umbrella that covers neighbouring ideas such as uncertainty, denial and even confusion. Given the dimensions of the subject, already large enough, I have opted for a relatively narrow definition of ignorance as absence. However, that choice does not mean a refusal to look beyond the definition. Like the German historians who study what they call 'conceptual history' (*Begriffsgeschichte*), I shall try to reconstruct a network of related ideas, centred on ignorance and including obstacles, forgetting, secrecy, denial, uncertainty, prejudice, misunderstanding and credulity.[56] Showing connections between this web of concepts and the phenomena to which they refer is a major aim of this study.

Obstacles to knowledge may be physical, including the inaccessibility of the object of knowledge (discussed in chapter five in the case of Europeans in Africa). They may also be mental, in the sense that old ideas that are not questioned stand in the way of accepting new ones. The cases of resistance to the ideas of Galileo and Darwin (among others) will be discussed in chapter four. Intellectual models or paradigms cast light, but since they simplify, they also have a dark side, getting in the way of whatever does not fit the model.[57] Obstacles may also be social – think of the former exclusion of women and the working class from higher education – or political, as in the case of cover-ups by governments.

The concept of forgetting, the move from knowledge back to ignorance, includes its metaphorical sense. The terms social, structural or corporate 'amnesia' refer to the conscious or unconscious remaking the past in the image of the present, as well as the loss of information to an organization.[58] Scholars also need to be aware of a tendency to what Robert Merton described as 'citation amnesia', a failure to refer to predecessors in their field.[59] In a cynical mood, I have sometimes thought that even the most conscientious scholars, happily acknowledging minor debts, sometimes forget to cite the predecessor to whom they owe most.

Secrecy too is obviously relevant to the topic of ignorance, since a secret involves not only a small group who are 'in the know' but also a larger group who are kept in ignorance, 'out of the loop'. Clandestine activities such as smuggling, drug-dealing and money laundering shelter under this umbrella and will be discussed in chapter ten. Denial is part of an arsenal of methods for keeping the public ignorant of embarrassing facts or events. Its history, especially its recent history, is all too familiar – denial of the Holocaust and other attempts at genocide, denial of the link between smoking and lung cancer, denial of climate change.[60]

What makes denial effective, like other forms of propaganda, is credulity, which might be defined as ignorance of both the importance and the techniques of criticism, especially the criticism of 'fake news' transmitted in a variety of media – rumour, newspapers, television, and more recently Facebook and Twitter. Credulity flourishes in situations of uncertainty. Uncertainty is the fate of all decision-makers, since we are all ignorant of the future. However, measures may be taken to prepare for it, thanks to risk analysis and other forms of forecasting, discussed in chapter fourteen. As for prejudice, it may be defined as a judgement made in ignorance, a classic case of not knowing that one does not know. Examples will recur throughout this book.

Misunderstanding depends on ignorance, and, like ignorance, it has played a large and insufficiently recognized role in human history.[61] Misunderstandings become particularly visible when members of one culture encounter members of another for the first time. A well-known example of that kind of situation is the encounter with the Hawaiians by Captain Cook and his crew in 1779, a meeting analysed in an essay by a leading American anthropologist, Marshall Sahlins. The Hawaiians had never seen Europeans before and vice versa. Each side discovered the other and tried to interpret their actions. Sahlins suggests, for instance, that since Cook had arrived at the time of the festival of their god Lono, the Hawaiians regarded him as an incarnation of the god. When the British undermined this interpretation by making an unexpected return, Cook was killed.[62]

As this chapter has suggested, ignorance is a more complex concept than it may appear at first sight. It is no wonder then that philosophers in different parts of the world have had a good deal to say about it. The views of some of them are the subject of the following chapter.

# 2

# PHILOSOPHERS ON IGNORANCE

Que sais-je?

Montaigne

Philosophers were the first to discuss ignorance, beginning more than 2,500 years ago. In ancient China, the collected sayings attributed to Kong Fuzi, known in the West as 'Confucius', include the following passage: 'Shall I tell you what knowledge is? It is to know both what one knows and what one does not know.'[1] In similar fashion, the classic of philosophical Taoism, 'The Book of the Way' (*Daodejing*), attributed to the 'Old Master', Laozi, includes the statement that 'To know what is not knowledge is the better part'. This passage has sometimes been interpreted as meaning that whatever can be said will necessarily miss the point. Since the 'Deep Way' is mysterious, attempts to describe it are no more than 'empty words'.[2]

For that reason, another famous Daoist text, attributed to Zhuangzi, approached the Way indirectly via a series of anecdotes such as the following. 'Nieh Ch'üeh asked Wang Ni, "Do you know what all things agree in calling right?" "How would I know that?" said Wang Ni. "Do you know that you don't know it?" "How would I know that?"'[3]

In ancient Greece, Socrates moved in a similar direction. According to his disciple Plato, Socrates claimed to be wiser than a man who 'thinks he knows something, when he does not', since Socrates himself does not 'think I know what I do not know'. In Plato's dialogues, Socrates revels in making other people (Menon, for instance) increasingly aware that they knew less than they had thought.[4] In a later source, Socrates is quoted as making the stronger claim that he 'knew nothing except just the fact of his ignorance'. Was this a genuine belief or a rhetorical device? Scholars continue to disagree.[5]

Socrates began what has been described as an 'epistemological turn' in Greek philosophy. Epistemology is a branch of philosophy concerned with how we acquire knowledge and know that it is reliable. Its opposite number, the epistemology of ignorance, is concerned with how and why we remain ignorant. These problems were discussed by Greek philosophers, in particular by the school of the Sceptics, notably Pyrrho of Elis. As in the case of Socrates, Pyrrho's opinions are only known from a late source, the *Outlines of Pyrrhonism* by Sextus Empiricus (*c.* 160–*c.* 210 CE).[6]

The school of the Sceptics went further than Socrates, questioning the reliability of different kinds of knowledge and making a method out of the distrust of appearances. Sceptics pointed out that 'the same impressions are not produced' on different people 'by the same objects', as in the case of an individual with jaundice who sees the world as yellow. They also noted that the same object looks different to everyone in different circumstances. An oar, for instance, appears to be bent when it is in the water but straight when it is pulled out.[7]

The sceptics did believe in 'investigation' (the original meaning of the term *skepsis*), in other words examining the case for and against a given belief and suspending judgement until knowledge had been attained.[8] To be more precise, there were two kinds of sceptic, the 'dogmatic' sceptic, who is sure that nothing can be known, and the 'reflexive' sceptic, who is not even sure of that.

Although a few medieval texts exist that 'complicate, problematize or refuse knowledge', the tradition of Greek scepticism was lost during the Middle Ages.[9] Classical scepticism resurfaced in the European Renaissance, when the text of the *Outlines of Pyrrhonism* was rediscovered. This rediscovery came at the right moment, the moment of what the philosopher-historian Richard Popkin called 'the intellectual crisis of the Reformation'. His point was that both Catholics and Protestants were more successful in their negative arguments than in their positive ones. The Protestants undermined the authority of tradition while the Catholics undermined the authority of the Bible.[10] What was left?

The most famous sceptic of the Renaissance, and 'the most significant figure in the sixteenth-century revival of ancient scepticism', was Michel de Montaigne, who experienced the wars between Catholics and Protestants at first hand when he was mayor of Bordeaux. Montaigne took as his personal motto the question, 'What do I know?' He was not alone. His follower, Pierre Charron, adopted the motto, 'I don't know', while a professor of philosophy at the University of Toulouse, Francisco Sanches, published a book arguing 'That Nothing is Known' (*Quod Nihil Scitur*). Charron and Sanches sound like 'dogmatic' sceptics, sure that nothing can be known. In contrast, Montaigne's motto suggests that he was a 'reflexive' sceptic, extending his scepticism to scepticism itself.[11]

In his *Discourse on Method* (1637), Descartes replied to Montaigne without naming him, practising what has been called a 'methodological ignorance' in order to move from doubt to certainty.[12] Nevertheless the tradition of doubt was continued by a number of French sceptics, notably François La Mothe Le Vayer, who 'inherited the mantle of Montaigne' and Pierre Bayle, the 'supersceptic'. The famous article on 'Pyrrho' in Bayle's *Historical and Critical Dictionary* (1697) presented the case both for and against scepticism, thus leaving readers as well as beliefs in suspense.[13]

Seventeenth-century scepticism might be regarded as a philosophical expression of a more general awareness of the gap between appearances and reality, an awareness that was central to the world-view of the 'age of the baroque'.[14] The famous play, 'Life is a Dream' (*La vida es sueño*, 1636) by the Spanish dramatist Pedro Calderón offers a dramatic illustration of the famous sceptical argument about the difficulty of distinguishing between dreaming and waking.

Two leading eighteenth-century philosophers, George Berkeley and David Hume, shared the seventeenth-century preoccupation with the problem of knowledge. In contrast, nineteenth-century philosophers tended to ignore ignorance, with the important exception of the Scotsman James Ferrier, the author of *Institutes of Metaphysic* (1854). It was Ferrier who coined the term 'agnoiology' to refer to the theory of ignorance (he also introduced the term 'epistemology' into English to refer to the theory of knowledge).[15]

A wider interest in ignorance was developing in Ferrier's time. Thomas Carlyle, for instance, described ignorance as 'the real privation of the poor' and emphasized the 'wide universe of Nescience', compared to mankind's 'miserable fraction of science'.[16] Karl Marx discussed social obstacles to knowledge, including the class interests of the bourgeoisie and the 'false consciousness' of members of the working class. A generation later, Freud discussed a psychological obstacle, the unconscious rejection of knowledge, including the tendency to forget embarrassing events.[17] The 'citation amnesia' mentioned earlier offers an example of what might be called 'the psychopathology of scholarly life'.

## SOCIAL EPISTEMOLOGY

In the 1980s, some philosophers made a social turn that led them to study knowledge and ignorance in a different way. Traditional epistemology had focused on the ways in which individuals acquire knowledge. In contrast, social epistemology focuses on 'cognitive' communities such as schools, universities, firms, churches and departments of government.[18]

As for the epistemology of ignorance, its programme has been defined as 'identifying different forms of ignorance, examining how they are produced and sustained, and what role they play in knowledge practices'.[19] In practice, the programme has focused on the ignorance imputed to genders, races and classes. There is an obvious social explanation for this focus. The influx into the academic arena of women, Black people and members of the working class, first as students and later as teachers and scholars, made them particularly aware of the ignorances and biases of the white middle-class males who once monopolized positions in this domain. It is time to look more closely at collective forms of ignorance.

# 3

## COLLECTIVE IGNORANCE

At some point we will have to elaborate the concept of
masculinist unknowing

Michèle Le Dœuff

In the previous chapters, the emphasis fell on the ignorances of individuals. In this one, I foreground the ignorances shared by cognitive communities, both large and small: organizations, social classes, races and genders.

### ORGANIZATIONAL IGNORANCE

The phrase 'organizational ignorance' has been coined to refer to the lack of knowledge sharing within a given organization.[1] This lack is sometimes an asset, at least in the case of clandestine organizations such as al-Qaeda, divided into 'cells', each of which is ignorant of the membership and activities of the others, so that the information that any one member might disclose under interrogation is strictly limited.

More often, though, organizational ignorance is a liability. For example, what is known on the shop floor may not be known by managers or CEOs. Employees who have worked in the same place for a long time acquire a store of implicit knowledge that may be lost when they retire or move elsewhere because they were not encouraged to share it. The loss of knowledge by failure to communicate within an organization is sometimes described as 'corporate amnesia'.[2]

A classic analysis of organizations by the French sociologist Michel Crozier concluded that 'A bureaucratic organization . . . is composed of a series of superimposed strata that do not communicate very much with each other.' At the clerical agency that Crozier studied, one of the female clerks told the investigator that the supervisors 'are too far above the actual work programme to understand what is actually going on'. The centralization of power in the organization produces a 'blind spot'. 'Those who have the necessary information do not have the power to decide, and those who have the power to decide cannot get the necessary information.'[3]

Failure to move information sideways also presents problems. The lack of communication between different departments of government is an obvious example. In early modern Europe, government finance was fragmented. Suppose that you were granted a pension by the king. That expenditure would be linked to a specific source of royal income. If, in a given year, that source failed to produce enough money, your pension would not be paid, even if the king's revenue was in surplus – since no one knew whether there was a surplus or not, no one saw the big picture.

A memorable example of a disaster caused by organizational ignorance is the explosion at Chernobyl in 1986. The engineers and the manager of the power plant were well aware of the dangerous situation. However, they took orders from officials in the Communist Party who imposed deadlines and quotas that were impossible to meet without cutting corners. The officials wanted certain results. They either did not know or did not want to know about the risks that were being taken in order to achieve these results.[4]

What went wrong has been described as an example of what has been called the 'Ch-Ch Syndrome', comparing Chernobyl with another disaster from 1986, when the American space shuttle *Challenger* burst into flames shortly after take-off. Both were catastrophes 'resulting from lapses of quality control . . . political pressure, incompetence and cover-ups'.[5] Chernobyl also offers an extreme example of the consequences of the lack of local knowledge, of what the anthropologist James C. Scott has called 'seeing like a state'.[6]

This 'local ignorance', as we might call it, can be found in many domains: in business, for instance, in politics or in war. The people working 'in the field' understand the local conditions, while headquarters, higher in the hierarchy of command, gives orders that ignore these conditions but cannot be questioned. Examples will be multiplied in later chapters. The big picture is more visible when viewed from the top, but the price of this visibility is blindness to much that is happening below.

## CLASS

Members of the upper classes in many places and periods have been ignorant of the lives of ordinary people, an ignorance symbolized by the famous (though apocryphal) remark by Marie Antoinette that if the poor lacked bread, 'let them eat cake' (*qu'ils mangent de la brioche*). Indeed, the upper classes have often viewed the lower orders as grotesque, more like animals than humans.

In tenth-century Japan, for instance, the noble lady Sei Shōnagon viewed the 'common people' at a pilgrimage as 'swarming like caterpillars' and described the 'odd' behaviour of carpenters eating their lunch in a hurry. In England, at the time of the peasant revolt of 1381, the poet John Gower wrote about the 'evil disposition' of the 'common people', comparing them to oxen who refuse to be yoked to the plough. In France, in a now famous passage in his *Caractères* (1688), Jean de La Bruyère wrote about the French peasants of his time as 'certain wild animals' burned by the sun, who when they get to their feet 'show a human face', using the technique of distantciation to shock his readers into recognizing their common humanity.[7]

There has also been much to say, especially by Marxists, about the way in which ruling classes have kept the 'lower orders' ignorant or misinformed in order to remain in control. This is the context for Marx's famous phrase, 'religion is the opium of the people' (*Die Religion . . . ist das Opium des Volkes*), offering them 'illusory happiness' so that the poor would remain content with their lot.[8]

A more complex version of Marxist theory includes the Italian philosopher Antonio Gramsci's idea of 'intellectual, moral and political hegemony'. Gramsci's basic point was that the ruling class does not rule by force alone but rather by a combination of force and persuasion, coercion and consent. The element of persuasion is indirect, at least in part. The subordinate or 'subaltern' classes (*classi subalterni*) learn to see society through their rulers' eyes.[9] Their knowledges were later described by Michel Foucault as 'subjugated' (*savoirs assujettis*).[10] The sometimes cryptic remarks in Gramsci's prison notebooks may be supplemented by an analysis by the British anthropologists Edwin and Shirley Ardener of what they called 'muted groups'. Since they lack a model of their own, these groups 'find it necessary to structure their world through the model (or models) of the dominant group'.[11]

## RACE

The phrase 'epistemology of ignorance' was coined by Charles W. Mills in the context of the analysis of racism. He noted the lack of philosophical studies of the subject, compared with studies of gender, and began to fill the gap. Mills argued that 'whites have agreed not to recognize blacks as equal persons', or even as persons *tout court*. He described ignoring black personhood as a form of ethnocentrism, an assumption of white superiority. Mills later called this implicit consensus 'white ignorance', a concept that has been taken up in studies of education.[12] The concept might also be employed to refer to other problems. One of these, an ignorance that is beginning to be remedied today, is ignorance of the importance of African slavery for the development of nineteenth-century capitalism. Another is the long-lasting lack of recognition by white people of the achievements of Black writers, artists and philosophers, a lack that reveals a mix of simple ignorance and deliberate or semi-deliberate ignoring.

A vivid example of this kind of ignorance, in the sense of failure to notice something significant, is offered by a famous passage in William Faulkner's novel *Intruder in the Dust* (1948). The passage refers to a form of what Freud called 'repetition compulsion', in this case the need for losers in a conflict to replay the past again and again in their heads. Faulkner's example is the fatal charge by General Pickett and his men at the battle of Gettysburg, leading to the loss of the battle by the South and with it the Civil War.

Faulkner remarks that 'For every Southern boy fourteen years old, not once but whenever he wants it, there is the instant when it's still not yet two o clock on that July afternoon in 1863', so that the fatal charge has not yet taken place. Faulkner was surely thinking of 'every Southern white boy'. His omission of the adjective 'white' is a Freudian slip, revealing something of his own identity and values.

## FEMALE IGNORANCE

A major stimulus to epistemology's social turn came from outside philosophy: the rise of feminism. Men have long ignored or devalued the knowledges and the credibility of females on the principle that 'what I don't know isn't knowledge'.[13] A common phrase for unreliable knowledge, from ancient Rome to early modern Europe, was *fabulae aniles*, 'old wives' tales'. Midwifery, an art long practised by women, was invaded by male doctors and surgeons in the eighteenth century, especially though not exclusively in England. The invaders, armed with a new instrument, the forceps, viewed their female competitors as ignorant. 'Midwives were caught in a double bind: they were ignorant of new methods and practices because they could not attend university . . . but they could not do so because they were women.'[14]

Female ignorance in many spheres was positively encouraged in early modern Europe. A classic articulation of the conventional male wisdom is the seventeenth-century treatise on the education of girls (especially those from good families) written by archbishop François Fénelon, a book that had considerable success not only in France but also in its eighteenth-century English translations and adaptations.

Fénelon recommended that girls be given religious instruction and taught how to manage a household and how to read and write. Arithmetic too was also recommended as useful for keeping accounts. On the other hand, the archbishop saw no point in girls learning foreign languages such as Italian or Spanish. Since women would not rule the state or become lawyers, priests or soldiers, they had no need to study politics, jurisprudence, theology or the art of war. They should also avoid what Fénelon called 'an indiscreet and insatiable curiosity' (*une curiosité indiscrète et insatiable*).[15]

In nineteenth-century England, the theme of female ignorance occurs in some famous novels (ironically enough, novels written by women). In Jane Austen's *Northanger Abbey* (1817), the narrator describes the heroine, Catherine Morland, as 'about as ignorant and uninformed as the female mind at seventeen usually is', while Catherine's friend Henry Tilney teases her about this. In George Eliot's *Middlemarch* (1870–71), there is – or was, before she deleted it – a reference on the final page to the 'modes of education that make a woman's knowledge another name for motley ignorance'.[16] In similar fashion, Virginia Woolf, who was born in 1882, feared that the gaps in her education made her a member 'not of the intelligentsia but of the ignorantsia'.[17]

In the language of the Ardeners, early modern women may be described as a 'muted group'. Nevertheless, a few early modern women, feminists before feminism, together with the occasional man, found words to protest against the imputation of ignorance to women and the restricted curriculum of the traditional regime of female education.

In fifteenth-century France, Christine de Pizan was already arguing that arts invented or discovered by women were more useful to humanity than those invented or discovered by men. In her book about the 'City of Ladies', the narrator, 'Christine', asks Lady Reason 'whether there was ever a woman who discovered hitherto unknown knowledge'. In response, 'Reason' recited a list of such women, including Minerva, inventor of armour, Ceres, inventor of agriculture, Arachne, inventor of tapestries, and Pamphile, who discovered how to make silk.[18]

In the seventeenth-century Dutch Republic, the polymath Anna Maria van Schurman wrote a treatise – in Latin – advocating a wider curriculum for girls. She argued that the study of all the liberal arts was 'entirely fitting for a Christian woman', and that women should not be excluded from theoretical knowledge of law, war and politics.[19]

Later in the century, a male philosopher, François Poullain de la Barre argued that the reason that women had not taken part in the different fields of learning was not that they lacked the capacity but because they had been 'excluded from learning' (*exclues des sciences*). In short, 'the mind has no sex' (*l'esprit n'a point de sexe*).[20]

At much the same time, the philosophers Gabrielle Suchon in France and Margaret Cavendish and Mary Astell in England were defending a broad education for women. Suchon investigated 'the source, origins and causes' of female ignorance and blamed 'those who want women to remain in the dark, deprived of the light of knowledge'. She argued that men exclude women from the means to acquire knowledge in order to dominate those 'whom they want to keep in a state of dependence'.[21] Cavendish, a noblewoman who herself had access to many books, complained that women were not 'suffer'd to be instructed in Schools and Universities'.

As for Astell, a merchant's daughter, she wrote that 'Ignorance is the cause of most Feminine Vices'. This ignorance, she continued, is not their fault, since they are excluded from access to knowledge: 'Women are from their very Infancy debarr'd those Advantages with the want of which they are afterwards reproach'd'. While boys are 'encouraged' to study, girls are 'restrain'd', driven away from 'the Tree of Knowledge'; 'if . . . they can't be kept so ignorant as their Masters wou'd have them, they are star'd upon as Monsters'. As a remedy for this ignorance she proposed to found a college for ladies.[22]

In the eighteenth century, female ignorance was discussed in two English texts, *Woman Not Inferior to Man* (1739), published under the pseudonym of 'Sophia', and the *Vindication of the Rights of Woman* (1792) by Mary Wollstonecraft. Both texts were translated into other languages in the early nineteenth century, though in its French and Portuguese versions, Sophia's text was attributed to Mary.[23]

Sophia blamed female ignorance on men 'for not giving them the means to avoid superstition'. Wollstonecraft claimed that 'the very constitution of civil governments has put almost insuperable obstacles in the way to prevent the cultivation of the female understanding' and that 'women at present are by ignorance rendered foolish or vicious'. She asked why women should be 'kept in ignorance under the specious name of innocence'.[24] To sum up: in early modern Europe, some women admitted their ignorance and blamed men for it.

## MALE IGNORANCE

In the late twentieth century, the situation described in the previous section was reversed. Feminists denied female ignorance and blamed men for ignoring female knowledge. The French philosopher Michèle Le Dœuff drew the conclusion that 'at some point we will have to elaborate the concept of masculinist unknowing'.[25] Where women were often aware of their ignorance, men were generally oblivious of theirs.

In the early modern period, a few women were already arguing in print for the equality (or occasionally the superiority) of women and complaining about male reluctance to recognize their achievements. Lucrezia Marinella suggested that the need to feel superior underlay male criticism of women, while Mary Astell noted that histories, which are 'writ by' men, 'recount each other's great exploits' and omit female achievements because the writers are 'envious of women'.[26]

The careers of nineteenth- and twentieth-century female scholars and scientists reveal the persistence of male reluctance to recognize their achievements, not least in cases in which they collaborated with men.[27] Notorious examples of the overshadowing of female scientists, surely cases of not wanting to know, include Mary Anning, Lise Meitner and Rosalind Franklin.[28]

Mary Anning is still often described as a fossil collector and dealer, a description that hides the contribution to palaeobiology that she made by identifying the remains of dinosaurs in Dorset in the first half of the nineteenth century.[29] The physicist Lise Meitner participated in the discovery of nuclear fission in the 1930s, but it was her male colleague Otto Hahn who received a Nobel Prize for this work.

The research of the crystallographer Rosalind Franklin, who has been described as 'the Dark Lady of DNA', was dismissed by James Watson, who received a Nobel Prize (together with Francis Crick and Maurice Wilkins) for the discovery. All the same, Crick and Watson made use of her X-ray photographs (without either permission or acknowledgement) in the paper in *Nature* that made their reputation. It has been suggested that the three prizewinners were part of a male conspiracy to exclude Franklin. At the very least, their failure to acknowledge her contribution offers one of the most notorious examples of 'citation amnesia' in the history of science.[30]

Turning to the humanities, the American scholar Alice Kober might be described as the Franklin of classics, since she was virtually omitted, for a time at least, from the famous story of the decipherment of the ancient Greek script known as 'Linear B'.[31] In the history of philosophy, some women, neglected earlier, have recently become objects of scholarly attention.[32] In similar fashion, in the case of art, major figures such as the Baroque painter Artemisia Gentileschi and the Impressionist Mary Cassatt have now been included in the pictorial canon, thanks to feminist art historians such as Linda Nochlin and Griselda Pollock.[33]

To reduce all these ignorances, feminists founded Women's Studies. A pioneering programme was launched at Cornell University in 1969. Journals followed, such as *Feminist Studies*, *Signs* and *Hypatia*. The multidisciplinary aspect of Women's Studies, which widened into Gender Studies, deserves emphasis. The Cambridge Centre for Gender Studies now draws on scholars in more than twenty departments in the university. Feminists had begun by pointing to the lack of research on women, their 'invisibility' to the scholars (mostly men) who ignored them.[34] Since 'adding women' to what was known about men was not sufficient to remedy the situation, they went on to make two general points about the gaps in what men called 'knowledge'.

The first of these points was a critique of scientific objectivity, faulted on the grounds of male bias and a lack of awareness that all knowledge is relative to a standpoint or social location.[35] The second point was that women have their own ways of knowing, usually ignored by men. It was argued that 'emotion' (viewed as female) 'is vital to systematic knowledge' and that male-dominated disciplines have institutionalized 'an emphasis on rationality that undervalues intuition'.[36] It was also argued that traditional (male) epistemology ignores 'knowing other people'.[37] In other words, men concentrate on *savoir*, women on *connaître*. If this is the case, the mind has sex after all!

In these publications and others like them, the contrast between male and female thinking as respectively objective and subjective is clearly too stark. For example, female scientists have no problem with using their reason, while some men make use of their intuition. In a classic analysis of the contrast, Evelyn Fox-Keller, a physicist as well as a feminist, argued that the 'association between masculine and objective, more specifically between masculine and scientific' was 'overshadowed' by individual variations. In any case the association was not genetic, but simply part of a belief system encouraged by the earliest experiences of males and females.[38]

# 4

## STUDYING IGNORANCE

It is still not entirely respectable to write about ignorance

Michael Smithson

Academic disciplines are a particular form of organization or cognitive community. Here too it is possible to identify institutionalized ignorance, in the sense of a collective lack of interest in certain kinds of knowledge and a failure to pursue research on them. It may therefore be illuminating to examine recent feminist approaches to particular disciplines.

A generation of women who had studied at university argued that the academic curriculum was not only taught by men but appeared to be designed with men only in mind. They noted what had been neglected, denied or even suppressed in male research. Since the 1970s, 'we have seen a huge collective exposure of absences of knowledge in many disciplines in the humanities and social sciences, and to a lesser extent in the natural sciences as well'.[1]

In one field after another, female scholars have identified blind spots, areas that have been ignored as a result of male bias. In the case of law, for instance, it is argued that the legal systems ignore the experiences and viewpoints of women, most obviously in the case of laws concerning rape.[2] In the case of politics, Carole Pateman claims that feminist writers have been excluded from the canon of theorists and that 'political theory, for the most part remains untouched by feminist argument'.[3]

Feminist geographers have studied the effects of location on inequalities between the sexes, as well as calling for a greater participation by women in geographical research and theory.[4] The Danish economist Esther Boserup pioneered a feminist approach to her discipline, noting that 'In the vast and ever-growing literature on economic development, reflections on the particular problems of women are few and far between.'[5]

In an early contribution to feminist sociology, Ann Oakley chose a topic that had been neglected by sociologists and economists alike: housework. In a broader critique of what she called 'Patriarchal sociology', Dorothy Smith argued that its 'methods, conceptual schemes and theories' had been 'built up within the male social universe' that ignored the experiences of women. She contrasted a male focus on impersonal rules with a female focus on everyday lives and personal experiences.[6]

## ANTHROPOLOGY AND ARCHAEOLOGY

In the case of anthropology, male researchers cannot be said to have ignored women but they do seem to have underestimated their importance in many societies and in any case, they were not always allowed to see or talk to them. However, a number of women entered the discipline relatively early, including, in chronological order, Ruth Benedict, Zora Hurston, Audrey Richards, Margaret Mead and Ruth Landes. The first impact of female anthropologists was to fill some gaps in knowledge by saying more about the experiences of women than their male anthropologists had been in a position to do. In Samoa, for instance, Mead was able to talk to the girls about sex. In Bahia, Ruth Landes emphasized the role of female priestesses in Afro-Brazilian religion.[7]

In all these areas, women identified blind spots that resulted from the domination of theses disciplines by males. At a second stage, female scholars began asking different questions from the ones posed by their male colleagues. Mary Douglas, for instance, has been described as bringing to anthropology 'the feminine concerns of her middle-class environment: with the house, its meals and upkeep, with domestic rituals of cleaning ... with shopping ... with the female body'.[8] At a third stage, anthropological theory was widened to explore formerly neglected topics such as gender.[9]

Female archaeologists lagged behind their colleagues in anthropology in their discovery of male bias but they were inspired by anthropologists in their efforts to correct it, thus 'engendering' archaeology.[10] They have had to face the problem of the lack of evidence for the sexual division of labour in a discipline that is essentially based on the study of material culture. This lack of evidence is one reason why the work of the Lithuanian scholar Marija Gimbutas, who argued for the existence of equality between the sexes in Neolithic Europe and claimed – like Christine de Pizan in the fifteenth century – that 'agriculture was developed by women', remains controversial.[11] However, new techniques of DNA analysis are allowing archaeologists to determine the gender of skeletons and to show that some Vikings who were buried with weapons were women.[12] In any case, what can be asserted with confidence is that a feminist approach has exposed traditional assumptions (that women gathered and cooked, for instance, while men hunted and made tools and pots) for what they are – assumptions.[13]

## WRITING ABOUT IGNORANCE

It has been well said that human ignorance is a 'vast, ungovernable and seemingly infinite topic'.[14] Imputing ignorance to oneself, as Socrates and Montaigne did, is one thing; imputing it to others is quite another. Young people impute ignorance to their elders and vice versa. The middle classes impute ignorance to the working classes or the 'masses'. Christians and Muslims impute ignorance to the 'heathen', so-called 'civilized' people impute ignorance to 'savages', and literate people impute it to anyone who cannot read and write.

It was as part of the revolution in the teaching of literacy associated with Paulo Freire, who was teaching in the north-east of Brazil in 1963, that he advised teachers of adults to give up the assumption that illiteracy equals ignorance and to be prepared to learn from their class, treating them as equals who are capable of examining their world critically. By abandoning what he called the 'banking' theory of education, the assumption that 'The teacher knows everything, and the students know nothing', Freire discovered that it was possible to teach adults to read and write in forty hours.[15]

As we saw in chapter one, it is commonplace to view earlier periods as ages of ignorance. It might be more exact as well as more modest to say that every age is an age of ignorance, for three main reasons.

In the first place, the spectacular growth of collective knowledge in the last two centuries is not reflected in the knowledge of most individuals. Although humanity as a whole knows more than ever before, most individuals know little more than their ancestors did.

In the second place, every age is an age of ignorance because the rise of some knowledges is often accompanied by the loss of others. The downside of the rise in the knowledge of world languages such as English, Spanish, Arabic and Mandarin is the accelerating rate of extinction of other languages. From 50 per cent to 90 per cent of the world's seven thousand languages are not expected to survive until the year 2100.[16] Knowledge that is stored only in the head and communicated orally is particularly at risk, as in case of tribes in the Amazon region today, since 'when the elderly members of a small tribe die, much if not most of the oral wisdom dies with them'.[17] At the conceptual level, when one model or paradigm replaces another, there is not only gain but also what is known as 'Kuhn Loss', in other words the loss of the ability to explain some phenomena, since each paradigm focuses attention on a few features of reality at the expense of others.[18]

In the third place, the rapid expansion of information, especially in recent decades, is not identical with the expansion of knowledge, in the sense of data that have been tested, digested and classified. In any case, organizations, especially governments and large corporations, conceal an increasing amount of the information they collect. It has been argued that in the USA in the year 2001, 'about five times as many pages' of classified documents were produced, compared with the pages of new books and articles in libraries, and that this proportion was continuing to rise.[19]

For all these reasons, the idea of an 'Ignorance Explosion', the title of a book published in 1992 by a Polish-American engineer, Julius Lukasiewicz, is not as paradoxical as it may seem at first sight.[20] It is often said that we live in an 'information society' or a 'knowledge society' in which 'knowledge workers' are replacing workers in industry and on the land. It might also be said that we live in an 'ignorance society'. As information continues to pile up, there is more and more for each one of us not to know.

How did we reach this situation? How different is it from the situation in earlier centuries? It is common to view the age in which one is living as quite different from the past, an attitude encouraged by frequent headlines in the media using phrases such as 'for the first time' or 'never before'. Writers in the movements we know as the 'Renaissance' and the 'Enlightenment' viewed them both in dramatic terms as liberations from ignorance. Already around the year 1400, the chronicler Filippo Villani described the role of Cimabue as restoring pictorial 'verisimilitude' after the deviation from this standard owing to the 'ignorance' (*inscicia*) of earlier painters.[21]

Even in a time like ours of accelerating cultural and social change, it is all too easy to exaggerate the gap between past and present. Continuities should not be forgotten, and it is one of the functions of the tribe of historians to remind the public of this point. In what follows I shall be offering such reminders from time to time, hoping not to exaggerate in my turn.

## THE POWER OF METAPHOR

Writers who discuss ignorance find it difficult to avoid certain recurrent metaphors. In the eighteenth century, leading participants in the movement that called itself the 'Enlightenment' regularly complained about the 'darkness' of ignorance, just as their predecessors had done in the Renaissance. The journalist Joseph Addison claimed that he founded *The Spectator* in order 'to dissipate the ignorance of the public', as if it was a kind of fog (some three hundred years later, another journalist would refer to 'the smog of ignorance').[22] The historian William Robertson presented the early Middle Ages as a time when 'the ignorance of the age was too powerful . . . the darkness returned and settled over Europe, more thick and heavy than before'.[23]

A variant of the metaphor was 'clouds of ignorance'. When Mary Astell published her 'serious proposal' for a college for women, her aim was 'to expel that cloud of Ignorance' that kept women in the shade.[24] The University of Alabama, founded in 1819, was expected to help in 'dissipating the clouds of ignorance and prejudice which have so long overshadowed and darkened the face of our land'.[25] This metaphor was represented literally in the British lawyer Edward Quin's *Historical Atlas* (1830), subtitled 'A Series of Maps of the World as Known in Different Periods', in which the maps were surrounded by black clouds representing the unknown.

Edward Gibbon described the barbarian invaders of the Roman Empire as 'immersed in ignorance', as if it was a stream or an ocean.[26] David Hume described thirteenth-century England as 'sunk in the deepest abyss of ignorance'.[27] The Enlightenment was supposed by the supporters of the movement to awaken humanity from the 'sleep' of ignorance, or to liberate the intellect from its 'bonds', 'chains' or 'yoke', a metaphor vividly illustrated in a painting by the Neapolitan artist Luca Giordano.

## EXPLORING IGNORANCE

Going beyond the metaphors to explore the causes and consequences of ignorance is more difficult than imputing it to others. As a topic for research, ignorance was itself ignored until relatively recently, although the possibility of such a study had been discussed by the philosopher James Ferrier in the 1850s. In this respect, writers of fiction were well ahead of scholars.

For example, a focus on ignorance is noticeable in George Eliot's *The Mill on the Floss* (1860) and difficult to miss in her masterpiece *Middlemarch* (1870–71). Maggie, the heroine of *The Mill*, first yearns for knowledge and then tries to resign herself to ignorance, provoking her friend Philip's comment that 'Stupefaction is not resignation, and it is stupefaction to remain in ignorance'. The author describes the period in which her novel is set, the period of her own youth, as 'a time when ignorance was much more comfortable than at present, without being obliged to dress itself in an elaborate costume of knowledge'.[28]

In *Daniel Deronda* (1876), Eliot asked, 'who hath duly considered or set forth the power of Ignorance?'[29] It is, however, in *Middlemarch* that Eliot's preoccupation with ignorance is most apparent. The finale of the novel, as a critic has suggested, 'exposes the difficulty of knowing other people'.[30] In this case the difficulty is dramatized by the ignorance of each other's feelings on the part of two leading characters, Dorothea and Will. However, the place of ignorance in the novel is much greater than that. The words 'ignorance' and 'ignorant' occur fifty-nine times in the novel (if I have not miscounted) and they refer not only to Dorothea's sense of her own ignorance but also to the ignorance of many other people in the fictional town in which the story is set.

Henry James was especially interested in private knowledge. In *What Maisie Knew* (1897), his real topic is what the child Maisie did not know about her parents. His most striking example of a focus on ignorance, a particularly appropriate theme for such a master of ambiguity and indirection, is *The Golden Bowl* (1904). The words 'knowledge' and 'ignorance' frequently recur in the text, while the plot focuses on the questions of how much or how little each of the main characters knows about a certain episode, including whether or not they know how much or how little the others know.[31]

## A MULTI-DISCIPLINARY ENTERPRISE

In 1993, the psychologist Michael Smithson could still begin an article on ignorance in science with the words, 'It is still not entirely respectable to write about ignorance.'[32] A similar point was made three years later by the French philosopher of science Théodore Ivainer.[33] Today, the situation is very different.

A few scholars and scientists arrived early at the scene. As we have seen, Freud was already concerned with ignorance in his *Interpretation of Dreams* (1899). In sociology, the pioneers in the study of ignorance include Georg Simmel, who was discussing nescience (*Nichtwissen*) at the beginning of the century.[34] In economics, uncertainty was discussed in the 1920s by Frank Knight and John Maynard Keynes, while Friedrich von Hayek published an article on 'coping with ignorance' in 1978.[35]

Given the interest shown by major writers such as George Eliot and Henry James, it is no surprise to find literary scholars producing studies of ignorance. One of them surveys the knowledge of ignorance 'from Genesis to Jules Verne', another focuses on 'unknowing' as a mark of modernist fiction, while a third, by Andrew Bennett, enquires how far authors, novelists as well as poets, are conscious of what they are going to do before they do it or aware of the meaning of what they write.[36] More generally, Bennett suggests 'that ignorance may be reconceived as part of the narrative and other force of literature, part of its performativity and indeed as an important aspect of its thematic focus'.[37]

In philosophy, where the problem of knowledge has long been a central theme, there was a turn towards an interest in ignorance in the 1990s, when the phrase 'epistemology of ignorance' was coined, as we have seen.[38]

In the case of medicine, institutionalization arrived unusually early. An anthropologist published a study of medical ignorance in 1981. An *Encyclopaedia of Medical Ignorance* was published in 1984. In an essay prefixed to a medical textbook, the polymathic doctor Lewis Thomas declared that 'we are not as candid as we ought to be about the extent of our ignorance ... I wish there were some formal courses in medical school on Medical Ignorance'.[39] A professor at the University of Arizona, Marlys Witte, who described Lewis Thomas as her 'mentor', put this suggestion into practice, including 'the things we think we know, but don't', 'the things we thought we knew, but didn't', and a discussion of what can be learned from failures, 'both our own and others". Despite some opposition, Witte's 'Ignorance 101' was launched in 1985 and was a great success, so much so that it was soon supplemented by an annual summer school for teachers and students outside the university.[40]

A dramatic reminder of medical ignorance comes from the appearance of unknown diseases, from bubonic plague to Covid (epidemics will be discussed later, in chapter twelve). The history of medicine also offers dramatic examples of institutional forgetting. In the seventeenth and eighteenth centuries, Western physicians discovered and sometimes made use of elements of Asian medicine, notably acupuncture and moxibustion. In contrast, from around the year 1800 onwards, Western physicians rejected these alternative medicines as 'unscientific', at a time when 'a single, increasingly dominant medical system . . . sought an absolute monopoly over healing practices and theories'.[41]

Early contributions to the study of ignorance by medics, philosophers and psychologists were more or less isolated from one another, like the disciplines from which they came. A few of them met in the early 1990s, thanks to an international conference on the subject held in 1991 and a session of the American Association for the Advancement of Science in 1993. The papers given at this session were concerned with ignorance as viewed from philosophy, sociology, journalism and medicine.[42]

Since that time, books and articles on ignorance have been appearing in increasing numbers. Sociologists from Germany to Brazil have offered contributions.[43] 'Agnotology' has become a multi-disciplinary enterprise. *The Routledge Handbook of Ignorance Studies* offers an overview of the state of the field with chapters by fifty-one authors who come from philosophy, sociology, anthropology, economics, politics, science, law and literature.[44]

Why such a strong interest in the study of ignorance should have developed in the last forty years or so is a question with more than one possible answer. One of these emphasizes the internal development of research. It has often proved illuminating, when studying a particular problem, to turn it upside down or inside out and examine its complementary opposite. Students of memory, for instance, have turned to the study of forgetting, while students of language now study silence as well. Success has long been an object of attention, but scholars now show interest in what can be learned from failure. Knowledge has attracted increasing attention from scholars, encouraged by the debate on the 'knowledge society', thus making it virtually inevitable that studies of ignorance would follow.

Turning to external explanations, the academic study of ignorance is clearly driven by the major concerns of our own century, especially the awareness of disasters in the recent past, such as 9/11, anxiety about disasters in the present (especially, in 2021, Covid), and the fear of

disasters to come. Academic interest is also encouraged by the spectacular demonstrations of ignorance by recent heads of state such as
Donald Trump and Jaïr Bolsonaro. At a popular level, the title 'The
Power of Ignorance' is shared by a number of self-help books (including
a parody of the genre).[45] It would be comforting, though it is probably
too optimistic, to suppose that the increasing interest in ignorance
offers evidence of a rise in collective humility.

# 5

# HISTORIES OF IGNORANCE

A history of knowledge that takes sufficient account of the history
of ignorance is yet to be written

Robert DeMaria

As in the case of the disciplines discussed in the previous chapter, historians too have been criticized for ignoring women, leading to attempts to
fill the gap and encouraging an interest in the history of that ignorance.

## WOMEN'S HISTORY

Women have sometimes been described as 'hidden from history',
implying that earlier historians were ignorant of the past of half of
humanity. In fact, three well-known examples of women's history – all
written by men – appeared in French, German and English in the eighteenth century: *Essai sur le caractère, les moeurs et l'esprit des femmes dans
les différens siècles* (1772) by Antoine Thomas; *Geschichte des weiblichen
Geschlechts* (1788–1800) by Christoph Meiners; and *The History of
Women* (1796) by William Alexander.[1] The authors and publishers were
clearly appealing to female interest in history, which offers further
evidence against the traditional assumption of female ignorance.[2]

Female scholars were able to fill gaps in historical knowledge that their
male colleagues had missed. Mary Ritter Beard argued that men 'miss the
force of women', their contribution to 'the making of history' as priestesses, queens, saints, heretics, scholars and mistresses of households.[3] Lucy

Salmon, who taught at Vassar College in the USA, published a study of domestic service and recommended a wide range of previously neglected sources for social history, including laundry lists and kitchen appliances.[4]

A more general turn took place in the 1970s, when feminists criticized male historians for ignoring women in the past. Natalie Davis, the doyenne of the subject in the USA, noted that 'most modern historians of the Reformation . . . scarcely mention women at all'.[5] In her best-known study, *The Return of Martin Guerre*, Davis inserted a discussion of the protagonist's wife Bertrande into the well-known history of the two Martins, the impostor who claimed to be her husband and the genuine one, who returned some years later. Bertrande's attitude to the man who claimed to be her husband was obviously a key element in the history, but it had been neglected if not ignored by earlier historians.[6]

Today, the number of professional historians studying women's work, women's bodies, women's religion and women's writing makes a dramatic contrast with the situation half a century ago.[7] It is often the case that the introduction of a new element into a system leads to other changes in the system in order to accommodate it.[8] Davis suggested that the rise of women's history 'should make some changes in the practice of the field at large'.[9] One is the rise of interest in private life, as in the *History of Private Life* originally published in French in five volumes from 1985 to 1987. Another is the increasing awareness of informal power, behind the scenes of the court and the household, whether it was exercised by women or men.

## HISTORIES OF IGNORANCE

Among the fifty-one contributors to the *Routledge Handbook* mentioned earlier there was not a single historian. In the study of ignorance, historians have come late to the table. Many have referred to ignorance in passing, but few have yet placed it at the centre of their enquiries.

Historians of science such as Peter Galison and Robert Proctor, who met when they were graduate students at Harvard in the early 1980s, were among the first historians to write about ignorance. Proctor was surprised by the lack of interest by his professors in the attitudes of ordinary people, from creationism to racism, while Galison, some of whose teachers in physics had worked on the atomic bomb, became interested in censorship and secrecy. Proctor in particular, together with another historian of science, Londa Schiebinger, has done much to launch what they call 'agnotology', the study of the way in which ignorance is produced or maintained, as opposed to 'agnoiology', the study of ignorance in general.[10]

On the other hand, plain or general historians have lagged behind their colleagues in the history of science.[11] Although interest in the history of knowledge has been growing for some time, 'A history of knowledge that takes sufficient account of the history of ignorance is yet to be written.'[12] This late arrival is rather odd, since in the case of history, as in that of philosophy, an interest in ignorance was awakened long ago by the need to answer sceptics. In the seventeenth century, some of these sceptics were already undermining the received accounts of the past, notably in a book on the uncertainty of history by François La Mothe Le Vayer.[13]

In the eighteenth and nineteenth centuries, some historians organized their books around the idea of progress, a movement from ignorance to knowledge. The early Middle Ages was often presented as a time of ignorance, the 'Dark Ages', against which the writers of the age of light, the 'Enlightenment', defined themselves. The philosopher-historian David Hume described the tenth and eleventh centuries as 'those days of ignorance' and 'those ignorant ages'. Voltaire too described the Middle Ages as 'ces siècles d'ignorance'.[14]

Ignorance was often linked to illiteracy. In his account of the origin of 'fables' (including what we call 'myths'), the French scholar Bernard de Fontenelle suggested that ignorance and barbarism began to decline after the invention of writing.[15] There is a similar emphasis on the role of writing, together with printing, in the most famous history written in terms of the progress of knowledge and the retreat of ignorance: the 'sketch' of the progress of the human mind by Nicolas de Condorcet, published posthumously after its aristocratic author had been guillotined in the course of the French Revolution.[16]

The tradition of studies of the war against ignorance lasted into the nineteenth century and beyond – an example from Victorian England is

David Nasmith's *Makers of Modern Thought* (1892), subtitled 'Five Hundred Years' Struggle (1200 AD to 1699 AD) between Science, Ignorance and Superstition'. The authors of books such as this wrote in what may be called a 'triumphalist' mode, confident that the war was being won and that their age was more enlightened than its predecessors. In other words, they accepted the so-called 'Whig' interpretation of history as the story of progress.[17]

Today, after a long interval, a few historians are returning to the subject of ignorance without committing themselves to Whig assumptions about its inevitable decline. Cornel Zwierlein and some of his German colleagues have been studying diplomacy and empire from this angle, while Zwierlein has also edited a collection of essays on the topic. Alain Corbin, a French historian who has long been known for his choice of unusual subjects – from smells to bells – has published a study of what was not known about the earth in the late eighteenth and early nineteenth centuries.[18] In 2015, a conference was held at the German Historical Institute in London on 'Ignorance and Non-Knowledge in Early Modern Expansion'. However, many other domains remain to be explored.

A history of schools or universities, for instance, might focus on what was not taught, described by the educational theorist Elliot Eisner as the 'null curriculum'. The idea underlying such a focus is that 'ignorance is not simply a neutral void; it has important effects on the kinds of options one is able to consider, the alternatives one can examine, and the perspectives from which one can view a situation or problem . . . a parochial perspective or simplistic analysis is the inevitable progeny of ignorance'.[19] In similar fashion, a study of successive editions of encyclopaedias might examine what was missing from them in different places and periods – especially what was removed because it was no longer thought to be either correct or important.[20]

## APPROACHES AND METHODS

Historians of ignorance face a fundamental problem: how to study an absence.[21] Social scientists can fill the gap by making their own surveys, of 'voter ignorance', for instance, but what possible sources and methods could there be for the history of what isn't there?

One response, a relatively traditional one, is to focus on the idea of ignorance in different periods. The letter 'On His Own Ignorance and That of Many Others' by the Renaissance poet-scholar Francesco Petrarca ('Petrarch') has often been discussed. Petrarch quotes Socrates on knowing he does not know, while defending himself against the claim by four young Venetians that he himself is ignorant.[22] The arguments about the limits to knowledge put forward by ancient and modern sceptics have often been discussed, as they are in this book. Theologians have studied the tradition of a 'negative route' to the knowledge of God, as we shall see in chapter six.

Recent responses to the challenge offer indirect approaches, akin to tracking pedestrians by looking at their shadows. One such approach may be christened the 'retrospective method', shifting the focus from the increase of knowledge to the gradual decline of ignorance. As the Spanish scholar Francisco López de Gómara pointed out in his *General History of the Indies* (1553), the discovery of America 'revealed the ignorance of the ancients, wise as they were' (*declaró la ignorancia de la sabia antigüedad*).[23]

The retrospective method resembles the 'regressive method' employed by the French historian Marc Bloch when he was studying agrarian systems.[24] However, Bloch was interested in discovering continuities, while the retrospective method emphasizes contrasts between past and present. It is thus closer to the approach of Bloch's colleague Lucien Febvre, who explored the limits to sixteenth-century French thought via absent concepts, words that had not yet been coined at that time.[25]

A second approach is to study what might be called 'eloquent absences', following the example of Sherlock Holmes. Investigating a missing race-horse, Holmes noted that the guard dog did not bark in the night, as he would normally have done when confronted with an intruder. The detective drew the conclusion that the robber was well known to the animal. In similar fashion, historians of ignorance can practise the comparative method to reveal significant absences, as the German sociologist Werner

Sombart did in a famous essay on the absence in the USA of what was very much present in the Germany of Sombart's time, Socialism.[26]

For example, Cornel Zwierlein, focusing on Western ignorance of the early modern Levant, noted the absence of certain books in private libraries, notably the work of the great Arab historian Ibn Khaldun, as well as the absence of certain information in the books to be found in those libraries.[27] This practice has been called 'null history', treating the absence of certain material in an archive, for instance, as a significant phenomenon.[28] Again, the comparison of texts written by different travellers to the same place reveals the gaps in each one, allowing the historian to notice what the author failed to see.

A third approach is to turn the traditional triumphalist narrative upside down, replacing the emphasis on the retreat of ignorance by an account of its advance or even (as suggested earlier) its 'explosion'. Such an account tells the story of the extinction of languages, the burning of books, the destruction of libraries, the collective forgetting of discoveries, the death of knowledgeable people and so on. In short, it offers an emphasis on losers rather than winners, failure rather than success.[29] The value of this approach is to reveal the one-sidedness of the traditional story, what historians used to call its 'bias'. Its weakness (if it is pursued in isolation) is that it is equally one-sided, the reverse of the medal.

A possible way towards such a reconciliation between these two interpretations of history was already suggested in the 1950s by C. S. Lewis, an Oxford don who is better known as a writer of fiction and as a lay theologian. Lewis's introduction to his history of English literature in the Renaissance carries the arresting title, 'New Learning and New Ignorance'. The author claimed that the hostility to medieval philosophy on the part of Renaissance humanists was a form of ignorance, and went on to generalize his point. 'Perhaps every new learning makes room for itself by creating a new ignorance . . . Man's power of attention seems to be limited; one nail drives out another.'[30] In this respect I shall be following Lewis, while adding a social dimension to his story, since ignorance, like knowledge, is socially situated.

## A SOCIAL HISTORY OF IGNORANCE

The history of ignorance, like the history of knowledge, forms part of intellectual history, but this intellectual history may be approached in different ways. This book emphasizes the social history of ignorance, the complementary opposite of the social history of knowledge. A key question in human affairs, as Lenin remarked in 1921, is 'Who-Whom?' (*Kto, Kogo?*). In a study of communication, the political scientist Harold Lasswell elaborated the question into a famous formula: Who is Saying What to Whom?[31]

In similar fashion, social historians of ignorance concern themselves with Who is Ignorant of What, distinguishing, for instance, the ignorance of ordinary people (the laity, the rank and file, the voters, the consumers) from that of elites (rulers, generals, scientists and so on), as well as examining the connections between them. This leads them to consider the uses of ignorance, notably its contribution to the dominance of one group (class, race or gender) over another. It follows from this approach that the term 'ignorance' – like that of knowledge – deserves to be employed in the plural, although the words 'ignorances' and 'knowledges' may still sound odd in English, unlike the French *savoirs* or the Spanish *saberes*.

Social historians might also study what Zwierlein calls 'coping with ignorance', in other words responses to awareness of particular ignorances, on the part of scholars, scientists, missionaries, colonial administrators etc. – performing experiments, conducting surveys, engaging in fieldwork and so on.[32]

Some forms of ignorance are virtually required of a given social group in a given culture. In early modern Europe, for instance, a gentleman was expected not to know – or not to know much – about money, or about skills associated with the crafts, since the upper classes looked down on manual labour. For their part, ladies were expected not to know about a variety of topics, from classical learning to sex (at least before they were married).

In the early twentieth century the British botanist Marie Stopes, better known as a campaigner for eugenics, women's rights and birth control, was shocked by the collective silence about sex in the world of middle-class women, resulting in the ignorance of girls until they married. Stopes quoted one who wrote to her saying that 'I married knowing practically nothing of what married life would be – no one ever talked to me and told me things I ought to have known – and I had a rude awakening.'[33] Michel Foucault, who liked to turn the conventional wisdom upside-down, claimed that what he called the 'Victorian regime' of sexuality was not one of silence and secrecy. On the contrary, it was 'that aspect of itself which troubled and preoccupied it more than any other'. As usual, however, it is necessary to distinguish between attitudes: official and unofficial, male and female, those of the parents and those of their children.[34]

On the other hand, other forms of ignorance have been widely regarded as culpable. In Protestant Europe, the devout were shocked by anyone who showed ignorance of the Bible (in Catholic Europe, on the other hand, interest in the Bible on the part of the laity might lead to the suspicion of heresy). For ladies, it was culpable ignorance not to know how to manage a household, to embroider, to write in an elegant hand, to sing, play the piano, read music and recognize works by famous composers.

As for males, a knowledge of the myths, history, literature and philosophy of ancient Greece and Rome, or at least a capacity to recognize allusions to the classics, was long considered to be essential for any educated man in the West, especially between 1500 and 1900. It was also culpable for a gentleman to be ignorant of heraldry, including its technical terms ('chevron', 'gules', 'impale', 'passant' and so on) and the ability to recognize the coats of arms of important families. In Walter Scott's novel *Rob Roy* (1817), set in the eighteenth century, an older man expresses amazement at a younger man's ignorance of the subject. 'What! Not know the figures of heraldry! Of what could your father be thinking?'

It is impossible to separate the social from the political history of ignorance. On a number of occasions, it will be necessary to ask who (men, the bourgeoisie, rulers, companies) keeps whom (women, the working class, the people, consumers) in ignorance and for what reasons.

The seventeenth-century English scholar Bathsua Makyn complained that women were 'kept ignorant on purpose to be made slaves', a point reiterated, as we saw earlier, by Mary Astell and Gabrielle Suchon in the seventeenth century and by the anonymous 'Sophia' in the eighteenth.[35]

As has already been noted, ignorance is an umbrella term and it is important to study it in the plural, as a series of specific ignorances with their own explanations and their own consequences. It is equally important to study it from different standpoints, with a place for the views of both missionaries and 'savages', elites and 'masses', men and women, workers and management, soldiers and officers and so on: in the hope of producing what is sometimes called a 'polyphonic' history.[36]

# 6

# IGNORANCE OF RELIGION

a man shall not say he knows or believes that which he has no
scientific grounds for professing to know or believe

T. H. Huxley

The material from which this chapter is drawn is both rich and various.
Ignorance plays various roles in both the theory and the practice of religion, most obviously in the apophatic tradition of theology, in which it is
claimed that humans can only say what God is not, allowing us 'to know
indirectly through our ignorance'.[1] Religion itself might be described as a
response to human ignorance, even though religious leaders are often
confident that they know the intentions of Jehovah, God or Allah.
Alternatively, religions have been explained as the deliberate creation of
mystery, as in the notorious treatise on the 'three impostors' (Moses,
Christ and Mohammed), first published in the eighteenth century.[2]

Ignorance has often been imputed to groups whose religion is not that
of the speaker, treating their beliefs as an absence of knowledge rather
than a different, rival knowledge. As we have seen, Muslims call the age of
polytheism before Islam 'the age of ignorance', while Christian missionaries have often referred to the 'ignorance' of non-Christians, along with
'idolatry' and 'superstition'. Within each religion, groups often accuse one
another of ignorance of the true faith, while believers in one of the major
world religions usually know very little about any of the others. Agnostics,
following the example of Socrates, impute ignorance to themselves.

This chapter will be concerned in turn with ignorance of the doctrines of their own religion on the part of both the clergy and the laity; with ignorance of the ideas of believers in other religions; with conscious ignorance of the divine in its two main forms, the 'negative way' to God and agnosticism; and finally, with the decline of interest in theology, a more or less conscious decision to ignore it.

## THE CLERGY

Like other large organizations, such as governments, companies and armies, churches are likely to be sites of what is known as 'organizational ignorance'. I am not thinking here of the cases of sexual abuse recently uncovered in both the Catholic Church and the Church of England, since the bishops in whose dioceses the abuse occurred may more plausibly be accused of covering up what was going on, rather than having been ignorant of it. More relevant here are the gaps in knowledge and communication between the parish and the diocese, still a neglected topic (so far as I know) on the part of ecclesiastical historians.

More is known about ignorance of the faith on the part of the clergy, in particular that of parish priests, an old problem that became a major issue for Catholics and Protestants alike during the European Reformation. In the Middle Ages, parish priests were not formally trained to carry out their duties. They picked up fragments of knowledge by a kind of informal apprenticeship, helping and watching their seniors.[3] This lack of formal training was already perceived as a problem: a thirteenth-century English church council produced an 'immensely influential and long-lived' plan for the instruction of the laity that is known by its opening words, 'The Ignorance of Priests' (*Ignorantia Sacerdotum*).[4] In the mid-sixteenth century, inspections of the diocese of Mantua revealed priests who were described as 'ignorant' (*nihil sciens*).[5] In 1561, the clergy of the diocese of Carlisle were described by their bishop as 'for the most part very ignorant and stubborn'.[6]

Martin Luther and his followers were particularly vehement in their denunciation of 'dumb dogs who cannot bark', in other words priests – and sometimes pastors – who lacked education and were therefore unable to preach the faith and correct the ignorance of their parish-ioners.[7] The phrase about 'dumb dogs' is a quotation from the Old Testament, where the prophet Isaiah also complained that God's watchmen 'are blind, they are all ignorant' (Isaiah 56.10), a reminder that the problem discussed here is not limited to Christianity, to Europe or to the age of the Reformation.

In response to these criticisms, seminaries were founded in the Catholic world from the later sixteenth century onwards in order to teach priests what to teach the people, while Lutheran and Calvinist pastors were increasingly expected to have studied at university. On the other hand, the parish clergy of the Orthodox or Eastern Christian churches lacked these opportunities. In Aleppo in 1651, a French Capuchin missionary noted that the patriarchs of the Syrians and Armenians 'are extremely ignorant' (*sono molto ignoranti*).[8] In 1762, when the Jesuit scholar Ruđer Bošković (who came from Dubrovnik) was visiting Bulgaria, he spoke to a village priest and later commented that 'His igno-rance, and that of all these poor people, is incredible ... they know neither the Pater Noster, nor the Credo, nor the essential mysteries of the religion'. A later discussion with another priest revealed that 'Of Rome he had no knowledge, neither of the pope, nor of any religious controversy, and he asked me if there were priests in Rome'.[9]

The case of missionaries, who have often been ignorant – though not always – of the belief system of the people they were attempting to convert, will be discussed in a later section.

## THE LAITY

Whether or not the Reformations reduced lay ignorance of the Christian faith in its various forms, they did at least produce sources that allow that ignorance to be studied. These sources include not only complaints by preachers but also the inspections or visitations of parishes. They allow historians to follow in the footsteps of the early modern clergy, Catholic and Protestant, who were concerned to discover what their flocks knew and often disconcerted to find out what they did not know about the faith.

In England, for instance, the testimony of sixteenth-century ministers included the claim that 'the poor people do not understand as much as the Lord's Prayer' and that 'Many are so ignorant' that 'they know not what the Scriptures are; they know not that there are any Scriptures'.[10] In Wales, the bishop of Bangor declared that in his diocese, 'Ignorance continueth many in the dregs of superstition'.[11] As for the German Protestant inspections, 'It was the appalling general ignorance of religion revealed in the Saxon visitation of 1527–9 that prompted Luther to write his two catechisms', simple accounts of the faith for simple people.[12] The most thorough investigations of the religious knowledge of the laity were probably those carried out in early modern Sweden, known as the *husförhör*. Pastors went from house to house to test the knowledge and understanding of the Bible – or the lack of them – on the part of every member of the household.[13]

The question-and-answer format of the catechism would be taken up by the Catholics for the same purpose, although the answers, learned by heart, may not always have been understood. The Church preferred ordinary people to believe rather than to understand religious doctrine, since the attempt to understand might lead them into heresy.[14]

In Italy, for instance, the questions asked during episcopal visitations were more concerned with the state of the churches and of the clergy than with the religious knowledge of their flocks. It was only gradually that bishops began not only to enquire about attendance at confession and communion but also to ask whether anyone in the parish 'criticizes the faith and the dogmas of the church' or 'is suspect of heresy'. Finally, in Venice in 1821, for instance, we find a parish priest in a poor parish criticizing the lack of concern that left his flock ignorant of religion.[15]

It is of course necessary to distinguish between lay knowledge of religious doctrine in different places, in different periods and among different social groups. In early modern Spain, for instance, the former Muslims who were forced to convert to Christianity after 1492 knew little about their new religion. The reason for their ignorance was that (after a short period of missions in Granada in the 1490s), they were not instructed in their new faith. A major obstacle to such instruction was the ignorance of Arabic on the part of most priests in the region.[16]

Converts from Judaism experienced a similar situation. At the end of the fifteenth century, 'the position of many *conversos* with regard to their new religion was one of profound ignorance'. They lacked 'systematic education in Christian beliefs and practices'.[17] Since they were no longer taught by rabbis, they also became increasingly ignorant of their old religion as well. Knowledge of the Jewish faith was sometimes passed on to the next generation, but in a simplified form that was sometimes defined against Christianity but sometimes borrowed from it.[18]

The laity were no better informed in some regions which had long been Christian. In early modern England, educated men, especially the clergy, often complained about the 'ignorant heathenish people', 'as ignorant of God . . . as the very savages'.[19] These complaints about lay ignorance focused on the 'dark corners of the land', especially the north and the west. For example, in the House of Commons in 1628, Sir Benjamin Rudyerd, a pious layman, lamented that there were places in northern England and in Wales 'where God was little better known than amongst the Indians'.[20]

Rudyerd was not alone in making this kind of comparison. In Italy and Spain at this time, parts of the countryside were known as 'the Indies over here' (*Indie di qua*) or 'other Indias' (*otras Indias*), since their inhabitants were in as much need of missionaries as the peoples of Asia or the Americas. Several Italian and Spanish missionaries who worked in the Apennines and the Abruzzi were inspired by what they had read about the Indies. One referred to Corsica as 'my India' (*la mia India*).[21]

## MISSIONS

The sixteenth century was not only the age of the European Reformation, but also the age of the expansion of Christianity outside Europe. The Jesuits in particular became a global order and made a major contribution to cultural globalization. The Catholic initiative was followed from the seventeenth century onwards by Protestant missionaries such as the Lutherans and Calvinists in India or the Moravians active in the Americas from Pennsylvania to Suriname.

Despite the difficulties under which they laboured, missionaries had one significant advantage over their colleagues at home. They knew that the people whom they were trying to convert knew nothing about Christianity. In South India, Catholic missionaries such as Roberto de Nobili and Protestant missionaries such as Bartholomäus Ziegenbalg used the Tamil term *akkiyanam* ('ignorance') to describe their converts.[22] In fact, the idea of the ignorance of their flocks is a commonplace in the writings of missionaries.[23] This view was sometimes held by the converts themselves. In Xhosaland (now part of South Africa), where a Methodist mission was active in the early nineteenth century, one man confessed that the Christian message had 'gone in at one ear and out at the other'. His case does not seem to have been an uncommon one.[24]

In the 'dark corners' of early modern Europe, the true situation was more obscure. Some missionaries began their visit to a particular region by asking questions, more ambitious than those asked in episcopal visitations. In the middle of the seventeenth century, in Eboli in southern Italy, some Jesuits encountered a group of shepherds. 'Asked how many gods there were, one replied "a hundred", another "a thousand", another a still higher number.' It is possible that Jesuit missionaries were instructed to ask this question, since a few years later, another of their missionaries, Julien Maunoir, active in Brittany, found that the inhabitants of the Isle of Ushant 'were unable to answer the question, how many gods there were'. A slightly more open-ended question was put to the inhabitants of Niolo in Corsica in 1652 by the missionaries of St Vincent de Paul: 'Whether there is one God, or many'.[25]

If the inhabitants of these three places had already known something about Christianity, they would have been extremely surprised by these questions from priests in their black robes and they would probably have searched for whatever answer would please their interrogators. The model of 'the Indies over here' may well have encouraged misunderstandings. Some of the clergy probably exaggerated the ignorance that they encountered, assuming, as literate people have done so often, that illiterates know little or nothing.

What has been discussed much less often than the ignorance of the laity is the ignorance of the missionaries themselves. They commonly knew little if anything of the culture to which they had been sent, beginning with its language.

Returning to Xhosaland, it seems that early nineteenth-century missionaries knew little or nothing about the traditional belief system of the people they were trying to convert, a system that included the idea of an impersonal divinity. This idea obviously made it difficult for the Xhosa to understand the Christian message.[26] In any case, in the early nineteenth century, many missionaries to Africa 'had little, if any, training and were even convinced that training, education and theology were rather pointless. What was needed was a good knowledge of the Bible, a great deal of faith, and a loud voice.'[27] The dangerous combination of ignorance and arrogance on the part of some missionaries has also been noted in a study of missions to Albania following the end of the Communist regime in 1991.[28]

It might be illuminating to approach the history of missions from the angle of the reciprocal ignorance of the two groups involved in this encounter, or three groups if we distinguish between the missionaries in the field and their superiors at their desks at home and so return to the theme of organizational ignorance that was introduced in chapter two. To quote William Burton, a Pentecostal missionary in the Congo in the early twentieth century, 'How many hundred missions have been handicapped by the fact that a home reference council had had the direction of the work. Men in their arm-chairs and their offices have dared to direct operations of a mission, in a field which they have never seen and under conditions of which they know nothing.'[29]

The main theme in such an approach to missions might be the ways in which each side learned to more or less understand the other. By the early twentieth century, some missionaries were devoting much of their time to studying not only the language but also the belief system of the people they were trying to convert. A few even published books on the subject – the Englishman John Roscoe, for instance, published an account of the Baganda (in what is now Uganda) in 1911; the Swiss Henri Junot, his *Life of a South African Tribe* (the Tsonga) in 1912; and the Belgian Placide Tempels, an interpretation of what he called 'Bantu philosophy' in 1945. These missionaries might be described as amateur anthropologists. A few actually turned professional in later life, notably Maurice Leenhardt, a French missionary in New Caledonia who became a professor in Paris.[30]

## IGNORANCE OF RELIGION IN THE TWENTY-FIRST CENTURY

In an age of surveys, including surveys of voters and consumers (to be discussed in later chapters), samples of the population of the United States and the United Kingdom have been asked not only about their religious beliefs but about their religious knowledge as well. In the UK in 2009, less than 5 per cent of the sample could name all the Ten Commandments (it is just as well that respondents were spared traditional questions about doctrines such as the Trinity or transubstantiation).[31]

In the USA in 2010, the Pew Forum's survey, 'Who Knows What About Religion', asked respondents to answer thirty-two simple questions, making the task easier by offering multiple choices. The average respondent scored sixteen out of thirty-two, but the survey showed considerable variation in knowledge.

> At the top end of that scale, at least eight-in-ten Americans know that teachers are not allowed to lead public school classes in prayer, that the term 'atheist' refers to someone who does not believe in God, and that Mother Teresa was Catholic. At the other end of the spectrum, just eight per cent know that the twelfth-century philosopher and Torah scholar Moses Maimonides was Jewish.[32]

## IGNORANCE OF OTHER RELIGIONS

Ignorance of other religions, often coupled with contempt, goes back a long way, not to mention ignorance of the 'other' in debates between

Catholics and Protestants or between Eastern and Western Christians. In the sixteenth century, for instance, the Greek Orthodox Church occupied 'a blind spot in early Reformation theology'.[33]

'Nature abhors a vacuum. So does the human mind.'[34] In the absence of more reliable knowledge, rumours flourish.[35] These rumours sometimes circulate so widely and are repeated so often that they may be said to solidify into long-lasting myths. This has been the case with Christian views of paganism, Judaism and Islam from the Middle Ages onwards, as well as with the views of Hinduism, Buddhism and other cults that spread in Europe after early modern travellers, merchants and soldiers penetrated Asia, Africa and the Americas. In all these cases, misinformation circulated widely.

In the ancient world, Christians were sometimes accused of the ritual murder of children and even of cannibalism, a vivid example of their perception as a threat to the rest of society.[36] In the Middle Ages, Christians accused the Jews of idolatry, ironically enough, given the fact that the Jews rejected holy images while the Christians accepted them.[37] Among the stories about the Jews that circulated at this time was that they worshipped the devil; that they desecrated the host (trampling on it, for instance) in order to test its power; that they poisoned the wells of cities and spread the plague. They were also accused, as early Christians had been, of ritual murder, kidnapping, killing and sometimes eating children: a dramatic example both of the long life of certain hostile stereotypes and their transfer from one group of outsiders to another. Accusations of this kind provoked pogroms in the later Middle Ages, or at least were used to legitimate violence for other reasons.[38] In these cases, it is difficult to distinguish the rejection of Judaism from the hatred of a minority whose dress, language and whole culture contrasted with that of the majority.

An alternative view on the part of the Church was that Jews were heretics, in other words that 'Judaism was not an independent faith but merely a perverse deviation from the one true faith'. This was actually worse than being regarded as an 'infidel', since as heretics, Jews became a target for official persecution.[39] Nicholas of Cusa was more accurate as well as more sympathetic, writing that 'The ancient pagans derided the Jews, who worshipped one infinite God of whom they were ignorant.'[40]

Christian scholars like Nicholas or the sixteenth-century German humanist Johann Reuchlin (who learned Hebrew to study Judaism) were and remained a minority. Reuchlin believed in the conversion of the Jews 'through reasoned disputation, gently and kindly'. As for Erasmus, his thought was 'permeated by a virulent theological anti-Judaism'. Following St Paul, Erasmus also criticized many Christians as 'Judaizers', in the sense of legalistic people who took the rules and the outward forms of religion too seriously at the expense of its spirit.[41]

Luther was more violent. In his treatise *On the Jews and Their Lies* (1543), he described them as 'full of the devil's faeces . . . which they wallow in like swine' and called for their synagogues and schools to be burned down.[42] In the seventeenth century, the witch-hunter Pierre de l'Ancre was not alone in denouncing what he called the 'absurd and indecent rites and beliefs' of the Jews. Meetings of so-called witches were often described by their persecutors as 'synagogues', which is surely a revealing detail.[43]

After the French Revolution, new myths were added to the repertoire of anti-Semitism, scapegoating Jews as a 'race' or ethnic group rather than adherents to a religion and accusing them of conspiracy on a global scale, plotting revolution in alliance with the Freemasons. A forged text first published in Russia, *The Protocols of the Elders of Zion* (1903), has often been used to justify the claim that the Jews were plotting to dominate the world.[44] After 1919, another myth, that of the 'stab in the back' (*Dolchstosslegende*), exploited by the Nazis, made Jews responsible for Germany's defeat in the First World War, conveniently letting the generals off the hook.[45] Luther's Anti-Semitism made Nazi Anti-Semitism more acceptable, at least to German Protestants. One pastor, Heinz Dungs, who was also a Nazi, compared Luther with Hitler as a great fighter.[46] Myths change but Anti-Semitism remains, still fuelled by a mix of hate, fear, credulity and ignorance.

Christian views of Islam were equally distorted, especially during what the distinguished medievalist Richard Southern called the 'age of ignorance' in Europe before the year 1100. In medieval texts such as the *Song of Roland* and Jean Bodel's *Play of St Nicholas*, followers of Islam were presented as worshippers of 'Mahomet' together with Tervagant and Apollo, viewed as an unholy trinity, an upside-down version of the Christian belief (as often happens, the unfamiliar was viewed in terms of the familiar).[47] It might be tempting to dismiss these views as examples of 'medieval credulity', but they do not differ all that much from the more recent ideas that all Muslims are fanatics or even terrorists.

Once again, Nicholas of Cusa was unusual in actually studying the Koran and viewing Muhammad neither as malicious nor an impostor but simply as someone ignorant of Christianity. Nicholas showed 'awareness of the limits of our judgement on those of other religions'.[48] In medieval Spain, following the invasion and settlement of the country by Arabs from North Africa from the eighth century onwards, Christians became relatively familiar with Islam. Indeed, when Spaniards arrived in Mexico in the sixteenth century, some of them referred to the local temples as 'mosques' (*mesquitas*), once again viewing the unfamiliar in term of the familiar.

On the other hand, Marco Polo's travels in Persia and elsewhere did not make him sympathetic to what he described as 'the accursed doctrines of the Saracens', writing inaccurately that 'The law that their prophet Mahomet has given them lays down that any harm they may do to one who does not accept their law . . . is no sin at all.'[49] 'It was only in the seventeenth century that scholars from other parts of Europe learned Arabic and produced more accurate if not always more sympathetic accounts of Islam.' Even then, it 'was not uncommon for these accounts to describe Mohammed as an "impostor"'.[50]

Western ignorance of other religions lasted longer. When Vasco da Gama landed in Calicut in 1498, his men believed all Indians to be Christians (as some, the 'St Thomas Christians', were). They mistook a Hindu temple for 'a large church' that included 'an image which they said represented Our Lady' and painted 'saints', each with 'four or five arms'. In other words, they were 'willing to see in any structure that was not obviously a mosque, a church of some sort'.[51] After the misunderstanding had been corrected, Hindu beliefs would be dismissed by westerners as 'fables' or as 'superstition', while images of the gods displayed in Hindu temples would be described by Western visitors as 'monsters' or 'devils' and often shown, like medieval images of pagans, as wearing horns.[52]

Even the intellectual baggage of missionaries (with distinguished exceptions such as the Italian Jesuit Matteo Ricci in China and the Dutch Protestant pastor Abraham Rogier in India) often included little more than the concepts of 'paganism', 'idolatry', 'superstition' and the conviction that indigenous cults were diabolical parodies of the true faith.

This conviction was shared by missionaries in Mexico. Juan de Zumárraga, bishop of New Spain, claimed to have destroyed many 'idols' of the 'devils' that the indigenous people worshipped. Diego Durán, a missionary in Yucatán, wrote about what he called 'counterfeit deities' and 'the false religion with which the devil was worshipped', while the bishop of Yucatán, Diego de Landa, declared that idolatry, like drunkenness, was one of the main 'vices of the Indians' (*vicios de los Indios*).[53]

It was not until the eighteenth century that some westerners rejected these hostile images and began taking Hinduism seriously as a religion. John Holwell, for example, an English surgeon who was for a time the governor of Bengal, noting the place of ignorance in encouraging 'presumption and contempt for others', declared himself 'amazed that we should so readily believe the people of Indostan a race of stupid idolaters, when to our cost in a political and commercial view, we have found them superior to us'. The Scottish soldier Alexander Dow found excuses for 'our ignorance concerning the learning, religion and philosophy of the Brahmins', but tried to correct it. Nathaniel Halhed, an Englishman in the service of the East India Company, compared Hindu belief in miracles with that of Christians in 'ages of ignorance' and illiteracy.[54]

A milestone in the spread of European knowledge about other religions was *Religious Ceremonies of the World* (1723–43), illustrated by Bernard Picart and explained by Jean Frédéric Bernard, which has been described as 'the book that changed Europe' and 'the first global vision of religion', allowing readers to compare and contrast different cults.[55]

Following a retrospective method, we can use the discoveries gradually made by the missionaries as indicators of their initial ignorance. When they first set foot in India, early modern missionaries were largely ignorant of indigenous religious traditions, especially Hinduism. It was only gradually that they, together with other Europeans who lived in India rather than simply visiting the country or reading about it, learned that the local gods were not monsters and discovered what they called 'Hinduism' – though some scholars have argued that they did not so much discover as 'construct' the religion by viewing regional cults as part of a general system.[56]

In similar fashion, Europeans discovered Buddhism, not suddenly but in the course of a long process of learning that began with the Jesuit encounter with Japan in 1549 and was still in progress when the Buddhist Society of London was founded in 1924. The Italian Jesuit Ippolito Desideri, who was sent to convert the Tibetans, studied for five years in what we might call a Buddhist 'theological college' in Lhasa, but his report on what he learned was not published until the twentieth century, apparently because Desideri's superiors in the Society of Jesus considered that he had displayed too much sympathy for Buddhism. Encounters with Buddhists 'made little impact on the understanding of Buddhism in the West' before the nineteenth century.[57]

## DISSIMULATION

Ignorance about the religion of others, whether individuals or groups, is sometimes the result of concealment, especially in the wake of forced conversions. It has often been suggested that the African slaves who were shipped to the New World and expected to accept Christianity remained loyal to their traditional West and Central African divinities. They kept their masters and the Christian clergy in ignorance of this loyalty by finding equivalents for their deities (*orishas*) among the Catholic saints. Ogun was disguised as St George, for instance, Shango as St Barbara, and so on. However, what began as disguise ended as pluralism, so that today, some Brazilians practise both Catholicism and the traditional African cult of Candomblé.[58]

Examples of minorities who keep outsiders in ignorance of their religion include the Crypto-Jews, Crypto-Muslims, Crypto-Catholics and Crypto-Protestants of early modern Europe.

Queen Elizabeth I is said to have made the famous promise not to open 'windows into men's souls'. Her attitude was not shared by Catholic inquisitors or indeed by Calvinist consistories, the assemblies that governed that Church. Those who did not share the dominant beliefs needed to keep their windows closed. As long as there is persecution of other religions there will be dissimulation, in other words the public practice of one form of religion by people who do not believe in it and practise another religion in private.

This recurrent response to a recurrent situation for Jews, Christians and Muslims was particularly necessary in the sixteenth century, thanks to the forced conversions of Muslims and Jews in Spain and to the conflicts between different kinds of Christian in Europe during the Reformation and Counter-Reformation.

In Arabic, dissimulation of this kind, long practised by the Shi'ites, is known as *taqiyya*, a word that also means 'fear' or 'prudence'. Prudence was certainly needed after the reconquest of Spain by the 'Catholic Kings' Ferdinand and Isabella in 1492, when Jews and Muslims were forced to convert to Christianity and became officially known as 'new Christians'.

In 1504 a mufti in Oran issued a fatwa allowing exterior conformity. 'Bow down,' he wrote, 'to whatever idols they are bowing to, but turn your intention toward Allah . . . If they oblige you to drink wine, you may do so, but let it not be your intention to make use of it . . . if they force pork on you, eat it but in your heart reject it.'[59] In other words, use external conformity as a way of maintaining the ignorance of the authorities.

Crypto-Jews and Crypto-Muslims present the historian today with the same problem that was faced by the early modern authorities: how to distinguish between genuine and feigned converts. Despite the problem, some perceptive studies have been published about these dissident groups.[60]

Within Christianity, dissimulation was also necessary on occasion, since heresy was a crime. After the Reformation and the consequent split of Western Europe into Catholic, Lutheran and Calvinist areas, individuals living in the 'wrong' area sometimes followed this practice, sometimes described at the time, notably by Jean Calvin, as 'Nicodemism', referring to the New Testament story of the Pharisee Nicodemus, who went to see Christ by night.[61]

## AGNOSTICISM

The term 'agnostic' comes from the Greek, meaning a lack of spiritual knowledge (*gnosis*). The first recorded agnostics were the Greek philosophers Xenophanes (*c.* 580–*c.* 470 BCE), who remarked that 'No man has ever seen nor will anyone ever know the clear truth about the gods', and Protagoras (*c.* 490–*c.* 420 BCE), who affirmed that 'About the gods I am able to know neither that they exist nor that they do not exist nor of what kind they are in shape: for many things prevent me for knowing this, its obscurity and the brevity of man's life.'[62]

According to Sextus Empiricus, who was discussed in chapter two, philosophical sceptics suspend judgement about the existence or non-existence of God.[63] Knowing that one does not know whether or not God exists – and believing that other people do not know either, whatever they may claim – is usually described as 'agnosticism', a term coined in 1869 by the British scientist T. H. Huxley. The term is also used in German – Nietzsche, for instance, refers to *Agnostikern* – and in French – Proust used the term *agnosticisme* – but discussions of the phenomenon are more common in the Anglophone world.[64]

In what might be called his confession of non-faith, Huxley declared his trust in the principle 'that it is wrong for a man to say he is certain of the objective truth of a proposition unless he can produce evidence which logically justifies that certainty. That is what agnosticism asserts and, in my opinion, is all that is essential to agnosticism.'[65] Huxley was one of a group of Victorian intellectuals who held a similar position, among them Herbert Spencer, Francis Galton, Leslie Stephen (author of 'An Agnostic's Apology', 1876) and probably Charles Darwin and Thomas Hardy as well.[66]

The debate over agnosticism was at its height in Britain between 1862, when the philosopher James Martineau discussed what he called 'religious nescience', till 1907, when the *Agnostic Annual*, founded in 1884, ceased to appear. Interest in the debate was already on the wane by 1903 when another philosopher, Robert Flint, published a history of agnosticism that began with the ancient sceptics.

What might be described as 'devout agnosticism' can be found in both Jewish and Christian traditions.[67] The idea of a 'hidden God' goes back to the Old Testament (Isaiah 45.15). The medieval Jewish scholar Moses Maimonides claimed that it is impossible 'to describe the Creator by any means except by negative attributes'.[68] Some of the Fathers of the Church, notably Gregory of Nazianzus, had made a similar point. So did some mystics, such as the anonymous fourteenth-century English writer of a book with the poetic title *The Cloud of Unknowing*.

The most famous expression of this idea is surely the treatise by the fifteenth-century cardinal Nicholas of Cusa, entitled 'Learned Ignorance' (*Docta Ignorantia*). By this phrase he meant that it was possible to attain the knowledge of one's own ignorance. Nicholas wrote that 'God is ineffable', so that he could only be approached by a negative route (*via negativa*), that is, by saying what he is not. Later, Martin Luther and Blaise Pascal both argued that God was unknowable by reason alone. According to them, Christianity could only be based on divine revelation.[69]

Since atheists believe in an absence – the absence of God – they might qualify for discussion here, but a stronger case can be made for including Deism. Eighteenth-century Deists believed in a God who created the world and then left it to its own devices, like a watchmaker whose watches function by themselves.[70] The poet Alexander Pope drew the moral: 'Presume not God to scan/The proper study of mankind is Man'.[71]

## THE SITUATION TODAY

In 2015, a survey of religious attitudes in the UK conducted for YouGov found that 7 per cent of respondents described themselves as 'agnostic', while 19 per cent were atheist. Whether the agnostics held opinions about the limits of knowability was not recorded. In the USA in 2019, a poll found that 23 per cent of Americans surveyed answered 'no religion' rather than choose a faith, while in Germany that same year, according to the Eurobarometer survey, the proportion was around 30 per cent (it was higher in the former GDR than in the west).[72]

These choices mean that the respondents do not believe rather than that they are totally ignorant of religion. Nonetheless, the figures suggest that for a quarter or more of the population of three large countries in the West, religious knowledge is scanty. Even believers often lack knowledge of their faith. Christian Fundamentalists sometimes claim that 'I don't need to read any books, I have the Bible', but as a retired American pastor recently pointed out, many of them do not know the Bible well either, while they are completely ignorant of the tradition of debate about its reliability and its diverse interpretations.[73]

One might have thought that in an age of globalization, knowledge of the world religions would increase. Although this knowledge has become increasingly accessible, and some conversions from one religion to another take place, ignorance remains widespread. Few westerners are as frank about their ignorance as Peter Stanford, a British journalist who has written about Christianity and presented programmes discussing Hinduism, Sikhism and Jainism. Stanford has admitted to knowing little about their core beliefs, 'failing, for example, to name the five Ks of Sikhism, or getting confused about what distinguishes the principal schools of Buddhism'.[74]

A survey carried out in the USA in 2008 revealed that 80 per cent of respondents did not know that the Sunnis are the largest group of Muslims worldwide. The Pew Forum survey of 2010 was more ambitious, asking Americans two questions on Judaism, two on Islam, two on Buddhism and one on Hinduism. On average, respondents answered correctly almost half the time – which means that more than half could not, for instance, name the Koran or say what Ramadan is. Another Pew Forum Survey, in 2019, found that over 70 per cent of respondents did not know that Islam is the religion of most Indonesians or that Rosh Hashanah is the Jewish New Year.[75]

One might have thought that the growth of the Muslim population of the UK in the last half century would lead to a better knowledge of their beliefs on the part of their fellow citizens. However, a survey by Ipsos Mori in 2018 found that the British public still knows little about Islam. They seriously overestimate the number of Muslims in the country (as one in six instead of one in twenty), while 'understanding of Islam is limited', especially among older people.[76]

Ignorance of other religions is not confined to the West. Another survey of the religious knowledge of a sample of thirty thousand adults in 2019–20 carried out by the Pew Research Centre, this time in India, found that a majority of Hindus admitted 'not to know much about India's other religions' (Muslim, Sikh, Jain and Christian).[77]

To sum up with a simple formula: over the long term, there have been several important shifts in religious knowledge. In medieval Christendom, many believed but few knew very much about their religion. The period 1500–1900 was an age of movements of evangelization at home and abroad, both in the Christian and in the Muslim worlds. Since 1900, religious knowledge has been available as never before, but it has come to have a low priority. More and more people choose to be ignorant of religion, though not in the Islamic world, where a religious reformation began spreading widely in the later twentieth century.

# 7

# IGNORANCE OF SCIENCE

The greatest of all the accomplishments of twentieth-century
science has been the discovery of human ignorance
Lewis Thomas

As was pointed out earlier, the history of ignorance has emerged from
the history of knowledge, which has in its turn emerged from the
history of science. It is scarcely surprising, then, that some of the most
important studies of the history of ignorance focused on the natural
sciences. For example, the book that founded the study of 'agnotology'
was edited by two historians of science.[1]

When a general symposium on 'Science and Ignorance' was organized at the American Association for the Advancement of Science in
1993, the philosopher of science Jerome Ravetz emphasized what he
called 'the sin of science', in other words the 'ignorance of ignorance',
encouraged by the training of scientists and by the triumphalist image
of scientific progress. For today's scientists, Ravetz claimed, 'Uncertainty
exists only as far as it can be managed interestingly, in the form of the
soluble research problems at the margin of our scientific knowledge.'[2]

In the past, some scientists, or as they used to be known, 'natural
philosophers', were well aware of their ignorance. The most famous
formulation of this awareness of how much there always remains to
know is associated with Isaac Newton, who is supposed to have said
that 'To myself I seem only to have been like a child playing on the

seashore, and diverting myself in now and then finding a smoother pebble or a prettier shell than ordinary, whilst the vast ocean of truth lay all undiscovered before me.' Even if Newton never said or never even thought this, the expression of the idea in an eighteenth-century text is itself significant.[3] In any case, Newton expressed his sense of his ignorance, in this case ignorance of what lies behind an everyday phenomenon, in another famous passage, admitting that 'the Cause of Gravity is what I do not pretend to know'.[4] In similar fashion, the agnosticism of T. H. Huxley extended to science as well as theology. 'I don't know whether Matter is anything distinct from Force,' he once wrote. 'I don't know that atoms are anything but pure myths.'[5]

At much the same time as Huxley, the British physicist James Clerk Maxwell wrote that 'Thoroughly conscious ignorance is the prelude to every real advance in science.'[6] Still more radical, the German physiologist Emil Du Bois-Reymond gave a celebrated lecture on the limits to science in 1872. He discussed not only what was not known at a given moment but also what could never be known. The title of his lecture was 'We shall not know' (*Ignorabimus*).[7]

The concern on the part of scientists with what they do not know has become even more obvious in the twenty-first century.

For example, in 2004, in his Nobel Prize acceptance speech, the American theoretical physicist David Gross asked the following question: 'As knowledge increases, could the pace of scientific discovery slow; as more and more problems are solved?' His optimistic answer was that 'The questions we ask today are more profound and more interesting than those asked years ago when I was a student . . . back then we did not possess enough knowledge to be intelligently ignorant . . . I am happy to report that there is no evidence that we are running out of our most important resource – ignorance.'[8]

A year later, in 2005, the 125th anniversary issue of the journal *Science* offered readers what it called a 'survey of scientific ignorance'. Again, an American professor of neuroscience, Stuart Firestein, began teaching a course on scientific ignorance at Columbia University in 2006, inviting scientists in different fields to speak to the students about what they do not know. The scientists 'come and tell us about what they would like to know, what they think is critical to know, how they might get to know it, what will happen if they do find this or that thing out, what might happen if they don't'.[9]

In what follows, I shall discuss the place of ignorance in the history of science; its place in new research; losses of knowledge; resistance to knowledge; and finally, the ignorance of non-scientists, the laity.

## DISCOVERIES OF IGNORANCE

One way of writing the history of science might be to present it as Alain Corbin has presented some episodes in the history of geography: as the story of increasing awareness of past ignorance. It was suggested in chapter one that ignorance is often revealed retrospectively. After a discovery is made, a community becomes aware of what its members did not know before. For example, Voltaire pointed out that before the seventeenth century, everyone was 'still ignorant of the circulation of the blood, the weight and pressure of the air, the laws of motion, the doctrine of light and colour, the number of the planets in our system'.[10]

Again, take the case of the age of the earth. In the seventeenth century, scholars believed the world to be about six thousand years old. With a precision that now seems comic, archbishop James Ussher declared that 'the beginning of time . . . fell upon the entrance of the night preceding the 23rd day of October' in 4004 BC.[11] A little over a century later, the Comte de Buffon's *Epochs of Nature* (1779) argued that the earth was about 75,000 years old. In the early nineteenth century, the German geologist Abraham Werner trumped Buffon by claiming that the earth's age was over a million years. In the 1860s, basing his estimate on heat loss, the British physicist William Thomson (Lord Kelvin), came up with the figure of a hundred million, which he later reduced to twenty million. His results came to appear too modest. Around 1915, the geologist Arthur Holmes came up with the figure of fifteen hundred million following his analysis of rocks in Mozambique. In 1931, however, speaking to a committee on the age of the earth, Holmes suggested three billion as a possible figure. Twenty years later,

Clair Patterson, studying meteorites, increased the figure to 4.5 billion, where it now stands. Each revision exposed the ignorance built into earlier estimates, only to be exposed in its turn.[12]

## HOW IGNORANCE DRIVES SCIENCE

When Yuval Harari described 'modern science' in his *Sapiens*, he entitled his chapter 'the discovery of ignorance', or more exactly of 'willingness to admit ignorance'.[13] This was not simply one of his favourite provocations, but an echo of statements by Herbert Spencer, Lewis Thomas and Stuart Firestein, whose book explores the paradox that 'science progresses through the growth of ignorance'.

In the nineteenth century, the British philosopher Herbert Spencer imagined science as 'a gradually increasing sphere': 'every addition to its surface does but bring it into wider contact with surrounding nescience'.[14] Each time a specific problem is solved, another problem becomes visible. The gaze of scientists is directed towards the future. The physicist Marie Curie confessed that 'One never notices what has been done; one can only see what remains to be done.'[15] As Firestein suggests, 'Scientists use ignorance to program their work, to identify what should be done, what the next steps are.'[16] According to the Irish chemist John Bernal, 'True research has to work into the unknown all the time.'[17] As the British molecular biologist Francis Crick once remarked, 'In research the front line is almost always in a fog', until the right idea comes to someone. The story of the discovery of the double-helix structure of DNA, in which Crick participated, bears him out.[18]

As the fog clears, scientists practise the 'selective' or 'specified' ignorance that was noted in chapter one: the deliberate ignoring of some of the data in order to concentrate on a particular problem. The neuroscientist Larry Abbott, speaking about his own research, stressed the importance of choosing 'precisely where along the frontier of ignorance I want to work'. This kind of choice might be described as the 'management of ignorance'.[19]

Sometimes the wrong choice is made – in cancer research, for instance, selectivity was a serious obstacle to solving a particular

problem.[20] In general, however, scientists might be described as practising what the American philosopher John Dewey called 'genuine'
ignorance, which is 'profitable because it is likely to be accompanied by
humility, curiosity and open-mindedness'.[21] 'Unanticipated ignorance'
refers to unexpected findings that turn up in the course of research.[22]

Ignorance leads to surprises, while 'Surprises can make people aware
of their own ignorance' and so open 'a window to new and unexpected
knowledge'.[23]

For a recent example that is as spectacular as it is invisible to the
human eye, we may take the muon, a heavy form of electron. It was
reported early in 2021 that a team of physicists, studying muons at
Fermilab in the USA, discovered that their behaviour did not fit the
model currently offered in particle physics. The physicists do not know
whether they have discovered a new particle or, what would be still
more spectacular, a new law of nature. In any case, their consciousness
of ignorance will drive further research, as in the case of 'dark matter',
which astronomers can map without being able to explain its distribution or indeed to say what dark matter is.[24]

## LOSSES OF KNOWLEDGE

Ignorance is sometimes the result of a loss of knowledge, a kind of
collective amnesia. A classic case is that of Greek science (including
mathematics), lost to western Europeans in the early Middle Ages. The
correspondence of two eleventh-century scholars, Raginbold of Cologne
and Radolf of Liège, shows them discussing what might be meant by
the phrase 'the interior angles' of a triangle in the famous theorem
attributed to Pythagoras. As a leading medievalist noted, this is 'a forc-
ible reminder of the vast scientific ignorance with which the age was
faced'.[25] Some of this ignorance was remedied by the Arabic translations of and commentaries on Greek texts that were made in Baghdad,
and the Latin translations of these Arabic translations in Toledo in the
twelfth and thirteenth centuries.[26]

In early modern Europe, the study of alchemy offers a vivid example
of what Martin Mulsow calls 'precarious knowledge', since individual

alchemists carried out their experiments in secret and recorded the results in manuscript. As a result, the risk of losing knowledge was high.[27]

Losses can still occur, despite the efforts to preserve knowledge in a variety of media. Particular observations or theories have sometimes dropped out of the collective scientific consciousness, until they are made or formulated all over again, rather like the rediscovery of America.

What has been described as 'one of the severest cases of collective amnesia in the history of science' concerns the history of the perception of different colours. Lazarus Geiger argued in 1867 that perception of colour over the millennia followed the sequence of sensitivity to red, yellow, green, blue, violet. However, 'In the decades following the First World War, Geiger's sequence was simply erased from memory.' Only in the 1960s was it rediscovered.[28]

More widely known is the fate of the research on the transmission of hereditary traits in plants carried out by the Augustinian friar Gregor Mendel. Mendel formulated his now famous principles of transmission in a paper published in 1866 in a local journal in Brno. The international scientific community took little notice of the publication at the time, so that Mendel's discoveries had to be made all over again a generation later by the German biologist Carl Correns and the Dutch botanist Hugo de Vries.[29]

## RESISTING NEW IDEAS

As we saw in chapter one, a major variety of ignorance is 'wilful', in other words not wanting to know, linked to what Karl Popper called 'active' ignorance in the sense of resistance to certain ideas, especially new ones. There is a famous story about Galileo's discovery of craters on the moon, showing that it was not, as Aristotle thought, a perfectly smooth sphere. Some Aristotelians are supposed to have refused to look at the moon through a telescope because they did not want to see the craters. This particular story is a myth, but the history of science offers many cases of resistance of this kind, leading the opponents of novelty to 'miss discoveries that are literally right before their eyes'.[30] They do not want to see what Thomas Kuhn called 'anomalies' in nature that cast doubt on theories that they were trained to accept.[31]

Examples of this blindness and of what Gaston Bachelard called 'epistemological obstacles' include resistance to the heliocentric theory of Copernicus; to Darwin's theory of evolution; to Pasteur's discovery of microbes; to Gregor Mendel's theory of genetic inheritance; and to Max Planck's quantum theory.

It was resistance to quantum theory that prompted Planck's bitter epigram that 'Science progresses from funeral to funeral'. His point was that 'A new scientific truth does not triumph by convincing its opponents and making them see the light, but rather because its opponents eventually die, and a new generation grows up that is familiar with it.'[32] Members of an older generation are often unwilling to abandon theories in which they may well have invested their professional capital. It is understandable, however regrettable, that they do not want to know that they were wrong.

It would be wrong to ascribe all the resistance to heliocentrism of Copernicus and its defence by Galileo either to simple ignorance or the desire not to know about evidence that contradicted both Aristotle and the Bible. The Galileo affair in particular has often been viewed as a major episode in the 'Warfare of Science with Theology', in the famous phrase of Andrew White, co-founder and president of Cornell University.[33] One problem with this formulation is the diversity of opinions of both theologians and natural philosophers (as scientists were known in Galileo's day), not to mention overlaps between the two categories. One historian of science has pointed out that defenders of geocentrism were a 'diverse group', while another has noted both 'anti-Copernican reliance on "scientific" arguments to support their views, and Copernican reliance on "religious" arguments to support theirs'.[34]

In the case of Galileo's opponents, there was a conflict between hard-line Dominican theologians, who opposed all discussions of heliocentrism, and Jesuits who followed a milder line, distinguishing between discussions that treated the idea as a hypothesis and belief that the sun really was in the centre of the universe.[35] The notorious condemnation of Galileo by the Church has often been misunderstood. Galileo was not condemned for his private opinions but for his public stand as a Catholic who tried to 'convert the Church' to the new science by arguing against literal interpretations of passages of the Bible such as Joshua commanding the sun to stop moving. Galileo was viewed as infringing the clerical monopoly of interpreting Scripture.[36]

Darwin was attacked by scientists such as Louis Agassiz as well as theologians such as Samuel Wilberforce because his theory of evolution by natural selection contradicted the biblical account of creation. Agassiz believed in what he called 'the direct intervention of a Supreme Intelligence in the plan of Creation'.[37] However, the history of Darwinism is not a simple story of the warfare between science and theology. Darwin was also criticized on scientific grounds – indeed, Wilberforce's critical review of *The Origin of Species* deliberately avoided theological arguments – while his book was defended by 'Christian Darwinians'.[38]

In France, resistance to Darwin's ideas was particularly strong, especially among the older generation that dominated the Academy of Sciences. Darwin's friend T. H. Huxley went so far as to write about a 'conspiracy of silence' among the French.[39] Huxley (like Planck later), believed that not wanting to know played a part in resistance to Darwin's ideas. Describing *The Origin of Species* as 'badly received by the generation to which it was addressed', Huxley went on to suggest that 'the present generation will probably behave just as badly if another Darwin should arise and inflict on them that which the generality of mankind most hate – the necessity of revising their convictions'.[40]

It would be comforting to think that scientists have become more open-minded since Huxley and Planck made their remarks, but the evidence is against this idea. Take, for example, the theory of continental drift, proposed by the German scientist Alfred Wegener in his book on the origin of continents (*Die Entstehung der Kontinente*, 1915).

Wegener was impressed, he explained, by looking at a map of the world and noticing how the east coast of Brazil appears to fit into the west coast of Africa like pieces of a jigsaw puzzle. He noted similarities between the rocks and the fossils of both sides of the divide, and drew the conclusion that they once formed a single region that later split into two. In the 1920s and 1930s, Wegener's theory was rejected by many geologists, especially in North America.

As Naomi Oreskes has argued, there were two main reasons for the negative reaction to Wegener's theory. One was opposition to what she calls 'the unmaking of scientific knowledge', a reluctance to give up the traditional geological paradigm of the stability of continents.[41] As one American geologist, Rollin Chamberlin, remarked, 'If we are to believe Wegener's hypothesis we must forget everything which has been learned in the last seventy years and start again.'[42]

A second reason for opposition to the idea of drift was the result of a conflict between disciplines and methods. The older discipline of geology was based on observation in the field, while the new discipline of geophysics was based on experiments in the laboratory, explaining drift by movements in the huge slabs of rock known as 'tectonic plates'. Patrick Blackett, a leading supporter of the theory of drift in the 1950s, was originally a nuclear physicist. As Charles Richter, a specialist on earthquakes who was also trained as a physicist, pointed out, 'We are all best impressed by evidence of the type with which we are most familiar.'[43]

Closer to our own time, in the 1980s and 1990s, a few well-known scientists became notorious for their protracted opposition to discoveries that contradicted what they wanted to believe. They cast doubt in public on what was becoming the scientific consensus about four threats to life and health in particular: the link between smoking and cancer, the problem of acid rain, the depletion of the ozone layer, and most important of all, the trend towards global warming.[44] These scientists include, in order of seniority, Frederick Seitz, William Nierenberg and Fred Singer. All three began their career as physicists. Seitz and Nierenberg were part of the wartime Manhattan Project, working on the production of an atomic bomb. They later rose to the top of their profession: Seitz became president of the National Academy of Sciences, while Nierenberg was a member of its council.

All three men were politically conservative. Seitz and Nierenberg were among the founders of a right-wing think tank, the George

Marshall Institute, while Singer was a Fellow of another one, the Alexis de Tocqueville Institution. All three men had links to industry and government. Seitz worked as a consultant to the tobacco industry, Nierenberg chaired the Acid Rain Peer Review Panel appointed by President Reagan, and Singer was chief scientist for the US Department of Transportation. All three were climate change sceptics. Singer published a number of books expressing his views on the subject, while Seitz and Nierenberg advised against taking measures to prevent or delay global warming, advice that presidents Reagan and George H. W. Bush clearly wanted to hear.

The evidence for their wilful ignorance is not the initial scepticism of the three scientists about the four threats – initial scepticism is a necessary element in evaluating new discoveries or theories – but rather, their continued refusal to accept the increasing evidence that the threats were real. In short, all three of them ignored or resisted information that pointed to what they did not want to know. As for industry and government, their campaigns to 'disinform' the public will be discussed in chapter nine.

Some of these campaigns are linked to what is known as 'Undone Science', the collective ignoring of problems and the 'areas of research that are left unfunded'. This 'systematic nonproduction of knowledge' illustrates the politics of science, the competition between groups with different agenda (government, industry, NGOs, foundations, universities and so on).[45] It might be illuminating to study 'undone social science' in this way and even, despite their chronic lack of funding, the humanities.

## MEDICAL IGNORANCE

As we saw in chapter four, medicine was a field in which ignorance was studied relatively early. Much has been written about charlatans and quacks as well as about more professional forms of 'bad medicine'.[46] In those cases it is necessary to discuss not only the problem of what is not known in a given field but also the much larger problem of what is not known by many individuals working in it, especially if their career is one of applying knowledge rather than carrying out research.

As the English doctor Ben Goldacre has pointed out, 'Today's medical students will qualify at the age of twenty-four and will then work for five decades . . . Medicine changes around you, unrecognizably over the course of decades: whole new classes of drugs are invented, whole new ways of diagnosing people, and even whole new diseases.' Doctors may try to keep up to date but given the number of articles published every year in medical journals, information overload makes this impossible, even in a particular speciality.[47] Lay people know even less, or resist the knowledge of hazards to health from nicotine, cholesterol or simple lack of exercise. Not wanting to know about some aspect of science or medicine is no monopoly of scientists or physicians.

## LAY IGNORANCE

The sharp contrast between professional scientists and the general public that we see today has not always existed. It emerged, like other forms of professionalization, in the early nineteenth century, the moment when the word 'scientist' was coined in English. Nonetheless, in earlier centuries, a rough distinction may be made between the learned and everyone else, including in 'learning' both medicine and natural science, which used to be known as 'natural philosophy'.

In the sixteenth and seventeenth centuries, studies of natural philosophy continued to be published almost exclusively in Latin, thus making their contents inaccessible to the majority of the population of Europe and even to the majority of the literate. In the sixteenth century, the Swiss physician and alchemist Paracelsus broke this rule by writing in German, and in the seventeenth century Galileo did the same by writing in Italian, choosing the dramatic form of a dialogue as a way to reach a wider public. However, many of their academic colleagues were shocked by this breach of convention.

Workers in different occupations – fishermen, midwives, miners, masons, blacksmiths, goldsmiths and so on – acquired specialized knowledges of nature, but these knowledges were rarely written down and it is unlikely that they were widely shared. Indeed, the guilds to which artisans belonged insisted on keeping their particular knowledges secret, as alchemists did, in order to avoid competition.[48]

If there was one domain where knowledge, or what was thought to be knowledge, was spreading in early modern Europe, it was medicine. In the case of patients, the problem of choosing between different medical practitioners offers a vivid example of decision-making in conditions of uncertainty. Another option for them was 'do it yourself', but this required the laity to remedy their ignorance of medicine. Paracelsus wished to see every man his own healer, boasting that whatever he knew, he had learned from his own experience, rather than depend on someone else's ignorance.[49]

In the wake of Paracelsus, medical books in vernacular languages aimed at a relatively wide reading public began to proliferate from the sixteenth century onwards. A famous English example of these vernacular books is *The English Physician* (1652), actually a guide to healing herbs produced by the apothecary Nicholas Culpeper. Culpeper, who was a republican and a radical Protestant, denounced publications in Latin as a means whereby the 'Commonalty' could be 'kept in ignorance that so they may the better be made slaves of'. He opposed the intellectual monopolies of priests and lawyers just as he opposed those of the College of Physicians, whom he accused of 'learned ignorance' in the pejorative sense of the term, not that of Nicholas of Cusa.[50] As the title page boasts, Culpeper's herbal was published in English and sold at the low price of threepence to enable every man 'to cure himself'. In similar fashion, his *Directory for Midwives* (1651) was not written for midwives but described itself as 'a guide for women' when conceiving, giving birth and nursing their babies.[51] A century later, the Scottish physician William Buchan's *Domestic Medicine* (1769) became a bestseller. Among its competitors, titles such as *The Poor Man's Medicine Chest* (1791) reminded readers that books of this kind were less expensive than doctors' fees.

A movement for the popularization of natural philosophy was spreading in the later eighteenth century. Some leading scientists participated in the movement. The Swedish botanist Carl Linnaeus, for example, produced small books, simply written and quickly translated, and so 'lowered the educational and financial entrance fee to the study of nature'.[52] A new group came into existence, professional popularizers.

One important means of spreading scientific knowledge in the eighteenth century was the popular lecture, a performance that often included 'demonstrations', in other words experiments carried out in public.[53] In the nineteenth century, the British scientist John Henry Pepper became famous for this kind of performance for a lay audience. In his lectures on the physics of light, for instance, a shadowy figure that seemed to be a ghost would appear on stage. Less showy, but at least equally successful, were the lectures on the cosmos given by Alexander von Humboldt to the general public in a music hall in Berlin in 1828. So was T. H. Huxley's famous lecture to the working men of Norwich in 1868 on 'a piece of chalk', introducing them by this means to chemistry, geology and palaeontology. Another form of popularization was the scientific magazine, for example the *Scientific American*, which was founded in 1845, targeting 'artisans and mechanics', and continues to this day.[54]

The nineteenth century was also a time of lay resistance to some scientific theories, notably Darwin's theory of evolution, with its implied criticism of the biblical account of creation in *Genesis* as well as of the argument that the design of the natural world proved the existence of God. Darwin sometimes used the term 'creationists' to refer to opponents of his views who believed that nature was a divine creation. Many of them are still active today, especially in the United States.

In Tennessee, a law passed in 1925 forbade teachers from contradicting the biblical account of creation, and one teacher, John Scopes, was taken to court for breaking this law (more exactly, Scopes agreed to challenge the law in court). Following extensive publicity, the trial was abandoned, but the law was not repealed until 1967.[55] What its supporters call 'scientific creationism' remains powerful. An Institute for Creation Research was founded in 1970, while the American Catholic biochemist Michael Behe, described as 'a modern Agassiz', opposes Darwinism and defends the argument for intelligent design.[56]

A survey of the USA carried out by Gallup in 2017 found that 38 per cent of adults in the United States still believed that 'God created humans in their present form at one time within the last 10,000 years'.[57]

Despite the resistance to Darwin, the nineteenth century now appears to have been a golden age for lay knowledge of science, followed by a slow decline ever since. The decline was famously lamented in a lecture given in Cambridge in 1959 by C. P. Snow, a former physical chemist turned novelist. In his lecture, Snow described science and the humanities as two separate cultures, claiming, probably correctly, that educated non-scientists were so ignorant of physics that they were incapable of citing the second law of thermodynamics, let alone understanding its importance. 'So the great edifice of modern physics goes up, and the majority of the cleverest people in the western world have about as much insight into it as their Neolithic ancestors would have had.'[58]

A few years after Snow, in 1963, the Scientists' Institute for Public Information was founded in the USA in order to assist the spread of scientific knowledge via journalism. It may be significant that the Institute considered it necessary to adopt an indirect approach, informing journalists who would in turn inform the public. Television programmes became particularly important in the process of popularization. In Britain, for instance, the BBC has commissioned a series on astronomy from the physicist Brian Cox as well as many series on natural history from the famous broadcaster David Attenborough. It would be good to know how much of the information presented to them on such programmes is remembered by viewers a few months or years later. A survey carried out in 1989 by John Durant, professor of the public understanding of science, concluded that 'The British and the Americans have a keener interest in science than they have in sport, films or politics, but they seldom possess a depth of knowledge that matches their curiosity on the subject.'[59]

Nonetheless, a minority of the laity is well informed about at least some aspects of some sciences. Evidence for this statement comes from the role of some citizens in mobilizing science in campaigns to defend the environment.[60] Another minority, officially described as 'dispersed non-expert volunteers', contributes to 'Citizen Science', observing the migration of birds or the effects of climate change in a particular location and sending the information via the Internet.[61] Another exception should be made for the public's knowledge of computers. The majority of us may still be ignorant of the second law of thermodynamics, but Moore's law, that the number of transistors in a dense integrated circuit doubles about every two years, is probably familiar to many members of the younger generation.

Despite ongoing initiatives such as these, science is becoming even more inaccessible to the general public than before, so much so that it may be no exageration to speak of the rapid growth of ignorance in this large domain. One reason for that growth is ever-increasing specialization, making it much more difficult than it was in the nineteenth century to see the big picture of science. 'Today,' as Stuart Firestein wrote in 2012, 'science is as inaccessible to the public as if it were written in classical Latin.'[62] Even scientists themselves have become part of the laity outside the particular field in which they work.

Specialization is not the only reason for this inaccessibility. It is also a consequence of the increasing remoteness of scientific experiments from everyday life. Nineteenth-century experiments were still visible to the naked eye, allowing popularizers such as John Henry Pepper to impress the public. On the other hand, electrons and chromosomes can only be perceived by specialists using complex apparatus. The movement for the 'public understanding of science' in the 1990s, including a journal with that title and chairs in the subject (one of them held by Richard Dawkins), is a sign of increasing awareness of the laity's ignorance in this vast domain, as well as of the desire to combat it.

# 8

# IGNORANCE OF GEOGRAPHY

Terra Incognita

Ptolemy

This chapter is concerned with ignorance of the earth's surface, what used to be the blank spaces on the map or the parts covered by gradually receding clouds illustrated in Edward Quin's triumphalist atlas of what was known about the world in different periods, mentioned in chapter one. It is of course necessary to ask (as Quin did not), On whose map (whether physical or mental) were the spaces blank? Who was ignorant of what?

Like historians, geographers worry about public ignorance of their discipline. In the UK, a survey by OnePoll, reported in the *Daily Mail* in 2012, found that over 50 per cent of British adults thought that Mount Everest was in Britain, while 20 per cent did not know the whereabouts of Blackpool. In the USA, the National Geographic Society has long been concerned with what it calls the 'Fight against Geographic Illiteracy'. A survey conducted in 2006 found that 'two-thirds of 18- to 24-year old Americans were unable to locate Iraq on a world map'.[1]

Wherever humans have lived, they have acquired local knowledge of their territory, and in a number of cultures, including the 'first peoples' of Canada and Australia, they have produced visual representations of that knowledge. What changes, sometimes in dramatic fashion, is the knowledge of outsiders, some of whom explored new territories with the aid of indigenous guides but went on to make their own maps.[2]

Some of the ignorance of outsiders, the colonizers, was so convenient that it must have been feigned. Whether or not the phrase 'no one's land' (*terra nullius*) was in use (a controversial question), the assumption behind it was certainly current among white settlers from the sixteenth to the nineteenth centuries. Like Columbus, when he took possession of 'the Indies' in 1492, British colonists did not want to know about the use of the land before their arrival, by the First Peoples in the Americas, the Maori in New Zealand and Aboriginal groups in Australia.

In 1824, for instance, Chief Justice Francis Forbes described New South Wales as 'uninhabited', although he cannot have been unaware of the presence of the indigenous inhabitants, while Sir Richard Bourke, governor of New South Wales, issued a proclamation in 1835 that the land was 'vacant' before the Crown took possession of it. This deliberate unawareness has been described as 'the conceptual erasure of those societies that had been there before'.[3]

This chapter follows the retrospective method described earlier. Like Alain Corbin in his recent study of the eighteenth and nineteenth centuries, it makes use of discoveries as reminders of what was not known before or of what was thought to be known but erroneous.[4] An obvious example is the assumption in medieval Europe that the world was divided into three continents. Another is the belief of the ancient Greek geographer Ptolemy that Scandinavia was an island, *Scandia insula*.[5] It would be fascinating to read a global study of what people in each part of the world did not know about the rest, but such a study would depend on a multitude of monographs that have not yet been written. What follows will therefore concentrate on the ignorance of Europeans concerning the world beyond them, as well as discussing their lack of knowledge about Europe itself. In Sicily, for instance, as late as the 1950s, an investigator was surprised to discover peasants who did not know where Russia was.[6]

Looking backwards, it is difficult to imagine how little Europeans knew about the rest of the globe in the year 1450 or even in 1750 (not to mention western European ignorance of eastern Europe).[7] It is true that in the Middle Ages, some Europeans had first-hand knowledge of parts of the world beyond Europe. Navigators, merchants, pilgrims, crusaders and missionaries all acquired some knowledge of the Middle East, especially of certain cities, centres of international trade such as Cairo, Aleppo, Caffa (now Feodosia), as well as the crusader city of Acre (now in Israel) and of course Jerusalem, the goal of many pilgrims.[8]

On the other hand, little was known about China (discussed below) or about India, apart from the existence of naked ascetics known as 'gymnosophists' (and later as 'yogis') and also of the so-called 'Nestorian' Christians, a branch of the Church supposed to have been founded by the apostle St Thomas.

One of the most dramatic examples of European ignorance in its day was displayed by Christopher Columbus. Columbus, who was sent on a mission to China, did not know – indeed, did not want to know – that the island of Hispaniola, where he landed, was not part of Asia. Indeed, it took some time for the public to accept the idea of a 'new world' that had been unknown to the ancient Greeks and Romans.[9] It was for this reason that the Mexican historian Edmundo O'Gorman entitled his well-known book on the subject the 'invention' of America rather than its 'discovery'. For the same reason, the sociologist Eviatar Zerubavel has written about 'the mental discovery of America'. In their own day, Amerigo Vespucci and Martin Waldseemüller, who accepted the evidence for a new continent, were in a minority.[10]

In any case, the 'discovery' of America by Columbus was actually a rediscovery on the part of Europeans. Around the year 1000, a Norse explorer, Leif Erikson, had reached what became known as 'Vinland' – part of the North American coast, perhaps today's Labrador. Recorded in thirteenth-century sagas under the name 'Markland', the existence of this territory in the west reached a fourteenth-century Italian friar, Galvano Fiamma, who called it 'Marckalada' and described it as inhabited by giants.[11] After that the knowledge seems to have been lost.

In the eighteenth century, the time of a boom in travel books in Britain, France and elsewhere, the ignorance that remained is revealed by what was left out or only published late in the century, including descriptions of 'Burma' and 'Abyssinia', as Myanmar and Ethiopia were known at this time. No wonder then that Jean-Jacques Rousseau could declare himself to be impressed by the enormity of European ignorance about the greater part of the world. 'The whole earth is covered by nations of whom we only know the names, yet we presume to make judgements about the human race!'[12]

## IMAGINING THE EXOTIC

The blank spaces on maps made by outsiders have often been populated by the imagination. As was noted earlier in the book, human nature abhors a vacuum. Driven by curiosity, hopes and fears, the collective imagination fills in the blanks. In the short term the vacuum is filled by rumours, in the longer term by legends or myths.[13]

A vivid example is that of the 'monstrous races'. In ancient Greece and Rome, it was commonly believed that non-human peoples could be found in distant parts of the world, in Asia or Africa. There were the dog-headed Cynocephali; the Sciapods, each with one enormous foot; the Blemmyae, 'whose heads beneath their shoulders grow', as Shakespeare's Othello describes them, and other 'Plinian races' as they are now known, since they were famously described in an ancient Roman encyclopaedia compiled by Pliny the Elder.[14] Stories such as these may have awakened the curiosity of some individuals, but to others they will have been a deterrent to travel.

Turning from fear to hope, a story was circulating in Christendom, especially between the twelfth and sixteenth centuries, regarding the ruler of a large empire in Asia, a Christian priest-king known as 'Prester John'.[15] This potential ally against pagans and Muslims was sometimes described as emperor of 'the three Indias', and he was supposed to have written a letter in Latin to the twelfth-century Byzantine emperor Manuel Comnenus describing his kingdom. This text was translated into many languages and in the course of its circulation, further details were added.

Where Prester John lived was a matter of debate.[16] The twelfth-century German chronicler Otto of Freising described him as living 'beyond Persia and Armenia'. Some thought he could be found in Central Asia: Marco Polo, for instance, mentions his 'great empire' and says that he was killed in a battle with Chinggis Khan. Since no trace of Prester John was found in Asia, the king was relocated to Ethiopia, which was, like India, a country in which Christians had been living for centuries. The fifteenth-century Spanish traveller Pero Tafur claimed that the Venetian traveller Niccolò de'Conti told him that he had actually visited Prester John's court.[17] When Vasco da Gama and his men reached the coast of Moçambique in 1498, they 'were told that Prester John resided not far from this place' though his court was situated inland, so that 'one could only go there on camels'.[18] In similar fashion, after 1492, the monstrous races, who had proved impossible to find in Africa or in Asia, were relocated to the unexplored Americas. When Walter Raleigh reached Guiana in the 1590s, for instance, he was told of headless men with eyes in their shoulders.

Relocation also occurred in the case of the Amazons, warrior women who were mentioned in the fifth century BCE in the *Histories* of Herodotus. In the thirteenth century, Marco Polo declared them to be found in East Asia. Columbus referred to 'The Island of Women, whom he thought were Amazons', but it was Francisco Orellana, a deserter from the conquest of Peru by Francisco Pizzaro, who claimed to have encountered them near the river that we still know, thanks to this encounter, as the Amazon.[19]

Some Spanish explorers had read a romance of chivalry published in 1510 and describing an imaginary island, 'California', ruled by Queen Calafia. Hernán Cortés and his men believed they had discovered that island, and what is now known as Baja California in Mexico was still represented on seventeenth-century maps as a long island off the west coast. This belief was challenged by the Jesuit Eusebio Kino, who argued in 1701 that California was a peninsula, but maps continued to represent it as an island until the middle of the eighteenth century.[20]

Like the story of Prester John, the myth of El Dorado offers a vivid example of what Freud described as wish-fulfilment. The story circulated after the Spanish leader Hernán Cortés discovered gold in the treasury of the Aztec emperor Moctezuma. In Cundinamarca in the Andes, still *terra incognita* to the Spanish conquerors in the 1530s, it was said that gold was so plentiful that the local chief or king was covered with gold dust every year. The story, influenced by the Greek myth of the golden fleece, expanded from reference to a person to a city or even a country. Like the Plinian races, El Dorado was relocated several times, 'from Colombia to the basin of the Amazon to the jungles of Guiana, as each site in turn failed to fulfill its glistening promise'. The many unsuccessful expeditions to find the city, at the cost of great effort and many deaths, included the last voyage of Walter Raleigh.[21]

## WESTERN IGNORANCE OF CHINA

The following two sections discuss Western ignorance of China and the converse, Chinese ignorance of the West. It will of course be necessary to avoid essentializing both 'China' and the 'West', making distinctions between the ignorances of emperors, literati, missionaries and merchants as well as between different periods and locales.

China (or 'Cathay') was a great unknown for Europeans until the Mongol invasion of Russia, Hungary and Poland in the thirteenth century, a threat that forced some westerners to try to remedy this ignorance.[22] In response to the invasions, missions were sent to the Khans of the Mongols by Pope Innocent IV and by Louis IX of France, attempting to discover the plans of the invaders and to make an alliance with them as well as to convert them to Christianity. The most famous of these missionaries were four Franciscan friars, three of them Italians (Giovanni da Pian del Carpine, Giovanni da Montecorvino and Odorico da Pordenone) and one a Fleming (Willem van Rubroeck). Three of the four wrote accounts of their travels, to Cathay via Persia, India and in Odorico's case, Sumatra. The interest evoked by Odorico's experiences in particular is shown by the survival of seventy-three manuscripts of his narrative, which was finally published in 1574.[23]

Even more successful with European readers was an account of the travels of the thirteenth-century Venetian merchant Marco Polo, the *Divisament dou monde*.[24] It was translated from the original French (more exactly, Franco-Venetian) into Venetian, Tuscan, Latin, Spanish, Catalan, Aragonese, German and Irish and became one of the best known books in late medieval Europe.[25] Marco, who entered the service of the Great Khan and spent seventeen years in Cathay, noted with some surprise the use of paper money. He was also impressed, whether at first or second hand, by Hangzhou's famous West Lake, writing that 'A voyage on this lake offers more refreshment and delectation than any other experience on earth.'[26]

Marco Polo did not visit all the places described in his travels, probably including most of those in central and southern China (though he began his return to the West from the southern port of Quanzhou).[27] Indeed, his book is not so much a travelogue as an informal treatise on geography. What is important for our purposes is that it was Marco's book, 'a very drastic revision of everything previously thought about the East', that placed China on the mental map of many Europeans, making its readers aware of a culture that was very different from their own.[28]

The kingdom of the Great Khan was also vividly described in another medieval 'best-seller', the travelogue attributed to 'Sir John Mandeville'. Over three hundred manuscripts of the book survive. It was translated from the original French into nine more languages: English, German, Dutch, Spanish, Italian, Latin, Danish, Czech and Irish, and read by individuals ranging from Christopher Columbus to the sixteenth-century miller Menocchio.[29] The (un)reliability of the text will be discussed later in this chapter.

When Columbus set off to find a new route to Asia, his expectations were shaped by his reading of both Marco Polo (whose book he carried with him) and Mandeville. He believed, like other Europeans, that China was still ruled by the Great Khan and hoped to deliver a letter to him at 'Quinsay' (otherwise known as Hangzhou). Columbus was unaware that his instructions were out of date by 124 years, since the Mongols had been replaced by the Ming dynasty in 1368.[30]

At this time, Western ignorance of China still extended to its geography, its history, its language, its system of writing, its medicine, its art, its political and social structure and its belief systems (Confucian,

Daoist and Buddhist). King Manuel of Portugal offers an early example of the mixture of ignorance with curiosity. His instructions to the captain of a ship sailing to Malacca in 1508 were to find out all that he could about the Chinese, not only 'when they come to Malacca', with how many ships and what merchandise, but also about their religion and form of government, including 'whether they have more than one king among them'.[31]

These gaps only began to be filled in the later sixteenth century, especially by three books: *Tractado de la China* (1569) by the Portuguese Dominican friar Gaspar da Cruz; *Reino de la China* (1577) by the Spanish soldier Bernardino de Escalante; and *El Gran Reyno de la China* (1585) by Juan González de Mendoza, a priest (later a bishop) who was active in Mexico. Mendoza's book was a great success, reaching forty-seven editions in seven languages by the end of the century. Montaigne owned a copy and made use of it in his essay 'On Coaches', where he wrote that 'We exclaim at the miracle of the invention of our artillery, of our printing; other men in another corner of the world, in China, enjoyed these a thousand years earlier'.

None of the three authors just mentioned had actually visited China, but their accounts were based on relatively reliable sources.[32] Less reliable as well as more vivid was the *Peregrinação* by the Portuguese traveller Fernão Mendes Pinto (published in 1614, but written in the 1570s).

Pinto's book was followed a year later by a published account of the Jesuit mission to China, based on the journal kept by the Italian Matteo Ricci and edited by a Flemish colleague.[33] This account, soon reprinted and also translated from Latin into French, was the first of a remarkable sequence of Jesuit reports on China that became the principal source of information about that country until the late eighteenth century. For about two hundred years the Jesuits played a major role as mediators, correcting both European ignorance of the Middle Kingdom and Chinese ignorance of the world beyond their empire.

For example, Ricci provided Europeans 'with more reliable geographic information on China'.[34] A second Italian, Martino Martini, who arrived in China in 1642, published an atlas of China, a history of the change of dynasty (from Ming to Qing, in 1644) and an account of the early history of the country. When he was living in Rome, Martini had been taught by the German Jesuit polymath Athanasius Kircher. The two men remained in contact and Martini supplied much information to his former professor, whose *China Illustrata* (1667) made its readers aware of – among other things – tea-drinking and acupuncture.

Martini's history of China, published in Latin in 1658, filled a major gap in Western knowledge but led to controversy because according to the Chinese chronology, their history went back at least six hundred years before Noah's Flood, undermining the biblical statement that the whole of humanity descended from Noah.[35] Some Western scholars did not want to know about the Chinese claim to antiquity. The famous *Discourse on Universal History* (1681) by the French bishop Jacques Bossuet did not mention China. In his *New Science* (1744), Giambattista Vico claimed that the history of the Hebrews was more ancient than the history of China. Voltaire, on the other hand, drew on Chinese history for ammunition in his critique of the Eurocentrism of Bossuet.

A group of Jesuit missionaries, which included the Fleming Philippe Couplet, made Europeans aware of Chinese philosophy by publishing texts in Latin translation. It is thanks to this book that the philosopher Kong Fuzi is still known in the West as 'Confucius'.[36] The German polymath Gottfried Wilhelm Leibniz was fascinated by China and learned as much as he could about it from Jesuit missionaries as well as from books. His enthusiasm is an early example of the admiration for China among scholars and men of letters during the Enlightenment, some of whom, including Voltaire, viewed that country as a paradigm of good government (thanks in part to ignorance of examples to the contrary).[37] Porcelain and other Chinese artefacts arrived in Europe in increasing numbers and created a fashion for what was known as *chinoiserie*, from interior decoration to the design of gardens.[38]

The new knowledge about China, including maps made for the emperor by Jesuits, was summed up in the four-volume *Description de la Chine* by their colleague Jean-Baptiste Du Halde (1735), who remained in France. In its English translation, the book's title became *Geographical, Historical, Chronological, Political, and Physical Description of the Empire of China and Chinese Tartary* (1738).

From this time onwards, ignorance of China could no longer be excused by lack of information. Nevertheless, it has persisted among the general public, who have sometimes been kept in ignorance of recent events by the lack of coverage or the unreliable coverage of that country in the media. In the early 1960s, for instance, the journalist Felix Greene published two books criticizing 'the accuracy of some of the reports about Communist China conveyed to the American people by the press, the experts, and by public officials'.[39] Are they more accurate today?

## CHINESE IGNORANCE OF EUROPE

It is of course an exaggeration to say that the Chinese lacked interest in the outside world, but from the sixteenth to the eighteenth centuries, when westerners became increasingly interested in China, there was relatively little reciprocity, producing a 'discrepancy in knowledge' that 'would dog China's relationships with the West down to the twentieth century'.[40] The Chinese government did not want to know or, more exactly, believed that it did not need to know about distant countries. It was the nineteenth-century threat from the West that compelled the Chinese to remedy their ignorance of the wider world, just as Europeans had been forced to do so by the Mongol invasion six centuries earlier.

Before the 1840s, what Chinese scholars had learned about Europe was largely the result of European initiatives, especially those of Jesuit missionaries. When Matteo Ricci arrived in China in 1582, he found that it was generally believed that the earth was flat and square, though surrounded by the 'rounded heavens' (in medieval Europe too, the earth had been regarded as 'a perfect square').[41] Ricci informed his Chinese interlocutors that the earth was a globe, as well as showing them maps of the world, improved in successive editions, and providing information about Europe, Africa and the Americas.[42]

In order to help his converts to understand Catholicism, Ricci sent home for religious engravings. These images also introduced the Chinese to perspective, although their painters, especially if they were scholars, largely refrained from adopting Western pictorial conventions, remaining faithful to their traditional, non-geometrical forms of representing space. Nevertheless, there are signs that awareness of Western conventions led to changes in Chinese painting, to what has been described as a 'convergence' between traditions. Learning of an alternative to their own tradition inspired some Chinese landscape painters to innovate in their own way.[43]

In the seventeenth century, other Jesuits made at least a few Chinese aware of other forms of what they called 'western learning' (*xixue*). The Italian Giulio Aleni published his 'Chronicle of Foreign Lands' (*Zhifang waiji*) in Chinese in 1623, including a map that informed readers about Europe, Africa and the Americas.[44] The Swiss-German polymath Johann Schreck wrote an introduction to Western anatomy and collaborated with a local scholar, Wang Zheng, on translating a description of what the Chinese title called 'The Strange Machines of the Far West' (*Yuanxi Qiqi Tushuo Luzui*, 1627).

When Schreck showed that he was able to predict the eclipse of 1629 more accurately than Chinese astronomers, he was invited by the last emperor of the Ming dynasty to reform the calendar, while the German Adam Schall von Bell was appointed director of the imperial observatory. Schall and his assistant the Fleming Ferdinand Verbiest carried on the reform of the calendar and took the opportunity to introduce the Chinese to Western astronomy – without mentioning Copernicus, to whom the Chinese were introduced only after the Church's ban on teaching heliocentrism was lifted in 1757.[45]

Under the new Qing dynasty, Verbiest became director of the observatory and tutor to the Kangxi emperor, whose reign began when he was seven years old. Kangxi, who disliked traditional Chinese acupuncture, showed interest in Western medicine as well as military technology. French Jesuits gave him quinine (known in Europe as 'Jesuit's bark') for his malaria, while he commissioned one of them, Jean-François Gerbillon, to write an account of Western medicine. Another French Jesuit, Joachim Bouvet, began a translation into Manchu of a Western textbook on anatomy.[46] How widely these introductions to Western medicine, anatomy and astronomy circulated is difficult to tell, but at least they were known at the imperial court.

Jesuits were also commissioned to map the empire, using scientific instruments such as quadrants, integrating Western methods with traditional Chinese practices and presenting their results to the emperor in 1717.[47] It has been suggested that Kangxi was using Western knowledge to lessen his dependence on his own officials.[48]

Kangxi's successor the Qianlong emperor was also interested in the West. He once interrogated a French Jesuit, Michel Benoist (who spent thirty years at his court, 1744–74) about European politics – about the relation between France and Russia, for instance, and the question of whether one European state could become supreme. It is worth emphasizing both the emperor's curiosity about the West and the ignorance of the European political system at the highest level of Chinese government.[49]

The success of these attempts to introduce Western learning, especially outside court circles, is difficult to measure. Some Chinese officials and scholars were certainly interested in these foreign ideas. For example, when Wang Pan, governor of Zhaoqing, heard of Ricci's knowledge of mathematics and cartography, he invited him to the city, where Ricci produced his map of the world in 1602. Wang Pan asked him to translate it, and had it engraved, 'as he wished to have it printed and made known throughout China' and 'began to give copies away as presents to all his friends in that province, and to send copies to other provinces'.[50] In Beijing, Ricci made friends with two scholars, Feng Yingjing and Li Zhizao, both of whom studied Western geography.

Another friend of Ricci, the scholar Xu Guangqi, was 'enthusiastic about acquiring new knowledge of the world', including the mathematics of 'the Western Countries'. His translation of Euclid's *Elements*, made together with Ricci, corrected Chinese ignorance of Euclidean geometry. Meanwhile, Chinese mathematicians were making studies of linear algebra that remained unknown to their opposite numbers in the West.[51]

Chinese scholars who were interested in Western learning also included Wang Zheng, who knew Schall and other Jesuits, became a convert, studied mechanical engineering and conceived the ambition of uniting Western and Chinese knowledges, as did Mei Wending in the following century.[52]

Apart from this handful of examples, however, there is little evidence of any serious Chinese interest in Western learning, especially in the early Qing period. In any case, there were considerable obstacles to pursuing this knowledge. Information 'was blocked and filtered at every point of interface'. The Chinese were not allowed to visit the West, while westerners could not go beyond Macao – a port that had been founded in the mid-sixteenth century to encourage international trade while keeping foreigners at a distance.[53]

There is also evidence of opposition to Western learning on the part of some of the literati. The scholar Wei Chün, for instance, declared that 'Matteo Ricci utilized some false teachings to fool people', criticizing him for failing to place China in the centre of the world.[54] Another scholar, Dong Han, wrote a critique of Aleni's account of Columbus's voyage to America, the conquest of Mexico, and Magellan's circumnavigation of the globe. He accused the author of 'fantastic and exaggerated' assertions 'without any basis whatever'.[55] The attachment to the Confucian tradition at a time when it was challenged by Western learning is illustrated in a late eighteenth-century novel, *An Old Rustic's Humble Words*, in which the followers of the superman hero visit 'Europe' (*Ouluoba*) and convert its people to Confucianism.[56]

Traditional Chinese cosmography and cartography continued to be practised, whether because map-makers were simply ignorant of the new information (including the idea of the earth as a globe) or because they deliberately ignored it.[57] It has been suggested that 'as late as the middle of the nineteenth century, the Chinese had little more information at their disposal about the West than had their ancestors of some 500 years before'. Once again, gaps in knowledge were filled by myths. Some Chinese believed that westerners were cannibals. One member of the first Chinese embassy to Britain and France wrote in his journal that 'Everything in England is the opposite of China', a response to the foreign reminiscent of what Herodotus wrote about the Egyptians.[58]

It was only in the age of the first 'Opium War' (1839–42), when British gunboats battered Chinese fortresses, that some members of the elite realized that self-defence required them to remedy their ignorance of the West, though conservative scholars continued to resist this idea.[59] Soon after that war, in 1844, the polymath Wei Yuan, who 'saw maps as essential for making foreign countries more accessible to Chinese readers', published an account of what he called the 'maritime king-doms' beyond China, focusing on maritime Asia and its penetration by the West. Wei Yuan criticized ignorance of this penetration, remarking that when the Chinese learned that 'England had established a wealthy and populous trading base in Singapore', no one 'knew where it was'.[60] He also informed his readers about Africa, Europe and the Americas.

Little had been known of Western history in earlier centuries, but Guo Songtao, the diplomat who led the embassy to the West in 1866, showed an awareness of the English Civil War, describing it in his journal as 'a struggle for power between the king and the people which caused much bloodshed'.[61]

Missionaries continued to play an important role in spreading Western learning in China, although Protestant missionaries were 'even more unanimous in opposing Darwin than the Jesuits had been contra Copernicus', while 'the western sciences were packaged via translation in a natural theology' that delayed the reception of Darwinism.[62]

Few translations from Western languages had been made between the sixteenth and the eighteenth centuries, but an official Translation Office was founded in Shanghai in 1867, located in the Arsenal – an appropriate symbol for the practical and especially the military reasons for the new interest in Western learning. The Englishman John Fryer, who worked there, translated seventy-eight books on Western science and technology as well as editing the first Chinese newspaper and writing scientific textbooks for use in Chinese schools (it would be fascinating to know how Fryer's readers understood and responded to his books).[63]

Ignorance of Western literature and ideas began to be replaced by acquaintance, thanks to the efforts of certain individuals. One was Lin Shu, a man of letters who did not know foreign languages himself but with the help of interpreters translated Dickens and Dumas. Another was Yan Fu, who studied at the Royal Naval College in London in the 1870s and translated Adam Smith, John Stuart Mill and T. H. Huxley.[64]

## JAPAN, KOREA AND FORMOSA

European ignorance of some other parts of Asia took longer to dissipate. Japan, for instance, had been visited by Europeans ranging from the Spanish missionary Francisco Xavier in 1549 to the English pilot William Adams, who arrived with his crew in 1600. The new shogun, Tokugawa Ieyasu, interrogated Adams, asking him what his religious beliefs were and whether his country had wars. Adams was made a samurai, given an estate and commanded to give advice on the building of a ship in European style.

However, Adams was forbidden to leave the country, where he died in 1620. After 1635, Japan was cut off from most contact with foreigners, a defensive response to the growing number of Japanese whom the Jesuits had converted to Christianity. The closure of Japan to foreigners encouraged ignorance on both sides.[65]

Despite this policy, the Dutch East India Company was allowed to set up an establishment in Japan. To minimize their contact with the Japanese, employees of the Company were confined – like Western merchants in Macao – to Deshima, a small artificial island near the port of Nagasaki. They were only allowed to leave this island to make official visits to the capital. European information about Japan, filtered through the Dutch, was limited.

For a long time, the fullest description of Japan in a Western language remained that of Engelbert Kaempfer, a German physician in the service of the Company, who had participated in the visits of Company officials to the capital and carefully observed the country on the way there and back (Kaempfer's manuscript was posthumously published in English translation in 1727, preceding the publication of the original German text).[66]

Conversely, the government discouraged the Japanese from taking an interest in Europe, although some individuals showed enthusiasm for Western learning – which they called 'Dutch learning' (*Rangaku*) – especially in the field of medicine.[67] Obstacles to knowledge of the West were only removed after the Japanese were forced out of their voluntary isolation in the 1850s. As in China, some of them began to study and to imitate Western culture, travelling to the USA and to Europe in order to remedy their ignorance.[68]

Even less was known by Europeans about other parts of Asia. Korea, for instance, was another closed country, nicknamed 'the Hermit Kingdom'.[69] It remained virtually unknown in the West until it became a protectorate of Japan in 1905. One of the rare foreign visitors – an unintentional one – was the Dutchman Hendrick Hamel. The author, a bookkeeper for the Dutch East India Company, was shipwrecked in Korea on his way to Japan. He was not allowed to leave the country, but after thirteen years in captivity he was able to escape and later wrote a journal describing his experiences. It was published in Dutch in 1668 and in French translation two years later.[70]

European ignorance of almost everything concerning Taiwan (once known as Formosa) may be illustrated by its exploitation by the eighteenth-century impostor who called himself George Psalmanazar. Psalmanazar – his real name is unknown – was a Frenchman who made a career out of pretending to be a Formosan, inventing, among other false information, a language and even an alphabet that he attributed to the islanders. Psalmanazar was invited to England to teach future missionaries to the island and became a temporary celebrity in London society. His deception was eventually exposed by members of the Royal Society, not because they had accurate information about Formosa but because they had become suspicious of the informant. Requested on two different occasions to translate a passage of Cicero into Formosan, Psalmanazar produced irreconcilable versions. When the astronomer Edmond Halley asked him about the duration of twilight on Formosa, he was unable to answer. Psalmanazar defended himself for a time, but eventually admitted his 'imposture' in his *Memoirs* (1747), explaining that he had chosen Formosa because 'his studies informed him that all Europeans were ignorant of that island'.[71]

## THREE MYSTERIOUS CITIES

Some famous Asian cities, notably Mekka and Lhasa, resisted European knowledge well into the nineteenth century. Mekka was out of bounds for non-Muslims, though a few bold travellers, including the English explorer Richard Burton and the Dutch scholar Christiaan Snouck Hurgronje, were prepared to risk visiting the city in disguise. Both travellers published accounts of the famous pilgrimage.[72]

Europeans knew little about the second city, Lhasa, and indeed little about Tibet before 1626, when an account of it by the Portuguese Jesuit missionary Antonio de Andrade appeared in print. Ninety years later, another Jesuit, Ippolito Desideri, arrived in Tibet. He spent five years in the country but his report on it remained buried in the archives until the twentieth century.[73] An Englishman, George Bogle, who was in the service of the East India Company, was sent on a diplomatic mission to Tibet in 1774, but he was not allowed to visit Lhasa. The country remained 'a no-go area for mapmakers' until spies sent by Thomas Montgomerie, a captain in the British army in India, surveyed it from 1863 onwards. One of these spies, Pundit Nain Singh, reached Lhasa in 1865 disguised as a Buddhist holy man and recorded the longitude and latitude of the city.[74]

Timbuktu, situated in an oasis in what is now Mali, had flourished in the later Middle Ages as a centre of trade and learning, but it later became – for Europeans – a symbol of remoteness and mystery. Even its location, like that of the river Niger, was generally unknown until the early nineteenth century, although geographical societies in both Britain and France sponsored expeditions to find the city. In Britain, the president of the Royal Society, Sir Joseph Banks, helped found the African Association for this purpose in 1788. Thirty-six years later, in 1824, with the city's location still undiscovered, the Geographical Society of Paris offered a prize to the first person to return from Timbuktu with a first-hand description. The explorer René Caillié finally collected the prize in 1830.[75]

## OBSTACLES TO KNOWLEDGE

To understand how European ignorance of these places lasted so long, it is necessary to consider the various obstacles in the way of outsiders who wished to explore them. As we have seen, some countries were officially closed to foreigners by the authorities, whether for political or religious reasons. Japan was more or less closed to westerners from 1635 until the 1850s. Tibet closed its borders to Europeans in 1792. Korea was closed to foreigners – apart from the Chinese – until the year 1905.

Elsewhere the problem was not prohibition but the difficulties and dangers of travel. Deserts long remained unmapped. These places could only be crossed on foot or on the back of camels, at the risk of death if supplies of food and water ran out. In 1865, an Indian clerk, Mohamed-i-Hameed, was sent by Thomas Montgomerie on a secret expedition to the Taklamakan desert, near the Himalayas. He died on his way back, but an English surveyor, William Johnson, recovered Hameed's notes and himself visited a lost city buried in the sand near Khotan (now in China), the former capital of a state located on the famous Silk Road. A few years later, in 1879, a botanist on an expedition supported by the Russian Geographical Society discovered another city buried in the sand in Turkestan, the former Uighur capital of Karakhoja, which had been conquered by a Chinese army in the year 640.[76] Other deserts were not mapped until the twentieth century, among them the 'Empty Quarter' (*Rub'al Khali*) in Arabia, visited by Jack Philby (father of Kim) in the 1930s, in search of another lost city, and crossed by the British explorer Wilfred Thesiger in 1946.[77]

Even when it was not dangerous, travel by land was more difficult and more expensive than travel by sea or by river. Hence knowledge of the coast of Asia, Africa and the Americas long preceded knowledge of the interior. In South America, Frei Vicente de Salvador, known as the 'Brazilian Herodotus', complained in his history of the country that the Portuguese had not bothered to explore the interior of Brazil, preferring to cluster along the coast 'like crabs'.[78] In the case of North America, little was known about what is now called the 'Middle West' until the expedition led by Meriwether Lewis and William Clark between 1803 and 1806.

## THE INTERIOR OF AFRICA

In similar crabwise fashion, the description of Africa published in Italian in 1550 by al-Hasan ibn Muhammad al-Wazzan, known in Europe as Leo Africanus, provided much more information about the coast of the continent than about its interior. This text would not have been published in Italian, and might never have been written at all, had the author, a Berber from North Africa, not been captured by Spanish pirates and presented to Pope Leo X, after whom he was christened 'Leo'.[79]

One part of Africa that long remained mysterious to westerners was Ethiopia, also known as Abyssinia. As in the case of Tibet, Jesuit missionaries were the first European visitors to return with information: an account of the country by Pedro Páez was published in 1622. After the Jesuits were expelled in 1633, however, it became difficult for foreigners to enter Ethiopia and still more difficult to leave it. The description of the country by another Jesuit missionary, Jerónimo Lobo, remained unpublished until 1728, while 'the few vague maps that existed were zealously guarded by the Jesuits'.[80]

A response to this challenge came from the Scottish laird James Bruce. Bruce was a figure larger than life, a big man and the author of a big book, telling the story of his travels in five volumes.[81] Appointed consul in Algiers by the British government, Bruce decided, in his own words, that 'the world shall have a true account of Ethiopia, with a map of those places which we have visited and their positions ascertained by most accurate observation with large instruments'.[82] He arrived with his quadrant, sextants and telescopes in 1769, disguised as a Syrian physician. Bruce was obsessed with finding the source of the Nile, describing European ignorance of it as 'a defiance to all travellers, and an opprobrium to geography'.[83] Bruce did find the source of the Blue Nile, describing it, with typical hyperbole, as 'that spot which had baffled the genius, industry and inquiry of both ancients and moderns for the course of near three thousand years', despite the fact that the source of the river had been known to his Jesuit predecessors.[84]

Although an agent for the Royal Africa Company, Francis Moore, had published an account of his *Travels into the Inland Parts of Africa* in

1738, the interior of Africa could still be described by an Englishman in 1790 as 'a wide extended blank'.[85] The source of the White Nile in Lake Victoria remained undiscovered by Europeans until 1856. Henry Stanley, who confirmed the discovery in the 1870s, used the phrase 'The Dark Continent' to refer to 'how much of the dark interior' of Africa 'was still unknown to the world'.[86]

The obstacles to exploring the interior of Africa were serious ones. Few rivers were completely navigable, while the vulnerability of horses to fatal attacks by the tsetse fly made it necessary to travel on foot or to be carried by porters. Guides were difficult to find, while the inhabitants of places on the route were often unwilling to give information to strangers. Travellers might be robbed and killed by local tribesmen; they might also drown in a river, die in the desert from lack of food or water or succumb to a fatal illness such as dysentery, malaria or sleeping sickness.

The dangers involved in filling the blank spaces on the map are vividly revealed by the misadventures of the leaders of expeditions to Timbuktu. Two explorers were killed on their way there, another was killed on his way back and a fourth never returned. The Frenchman René Caillié successfully completed the task, received the prize of 9,000 francs from the French Geographical Society and published an account of his travels – but he died at the age of thirty-nine from an illness that he had contracted in Africa.[87]

For another example of difficulties and dangers, we might turn to *Travels in the Interior Districts of Africa* (1799), a book written by the Scottish explorer Mungo Park, a former surgeon in the service of the East India Company. As the title page of his book makes abundantly clear, Park's travels were 'Performed under the Direction and Patronage of the African Association'. On his first expedition, in 1795, he was captured by a 'Moorish' chief but released after three months, without his money or supplies. He was robbed again later on his journey, losing his horse and his spare clothes. Despite these experiences, Park returned to West Africa in 1805 to discover the source of the river Niger. On this occasion he experienced the hostility of Muslim traders, who viewed him as a competitor, while his team learned that it was only prudent to stay well away from the shore while navigating the river. They were regularly pursued by hostile canoes, which caught up with them when their boat ran aground. In the subsequent fight, Park was drowned.[88]

Another explorer, the Irishman James Tuckey, died in 1816 in an unsuccessful attempt to find the source of the river Congo. No wonder then that as late as 1878, Henry Stanley (who did find the source of the river) began his travelogue with 'thanks to Divine Providence for the gracious protection vouchsafed to myself and my surviving followers during our late perilous labours in Africa'.[89]

Given these problems, the British Prime Minister Lord Salisbury may not have been exaggerating very much in his comment on ignorance of the European governments when they divided the spoils at the Berlin Conference (1884–5), at the time of the 'scramble for Africa': 'We have been giving away mountains and lakes and rivers to each other, only hindered by the small impediment that we never knew exactly where the mountains rivers and lakes were.'[90]

## SECRET MAPS

Even when discoveries were made, the information often remained secret, keeping foreigners in ignorance. At first sight, the history of cartography over the last five hundred years or so appears to support the idea of a steady progress in knowledge, as more and more parts of the world were mapped and the maps themselves became more and more accurate, thanks to technical improvements in surveying. However, official secrecy presented a major obstacle to knowledge of the wider world.

In a pioneering study of what he called cartographic 'silences' (a term he preferred to the traditional phrase, 'blank spaces'), the British geographer Brian Harley noted the paradox that just at the time that printed maps were spreading geographical knowledge more widely, 'some states and their princes were determinedly keeping their maps secret', attempting to ensure that their political or economic rivals would remain ignorant of their resources.[91]

In the sixteenth century, the Portuguese, who were establishing outposts of trade and empire in India, China, Africa and Brazil, generally kept their information to themselves, including their maps. In 1504, for example, King Manuel I forbade chart-makers to show the West African coast beyond the Congo and required existing charts to be censored. The *Suma Oriental*, an account of his travels in the East by the Portuguese apothecary Tomé Pires, addressed to King Manuel, could not be published because of the information it gave about the spice trade.[92] The Portuguese preoccupation with the secrecy of information lasted for a long time. In 1711, a treatise on the economy of Brazil written by an Italian Jesuit was suppressed immediately after its publication, apparently out of fear that foreigners would learn the routes to the Brazilian gold mines.[93]

Competitors with the Portuguese naturally made attempts to acquire this information. In 1502, for instance, an Italian, Alberto Cantino, smuggled a Portuguese chart out of Portugal, a map now known as 'the Cantino Planisphere', while in 1561 the French ambassador to Lisbon was instructed to bribe a Portuguese cartographer to provide a map of southern Africa.[94]

Although the Portuguese were notorious for their policy of secrecy, they were not alone. Maps were also kept secret from foreigners in other places at this time. Knowledge of the Spanish Empire was controlled by the government, while 'cosmographers teaching classes aimed at pilots swore oaths not to share their knowledge with foreigners'.[95] A Dutch merchant living in Muscovy in the late sixteenth century found himself unable to obtain maps of the territory because divulging them was forbidden under pain of death.[96] This kind of secrecy was not confined to European governments. In 1522, Korean visitors to China were confined to their quarters after buying an illustrated handbook to the Ming Empire.[97] Maps of Japan were considered to contain secrets of state and it was forbidden to take them out of the country.

In the seventeenth century, when the Dutch replaced the Portuguese as the masters of intercontinental trade, their East India Company, the VOC, followed a 'strategy of secrecy'.[98] Their maps were kept in a special room at the headquarters of the Company in Amsterdam. The knowledge of routes was especially sensitive. Chart-makers had to swear an oath before the burgomasters of Amsterdam not to print the information in these charts and not to disclose it to anyone who was not a member of the Company. The charts were lent to pilots for use on voyages but were supposed to be returned. All the same, they were sometimes made available to foreigners at a price. A Dutch chart now in a French archive carries the inscription 'bought from a Dutch pilot'.[99] Those who did not pay the price remained in ignorance.[100]

In the eighteenth and early nineteenth centuries, the British East India Company was responsible both for the production of maps and for restricting their dissemination. In 1811, the Company's Board of Control prevented the publication of some maps of India so that they might not, 'in some future period, get into the hands of Europeans acting in hostility to the Company', in particular their French rivals.[101] The French reciprocated: some of the maps made in Egypt during Napoleon's expedition there in 1798 were kept secret, with the British in mind. They were kept secret until the fall of the Napoleonic regime.[102]

Even in the twentieth and twenty-first centuries, some regimes and corporations have continued the policy of secrecy. In the Soviet Union, for instance, the *naukograds*, cities where scientific research was carried out, were absent from maps of the region. Today, Google Maps does not allow its users to view certain locations.[103]

## THE EPISTEMOLOGY OF TRAVEL

For thousands of years, knowledge of foreign parts came from observations made by travellers, rather than from systematic surveys by specialists. The reliability of travelogues has long been the subject of debate.[104] In the ancient world, for instance, Herodotus was often accused of lying, while the geographer Strabo discussed the unreliability of travel writers. Unreliability varies. In a relatively mild form, it consists of basing statements on a hurried visit, turning a single experience into a generalization, claiming a more central role in events than was actually the case, or trusting the word of earlier travellers or half-understood information from locals.

In extreme form, unreliability includes pretending to have visited the place described or even failing to exist, as in the notorious case of 'Sir John Mandeville' of St Albans (alias Jean Mandeville of Liège), the supposed author of a book describing a visit to the East in the fourteenth century. The book turned out to be a collage of fragments of reports by earlier travellers, notably Odoric of Pordenone on East Asia and the German pilgrim Wilhelm von Boldensele on the Holy Land. Included in the first edition of Richard Hakluyt's anthology of travelogues, *The Principal Navigations* (1589), 'Mandeville' was excluded from the second edition, presumably because the report on 'what I have seen' no longer inspired trust.[105]

Marco Polo's *Travels* (the *Divisament dou monde*) offers a celebrated example of more or less unreliable travelogues. The popularity of his book, from the Middle Ages to the present, has always owed something to the love of a good story. Describing India, for instance, through which he passed on his way to China, Marco mentions yogis who live for '150 or 200 years' thanks to eating little and drinking a concoction of 'sulphur and quicksilver'.[106] Although he is unlikely to have visited Japan, which he describes as 'a very big island', Marco claimed that there was gold there 'in measureless quantities' and that the ruler 'has a very large palace entirely roofed with fine gold'.[107] In other words, he offers an earlier example of a hope that later crystallized into the myth of El Dorado.

The most famous part of Marco's book is the account of China in the age of Kubilai Khan. However, if Marco did live in China for seventeen years, as the text claims, some of the omissions from his description are extremely surprising. These omissions include tea, chopsticks, the writing system, printing, female foot-binding and the Great Wall.[108] Another puzzling feature of the *Travels* is that it gives the names of places in Persian, making clear the author's ignorance of Chinese and implying that much of the information he offered was not obtained at first hand. In fact, the prologue to his book admits that while some of his observations were seen 'with his own eyes', some had been heard from others, described as 'men of credit and veracity'. Marco probably saw Mongolia for himself, but viewed China through 'Mongol, Turkish and Persian eyes'.[109]

We should also remember that Marco's book, unlike the accounts of the three thirteenth-century friars mentioned earlier, was ghostwritten by a professional storyteller, Rustichello da Pisa, whom Marco met when they were both in prison in Genoa. Rustichello also wrote fiction, more exactly romances of chivalry, and Marco's account of his arrival at the court of Kubilai Khan has been compared by an Italian scholar to Rustichello's romances, especially his account of the reception of the knight Tristan at the court of King Arthur.[110]

No wonder then that Robert Burton, author of the famous *Anatomy of Melancholy*, rejected what he called 'Marcus Polus lyes'.[111] A recent study concluded that although an earlier expedition by his uncles is 'credible', Marco himself 'probably never travelled much further than the family's trading ports on the Black Sea and in Constantinople'.[112] His ignorance of central and southern China in particular has also been noted.[113]

Another example of questionable reliability, this time from the sixteenth century, is offered by Fernão Mendes Pinto, a Portuguese who spent twenty-one years in Asia and wrote an account of his travels, the *Peregrination* (posthumously published, 1614) in which he claimed to have visited China. Some of his seventeenth-century readers described him as a liar, although one of them, the gifted letter writer Dorothy Osborne, declared that 'his lies are as pleasant harmless ones as lies can be'.[114] A British historian of China, Jonathan Spence, is prepared to 'guess that Pinto never travelled in China at all', though he probably visited Macao and perhaps other ports. Spence's verdict is that it is impossible 'to decide what actions Pinto really performed, which ones he saw at first hand, which he heard about from others, which he read about . . . and which he made up'.[115] In this respect Pinto did not differ greatly from many authors of travelogues, although his stories are more picturesque than most of theirs.

In the age of the 'Scientific Revolution', books by travellers continued to be a major source for knowledge of the natural world. In order to make future sources more systematic and more reliable, a number of questionnaires were drawn up by the Royal Society in the 1660s. In the eighteenth century, these instructions for amateurs were replaced by scientific expeditions which included observers specializing in astronomy, geology, botany and zoology.

The reliability of travelogues continued to be controversial. When James Bruce returned to Britain from Ethiopia, for instance, he encountered a sceptical response to his descriptions of what he had seen. Bruce himself had accused Jerónimo Lobo of being 'the greatest liar of the Jesuits', but Samuel Johnson, who had translated Lobo and used information from it in his novel *Rasselas*, turned the accusation back on Bruce himself.[116]

In the twentieth century, Laurens van der Post and Bruce Chatwin, both of whom published novels as well as travelogues, were accused of confusing the two genres, exaggerating their own achievements as travellers. Van der Post's *Venture to the Interior* (1952), describing his ascent of Mount Mulanje in Nyasaland (now Malawi), has been criticized for claiming that the area was a remote one, although it was 'frequently visited by local expatriates and colonial officials', while its author has been accused of 'obsessive need to fantasize'. Chatwin's *In Patagonia* (1977) has met with similar criticisms.[117] Both Post and Chatwin may have gone too far in the direction of fiction without admitting this to their readers (or possibly to themselves), but as in the case of autobiography, an account of personal experiences will never be able to conform completely to objective standards of reliability.

## FROM GEOGRAPHY TO ECOLOGY

In the twenty-first century, now that ignorance of the earth's geography has been reduced by exploration, scientific research, and in the case of a wider public, the foundation of Google Earth (2005), our remaining ignorance and its tragic consequences have been revealed by debates about nuclear weapons, pollution, the decline of biodiversity and above all by forecasts of climate change.

Nuclear weapons have been a subject of public debate ever since atomic bombs were dropped on Hiroshima and Nagasaki in 1945. The effects of the bombs on the inhabitants of the two cities are well known, leading both Einstein and Bertrand Russell to warn the world about the possible extinction of humanity, while the philosopher Toby Ord dates the beginning of 'the Precipice', defined as 'our age of heightened risk', to 16 July 1945, when the first atomic bomb was detonated in New Mexico.[118] What remains uncertain is the effect of a war in which numbers of the much more powerful bombs available today are actually used. Besides killing hundreds of millions of people, such a war might lead to a 'nuclear winter' (a drop in temperature owing to the blockage of sunlight) and even to 'the death of the earth', in other words the extinction of life on the planet. We simply do not know.[119]

Concern for the environment became increasingly widespread in the later twentieth century, encouraged by books such as the American biologist Rachel Carson's eloquent *Silent Spring* (1962) as well as by organizations such as Friends of the Earth, founded in San Francisco in 1969. *Silent Spring* is concerned with the toxic effects of pesticides on the earth, rivers, plants, animals, humans and birds (it is the absence of birdsong to which the title 'Silent Spring' refers).

Carson's wake-up call was a response to what was then a relatively new trend (she dates the beginning of the mass use of pesticides to the 'mid 1940s'). Rereading the book today, the author's repeated references to ignorance spring to the eye. She contended that toxic chemicals had been placed 'in the hands of persons largely or wholly ignorant of their potentials for harm', and that they were made available 'with little or no advance investigation of their effect'. She quoted the confession of Rolf Eliassen, an American specialist on environmental engineering: 'What is the effect on people? We don't know.' She also quoted the Dutch biologist C. J. Briejer: 'We do not know whether all weeds in crops are harmful or whether some of them are useful.' Carson herself noted that the ecology of the soil 'has been largely neglected even by scientists and almost completely ignored by control men'.[120]

*Silent Spring* became a classic, with special editions for the fortieth and fiftieth anniversaries of its original publication. In the next generation, a book by the American journalist Bill McKibben with a striking title, *The End of Nature* (1989), enjoyed a similar success. 'By the end of nature,' the author explains, 'I do not mean the end of the world. When I say "nature", I mean a certain set of human ideas about the world and our place in it . . . One reason we pay so little close attention to the separate natural world around us is that it has always been there and we presumed it always would.'[121] In that sense, we ignored it.

It is intriguing to note that a few years before McKibben's book, the historian Keith Thomas had published a study entitled *Man and the Natural World* (1983), making a similar case – but for the period between 1500 and 1800. In England, 'New sensibilities arose towards animals, plants and landscape. The relationship of man to other species was redefined; and his right to exploit those species for his own advantage was sharply challenged.'[122] Why? The explanation offered in the two cases is a similar one. Destruction, or the threat of destruction, as a result of two phases of industrialization, awakened interest in what was threatened.

In the later twentieth century, attention focused on the local and all too perceptible effects of industrial pollution, as in the court case in the USA associated with the whistleblower Erin Brockovich, that will be discussed in chapter thirteen. These effects continue to cause concern, highlighted by disasters such as oil spills or more recently by research on the effects on marine life of the dumping of vast amounts of plastic in the oceans.[123] However, the recent debate on global warming, including its denial, has revealed new ignorance about the earth as well as presenting new challenges to all its inhabitants.

The decline of biodiversity, for instance, is now in the public eye. In 2014, Elizabeth Kolbert published *The Sixth Extinction*, written for the general public and placing the recent decline in the context of the 'Big Five' mass extinctions in the history of the earth, from the impact of a giant asteroid 66 million years ago that wiped out three-quarters of all species, to the 'megafauna extinction' including the mammoth and the mastodon, a mere thirteen thousand years before our time. A United Nations report on the 'unprecedented' decline of biodiversity all over the globe was published in 2019.[124]

The public debate on climate change is also relatively new, although the knowledge of the problem is considerably older. It was in 1896 that a Swedish physical chemist, Svante Arrhenius, predicted global warming (as readers will have guessed, his predictions were dismissed by his senior colleagues at the time). In 1938, a British engineer, Guy Callendar, demonstrated that this warming had been taking place for the previous half-century. These scientists were aware that global warming is the result not of a natural cycle but of what is now known as the 'greenhouse effect' of the burning of fossil fuels. As so often happens in the case of bad news, their findings were largely ignored and sometimes denied altogether. Now that they are widely discussed, we just have to hope that practical responses will come in time and also on the necessary scale, rather than (as in the case of the catastrophes described in chapter twelve), too little and too late.

# PART II

# CONSEQUENCES OF IGNORANCE

As the discussion of the environment at the end of the previous chapter suggests, the consequences of ignorance for decision-makers are often serious and sometimes fatal. The moral to be drawn is the necessity of education. In a famous presidential debate in Brazil in 1989, when Fernando Henrique Cardoso complained about the cost of education, the riposte of his rival Leonel Brizola was that 'Education isn't expensive. What's expensive is ignorance' (*Educação não é caro. Caro mesmo é a ignorância*).[1]

This point will be illustrated in chapters nine, ten and eleven, concerned in turn with war, business and politics. The role of ignorance in different kinds of disaster – famines, floods, earthquakes, pandemics and so on – is discussed in chapter twelve. The ignorance of the public, and the ways in which they are kept in ignorance, is the theme of chapter thirteen. Chapter fourteen is concerned with attempts to remedy our ignorance of the future, while chapter fifteen turns to the unhappy consequences of ignorance of the past.

According to Edward Gibbon, 'the crimes, follies and misfortunes of mankind' make up the great part of human history. Whether or not this is the case, they make up the great part of the following chapters.

# 9

# IGNORANCE IN WAR

War is the realm of uncertainty

Clausewitz

Wars are not only 'a continuation of politics by other means', as the Prussian general Carl von Clausewitz famously wrote: they are even more extreme cases of the problem of taking decisions in conditions of uncertainty, planning for the future despite knowing that the future will not go according to plan. To quote another famous military theorist, Sun Tzu (Sunzi, *c.* 544–496 BCE),

> There are three ways in which a ruler can bring misfortune on his army: By commanding the army to advance or to retreat, being ignorant of the fact that it cannot obey . . . By attempting to govern an army in the same way as he administers a kingdom, being ignorant of the conditions which obtain in an army . . . By employing the officers of his army without discrimination, through ignorance of the military principle of adaptation to circumstances.[1]

Even in peacetime, armies, including the divisions, corps and regiments into which they are divided, are sites of the 'organizational ignorance' discussed elsewhere in this book. I know of no historical study of this problem but in this case I have something to say as a witness. When I served as a pay clerk in Singapore District Signal Regiment in 1956–7, a regiment that was mainly composed of Malays, the British officers were clearly ignorant of much that was going on behind their backs, especially in the hours (from four in the afternoon to six in the morning) when they were away in their own quarters. Material from the quartermaster's stores turned up in the centre of town in the so-called 'Thieves' Market', while some soldiers took protection money from shops in the neighbourhood. The most profitable scheme was probably the one organized by a dignified Indian civilian whose day job was serving tea to the various offices, including the one in which I worked. His night job was as an entrepreneur, renting out space for civilians to sleep in the barracks at a time of housing shortage. As an innocent eighteen-year-old who had left school only a few months earlier, I observed these operations with a mixture of incredulity and amusement, but I never thought of telling the authorities about them. At school we would have called that 'sneaking'.

In the case of war, military operations are, among other things, battles between ignorance and knowledge, attempting to keep the enemy ignorant of one's plans while trying to discover theirs. As the Duke of Wellington liked to say, 'the whole art of war consists in getting at what is on the other side of the hill'. The penalty for failure is high: war is a zero-sum game in which rapid response to the enemy's moves is crucial. The British prime minister Harold Wilson liked to say that 'A week is a long time in politics'. In battle, fifteen minutes is a long time.

Errors on the battlefield are punished more rapidly and more visibly than in politics or business. There are many biographies of winners in this game, but much can also be learned from the few biographies of losers such as Ludwig von Benedek, remembered today for his role in the Austrian defeat at the battle of Königgrätz (otherwise known as Sadowa) in 1866. Benedek was 'badly served by his Intelligence Service'. His misreading of the situation led him to divide his army into two and so to disaster.[2]

At this point it may be useful to introduce the idea of relative ignorance. In war, both sides suffer from ignorance: the victor is the one who makes fewer mistakes or lesser ones, thanks to being somewhat better informed. For example, in Napoleon's campaign against the Russians in Central Europe in 1806–7, he made a 'false assumption' at the battle of Jena, misjudging the position of the larger part of the Prussian forces. At the battle of Eylau it was the turn of the Russian commander, Theophil von Bennigsen, who was unaware that Napoleon had used up his reserves and so missed an opportunity for victory. At the battle of Friedland, Napoleon overestimated the strength of the Russian forces because he did not know that 25,000 troops had been detached from the main body and sent to Königsberg.[3] During the 'Peninsula War' in Spain, the French knew less of what was happening than the British, since the Spaniards were helping their allies find their way in unknown terrain as well as passing them captured French dispatches.[4]

The ignorance that matters is the ignorance of commanders. Ordinary soldiers are usually left in the dark about the time and place of their next attack or retreat. Once again, a vacuum of knowledge is filled by rumour. After he returned to civilian life, the French historian Marc Bloch, who served in the First World War, wrote a pioneering study about the 'false news' that had circulated in the trenches between 1914 and 1918.[5]

The fundamental question whether battles and wars can be won by planning remains controversial. On one side, in two famous nineteenth-century novels, Stendhal's *Charterhouse of Parma* (1839) and Tolstoy's *War and Peace* (1869), battles – Waterloo in the first case and Borodino in the second – are presented as sheer chaos in which everyone is equally ignorant of what is happening more than a few yards away. Stendhal describes Waterloo through the eyes of the seventeen-year-old Fabrice, who has never witnessed a battle before. Fabrice experiences 'confusion' and sometimes, peering through the smoke of cannon, is unable to see what is going on. In similar fashion, Tolstoy describes Napoleon at Borodino, standing on a hill and looking through his binoculars but seeing nothing but smoke. The author repeats the term 'impossible'. 'It was impossible to tell what was being done'; 'it was impossible to make out what was taking place'; 'it was impossible in the heat of battle to say what was happening at any given moment'. Orders from Napoleon and his generals were not carried out. 'For the most part, things happened contrary to their orders.'[6]

On the other side, some commanders, notably Napoleon and Wellington, appear to have exerted a considerable degree of control over the battles that they won. Wellington, armed with his telescope, would look for a hill or a tower from which to observe the lie of the land and the position of the enemy, and then move round the battlefield on horseback, ready to respond to both threats and opportunities. Wellington was 'adept at absorbing information', while 'His powers of concentration were prodigious' and he put these qualities to good use, on as well as off the battlefield.[7] Stendhal and Tolstoy may be said to have loaded the dice in the favour of their chaos theory by presenting the two battles to their readers through the eyes of observers who were ignorant of war.

Nonetheless, the testimonies of these two novelists are worth taking seriously because both of them had experience of battle. Stendhal, a former lieutenant in a regiment of cavalry, served in Napoleon's army in Russia in 1812. Tolstoy (whose father had served on the other side) himself served as an officer in the artillery in the Crimean War, participating in the siege of Sebastopol and the battle of the Chernaya.[8] The emphasis on chaos by these two novelists received some support from a later military theorist, the Englishman Colonel Lonsdale Hale, who coined the memorable phrase 'the fog of war'. Hale described this fog as 'the state of ignorance in which commanders frequently find themselves as regards the real strength and position, not only of their foes, but also of their friends'.[9] The metaphor was surely suggested by the smoke from artillery (in which case the phrase 'fog of battle' might be more exact).

The idea of ignorance on the battlefield has been described in more concrete detail by a specialist on early modern warfare:

Messengers were waylaid and headquarters forced to move, breaking communications. Formations were driven into each other, jamming the roads and confusing command ... Hasty withdrawals and retreats led to entire units being lost, often without realizing it, rendering their reports to headquarters late and inherently incorrect, even incomprehensible. At headquarters, as the staff's grasp of the situation became more tentative, uncertainty and indecision began to slow decision-making.[10]

Two famous battles in which Napoleon was in command reveal both ignorance and planning: Austerlitz (where the phrase 'fog of battle' came true in the literal sense) and Waterloo. At Austerlitz, the position of the Austro-Russian army, 'based on erroneous assumptions regarding the French strength and intentions', placed it 'in a situation where defeat was likely from the outset'. As the fog lifted, Napoleon, observing from the Zuran Hill, was able to plan his moves and to modify them in rapid response to those of the enemy. He decided 'to draw the enemy into a position from which they would attempt to attack his right flank', thus luring them to expose their rear to his forces. Although the French army was outnumbered by the Russians, Napoleon and his generals made good use of 'local numerical superiority'. As Tsar Alexander admitted afterwards, his army never had time to reinforce the places where the French attacked: 'you were everywhere twice as numerous as we'.[11]

Before Waterloo, Wellington was uncertain about Napoleon's intentions. When he learned the true direction of the French forces, he burst out: 'Napoleon has humbugged me, by God; he has gained twenty-four hours' march on me.' On the battlefield, Wellington expected an attack on his flank that did not in fact occur. Nevertheless, he was able to respond adequately to French challenges until the arrival of the Prussian forces placed victory within his reach.[12]

## MILITARY TECHNOLOGY

Battles may be lost owing to different kinds of ignorance. One of these is the result of arrogance, underestimating the enemy. A vivid medieval example is the battle of Crécy, where the French knights did not take the English bowmen seriously and were killed trying to ride them down. In that case, their weakness was the result of what we would call 'class prejudice'. Another kind of ignorance is the result of failure to keep up with new developments in military technology, including unawareness that the enemy had guns capable of firing more rapidly, more accurately or at a longer range than the home side. What was once an effective tactic, the charge for instance, became suicidal, as two famous examples from the nineteenth century, the Charge of the Light Brigade (1854) and Pickett's Charge (1863), may remind us.

The charge of the British light cavalry against Russian guns took place at the battle of Balaclava, during the Crimean War, when Britain supported the Ottoman Empire against Russia. The charge into the so-called 'Valley of Death', apparently the result of the misunderstanding of an order, led to the destruction of the brigade. In contrast, Pickett's Charge was an infantry attack by the Confederates at the battle of Gettysburg during the American Civil War. In the attack, under heavy fire, half the attackers were either killed or wounded. The Confederates lost the battle, and soon afterwards they lost the war as well.[13]

These charges took place at a time when improvements in artillery were making attacks of this kind an invitation to a massacre, even in situations where the two sides were more or less equally matched. However, there was no equality at the battle of Omdurman (1898), an encounter between the British army, with their cannon and Maxim guns (an early form of machine gun) and the followers of the Mahdi (an Arab Messiah), armed only with swords and spears. The Arabs may well have been ignorant of the consequences of charging at guns. To quote the sarcastic verses of the Anglo-French writer Hilaire Belloc, 'Whatever happens, we have got/ The Maxim gun and they have not'.

## STRATAGEMS AND SURPRISES

In the cases just mentioned, the artillery was visible, but it has sometimes been possible to conceal it, leading the enemy into a trap with devastating effects. Some of the most famous commanders in history – Hannibal, Scipio Africanus, Napoleon, Nelson – were masters of deception, devising plans that surprised and wrong-footed the enemy.

Hannibal, for instance, destroyed a larger Roman army at the village of Cannae in Apulia by devising a trap. He presented an apparently weak centre to the enemy to encourage an attack that allowed him to surround the attackers with a pincer movement.[14] In Hannibal's own time, his enemy and rival Scipio Africanus won two major victories against the Carthaginians by his surprise night attacks. He has been described as 'greater than Napoleon'.[15]

Hannibal's stratagems were admired by leading generals in the nineteenth and twentieth centuries, among them Helmuth von Moltke the elder, architect of Prussian victories against the Austrians and the French in 1866 and 1870; Alfred von Schlieffen, the chief of the German General Staff, whose plan of attack was followed in 1914; and more recently, Norman Schwarzkopf, the US commander in the First Gulf War (1991), in which the deception of the Iraqi forces played a significant part.

Napoleon studied the battles of the most famous European commanders of the past and sometimes won by setting traps for the enemy. At Austerlitz, for instance, he pretended to retreat so as to lure the Austrians and Russians to attack, and made his right flank appear to be weak, distracting the enemy while he attacked their centre. At Waterloo, as we have seen, Napoleon deceived Wellington by moving his forces in an unexpected direction.

For his part, Wellington surprised the French on occasion with a pretended attack in one direction that hid a more serious attack in another part of the field. A French general praised Wellington's tactics at the battle of Salamanca because 'he kept his dispositions concealed for almost the whole day'. On campaign in Portugal, Wellington had the 'lines of Torres Vedras' constructed, ramparts that delayed the enemy and made them vulnerable to fire from hills nearby. The French general André Masséna knew nothing about these obstacles until he reached them, and had to retreat in order to avoid heavy losses.[16]

In the war against Napoleon at sea, the British Admiral Horatio Nelson surprised the enemy by disregarding the prevailing conventions for sea battles. At the battle of the Nile, his first major victory, the French were at anchor, off guard because, as the larger force, they did not expect the British to attack at all. Nelson ordered his attack when it was 'nearly dark', whereas the normal decision would have been to wait till the next day. The French commander expected an attack on the outer or starboard side of his ships, which was the normal procedure, but the captain at the head of the British line did the opposite, in order 'to find the Frenchman unprepared for action on the inner side'. The ships behind him did the same.[17]

In the Second World War, deception once again played an important part in victory.[18] For example, the surrender of the Germans in Stalingrad in January 1943 followed the encirclement of their forces by Marshal Zhukov in Operation Uranus. Deception was maintained during the operation by reducing communication by radio or in writing, by marching at night, and by giving the Germans the impression of activity in other sectors. While encirclement was taking place, the German army was 'blinded by the absence of clear information'. On the day of the Russian attack, 19 November 1942, there was a freezing mist followed by a blizzard, so that it was 'not even possible to get an overview of the situation through air reconnaissance', as one of the leading German generals noted at the time. As in the case of Austerlitz, the well-known phrase of the 'fog of war' came true in a literal sense as well as a metaphorical one.[19]

In some major battles, then, the plans of the victors succeeded largely because the enemy did not expect what actually happened. In other words, commanders failed to consider their adversary's possible options. Can wars as well as battles be described as triumphs of knowledge over ignorance?

## THE FRANCO-PRUSSIAN WAR

One nineteenth-century war in particular supports Tolstoy's argument about the chaos of battles: the Franco-Prussian War of 1870–71. The author must have felt vindicated when he read about a war that broke out only a year after the publication of his famous novel. In his story of the French defeat, *La Débâcle* (1892), Émile Zola made a leading character, Maurice, accuse himself of 'a crass ignorance of everything that it was necessary to know' (*une ignorance crasse en tout ce qu'il aurait fallu savoir*).[20] Zola was doubtless aware of *War and Peace*, but he also carried out careful research before writing his novel. In any case, his reflections on ignorance are abundantly confirmed by the classic account of the war, written by one of the leading military historians of our day, Michael Howard.

Howard himself served in the Second World War and won the Military Cross for his bravery. 'Much later, asked about these events, he said that it was only because he was so young (still only 20), and so ignorant, that he could perform such an act.'[21] In his book, however, what Howard emphasizes is the ignorance of the French generals – ignorance of the topography of the terrain in which they were fighting and especially of the positions of both their own armies and those of the enemy. There were 'no maps available, except maps of Germany', since the French had expected to invade rather than to be invaded. In the case of one battle, the French commander, Marshal Achille Bazaine, would later complain about 'the total absence of information from civil authorities about the German advance on his left'. At the battle of Sedan, where the defeat of the French led to their surrender and the effective end of the war, the commander, Marshal Patrick MacMahon, felt that he did not have enough information to decide what to do, while his second in command 'did not know the position of the other corps, nor of the Germans, nor what supplies were available'.[22]

The Prussians too suffered from ignorance. At the battle of Beaumont, where Marshal Helmuth von Moltke was in command, his 'principal difficulty in planning his advance lay in his ignorance of the position of the enemy army', while his subordinate Marshal Leonhard von Blumenthal 'grumbled about the constant change of orders on the basis of inadequate information'.[23] The Prussians won not because they were omniscient but because they were less ignorant of the terrain and the enemy than the French were.

The French learned their lesson, just as the Prussians had learned it some sixty years earlier. After Prussia's defeat by Napoleon at the battle of Jena in 1806, more geography was taught in their schools. In similar fashion, after the French defeat in 1870 in a war described by an American geographer as 'fought as much by maps as by weapons', the study of geography was given more importance in French education.

## GUERRILLA WARFARE, 1839–42 AND 1896–7

Disasters are particularly likely to happen in encounters between regular armies and local guerrillas, when arrogant and 'breathtakingly ignorant' generals underestimate the enemy. A comparative study of 'Great Military Disasters' offers eleven examples from this category.[24]

The First Afghan War remains memorable for the tragic retreat of the British army from Kabul in 1842, when the force was virtually annihilated. In hindsight, it can be said that the British made every mistake in the book. These mistakes were essentially due to their ignorance of local conditions: the terrain, the weather and the weapons of the enemy. The British commanders had not realized how easy it would be for the Afghans to lay an ambush for the army while it marched through the narrow mountain passes. To make matters worse, the British also seem to have been unaware that the Afghan muskets, the famous *jezails*, had a longer range than British muskets, so that Afghans could fire down on the army from the top of the cliffs, secure in the knowledge that British bullets could not reach them.[25]

The British also made the mistake of retreating during the winter, despite the fact that Shah Shuja, whom the army had re-established on his throne, had advised them to postpone their departure until the spring. Lacking winter clothing, the soldiers froze to death at night. If they survived, their frostbitten hands and feet rendered them ineffective against the enemy. In the narrow Jugdulluck Pass, an ambush turned into a massacre. Only one man returned to tell the tale, represented in Lady Butler's painting, *Remnants of an Army* (1879).[26] The traveller Richard Burton, who prided himself on his knowledge of the 'East', believed that the British defeat was the result of 'crass ignorance concerning the Oriental peoples'.[27]

Returning to the theme of relative ignorance, it should be noted that the Afghans also made mistakes, especially before they learned that

British troops usually won when they were doing what they had been trained to do – engaging in a pitched battle on a plain. However, the Afghans rapidly learned from defeat and made fewer errors. The British eventually learned their lesson. The so-called 'Army of Retribution' marched to Kabul in the summer of 1840 and made sure to command the heights before marching through a mountain pass. Breech-loading rifles made *jezails* obsolete. By the late nineteenth century, manuals had been published advising on the appropriate tactics in mountain or 'savage' warfare on India's North-West Frontier.[28]

As we shall see in chapter fifteen, similar mistakes were made in our own time in the course of the Russian and American invasions of Afghanistan.

## THE REVOLT OF CANUDOS

The 'Revolt of Canudos' (1896–7) offers an example well known in Brazil, though not elsewhere, of the fatal combination of arrogance with ignorance on the part of professional soldiers fighting guerrillas. The revolt was immortalized by a major writer, Euclides da Cunha, a former cadet at a military school turned reporter for a newspaper, *A Província de São Paulo*, which sent him to cover the event. It was elaborated into a book, 'The Backlands' (*Os Sertões*), published in 1902, which has become a classic of Brazilian literature. It equally deserves to become a classic in the history of guerrilla warfare.

Canudos was a small town in the north-east of Brazil that became a refuge for opponents of the newly founded Republic (proclaimed in 1889). Their leader was the charismatic Antonio Conselheiro, a wandering prophet who foretold the imminent return of King Sebastian of Portugal, who died fighting the Muslims in North Africa in 1578. In November 1896, a small military force was sent to suppress the so-called 'revolt' – even though the monarchists had not taken any aggressive action. The force was soon compelled to retreat. A larger force of nearly eight hundred men was sent soon afterwards, with similar results. Early in 1897, a third, still larger force was defeated and its commander, Moreira César, was killed.[29]

Moreira César, a successful professional soldier, had made the classic mistake of underestimating his enemy, regarding them as mere amateurs. Racial prejudice probably played its part: many of the defenders were 'half-breeds' (*mestiços*), mixtures of European, indigenous and African origin. The commander also suffered from simple ignorance. He was unaware that the town was defended by a substantial group of *jagunços*, irregular soldiers who knew their job. The defenders sent out spies to observe and report on the movements of the enemy, dug trenches, camouflaged their position with branches and moved with ease through tropical vegetation which was unfamiliar to most of the troops sent against them. Like the Afghans in 1840, the *jagunços* controlled the heights above Canudos and fired down on the enemy, as they did from the church tower when the soldiers entered the town. In the house-to-house fighting that followed the assault, the inhabitants had the advantage of local knowledge and could easily surprise their attackers.

In short, Moreira César suffered, according to Euclides da Cunha, from 'ignorance of the elementary principles' of the art of war (*a insciência de princípios rudimentares da sua arte*).[30] For example, he ordered the attack when his troops were exhausted, following a long march in the tropical heat. It was only when the defenders suffered a fourth attack, this time by more than eight thousand soldiers, complete with machine guns and artillery, that they were finally overwhelmed.

## THE VIETNAM WAR

The role of American ignorance in the Vietnam war was a crucial one. As James Gibson, a professor of sociology, remarks in his study of the war, there were many 'absences of knowledge'. 'Some are simply blank spaces', while others 'indicate places where knowledge about the war was discounted and ignored for various reasons'. For example, 'military bureaucracies have no interest . . . in estimating civilian casualties', since 'military units are rewarded for efficiency' and civilian casualties detract from this.[31] At a conference held in 1983 to reconsider the war and to learn from it, 'there runs like a red thread the question of ignorance – the ignorance of the policymakers; the ignorance of the military; the ignorance of the public; the ignorance of the press as to what Vietnam was, what it was about and even where it was geographically'.[32] These multiple ignorances all deserve discussion.

The American commanders made similar mistakes in Vietnam to the ones that they would make some decades later in Afghanistan. In both cases they were encouraged by awareness of their superiority in artillery, bombs, helicopters and technology in general for fighting what Gibson calls a 'technowar' against 'a nation of peasants with bicycles'.[33] What they did not take into account was the force of ideas and the willingness of a people to fight in defence of their fundamental values, as the Americans themselves had done in 1776.

The great military disadvantage of the invaders was that they were outsiders, most of them ignorant of the language, the customs and the terrain (including the tropical climate) of the country in which they were fighting. Ignorance of the language meant that 'Most of the Americans were unable to communicate with their so-called Vietnamese counterparts.'[34] They were a regular army confronting a force of guerrillas, the Viet Cong, who possessed both local knowledge and the support of the civilian inhabitants of the country.

The Americans paid a high price for these ignorances: twenty years of fighting (from 1955 to 1975), nearly sixty thousand American dead, $168 billion spent, and despite that, ignominious defeat. Like the military, the American government failed to take ideas into account. They did not learn from the past, since 'the longevity of Vietnamese resistance to foreign rule could have been learned from any history book on Indochina'.[35] The government was aware of Vietnamese nationalism and anti-colonialism, side by side with Communism, but 'ignored the implication of this information, that outside intervention made revolution more, not less viable'.[36] In other words, they did not want to know that most Vietnamese were against them, in the South as well as the North.

The government was itself starved of essential information. For example, the CIA had not studied the possible effects of the bombing of the North (operation 'Rolling Thunder'), so that President Johnson 'was left to stumble into one of the most crucial decisions of the war with no intelligence guidance'. The CIA itself suffered from organizational ignorance. Some of its field agents were well aware of the corruption of the South Vietnamese army, but they were forbidden by their immediate superiors to mention this in their reports to headquarters.[37]

A study of the war by a former participant concludes that 'each side grossly underestimated the determination and staying power of the other'. The American failure 'was a failure of understanding and imagination'.[38] To make matters worse, organizational ignorance once again played a part in failure. Robert McNamara, the American secretary for defense from 1961 to 1968 (and a former general manager of Ford Motors), failed to realize that 'the intense pressure he placed on the military to provide palpable signposts of progress led many of those who reported to him up and down the line to fabricate the information they were providing', especially the body counts. There was 'systematic falsification of battle reports' in order to meet what Gibson calls the 'production quotas' ordered by management. In other words, there was a serious knowledge gap between the men with boots on the ground of Vietnam and the managers far away in Washington.[39]

McNamara came to believe that the war was a mistake and listed eleven reasons for American failure. His fourth reason was that 'Our misjudgments of friend and foe alike reflected our profound ignorance of the history, culture and politics of the people in the area.'[40] Arguing for the need to 'empathize with your enemy', McNamara added, 'In the case of Vietnam, we didn't know them well enough to empathize. There was total misunderstanding as a result.'[41] Other commentators have also emphasized the place of ignorance in the American defeat, and some of them mention arrogance as well.[42] Prejudices, including racism, played a part. The American commanders, professional soldiers, regarded the enemy leaders as amateurs, while ordinary soldiers despised the Vietnamese, whom they called 'gooks'. As in Canudos and Afghanistan, underestimating the enemy had fatal consequences.

The American press also suffered from ignorance. Looking back, the journalist Robert Scheer confessed that 'We had not noticed Vietnam until our government noticed it – so that everything that happened before 1950 was totally uninteresting to us.' Hence they were 'woefully ignorant of the setting of the conflict'.[43] At the time, the reporters blamed both the military (in their regular briefings), and also the government for lying to them, exaggerating successes, minimizing casualties and hiding atrocities.[44] The bombing of Cambodia was covered up, and so was the massacre of hundreds of civilians in the village of My Lai in 1968. 'Everybody was covering everybody's ass.' The cover-up of the massacre was exposed by the freelance journalist Seymour Hersh, whose independence allowed him to pursue the story.[45]

Reporters in the field, however unprepared for understanding what was happening, learned from experience. However, in yet another case of organizational ignorance, 'the vast complex we term "the press" did not really catch up with the correspondents in the field'. The magazine *Life* rejected Hersh's story, which was eventually published in a relatively obscure outlet, the *Dispatch News Service*. 'The massacre was now out of the box' and thirty-five newspapers carried the story.[46]

As for the American public, they 'were poorly informed by their political leaders' about the implications of commitment to South Vietnam.[47] When the war began, they had little chance to understand what was going on, given the misinformation and disinformation that filtered down – not to mention the information that failed to reach them.

## A MIDDLE WAY?

Are defeats and victories the result of planning or chaos? In the controversy between admirers of famous generals and followers of Tolstoy, the truth probably lies, as usual, between the two extremes. Clausewitz claimed that war is the realm of uncertainty, since 'all action takes place, so to speak, in a kind of twilight, which, like fog or moonlight, often tends to make things seem grotesque and larger than they really are', a simile that inspired Colonel Hale's famous phrase about the 'fog of war', quoted earlier.[48] Despite this pessimistic statement, Clausewitz continued to believe that the courage, self-confidence and intelligence of generals did make a difference to their results.

Another testimony in favour of this middle way comes from Vasily Grossman, a Russian reporter who covered the siege of Stalingrad in 1942 and made use of this experience in two novels, *Stalingrad* and *Life and Fate*. Grossman often refers to *War and Peace*, a book that he clearly wishes to emulate, although he sometimes disagrees with the author's generalizations. In *Stalingrad*, staff officer Novikov 'was surprised by his ability to make sense of a chaos that often seemed beyond understanding', while *Life and Fate* describes a kind of military intuition, 'the sense that allows a soldier to judge the true correlation of forces in a battle and to predict the outcome'. Grossman sometimes uses the term 'chaos', but his narrative suggests that this chaos is more apparent than real.[49]

Distinctions are of course in order: between pitched battles (Borodino, Waterloo) and guerrilla warfare (in Afghanistan, Brazil and Vietnam); between war on land and war at sea or in the air; between theatres of war and between periods of history. There are also major differences between planning tactics and ensuring that the troops have enough food, ammunition, appropriate clothing and means of transport such as horses, trucks and the trains that were crucial to Prussian success in 1870. In all periods and places, though, ignorance can be literally fatal.

The German invasion of Russia in 1941 offers a spectacular case of the toxic combination of ignorance and arrogance. One of the major weaknesses of the campaign was Hitler's determination to control what his generals were doing, although they were on the spot while he was distant, indeed virtually isolated, issuing orders from his 'wolf's lair' in Rastenburg (which is now in Poland). Such remote control would have been physically impossible before the invention of the telephone. In this case, it turned out to be unwise.

A messenger who reported to Hitler in January 1943 on the dire situation of the German forces watched him look at the map studded with flags representing German divisions, as if he was ignorant of the fact that these divisions were no longer at full strength. The messenger later commented, 'I saw then that he had lost touch with reality. He lived in a fantasy world of maps and flags.'[50] This incident offers a vivid illustration of the anthropologist James Scott's concept of 'thin simplifications', including taking the map for the reality that it is supposed to represent. On a larger scale, the whole campaign testifies to the risk involved in the attempt to control military operations from the rear. Unaware of or uninterested in the situation, Hitler forbade retreat when it became necessary and robbed commanders in the field of the opportunity to respond to unexpected events with the necessary flexibility.[51] More generally, his self-confidence, not to say arrogance, prevented him from learning the lessons of Napoleon's Russian campaign of 1812. Chapter fifteen offers further discussion of failures to learn from the past.

# 10

# IGNORANCE IN BUSINESS

If only we knew what we know at HP

Chairman of Hewlett-Packard

In the world of business, as in the worlds of war and politics, decisions have to be taken about the inevitably uncertain future. As in the case of science, the ignorances of the professionals – in this case farmers, merchants, financiers and industrialists – will be distinguished from those of the public, whether as consumers or as investors.

## AGRICULTURE

The dangers of ignorance in agriculture are particularly clear when the farmers have arrived only recently in the land they are cultivating, as in the case of settlers in New England in the seventeenth century or in Australia and New Zealand in the nineteenth. In New England, 'most colonists anticipated that they would be able to live much as they had done in England', but the new arrivals were not aware of the harsh winters and died of starvation because they had not brought a sufficient supply of food to last until spring.[1] In Australia and New Zealand, 'Farmers and ranchers pushed into new country with high hopes and little information. Some were ruined by drought, frost or heat, others failed as their farming or grazing techniques exhausted the land.'[2] They brought familiar animals, notably rabbits, without awareness of the consequences of their rapid reproduction, creating a 'pest' that it was impossible to eradicate: 'not only could the settlers not halt it, they had no way to explain it'.[3] Ignorance again.

According to a major landowner, the prince of Trabia, the main reason for the decline of agriculture in Sicily was the ignorance of the local workers.[4] Ignorance was often attributed to the peasantry by the upper-class members of the many agricultural societies founded in Europe in the age of Enlightenment, beginning with the 'Society of Improvers in the Knowledge of Agriculture' founded in Edinburgh in 1723.

Indeed, it was in the context of agriculture that the term 'improvement', an Enlightenment keyword, was originally employed. It referred to crop rotation, the use of a new form of plough and other aspects of what is known as the 'Second Agricultural Revolution', promoted by the landowners. Among the many societies of this kind founded in the eighteenth century were the Society for the Advancement of Agriculture and Manufacture in Dublin, the Accademia economico-agraria dei Georgofili in Florence, the Société d'agriculture in Paris, the Gesellschaft des Ackerbaues in Klagenfurt and the Spanish network of Sociedades Económicas de los Amigos del País.[5] It is worth noting that these societies all met in cities.

A further step in making agriculture a science was taken in the nineteenth century by Justus von Liebig, professor of chemistry at the University of Giessen. Liebig was interested in applying organic chemistry to agriculture, increasing yields by using fertilizers containing nitrogen. Retrospectively, his discoveries reveal the earlier ignorance of farmers, just as the more recent critique of chemical fertilizers shines a spotlight on what Professor Liebig did not know.

If the work of the societies and of Liebig, like the Green Revolution of the mid-twentieth century, illustrate the success of campaigns to improve agriculture from above, other examples reveal the dangers of imposing changes in defiance of local knowledge. If we are looking for disasters that were due to ignorance, the economic domain, and agriculture in particular, comes a close second to war. Again and again, disasters have followed central planning that failed to take local knowledge into account. Disasters of this kind are the central theme in James

Scott's comparative study, *Seeing Like a State*, which demonstrates 'how certain schemes to improve the human condition have failed'.[6]

For a British example, one might cite the Groundnut Scheme (1947–51), a project of the Labour government (especially the minister of food, John Strachey). The plan was to grow peanuts in Tanganyika (now part of Tanzania) by clearing five million acres of land. The failure of the project, at a cost of some £36 million (at 1951 prices) to the taxpayer, was essentially due to the British government's ignorance of local conditions – the lack of necessary rainfall, the hard soil and a workforce that was not trained, or not trained well enough, to operate the machines provided. As in the case of war, the recipe for disaster was the combination of ignorance with arrogance, in this case, the idea that 'Whitehall knows best'.[7] On a much larger scale, think of the human cost of Mao Zedong's failed 'Great Leap Forward' (1958–62).[8]

In other cases, disaster followed decisions made by the farmers themselves, as in the well-known case of the 'Dust Bowl' in the Great Plains of the Middle West of the USA in the 1930s. When the price of wheat was high, grassland was ploughed up at an unprecedented rate, leaving the soil vulnerable to erosion. This was not the result of pure ignorance but of (mis)calculated risk-taking on the part of entrepreneurs in agribusiness who did not want to know about the danger of ploughing up the land in this way. They learned their lesson in the droughts of the 1930s.[9]

The damage is sometimes the result not of ignorance but of short-term self-interest, as in the case of the long history of deforestation in Brazil, first in the Atlantic Forest and now in the Amazon, clearing the land first for sugarcane, then for coffee and now for soya. One group, the farmers, have reaped the short-term benefits, while other groups, the indigenous peoples and humanity in general, have paid or will pay the price.[10]

## TRADE AND INDUSTRY

Some kinds of ignorance may be beneficial in business, at least to someone. In auctions, for instance, sellers benefit when bidders do not know how high their competitors are prepared to go. It has been argued that trade benefits from the 'symmetric ignorance' of the two parties to a transaction.[11] Asymmetrical ignorance is more common. A famous example was offered by the American economist George Akerlof. On his now famous 'Lemons Principle', bad second-hand cars ('lemons') drive out good ones, since the good ones are cherished by their owners and so remain outside the market. Ignorance leads to the disappointment of buyers.[12] Other kinds of ignorance lead to the failure of sellers, measured by the rate of bankruptcies.

No wonder then that the study of the role of information in economic life has become a major field within the discipline of economics. One major contribution to the field was made jointly by the economist Oskar Morgenstern and the polymathic mathematician John von Neumann, making use of the theory of games. Economic behaviour has basic elements in common with games: players, strategies and payoffs. It resembles one type of game in particular, games in which players are ignorant of one another's choices. The problem is to discover the best strategy in this situation.[13]

The economist Kenneth Arrow became famous for his analysis of the problem of buying and selling information. 'Arrow's paradox' notes the incompatibility between the need of customers to know in advance what they are buying and the equal need of sellers not to divulge information fully before they are paid.[14] As in the case of war, relative ignorance is key. All participants are ignorant to some extent, but the least ignorant ones are likely to be the most successful.

It is important to distinguish domains as well as degrees of ignorance. In business, ignorance has usually been greater in international trade than in the domestic variety. The 'reciprocal ignorance' of European merchants and Ottoman merchants in the early modern Mediterranean has been noted in a recent study. In the case of England, 'Overseas trade was necessarily a high-risk area to the eighteenth-century business community.'[15] In an age of sailing ships, the risk of shipwreck and the loss of the cargo was particularly high. It was a major 'known unknown' for merchants as well as for the crew. No wonder then that the history of insurance began not with lives or even houses, but with ships.

War was and remains another major hazard. In eighteenth-century England, 'Wars created a high degree of uncertainty by cutting flows of information, money and goods and disrupting access to markets.' Uncertainty is also produced by innovation. 'New methods of production or marketing are inevitably more risky than old ones.' Ignorance of new opportunities is particularly likely when communication is slow and infrequent. During the Industrial Revolution, for instance, 'A corn merchant in Hemel Hempstead in Hertfordshire could hardly hope to know enough about the market for cotton goods to pack up his bags and troop off to Bolton in the 1780s to set up as a cotton manufacturer.'[16]

Another area of ignorance concerns 'the other side of the hill', in other words the policies and techniques of rivals. Knowing whether competitors are making use of new techniques is obviously important, like attempting to keep them ignorant of one's own recipes, technology, clients, projects for the future and so on. In order to keep knowledge of his technical processes secret, the eighteenth-century English manufacturer Benjamin Huntsman is said to have operated his steelworks only at night.[17]

Industrial espionage has a long history. In the seventeenth century, the secrets of Venetian glassmakers, for example, were coveted by their opposite numbers in France and England. In the age of the Industrial Revolution, some Swedish visitors to England reported back to the Board of Mines and the Iron Office in their own country about the new machinery that they had observed and sketched. In the 1780s, a French engineer visited England to collect information about Wedgwood pottery, stocking looms and other machines and took home with him three workers 'without whom the machines themselves would be quite useless'.[18] During the Cold War, spies from the Communist bloc successfully stole technical information from Western countries.[19] As for the situation in the twenty-first century, among the revelations of Edward Snowden, to be discussed below, was the fact that the National Security Agency had spied on German companies that competed with the Americans.

Yet another important area of ignorance in business is lack of knowledge of possible markets. Mistakes can be expensive, as in the case of the early history of the English South Sea Company, when it was still engaged in trade with South America, and shipped woollen cloth to Cartagena in 1714 without realizing that the tropical climate made that type of clothing inappropriate.[20] An early attempt to remedy this kind of situation was made by the Dutch East India Company. Thanks to one of its directors, Johannes Hudde, sales figures were already being analysed in 1692 in order to determine the future policy of the company on pricing and the ordering of pepper and other commodities from Asia.[21] Systematic market research is much more recent. Returning to retrospection, the history of market research reminds us of earlier ignorance on the part of managers concerning the kind of person who bought a particular product (male or female, young or old, middle class or working class) as well as their reasons or motives for choosing one brand over another.

An American psychologist, Daniel Starch, founded a company to engage in market research in 1923, focusing on the effectiveness of advertising. Where Starch and his assistants simply asked people about their preferences, the Austrian-American psychologist Ernst Dichter, active in the 1940s, adopted a Freudian approach in his 'motivational research', focusing on the unconscious desires underlying the consumer's choice of products ranging from soap to cars and so helping sellers to target them through advertising. Today, this kind of 'hidden persuasion' has become commonplace.[22]

Organizational ignorance is a serious problem for businesses as well as for governments. Indeed, it was in the economic domain that studies of this type of ignorance developed. In the United States from the beginning of the twentieth century onwards, 'small companies were combined into large ones'.[23] As firms became larger they acquired more information but also more layers of management, interposed between the top and the bottom of the company. With this development came a new weakness, 'organizational silence', in other words a failure to communicate, to transfer knowledge from one part of the firm to another.[24]

For example, workers on the shop floor of a factory acquire by experience a knowledge about the process of production that managers and the CEO may lack, just as the workers may be ignorant, or be kept ignorant, of the CEO's plans. Workers and management have often resembled 'two cultures' (to adapt C. P. Snow's phrase about the sciences and the humanities). Each side is ignorant of the other side's knowledge. The problem has been described as that of 'sticky knowledge', which does not move easily.[25] If we imagine knowledge as a 'flow', it is one that is sometimes interrupted by barriers and may be 'filtered'. Unwillingness to listen on the part of management leads to unwillingness to speak out, a 'climate of silence'.[26] In extreme cases, managers are afraid to tell bosses what they think the bosses do not want to hear, a problem that will surface again in a political context in the following chapter. As a result, serious problems are ignored. Striking examples of organizational ignorance have come from factories in Communist countries, from Hungary to China, where the managers did not know or pretended not to know that workers were absent, slacking or stealing.[27]

One writer on firms introduced the metaphor of the 'iceberg of ignorance': the higher in the hierarchy one climbs, the less one knows about the workers below, including what these workers know about the firm and its products. As a chairman of Hewlett-Packard ruefully remarked, 'If only we knew what we know at HP.'[28] Organizational 'forgetting' is a similar problem. Employees who work in the same firm for decades acquire 'tacit knowledge', in other words knowledge that that they may not know they possess. They often do not write down this knowledge or pass it on to their successors, so it is lost to the firm when they retire. As the management consultant David DeLong puts it, thinking in particular of the decade following 2004, 'that giant sucking sound you will hear is all the knowledge being drained out of organizations by retirements and other forms of turnover'.[29] The problem is not of course confined to business, but also affects governments, churches, armies and other organizations. However, companies, especially in Japan, have been pioneers in attempts to overcome the problem.[30]

Not all the official policies that have led to economic decline have been the result of simple ignorance. Some governments have treated prosperity as a lower priority than religious orthodoxy, as in two well-known cases from early modern Europe, the expulsion of the Moriscos (descendants of Arabs suspected of loyalty to Islam) by Philip III of Spain in 1609 and the expulsion of Protestants from France by Louis XIV in 1685. Expulsion meant the loss of many skilled workers. In both cases, the rulers acted for religious reasons. Nonetheless, we can say that these governments ignored the economic consequences of the loss.[31]

## CONSUMER IGNORANCE

Like businesses and governments, consumers take economic decisions in conditions of uncertainty. Economists have often analysed their behaviour as if their choices were completely rational, in which case the extent of their knowledge or the opposite, the extent of their ignorance, is obviously important. Psychologists such as Starch and Dichter, on the other hand, have sometimes analysed consumer behaviour as irrational (or at least non-rational, the product of unconscious desires), in which case ignorance is irrelevant. In practice, it might be more illuminating to make distinctions not only between individual consumers but also between products. Unconscious desires are surely more important in choosing a car than in choosing eggs in a supermarket.

Choices were relatively simple in the preindustrial world of limited goods, offered for sale in markets, at fairs and outside the workshops of artisans. Even in that world, however, there was still too much information to master. Many prices were not fixed but negotiated, so buyers needed to know whether a particular seller was flexible or obstinate. Visiting different stalls or shops allowed comparison of the quality as well as the price of different products. On the other hand, in the case of substantial purchases, buying a horse for instance (as in the later market for second-hand cars), it was easy for an uninformed buyer to be cheated by a cunning dealer. 'Let the buyer beware' (*caveat emptor*) is an ancient admonition.[32]

The situation became more complex, at least for the relatively wealthy, from the seventeenth century onwards, when the rise of fashion, particularly in clothing, required consumers who wished to follow the latest trends to discover what these trends were, sometimes by reading specialized magazines such as *Le Cabinet des Modes* (1785). Complexity increased still further in the age of industrialization, with a dizzy rise in the numbers and variety of goods for sale. Consumers began to study catalogues and view advertisements in print before making choices, while named brands of commodities became more and more common.

Advertisements, originally designed to inform the buyer, gradually turned into a form of persuasion, appealing to desires that consumers did not know they had.[33] It is obviously too simple to suggest that if buyers possessed more knowledge, they would never be persuaded. On the other hand ignorance, especially ignorance of the strategy of advertisers, makes consumers more vulnerable to manipulation, as in the case of many scams.[34] To respond to this problem, inform consumers and encourage discrimination, institutes such as Consumer's Research (1929) have been founded and magazines such as *Which?* (1957) have been published. Research into products for the sake of consumers now takes place side by side with research into consumers for the sake of selling products. Even so, many consumers remain ignorant of rival products, not to mention what materials go into a particular product or the effect of its manufacture on its workers or the environment.

The problem is that to evaluate some products – especially if they are legal, medical or financial – requires specialized knowledge, making the ordinary consumer dependent on the advice of intermediaries. In today's specialized world, this is even the case for doctors, especially GPs who need to know which drug to prescribe to a patient. As was remarked in chapter seven, it is impossible to keep up with the articles on new drugs published in medical journals, leaving the GP at the mercy of drug companies who may offer misleading information, including academic articles ghostwritten by employees of the company.[35]

In short, to consume wisely without assistance has virtually become a full-time job. A similar point may be made about finance: about accounting and especially about investment.

## ACCOUNTING ILLITERACY

In the world of finance, phrases such as 'financial literacy' and 'accounting literacy' have become commonplace. The Accounting Literacy Foundation (which was set up in 1982 and became a foundation in 2020) defines this form of literacy as 'the ability to read, interpret and communicate a financial situation or event, typically reflected in the five elements of the balance sheet and the income statement: Revenue, Equity, Liabilities, Assets and Expenses'.[36]

What interests us here is the reverse, 'accounting illiteracy' and its consequences, for small businesses that cannot afford to appoint a financial specialist or for ordinary people who are planning for retirement. In the latter case, it has been noted that 'Women are less financially literate than men' and that 'the young and the old are less financially literate than the middle-aged'.[37]

Going back in time, it was the need to record the storage and flow of goods that led to the invention of writing on clay tablets in ancient Babylon. Instructions for book-keeping by double entry (debits on one side, credits on the other) could be found in manuals for merchants in Italy from the fifteenth century onwards and later for householders in many European cities. On the other hand, rulers such as Philip II (discussed in chapter eleven) and their nobilities were content to be illiterate in accounting, while most of the rural population of Europe were still unable to read and write in the year 1800.

In the nineteenth century, accountants emerged as a separate profession while accounting became more complex, a process that has continued ever since.[38] It has been argued that accounting is itself 'a technology of ignorance'. For example, a study of seventeen corruption scandals in Italy reported between 2014 and 2018 concluded that 'Accounting plays a role in producing and sustaining ignorance'.[39] To this it might be retorted that – on the analogy of the well-known epigram that 'statistics don't lie, statisticians do' – accounting does not lie, while individuals and companies can and do lie in balance sheets. The price of accounting illiteracy is the failure to detect these lies.

## INVESTING IN IGNORANCE

From a lay person's point of view, the dangers of financial illiteracy are greatest in the domain of investment. This has long been the case. Among the institutional innovations of the late Middle Ages and the early modern period was the joint stock company. Famous examples include the East India Company in Britain, founded in 1600, in which a group of merchants held shares, and its Dutch rival the VOC (*Vereenigde Oostindische Compagnie* or 'United East India Company'), founded in 1602, which appealed to small investors as well as to the rich. Another innovation was the stock exchange, notably the Amsterdam Bourse (1602).[40] Earlier bourses had offered opportunities for buying and selling commodities, but the Amsterdam Bourse was for buying and selling 'stock', in other words shares in companies. Its London equivalent was 'Change Alley', close to but separate from the Royal Exchange, while its New York equivalent was Wall Street. Stockbrokers met under a tree in Wall Street before founding the New York Stock Exchange in 1792.[41]

Like the VOC, stock exchanges mobilized the resources of many small investors. Then as now, investors included both professionals (merchants and speculators) and amateurs. The ignorance of investors, like that of consumers, has not been the object of systematic research. However, the rapid fluctuations of the stock market over the centuries, its booms and busts, would be difficult to explain without the presence of many 'inexperienced investors'.[42]

As in the case of consumers, the language of psychology, often old-fashioned collective psychology, has often been employed to describe the behaviour of investors, treating them as a 'herd' rather than as individuals and employing terms such as 'exuberance', 'mania', 'panic' or 'hysteria'.[43] Once again, distinctions are surely in order, between cautious and incautious investors as well as between investment in normal times and in moments of economic boom, when more and more individuals want a share in the action. Innovation in technology may lead to a rapid growth in speculation, thanks to the 'excitement surrounding technology' combined with ignorance, or more exactly 'limited information with which to value the shares accurately'.[44]

The result of these conditions is the rapid expansion and even more rapid bursting of 'bubbles': the railway bubble, the bicycle bubble and more recently the 'dot-com bubble'. A crucial factor in the process is the ignorance of investors (insiders apart) of the state of the finances of the company in which they are investing, knowledge that would have allowed them to sell their shares before the bubble burst. All investment involves uncertainty, but in the case of bubbles such as the South Sea Bubble of 1720 or crashes such as the Great Crash of 1929, discussed below, ignorance and its companion, credulity, also played an important part.

Investing has often been compared to gambling. That is actually part of its appeal. For some people, a certain degree of risk with the possibility of large gains is preferable to the greater security and the lower return of lending money to banks. Some gamblers study the 'form' of particular horses before the race, or the statistics of gains and losses at the roulette table, while others do not bother. The situation appears to be the same in the case of investors. Some study the fortune of particular commodities. Some take the advice of stockbrokers. Some consult books or watch television programmes by freelance advisers like the American Suze Orman, a best-selling author who also hosted a show of this kind on the business news channel CNBC from 2002 to 2015.

Others simply buy and sell shares because others are doing so or allow themselves to be taken in by swindlers such as Charles Ponzi, who was active in the USA in 1920. Ponzi offered investors unbelievably high rates of profit but he financed his pay-outs to earlier investors from the investments of clients later in the queue. Sooner or later the scheme was bound to collapse, as it did within a year of its launch. Ponzi was imprisoned for fraud, while the investors lost almost everything, illustrating the maxim that 'If something sounds too good to be true, it probably is.'[45]

As we have seen in earlier chapters, a vacuum of reliable knowledge is quickly filled by rumour, circulating orally and spread further in print and other media. It has been observed that the history of speculative bubbles 'begins roughly with the history of newspapers', in the early eighteenth century. The media have continued to encourage or discourage investment in the ages of the telephone (so important in the stock market), the radio, television and the Internet.[46] Once stock exchanges were founded, some speculators did not take long to discover that they could manipulate the market by spreading what we now call 'fake news'. A story about the loss of a cargo of spices at sea, for example, would push up the price of a particular commodity.

Political rumours also had this effect. A rumour of the death of Napoleon was deliberately spread in dramatic fashion in 1814, when a man dressed in the uniform of an aide-de-camp arrived in Dover and let it be known that the emperor had been defeated and cut down by Cossacks. This 'fake news' led to a sudden rise in the price of shares on the London Stock Exchange, allowing a small group or syndicate of people who were in on the secret to take advantage of the public's temporary ignorance of the true state of affairs to sell their shares at a high price before the truth was discovered. Until this time the Stock Exchange had turned a blind eye to the deliberate spread of rumours, but on this occasion a trial for 'conspiracy to fraud by means of false reports' took place and led to convictions.[47]

In similar fashion but with opposite effects, rumour has often bred panic, the selling of shares and a run on the banks. In the USA in the nineteenth century, panics were common enough – in 1819, 1837, 1857 and 1873 – to be regarded as a kind of institution, although they were minor events in comparison with the Great Crash of 1929 or the world financial crisis of 2008–9.[48]

Rumours are effective because they play on two powerful emotions, hopes and fears. Stock exchanges might be viewed as amplifiers of rumour, encouraging investors to buy or sell simply because others are doing so.[49] A rise in the price of stock encourages buying, which in turn drives up the price in a kind of chain reaction or 'feedback loop'.[50] Hence the history of the stock market is punctuated by regular booms, moments of what Alan Greenspan, the former chair of the US Federal

Reserve, called 'irrational exuberance'. The booms, known since the eighteenth century as 'bubbles', are followed, as inevitably as a hang-over, by 'crashes', sometimes because the supply of buyers has run out and sometimes as a result of bad news, true or false. Once again, there is a chain reaction, selling shares because others are doing so.

Relatively recent examples include the dot-com bubble in the stock of companies concerned with the Internet (1995–2002), and the housing bubble in Spain from 2005 to 2008, which ended with many houses left half-built. Professional speculators observe what is going on and calculate the moment to sell before the bubble bursts, alighting from the train just before it crashes. Indeed, on occasion they set the train in motion. The mechanism was described as early as 1690 by the English Commissioners for Trade, condemning the practice of founding a company only for the purpose of selling shares in it to 'ignorant men, drawn in by the reputation, falsely raised and artfully spread, concerning the thriving state of their stock'.[51] This description looks like a prophecy of events in Britain thirty years later: the vertiginous rise and the rapid bursting of the notorious 'South Sea Bubble'.[52]

## THE SOUTH SEA BUBBLE

This 'Bubble' is a classic case of investor ignorance that led to credulity and so to disaster. Robert Harley, Queen Anne's chief minister, founded the South Sea Company in 1711 in order to trade with South America, still viewed at this time as a kind of El Dorado. Unsuccessful in this domain, the Company turned to a scheme to eliminate the national debt. The Company manipulated the public.[53] To launch the stock, important people were allowed to buy at a preferential rate or credited with fictitious stock, while the Company lent money to would-be investors, encouraging them to buy shares that some of them could not afford. As a result, the stock went up in value, more people invested, and the increase in the demand for shares pushed the price still higher. It was a kind of multiplier effect, described at the time as a 'frenzy', or as 'selling the bear's skin' before killing the bear.[54] The investors were a miscellaneous group, including King George I, Isaac Newton and the poet Alexander Pope alongside politicians and financiers. Many women were said to have invested, ranging from duchesses to the fishwives of Billingsgate market.[55]

Some individuals sold out early and made a profit. The chancellor of the Exchequer, John Aislabie, was 'one of the first to foresee the crash'. He advised King George I to sell because 'the stock was carried up to an Exorbitant height by the madness of people' so that 'it was impossible it should stand'. Like Aislabie, the duchess of Marlborough got out in time, foreseeing 'that this project must burst in a little while' because of the weight of credit compared to cash.[56] Others, described at the time as 'a credulous Multitude' (including King George), held on to their shares, which continued to rise as if by magic, assisted by puffs inserted in the newspapers.[57]

The bubble burst in September 1720. It was to this event that Rishi Sunak, the British chancellor of the Exchequer, was referring in 2020 when speaking of 'the worst recession for three hundred years'. The crash was followed by a wave of suicides and the fall of the government. Robert Walpole, the new prime minister (a term first applied to him), covered up much of what had happened in a manoeuvre that gained him the title of 'Screenmaster General' (cover-ups will be discussed in chapter thirteen).[58]

The 'thousands and thousands of unwary people', deceived by 'artful management of the spirit of gaming', were not the only ignorant ones.[59] If the investors 'were ignorant of the way high finance worked', the speculators, like the political leadership of the country, were ignorant of the actual economic forces which were propelling the country forward.[60]

For a balanced verdict on the affair it is difficult to improve on Adam Smith, who remarked that the South Sea Company 'had an immense capital dividend divided among an immense number of proprietors. It was naturally to be expected, therefore, that folly, negligence and profusion should prevail in the whole management of their affairs.' Smith also noted the role of what he called 'knavery': 'the negligence, profusion and malversation of the servants of the Company'.[61] Smith identified the perpetrators and the victims of most if not all bubbles and crashes: on one side the

**1.** The recurrent metaphor of the 'bonds' or 'chains' of ignorance is vividly portrayed in this Baroque painting. Knowledge gives humanity wings!

**2.** The triumphalist rhetoric of Enlightenment narratives of the defeat of ignorance is illustrated here in a dramatic image that draws on traditional representations of the fall of Lucifer.

**3.** Ignorance is the central figure in this engraving, depicted, as was or became traditional, with ass's ears, illustrating the common assumption that ignorance results from stupidity.

PAVLVS SARPIVS VENET$^{VS}$
CONCILII TRIDENTINI
EVISCERATOR

**4.** A seventeenth-century 'whistleblower', the Venetian friar Paolo Sarpi became famous or notorious for his *History of the Council of Trent* (which was summoned to reform the Church), emphasizing the manipulation of the Council by the popes in order to increase their power.

Voicy du grand Montaigne vne entiere figure
Le Peinctre a peinct le corps, et luy son bel esprit,
Le premier par son art egale la Nature,
Mais l'aultre la surpasse en tout ce qu'il escrit,
Thomas de Leu fecit,

**5.** Montaigne's motto, 'What do I know?', reveals both his awareness of his own ignorance and his doubts about the reliability of so-called 'knowledge'.

A Serious

# PROPOSAL

To the

# Ladies,

*For the Advancement of*
*their true and greatest*
*Interest.*

*By a Lover of Her SEX.*

*L O N D O N,*
Printed for R. Wilkin at
the *King's Head* in St. *Paul's*
*Church-Yard.* 1694.

**6.** Long before the rise of the feminist movement, the seventeenth-century Englishwoman Mary Astell complained that girls were driven away from 'the Tree of Knowledge' and proposed founding a college for ladies to remedy the situation.

7. Unlike Astell, Mary Wollstonecraft achieved international fame after publishing her *Vindication of the Rights of Woman* in 1792.

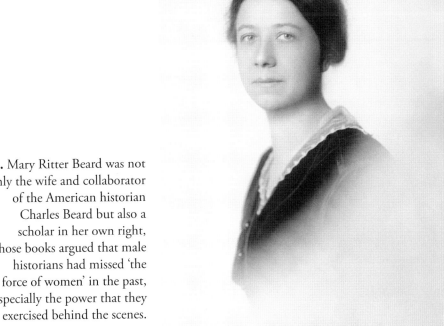

8. Mary Ritter Beard was not only the wife and collaborator of the American historian Charles Beard but also a scholar in her own right, whose books argued that male historians had missed 'the force of women' in the past, especially the power that they exercised behind the scenes.

THE ENGLISH
PHYSICIAN
OR AN
Aftrologo-phyfical Difcourfeof
the vulgar Herbs of this
NATION.

Being a compleat Method of Phyfick,
whereby a man may preferve his Body in
health; or cure himfelf, being fick, for
three pence charge, with fuch things one-
ly as grow in *England*, they being moft fit
for Englifh Bodies.

*Herein is alfo fhewed*,
1. The way of making Plaifters, Oyntments, Oyls,
Paltilles, Syrups, Decoctions, Julips, or Waters of
all forts of Phyfical Herbs, that you may have them
ready for your ufe at all times of the year.
2. What Planet governeth every Herb or Tree
(ufed in Phyfick) that groweth in *England*.
3. The Time of gathering all Herbs, but vul-
garly, and aftrologically.
4. The way of drying and keeping the Herbs
all the year.
5. The way of keeping the Juyces ready for ufe
at all times.
6. The way of making and keeping all kinde of
ufefull Compounds made of Herbs.
7. The way of mixing Medicines according to
Caufe and Mixture of the Difeafe, and Part of
the Body afflicted.

By *N. Culpeper*, Student in Phyfick and Aftrology.

LONDON,
Printed by *William Bentley*, 1652.

**9.** Nicholas Culpeper, a seventeenth-century English apothecary, criticized both the ignorance of physicians and their attempts to keep the public ignorant. He published his herbal in support of 'do-it-yourself' medicine.

**10.** The English nurse Florence Nightingale was a critic of public ignorance of hygiene and a believer in the importance of frequent hand-washing.

**11.** The English physician John Snow became famous for his detective work during the epidemic of cholera in London in 1854. He remedied ignorance of the diffusion of the disease, following clues showing that it spread via contaminated water.

**12.** The photographs made by the crystallographer Rosalind Franklin made a crucial contribution to the discovery of the structure of DNA, the famous 'double helix', but her role in the discovery was ignored, or at least insufficiently acknowledged, by her male colleagues.

**13.** The explosion at the power station of Chernobyl in 1986 was both a tragic example of the results of ignorance and a dramatic illustration of attempts by the Soviet government to cover up the disaster.

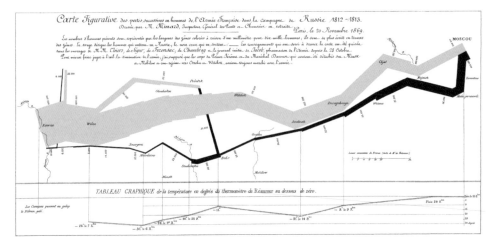

**14.** This vivid image of the virtual destruction of Napoleon's army during its retreat from Moscow in 1812 might be described as a map of the fatal results of ignorance, in this case ignorance of the severity of a Russian winter.

**15.** One of the greatest military theorists of all time, the Prussian officer Clausewitz is best known for his analysis of the 'fog of war', a vivid phrase that describes the ignorance of both sides on the battlefield.

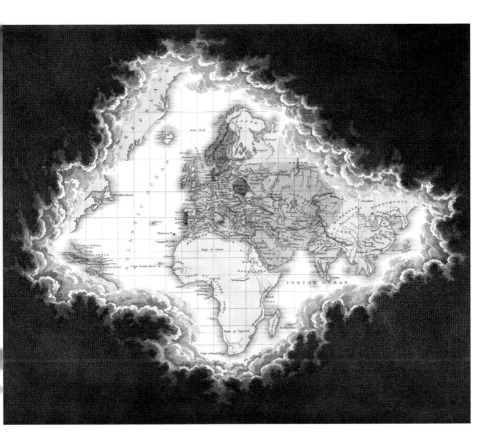

**16.** Quin's atlas of what was known – in the West – about the world in different periods offers equally vivid illustrations of what was not known at those times.

**17.** This print satirizes both the ignorance of many investors in the South Sea Company and what the economist Adam Smith called the 'negligence' and 'malversation' on the part of the Company itself, which led to the bursting of the 'Bubble' in 1720.

**18.** As in the case of the South Sea Bubble, unrealistic hopes of 'getting rich quick' by buying shares on the New York stock market were followed by a scramble to sell the shares as they plummeted in October 1929.

**19.** At the Peace Conference in Paris in 1919, President Wilson embarked on a task for which he admitted that he had insufficient knowledge, redrawing the map of Europe in the name of national self-determination.

**20.** The protests against Trump are a reminder that fake news can be detected and that as Abraham Lincoln is said to have remarked, 'you can't fool all the people all the time'.

insiders, the professionals, who make false promises, and on the other the outsiders, the amateurs, who trust them, either out of simple ignorance or because the promises were what they wanted to hear. For these reasons, the insiders were able 'to intoxicate the minds of the people' in 1720.[62]

## THE GREAT CRASH[63]

According to a famous American economist, the cultivated and flamboyant John Kenneth Galbraith, the 'Great Crash' of the New York stock market in 1929 was 'the greatest cycle of speculative boom and collapse in modern times – since, in fact, the South Sea Bubble'.[64] Writing in an Olympian and ironic manner, Galbraith presented the Crash as an example of what Gibbon called 'the crimes, follies and misfortunes of mankind'.

Galbraith's account of the decline and fall of the stock market presented the Crash as a 'speculative orgy', revealing 'the seminal lunacy which has always seized people who are seized in turn with the notion that they can become very rich'. He suggested that in the 1920s, the American people showed 'an inordinate desire to get rich quickly with a minimum of physical effort'. He also noted the importance of 'mood', 'a pervasive sense of confidence and optimism and conviction that ordinary people were meant to be rich'.[65] Investment was encouraged by publicity, including an article in the *Ladies' Home Journal* entitled 'Everybody Ought to be Rich'. Investors, especially women (according to Galbraith) did not know that they did not know what they were doing.[66]

When stocks began to fall, there was another chain reaction. Investors sold because others were selling and so drove down the price still further. The crash came in October 1929. There was a 'panic', a 'mad scramble to sell' as a result of 'blind fear'. 'Rumour after rumour swept Wall Street.' As in the case of the South Sea Bubble, there were suicides, although their relative number has been exaggerated.[67]

Elsewhere in his study, however, Galbraith undermined his own generalizations about the irrationality of amateur investors. In the first place, he noted that the democratization of shareholding, in this case as in that of the South Sea Bubble, had been exaggerated: 'at the peak in

1929 the number of active speculators was less – and probably was much less – than a million'.

In the second place, Galbraith showed that the amateur investors were manipulated by the professionals. Sometimes 'a number of traders pooled their resources to boom a particular stock'. Investors were often encouraged by advice from investment trusts, an increasingly successful institution in the 1920s. Trusts owed their success to public respect for the expert, the professional financier, who enjoyed a 'reputation for omniscience'. The problem was that the trusts could not be trusted. Adam Smith's term 'knavery' is surely applicable here.

In the third place, Galbraith noted structural reasons for the Crash. The supply of new investors was limited, and when it was exhausted demand fell and the price of shares stopped rising, thus weakening confidence. When the fall began, the 'stop-loss' system (in other words, automatic sales when a given price was reached) amplified the trend. 'Each spasm of liquidation thus ensured that another would follow.'[68]

A more nuanced explanation of the behaviour of the amateurs is offered by the German historian Daniel Menning, who emphasizes information overload. Too many figures appeared on the ticker tape and they changed too fast for viewers to keep up. Small speculators did not know how to analyse the information and this ignorance led them to disaster.[69]

In short, investor ignorance was a necessary condition for the Crash, but not a sufficient one. Galbraith's assumption of the irrationality of investors also needs to be questioned. Buying shares that are appreciating in value looks like a rational choice. So is cutting one's losses when the shares are going down. The problem was that what made sense for individual investors had unintended and disastrous consequences when many people made the same choice at the same time.

## CLANDESTINE BUSINESS

Some of the business activities already described took place on the frontier of legality. Illegal business, which depends on dissimulation or 'strategic ignorance', in the sense of keeping some people ignorant of what is going on, deserves a section of its own. It includes the production of banned goods (such as alcohol, drugs and fakes), their transport (smuggling) and their sale (the black market), as well as the provision of illegal services ranging from sex to protection and contract killings. All this business is clandestine, supposedly invisible, although a social historian must always ask, Invisible to whom?

In this case the ignorant (at least in theory) are the customs officials, the tax collectors and the police. In practice, many people, including individuals in high positions in government, know what is going on, though fewer know exactly when and where.[70] In any case the fiction of ignorance, if not ignorance itself, has to be maintained. It is in the analysis of business and politics that the concept of 'feigned ignorance' is most useful.

Some of this business was and is small-scale, from the farmer who makes his own calvados to the plumbers who charge less if you pay them in cash or the street traders who may not have a licence to trade or whose produce may counterfeit well-known brands. If genuine, the goods may have been smuggled or stolen. As they said in the London of my childhood, 'they fell off a lorry'. The whole system is variously known as the grey, informal, parallel, alternative or 'shadow' economy.

In times of crisis, this unofficial economy is particularly important. In the USA, in the age of 'Prohibition', from 1920 till 1923, alcohol was outlawed. In response, some people produced their own booze, some smuggled it in from Canada in fishing boats (a practice known as 'rum-running') and others sold it by the glass (or teacup, the better to disguise it) in 'speakeasies', private houses that were open to those who knew. In the words of its historian, 'Prohibition offered a graduate course for training in the crime industry' and made the fortune of the young Al Capone.[71] Historians would of course love to know who was in and who was out of the loop. Since potential customers needed to know what was available, when and where, the police (or some of them) probably knew as well, while feigning ignorance when it was made worth their while to do so.

In China during the age of the great famine of 1958–62, an informal distribution system came into being, or at least became much more important. Members of the Party 'showed endless guile in devising ways to defraud the state'. A 'parallel economy' developed that included

barter and fake permits. There was 'trade in dead souls', since production units inflated the numbers of workers in order to receive more
rations.[72] Officials, including the police, either did not know what was
going on or they turned a blind eye – at a price.

Needless to say, economists find it difficult to estimate the size of the
unofficial economy. A study of 151 countries from 1999 to 2007
suggested that this section of the economy was smallest in Switzerland
and the USA (from 8 to 9 per cent of GNP) and largest in Bolivia and
Georgia (from 68 to 69 per cent).[73] Historians find it even more difficult
to make similar estimates for the past. In the case of sixteenth-century
Spain, for instance, they are well aware that the official figures for the
amount of silver from the New World that arrived in Seville every year
are underestimates. What they do not know is the scale of the unofficial
operation. All that can reasonably be done is to make a few general
contrasts between different periods. Before the rise of income tax in the
nineteenth century, there was no need to disguise one's earnings (earlier
governments obtained much of their revenue from customs and excise,
hence their running battles with smugglers). Before the rise of govern-
ment-organized welfare in the twentieth century, cases of individuals
receiving unemployment benefit while secretly working would not have
arisen.

Much clandestine business has taken place on a much grander scale
than the petty transactions of the unofficial economy. A notorious
example is that of trade in forbidden drugs. In this trade, the clandestine organizers are opposed by equally clandestine agents – the FBI, the
DEA and so on – in a kind of hidden war. Production is often secret,
including underground factories in the mountains of Fujian processing
cannabis grown in containers in 'enormous holes in the forest' in British
Columbia.[74] Cocaine was usually refined in secret laboratories in private
houses, but with characteristic flamboyance, the drug lord Pablo
Escobar and his partners the Ochoa brothers had a complex of laboratories constructed in the Colombian jungle, complete with landing
strips for aircraft and dormitories for workers (the complex, known as
Tranquilandia, was discovered and destroyed in 1983).[75]

Turning now from production to distribution, illicit items have been smuggled by secret routes such as mountain paths or tunnels, carried on the backs of porters or donkeys or hidden in private cars, planes and ships and even in the bodies of human 'mules'. 'Many illicit goods pass through the same physical space.'[76] Arms may travel a given route in one direction, drugs in the other. Some of the routes for exporting cocaine from Columbia had already been employed by smugglers of emeralds, cigarettes and marijuana.

The diamond trade has been described as 'secretive, perhaps more secretive than any other', since it comprises small objects of great value that are easy to conceal.[77] Diamond miners smuggle out some of their finds, and what they hand over is smuggled across international borders, an 'invisible export' that surfaces as a legitimate commodity in Antwerp and other cities.

Leading players in these clandestine fields use a variety of names and passports and frequently move from one hideout to another in order to keep the police and other agencies ignorant of their identities and whereabouts. Their wealth has been hidden in 'offshore' accounts or 'tax havens' since the nineteenth century, beginning with Switzerland and the Channel Islands. They 'launder' their money by moving it from one account, bank or company to another and another, to keep police and tax inspectors ignorant of their activities.[78]

Secrecy is of course essential to operations on the margin of, if not well outside, the law. In Switzerland, 'financial secrecy has existed for centuries', culminating in the notorious Banking Secrecy Law of 1934. This tradition of 'client privacy', combined with the country's long tradition of neutrality, explains how foreign capital 'poured into Swiss banks' during the First World War and again during the Second.[79] It was where the Nazis, the American Mafia, the emperor Haile Selassie of Ethiopia, the shah of Iran and (among others) presidents Perón of Argentina, Mobutu of Zaïre and Trujillo of the Dominican Republic all hid their money.[80]

Money-laundering is one major part of the clandestine service industry. Another major part is protection, a kind of tax paid to gangs of criminals by individuals and businesses. The Sicilian Mafia, which has been studied more than once by economists and sociologists such as Pino Arlacchi and Diego Gambetta, has been involved since the nineteenth century in the business of selling protection to small businesses (protection from other criminals, but also from the Mafia themselves). Protection has also been a major source of income for gangs in China, where the secret societies known as 'Triads' already existed in the eighteenth century, and in Russia since the breakup of the USSR. The Russian gangs speak of 'creating a problem' and then offering to solve it.[81] The sale of protection is subject to the laws of supply and demand. The demand comes from owners of assets who fear to lose them in a society with a deficit of law and order. The supply comes from ex-soldiers, ex-policemen and other individuals who specialize in violence.[82]

As in the case of the informal economy in general, criminal business flourishes in times of crisis. People smuggling has become a bigger and bigger business from the 1990s onwards. The illegal trade in arms has often taken advantage of revolutions and civil wars. During the Mexican Revolution of 1911, for instance, arms were smuggled in from the USA via the port of Veracruz.[83] An analysis of what the author calls 'the clandestine political economy of war and peace' presents a case study of the civil war in Bosnia in the 1990s and argues that 'access to supplies through smuggling networks and the involvement of quasi-private criminal actors are critical in explaining the outbreak, persistence, termination and aftermath of the war'.[84]

It was also in the 1990s that Viktor Bout (or Crout), later described as 'The Merchant of Death', became notorious for smuggling weapons to theatres of civil war such as Afghanistan, Angola, Liberia, Sierra Leone and the Congo. Bout, who once worked for Soviet intelligence, acquired a fleet of old Russian cargo planes and used them to sell arms (sometimes to both sides) in the civil wars in Afghanistan, Angola, Sierra Leone, the Democratic Republic of the Congo and elsewhere. The weapons were second-hand, bought in Bulgaria and the Ukraine. The planes were registered in places such as Liberia, where blind eyes were turned and no questions asked, while the cargoes were supplied with forged 'end user certificates' to make them appear legitimate.[85]

Smuggled arms have become so much part of everyday life on the borders, notably the 'Ilemi Triangle' where Kenya, Uganda, Ethiopia and Sudan all meet, that a visitor noted that 'a bullet can be used as bus fare or to buy a glass of beer or a bottle of Coca-Cola'.[86]

Clandestine business is often a response to monopolies and prohibitions. Bout, for instance, flouted UN arms embargoes, just as Al Capone flouted Prohibition. The clandestine trade in antiquities is a response to the refusal of export licences to items considered to be part of the national heritage (although these antiquities may also have been looted or faked at an earlier period). Legitimate commodities that have been smuggled at some time or other to evade taxes and monopolies include silk, spices, salt, silver, brandy and cigarettes.

In other cases, the smuggled commodity has itself been branded as illicit. For example, printed books that were banned because they were considered to be heretical, subversive or pornographic have long circulated under cover. In the sixteenth century, after the Catholic Church banned the works of Erasmus and Machiavelli, copies of their books continued to reach Venice in the 1570s and 1580s.[87] Heretical books were sometimes concealed in barrels topped with fish (like gin or whiskey in trucks supposed to be carrying lumber in the age of Prohibition).

In the eighteenth century, there was a lively trade in forbidden books (known as 'philosophical books') in France. The books were smuggled from Neuchâtel in Switzerland and carried by porters along secret trails over the Jura mountains in crates that also contained innocent material, to be sold in France under the counter or as they said at the time, 'under the cloak'.[88]

During the Cold War, famous cases of evading the official censor included smuggling manuscripts from the USSR to be published in the West, among them Boris Pasternak's novel *Dr Zhivago* (first published in Italy by Feltrinelli in 1957) and works by Andrei Sinyavsky and Yury Daniel that criticized the regime and led to their imprisonment on a charge of 'anti-Soviet activity' in 1966. The technique is not a new one: in the seventeenth century, the manuscript of the anti-papal *History of the Council of Trent* by the Venetian friar Paolo Sarpi had been smuggled out in sections, code-named 'songs', so that it could be published in London both in Italian and in English translation.[89]

As for the so-called 'piracy' of books, in other words the production of unauthorized editions in defiance of copyright laws, it goes back for centuries and continues to this day. Dublin was a major centre of pirate editions in the eighteenth century and Taiwan in the 1960s, when counterfeits ranged from *Lord of the Rings* to the *Encyclopaedia Britannica* (an earlier edition had been pirated at least twelve times by American publishers between 1875 and 1905).[90]

In an age when designer brands attract so much interest from consumers, counterfeiting them has become big business. Around the year 2007, from 20 to 25 per cent of Chinese exports were counterfeits. At the low end, they included cigarettes and DVDs and at the high end, Armani jackets, Vuitton bags and even a Mercedes.[91] It would be interesting to learn how many purchasers are genuinely ignorant of the faking, and how many do not want to know, or at least do not want to be known to know.

A classic study of counterfeiting and smuggling is the work of the Italian journalist Roberto Saviano, who not only described the activities of a secret society, the Camorra, but also named names. After his book was published, Saviano had to go into hiding.[92] Saviano vividly described the imitation of designer clothing by skilled tailors, often illegal immigrants from China or Vietnam, in secret workshops in Secondigliano, on the outskirts of Naples.[93] He also described how other counterfeits were smuggled from China to Europe via the port of Naples. All the containers arriving in the port were numbered in order to facilitate official control, but the Camorra made sure that the same number was given not only to one legitimate container but also to several illegitimate ones so that customs officers would remain ignorant of the smuggled goods.[94]

The marketing of these commodities is semi-clandestine, a difficult balancing act. The sellers obviously need potential consumers to know about their wares, but they also need to keep everyone else ignorant. Drugs are distributed by a network of runners and small-time dealers, while counterfeit or stolen goods can be found for sale if you know where to go. Notorious markets include Canal Street in New York, Rua

Santa Ifigênia in São Paulo and the suburb of La Salada in Buenos Aires, 'the Mecca of Counterfeits', and even whole cities such as Shenzhen in China or Ciudad del Este, Paraguay (on the border with Brazil).[95] Necessary to these enterprises is feigned ignorance, the official 'blind eye', 'a systematic non-enforcement of the law performed by police and inspectors in order to thrive'.[96]

Who has profited and who still profits from the enormous volume of illegal and largely hidden trade? Some of it is in the hands of small gangs, but it is probable that a high proportion (obviously impossible to measure) is organized by large ones. These include a number of secret societies such as the Mafia, which shifted in the 1970s from its traditional concentration on protection into new profitable activities, from construction to trafficking in 'drugs, arms and dirty money', 'with the tacit consent and studied ignorance, if not the outright encouragement, of elements of the Italian establishment'.[97]

For a long time Mafiosi were virtually untouchable, defended by the obedience of potential witnesses to the unwritten rule of *omertà*, the pretence of ignorance. Only in the 1980s was this rule of silence broken by Tommaso Buscetta and the colleagues who followed his example and described the working of the system to the authorities. The Mafiosi themselves were and are bound to secrecy, an obligation that explains their otherwise inexplicable abstemiousness. As Buscetta told his interrogators, 'a drunken person has no secret while a Mafioso must keep self-control and decency in every circumstance'.[98] Trust is particularly important in illicit business, since aggrieved parties have no recourse to the law.[99] Hence secret business is often carried on by secret societies, with complex rituals of initiation and codes of honour that help to create solidarity between members, as in the case not only of the Mafia but also the Triads and the Japanese Yakuza.

Clandestine crime has to be fought by clandestine methods, including informers as well as plain-clothes detectives who observe and sometimes infiltrate the organizations that they are fighting. The parallel with the political world of spies and secret police is an obvious one. Ignorance in politics is the subject of the following chapter.

# 11

## IGNORANCE IN POLITICS

If a nation expects to be ignorant & free, in a state of
civilisation, it expects what never was & never will be

Thomas Jefferson

The many publications of Michel Foucault have helped many people to see
the relation between power and knowledge more clearly than before. It is also
illuminating to examine the relation between power and ignorance.[1] Three
main forms of political ignorance will be discussed here. In the first place, the
ignorance of the people, those who are ruled. In the second place, the ignorance of rulers, whether they are kings, prime ministers or presidents. And
finally, the organizational ignorance built into the political system, the
machinery of government. The consequences of these ignorances are often
unintended, unpredictable and not infrequently disastrous. As Foucault
once remarked, 'People know what they do; they frequently know why they
do what they do; but what they don't know is what they do does.'[2]

### THE IGNORANCE OF THE RULED: AUTOCRACIES

The ignorance of ordinary people is an asset for authoritarian regimes
but an anxiety for democracies. To qualify this simple statement, it may
be sufficient to observe that the contrast between democracy and despotism (or to use a more neutral term, 'autocracy') is a difference in degree
rather than a difference in kind. Regimes are more or less authoritarian
or more or less democratic.

In seventeenth-century France, in an age of 'absolute monarchy', when the country was ruled by King Louis XIII with the assistance of the powerful Cardinal Richelieu, the latter observed, with a brutal clarity worthy of Machiavelli, that although ignorance 'is sometimes harmful to the state' (*préjudiciable à l'Estat*), so, on occasion, is knowledge. The education of peasants and farm workers, for instance, would ruin agriculture and make it difficult to recruit soldiers. Besides, education for everyone would produce more people 'capable of raising doubts' than people able to resolve them. In other words, implied rather than stated, Richelieu believed that education for all would produce too many critics of both the government and the Church. A century later, the Academy of Rouen discussed whether peasants who could read and write were an advantage or a disadvantage for the state.[3]

Voltaire seems to have agreed with Richelieu, thanking the magistrate Louis-René de La Chalotais in 1763 for arguing that labourers should be excluded from education (he revised his ideas later). In similar fashion, two hundred years later, King Frederick VI of Denmark, who ruled from 1808 to 1839, declared that 'The peasant should learn reading and writing and arithmetic: he should learn his duty towards God, himself and others, and no more. Otherwise he gets notions into his head.'[4]

Henry Oldenburg, a German who lived in England, became secretary of the Royal Society and spent his professional life circulating knowledge, made a similar suggestion in 1659 from an opposing point of view. Oldenburg wrote that the Ottoman sultan (a leading example of what was becoming known as 'oriental despotism') 'finds it to his advantage to have such a people on whose ignorance he may impose'.[5]

The Polish journalist Ryszard Kapuściński agreed with Oldenburg. In 1982, in his report on Iran under the shah, he wrote that 'A dictatorship depends for its existence on the ignorance of the mob; that's why all dictators take such pains to cultivate that ignorance.'[6]

To maintain ignorance, especially ignorance of alternatives to the official line, authoritarian regimes in both church and state have long engaged in censorship, which will be discussed in chapter thirteen.

Keeping the people ignorant may solve some problems for autocrats but it raises others. In the case of politics as in business and geography, the lack of information available to ordinary people is filled by rumour, which flourishes when the demand for news exceeds the supply.[7] As the Calcutta newspaper *The Statesman* commented in 1942, during the exodus of the city following Japanese bombing, 'When authority fails to put forth reliable information promptly or in adequate amount about local happenings, it is inevitable that rumours should gain currency.'[8] In Stalin's Russia, where people did not believe what was printed in the official newspapers *Pravda* and *Izvestiya*, rumour was their main source of information.[9]

Ignorance of what is happening behind the scenes encourages conspiracy theories, so it is scarcely surprising that plots have been a major theme of rumour in the past, as indeed they still are. A well-known example from English history is the so-called 'Popish Plot': in other words, the story, widespread between 1678 and 1681, of a Catholic conspiracy to assassinate King Charles II. The king himself did not take the story seriously, but much of the country did. The official *Gazette* made no mention of the story, but the vacuum was filled by rumour, creating what sociologists call a 'moral panic' that took three years to subside.[10] The plot was the subject of a monograph by a leading British historian that illustrates both the strengths and the weaknesses of a common-sense empiricist approach.[11] The author, John Kenyon, was concerned to establish 'what actually happened', and dismissed the stories in circulation at the time as examples of 'mass hysteria', without further analysis.

However, the Popish Plot also requires to be studied as a media event, a case study of the spread, reception and transformation of rumours, including their contamination by or assimilation to existing cultural stereotypes such as the Protestant stereotypes of the pope and the Jesuits. Over a century ago, an American historian, Wilbur Abbott, noted parallels between the narratives of the Popish Plot and earlier accounts of conspiracies, such as the even more notorious Gunpowder Plot of 1605, when Guy Fawkes and some other Catholics attempted to blow up Parliament. Hence Abbott wrote not of the 'invention' of a new story but of the 'adaptation of old stories to new circumstances'.

This point has been amplified and theorized by later social scientists.[12] In the USA in the 1850s, a similar belief in a Catholic conspiracy activated members of the American Party, better known as the 'Know Nothings'. In the last few years, rumours have circulated accusing Hillary Clinton of a range of misdeeds, from assassinating opponents to drinking the blood of children. Still more recently, public suspicion of vaccines has been encouraged by stories circulating on the Internet. Another story has claimed that vaccines implant microchips that allow anyone vaccinated to be tracked.[13]

Needless to say, conspiracies are not always imaginary. Every *coup d'état* is plotted in advance. Governments employ secret informers and secret agents and have done so for centuries, as in the case of early modern Venice, even though the growth of secret agencies has accelerated in the last hundred years.[14] Secret societies are sometimes involved in politics at the highest level. In late nineteenth-century Italy, for instance, Prime Minister Francesco Crispi was a Mason; a hundred years later, Prime Minister Giulio Andreotti was linked to the Sicilian Mafia. In any case, a large part of political activity always takes place behind the scenes. Even the best-informed citizens are aware of only a small proportion of what is going on.

Everyday forms of resistance also make use of ignorance, notably pretending not to know the answer to awkward questions. The American Party, originally a secret society, acquired the name of the 'Know Nothings' because members were advised to say 'I know nothing' when faced with questions about their organization. Such resistance is sometimes described as 'strategic ignorance', although the same phrase sometimes has the opposite meaning of ignorance as a means of domination.[15]

## THE IGNORANCE OF CITIZENS: DEMOCRACIES

If the ignorance of the ruled is cultivated by autocrats, it is a source of anxiety for democratic regimes. Americans remember the argument of Thomas Jefferson that 'if a nation expects to be ignorant & free, in a state of civilisation, it expects what never was & never will be', seconded by James Madison, who noted the need for 'popular information' since 'knowledge will forever govern ignorance'.[16] Opposition to extensions of the franchise has often relied on the argument that the working class, or ex-slaves, or women, simply do not have the knowledge required for a rational vote.

In Britain in the early nineteenth century this argument was rejected by supporters of popular education such as the Baptist minister John Foster and the Radical Member of Parliament, John Roebuck. Foster's essay 'on the evils of popular ignorance' called for a national system of education and rejected the argument (reminiscent of Cardinal Richelieu) 'that a material increase of knowledge among the people would render them unfit for their station'.[17] For his part, Roebuck placed a resolution for the extension of national education before the British Parliament in 1833, accusing the government of 'fostering and perpetuating ignorance among the people'. The Conservative government was not interested in Roebuck's plan, but he went on to publish *Pamphlets for the People* (1835–6), to remedy the ignorance of future voters.[18] Some leaders of the popular movement known as 'Chartism' (after the 'Great Charter', Magna Carta), notably William Lovett, proposed a reform of education, since – to quote an article in the Chartist newspaper *Northern Star* – 'the ignorance of the masses has made them in all ages the slaves of the enlightened and cunning'.[19]

A later British government was forced to take popular education more seriously. In 1867, when the Second Reform Bill extended the vote to the skilled male working class, leading intellectuals such as John Stuart Mill and Walter Bagehot expressed their anxiety about ignorance 'sitting in judgement' on knowledge and 'the supremacy of ignorance over instruction'.[20]

It was no coincidence that the Education Act of 1870, making schooling compulsory for all children, was passed so soon after the extension of the franchise. The link between education and franchise was pointed out by an opponent of that extension, the chancellor of the Exchequer Robert Lowe, still famous for the epigram 'We must educate our masters'.[21] Oscar Wilde's Lady Bracknell was not alone in her disapproval of 'anything that tampers with natural ignorance . . . if it did, it would prove a serious danger to the upper classes'.[22]

The problem of citizen's ignorance did not go away. Take the case of Sicily in the 1950s, as it appears in a famous investigation by Danilo Dolci, an Italian engineer turned sociologist and activist. One of the eleven questions he put to five hundred men in his social survey was, 'What do you think the Italian political parties should do?' Forty-five members of the group evaded the question or insisted on their ignorance: 'How could I know?'; 'We don't take a newspaper'; 'The government should know'; 'I am illiterate'; 'I am a poor ignorant person', and so on. It is difficult to know whether to take these answers literally or as examples of 'strategic ignorance', employed, like the famous *omertà* of the region, in self-defence against intrusive enquiries.[23]

Today, most people learn more about politics from watching television or reading messages on social media than from the newspapers, but the problem of citizen's ignorance still remains. 'Voter ignorance' has been the object of a number of surveys and studies in the USA and elsewhere. John F. Kennedy once declared in a speech to students that 'the educated citizen knows that . . . only an educated and informed people will be a free people – that the ignorance of one voter in a democracy impairs the security of all'.

Kennedy would doubtless have been shocked to learn that at least a third of American citizens in the early twenty-first century are politically ignorant, giving wrong answers or no answers at all to two-thirds of the questions asked in surveys of political knowledge.

An even larger group failed to answer simple questions of this kind. In the year 2008, 58 per cent of those surveyed did not know that Condoleezza Rice was secretary of state, while 61 per cent did not know that Nancy Pelosi was speaker of the House of Representatives. In 2014, only 38 per cent of Americans knew which party controlled each of the two houses of Congress.

Americans were and are especially ignorant of foreign affairs, at least relative to Europeans. In 1964, only 38 per cent were aware that the

USSR was not a member of NATO, while in 2007, only 36 per cent of respondents could name the president of Russia (down from 47 per cent in 1989). The surveyors concluded that 'public knowledge of current affairs' has been 'little changed by news and information revolutions'.[24]

The economist Anthony Downs coined the phrase 'rational ignorance' to describe people who think that informing themselves is not worth the trouble, since each of them has only one vote among millions.[25] A rather different adjective is required to describe the ignorance displayed by many voters for Donald Trump in 2016. As the feminist philosopher Linda Alcoff has remarked, this ignorance

> goes beyond a lack of knowledge. It's not just that folks are not knowledgeable. It is that their lack of knowledge is the product of some concerted effort, a conscious choice or, in actuality, a series of choices. Certain news articles, or news sources, are avoided, certain college courses are kept away from, certain kinds of people are never asked for their opinion on the news of the day.[26]

Ignorance of certain facts is easy to discover but may not be as significant as credulity, believing the promises of candidates for election or taking fake news for real without checking where it came from. In any case, the political consequences of voter ignorance are not limited to ignorance of politics. Ignorance of science, for instance, may lead voters astray when science policy or climate change is one of the issues debated in an election. Allowing technical issues to be subject to a majority vote is what the philosopher Philip Kitcher calls 'vulgar democracy' and describes as a 'tyranny of ignorance', expressing the anxieties of Mill and Bagehot in a more precise form.[27]

Needless to say, American voters are not the only ignorant ones. They are simply the ones whose ignorance has been surveyed most often. In the UK, for instance, there was widespread ignorance about the effects of Brexit at the time of the crucial referendum of 2016. Again, it is commonly believed that the crime rate in Britain is increasing, although it has actually been falling in recent years.[28] In the European Union, so it has been argued, political ignorance is on the rise, owing to what has been described as 'market censorship', in other words a flood of 'redundant material' that drowns the information that is relevant.[29]

Going a little further in this direction, the idea of 'voter ignorance' might be extended to include people who rely on suspect information because they have not learned to be critical, either of bias in the media or of the possibility of 'fake news'. They are vulnerable to 'disinformation', a practice that will be discussed in chapter thirteen.

## THE IGNORANCE OF EARLY MODERN RULERS

If ordinary people suffer from political ignorance, they are not alone. Rulers too have often been ignorant of much of what they needed to know. One reason for this is social distance, the bottom of society being scarcely visible from the top. Take the case of Eduardo Suplicy, who is a member of both the Brazilian ruling class and the Workers' Party. When asked about the price of a bread roll in a live interview on television by the well-known presenter Boris Casoy, Suplicy was unable to answer.[30]

In early modern Europe, the problem of the ignorance of rulers was exacerbated by the fact that ruling was a family business in which the young members learned the job not by formal training but from the advice or the example of their elders, which they were free not to follow once they were on the throne. Some kings had little interest in acquiring information about their kingdoms. They preferred to go hunting. Indeed, when foreign diplomats wanted to discuss business with a particular monarch (Francis I, for instance, or James I), they sometimes needed to look for him in the forest. These rulers might be described as taking their political decisions in the intervals of hunting rather than the other way round (it has been suggested that James 'spent about half his waking life on the hunting field').[31]

Even conscientious rulers found it difficult to obtain the information they needed. Paying attention to one source of information left an individual little time to attend to others. The emperor Charles V spent most of his life travelling between his different European dominions, partly because he believed in seeing for himself how his subjects lived. The downside of this hands-on – or, more exactly, this eyes-on – approach was that the emperor had little time to read state papers, including the letters that were sent to him from his dominions in the New World to inform him about conditions there. He was necessarily ignorant of much that went on in his empire. When Charles was elected emperor, at the age of nineteen, his chancellor advised him that 'To speed up business and avoid keeping those who need a decision waiting, Your Majesty must listen to three or four items of business every morning as you arise and get dressed.'[32] Whether or not the young man took this advice, three or four items were nothing compared to the increasing demands on Charles's time by the business of his empire.

In any case, the emperor was not prepared to work all the time. He too liked to hunt. As his grandfather the emperor Maximilian I had observed, it was good that Charles took pleasure in hunting at an early age, 'otherwise one might think he was a bastard'. In his thirties, 'Hawking and above all hunting could keep Charles away from his desk for days on end.' In his forties, the emperor confessed that 'we spend all our days hunting and hawking'. He found time for other sports as well, once keeping an English ambassador waiting for most of the day because he was playing a kind of tennis.[33]

Much official business was left to secretaries such as Francisco de los Cobos, who 'would read, open and summarize thousands of letters addressed to Charles . . . and prepare responses for his master's approval and signature'. As Charles's confessor once told him, Cobos 'knew how to make up for your negligence'. However, as Charles's empire expanded, more assistants became necessary, dividing the labour between them. Nicolas de Granvelle, keeper of the seals, became responsible for Northern Europe, Cobos looked after the Mediterranean and the Americas while his nephew Juan Vázquez took over Spanish affairs. Charles was aware of the risk of relying on his assistants, advising his son Philip about their equally dangerous 'animosities and alliances' and noting that each minister 'will attempt to come to you under cover of darkness in order to convince you to rely on him alone'.[34] Yet given the increasing volume of business, the emperor had no choice.

Charles's son Philip II of Spain, who became king in 1558 and was one of the most conscientious monarchs of his time, chose the opposite solution to his father, advising his own son that 'travelling about one's kingdoms is neither useful nor decent'. Philip preferred to read and to write comments in the margins of the thousands of papers that were sent to him (about ten thousand of the documents sent to or from Philip have survived). He usually spent eight hours a day at his desk, as well as reading documents in bed and taking a small desk with him when travelling with his family on a boat on the river Tagus.[35] Philip was an early victim of 'information overload', toiling over what he called 'those devils, my papers'.[36]

Philip was or became a shrewd analyst of political situations, but his weak point – like that of so many early modern rulers – was finance. His government could not have functioned without loans, from the bankers of Genoa in particular. However, the king confessed to financial illiteracy, writing that 'I have never been able to get this business of loans and interest into my head' and that 'I am absolutely ignorant in these matters. I cannot tell a good account book or financial report on the subject from a bad one. And I do not wish to break my brains trying to comprehend something which I do not understand now, nor have I ever understood in all my days.'[37] He did not want to know about finance.

In this respect, Philip was not eccentric but typical of early modern monarchs, who shared with their nobilities the idea that making or saving money or even thinking about these activities was beneath their dignity. Money was for spending, to demonstrate their magnificence. Although the young Louis XIV was persuaded by his minister Jean-Baptiste Colbert to carry an account book in his pocket, and even wrote to his mother about 'the pleasures to be found in working on finances myself', the king gave up this practice after Colbert's death. He apparently 'preferred ignorance'.[38]

The many hours that Philip spent at his desk may be regarded as a weakness as well as a strength. The king became virtually marooned in his palace of El Escorial, more than fifty kilometres from Madrid, a palace in which he spent more and more time from 1566 till his death in 1598, virtually isolated from the society that he ruled, like the managers in the bureaucratic organizations described by Michel Crozier in chapter three.

A folktale current in many parts of the world reveals the general awareness of the problem of the isolation of monarchs. A certain ruler – Harun al-Rashid in Baghdad, Henry VIII in London or Ivan the Terrible in Moscow – decides to disguise himself and walk the streets of his capital at night in order to discover what ordinary people think of him. After all, how else could he make this discovery? There was no point in asking his ministers, since ministers were likely to tell their monarch only what they thought he would want to know.

This point is supported or at least symbolized by the famous story of 'Potemkin villages'. Grigory Potemkin was both the lover and the minister of the Empress Catherine the Great of Russia. When the empress decided to visit the south of Russia in 1787, taking a barge down the river Dniepr, Potemkin is said to have made sure that she saw only the most prosperous villages, having the buildings, or their facades, moved from place to place in order to deceive his employer.

This story was already in circulation before the imperial inspection took place, and was repeated soon afterwards by a Saxon diplomat, Georg von Helbig. The Belgian Prince de Ligne, who was present during the imperial visit, dismissed this 'ridiculous story' about 'pasteboard villages'. Nevertheless, Ligne was well aware that 'the empress was shown only the fairest side of her southern provinces'. It seems reasonable to conclude that there is a kernel of truth in the story, although it was embellished in the telling, while Potemkin was not the only person responsible for deceiving Catherine, since the governor of Kharkhov and Tula 'did conceal things from her and may have built false houses'.[39]

In similar fashion, according to the German intelligence service, Mussolini was deceived by his air force: 'on his summer inspection tours of the aviation squadrons, he was several times shown the same military contingents, without suspecting anything'.[40]

The ruler might of course employ informers to listen to conversations in taverns and other public places and report to the palace what they claimed to have heard. However, their information could not be trusted, since they were paid to produce it regularly, whether they actually heard seditious talk or not.[41] In any case, even looking and listening in the streets would not have offered the monarch the opportunity to learn everything that he either wanted or needed to know.

To sum up in the words of James Scott's classic study, *Seeing Like a State*: 'The premodern state was, in many crucial respects, partially blind; it knew precious little about its subjects, their wealth, their landholdings and yields, their location . . . it lacked anything like a detailed "map" of its terrain and its people.'[42] Late modern governments usually possess this kind of information, but it comes at a price, as we shall see.

## LATE MODERN RULERS

The ignorance of modern presidents and prime ministers has become a more topical subject than I could have imagined or feared when I began research for this book. Donald Trump and Jaïr Bolsonaro offer conspicuous examples of ignorance, most obvious and most dangerous in their public response or lack of response to the spreading of the Coronavirus. However, they are not alone in their ignorance. Think, for instance, of the apparent ignorance of the conflicts between Sunni and Shia Muslims on the part of President George W. Bush when the decision was taken to invade Iraq in 2003. The president is also said not to have known where the country was on the map. Today, the consequences of that ignorance are difficult to miss.[43]

Presidents and prime ministers have usually been trained in a very different way from early modern monarchs. Before entering politics, they have often studied and practised law (like Tony Blair and Barack Obama) or administration (like Emmanuel Macron). They have also had time to acquire political experience in parliaments or town halls before reaching the top, an experience all the more necessary for leaders who are expected to share power with their ministers. Prime ministers have often had personal experience of foreign affairs as diplomats. Otto von Bismarck, for instance, who was chancellor of the new German Empire from 1871 to 1890, had already served as an ambassador abroad. Lord Salisbury, three times British prime minister in the late nineteenth century, had previously served as secretary of state for India and as foreign secretary.

Other leaders had experience in other departments of state. The famous liberal prime minister William Gladstone served four times as chancellor of the Exchequer. Ludwig Erhard was minister of economic affairs under Chancellor Konrad Adenauer before becoming chancellor himself. Amintore Fanfani, who was five times prime minister of Italy, had served as minister of agriculture and minister of economic planning. Some presidents and prime ministers studied economics or even 'political science'. Fanfani was a professor of economic history before he entered politics. President Woodrow Wilson was a professor of political science who became president of Princeton University before he moved on to become president of the United States.

However, professional training involves specialization, while the job of president or prime minister requires wide-ranging knowledge. Gaps are inevitable. A study of the use of statistics by the German state notes the fact that in 1920, in the crisis of transition from the German Empire to the Weimar Republic, 'the vacuum of knowledge' about the state of the German economy 'was almost complete'.[44] More generally, the economist Frank Cowell has pointed to the problem of 'the lack of omniscience' of governments and its influence on the design of tax systems.[45] The ignorance of officials allows direct taxes to be evaded. Indirect taxation avoids the problem of individual and corporate dishonesty but has the disadvantage of weighing more heavily on the poor than on the rich.

Ignorance of other countries is not uncommon among political leaders. Nikita Khrushchev, for instance, was described as 'alarmingly ignorant of foreign affairs'.[46] Some British prime ministers and foreign secretaries have not done very well in this domain. When he was in London in 1862, Bismarck noted that 'The British ministers know less about Prussia than about Japan and Mongolia': 'Palmerston and, to an only slightly lesser degree, Lord Russell too were in a state of complete ignorance.'[47] Edward Grey, foreign secretary, at a time (1914) when international affairs mattered, 'knew little of the world outside Britain, had never shown much interest in travelling, spoke no foreign languages and felt ill at ease in the company of foreigners'.[48]

David Lloyd George, British prime minister from 1916 to 1922, also shows up badly in this respect. The French prime minister Georges Clemenceau found him 'shockingly ignorant, both of Europe and the United States'. In 1916, he had asked, 'Who are the Slovaks? I can't seem to place them.' In 1919, he mixed Ankara up with Mecca.[49] A recent study of the negotiation of the frontier between Poland and Germany claims that 'The ignorance of the British Prime Minister David Lloyd George . . . in international affairs, has passed into legend. By way of example, one could mention his confusion of the Spanish province of Galicia with Eastern Galicia.'[50] In the case of the problem of Shandong, a major item on the agenda of the Peace conference of 1919, it has been observed that Lloyd George 'did not possess a profound knowledge of, or even a deep interest in, Eastern Asia'.[51]

Some of the prime minister's advisers were in the same boat. A civil servant present at the Peace Conference complained that there was no one on the British side 'with actual knowledge of the Galician question'.[52] Lloyd George was not of course alone in his lack of interest in the world beyond Britain and its empire. Among later prime ministers, Stanley Baldwin was 'bored with foreign affairs', while his successor, Neville Chamberlain, notoriously referred to Hitler's demands on Czechoslovakia in 1938 as 'a quarrel in a far-away country between people of whom we know nothing'.[53]

President Woodrow Wilson was not much better informed. One of his weak points was his ignorance of Continental Europe, described by the Austro-Hungarian ambassador to the USA as 'utter ignorance of facts and of geography'.[54] In spite of this handicap, following American intervention in the First World War, Wilson became one of the arbiters of the new Europe that was under construction at the Peace Conference of 1919 and included the redrawing of national borders. His role was unprecedented for an American president and one for which he was unprepared. Indeed, when he took office, Wilson admitted that 'all my preparation has been in domestic matters', so that 'It would be an irony of fate if my administration had to deal chiefly with foreign problems.'[55] The French prime minister, Georges Clemenceau, was shocked by Wilson's 'ignorance of Europe'.[56] To be fair, 'No American President has ever been as interested in Eastern Europe as Woodrow Wilson', and although his knowledge was still 'very limited' in 1914, he filled some of the gaps later, accumulating more and more maps and reports by specialists.[57]

Although Wilson asked specialists for information, 'he was seldom prepared to listen to them when they ventured to tender advice'. He virtually ignored the question of reparations, confessing that he was 'not much interested in the economic subjects'. Mistakes were certainly made, partly in response to pressure from other nations but also from a simple lack of knowledge. For example, Wilson allowed Italy to take over the German-speaking South Tyrol, explaining later that 'I was ignorant of the situation when the decision was made'.[58]

Wilson's colleagues were little better informed, if not worse. The historian R. W. Seton-Watson, a specialist on Central Europe who attended the Paris Conference as an adviser, described participants in a private letter as 'a crowd of incompetents, too worn out and too ignorant to solve the vast series of problems that await decision'. Much later in his career, Seton-Watson gave a seminar at Oxford about the conference, arguing that many decisions were 'made by ignorant politicians who had no idea of geography'.[59] Elsewhere, he noted the 'abysmal ignorance' of the South Slavs on the part of Russian politicians.[60]

Recent displays of presidential ignorance, especially of foreign affairs, go well beyond Wilson's, but in this competition, Donald Trump would probably overtake both Ronald Reagan (whose ignorance of current affairs sometimes led to embarrassment at press conferences) and George W. Bush. Like his follower President Jaïr Bolsonaro of Brazil, Trump suffers from ignorance in its acute form, that of not knowing that he does not know. The response of both presidents to the Coronavirus crisis of 2020 was to refuse to take the crisis seriously, to ignore inconvenient facts, to criticize the epidemiologists and to advocate dubious remedies such as hydroxychloroquine. In Belarus, President Alexander Lukashenko went one better, or more exactly one worse, by dismissing fear of the virus as 'psychosis' and claiming that the infection could be cured with vodka.[61] The expert is not always right, but it is obviously dangerous to ignore their advice during a crisis, as the number of deaths from the Coronavirus in both the USA and Brazil made all too clear in 2020.[62]

As for climate change, Trump and Bolsonaro are both in denial. Trump has called the idea of global heating a 'hoax', while Bolsonaro's alliance with agribusiness in the Amazon means that he too does not want to know about the consequences of deforestation for the world's climate. Denial means not wanting to know, or more aggressively, wanting not to know. There are far too many examples to cite here of this kind of wilful ignorance on the part of rulers, or more generally of governments: denial of genocide, for instance, denial of famines or denial of the threat to the environment posed by polluted rivers or by acid rain.[63] Denial will be discussed further in chapter thirteen.

## ORGANIZATIONAL IGNORANCE

As noted in chapter three, ignorance is to be found not only in individuals but in organizations as well.[64] Organizational ignorance is usually studied in business, but political organizations, such as the apparatus of the state, also contain various levels, and once again what is well known at one level may be quite unknown at another. As governments come to know more and more about the people they govern, individuals in the administration, even at the top, are aware of a smaller and smaller proportion of that knowledge, as well as facing the problem of 'having to process more information than you can manage or understand'.[65]

In what follows I shall explore this problem in two periods of history, focusing on what scholars call the first and the second revolutions in government. These revolutions have often been celebrated as improvements in efficiency, but they will be examined here with particular attention to their negative side, the rise of ignorance.

## THE FIRST REVOLUTION IN GOVERNMENT

The phrase 'revolution in government' was coined by the historian Geoffrey Elton in a study of the reign of Henry VIII that focused on the achievement of the king's secretary of state, Thomas Cromwell, in the years before his execution at Henry's orders in 1540. Cromwell, a man of humble birth, was hated by the nobility because he ignored their traditional role in government. Attributing the revolution to Cromwell was something of an exaggeration, since the changes that Elton describes took place more gradually, while the process was not confined to England but can also be discerned in a number of European states.[66] These changes may be summed up in a single word, 'bureaucratization', in the sense that the historical sociologist Max Weber gave to the term – impersonal government according to fixed written rules in which the role of each participant is carefully defined.[67] Central to the new form of government was a new institution, the council. Rulers had long been surrounded by their advisers, but it was in the sixteenth century that counsellors turned into councillors.

Since the business of government was increasing, rulers needed more and more help in their task, not only from councils but also from secretaries who could handle the proliferating paperwork. As we have seen, Charles V depended on secretaries to summarize incoming papers and draft outgoing ones. In Sweden, nobles who resented losing their former participation in government referred to the 'rule of the secretaries' (*sekreterareregementet*). They were thinking in particular of Jöran Persson, the powerful secretary to King Erik XIV. Persson was a kind of Swedish Cromwell. He too was of humble birth. He too was hated by the nobility. He too was executed, in his case in 1568 after Erik had been deposed and replaced by his brother John III.[68]

Cromwell, who employed secretaries of his own to manage government business, was effectively the king's chief minister, like Cardinal Richelieu in the case of Louis XIII. The rise and consequent institutionalization of this role is a sign that kings were allowing themselves to become increasingly ignorant of the actions of their government. Thanks to ever-increasing paperwork, secretaries might even be authorized to forge the royal signature.[69] The ruler's agreement was needed but information might be filtered.

Given the extent of the lands that he ruled, Philip II offers an extreme case of this process of bureaucratization. He was what we might call the CEO of a huge empire, in Europe (including Spain, the Netherlands, parts of Italy, and eventually Portugal) and in the Americas (Mexico and Peru), as well as the newly acquired 'Philippines', administered from Mexico. To govern all these regions, the machine of government had to be enormous for its time. At the beginning of his reign, Philip was already advised by fourteen councils, which included nobles and clerics but were largely staffed by the so-called *letrados*, individuals who had been trained as lawyers but became full-time officials. The councils met regularly and each time they sent a paper with their recommendations to the king. In the course of the reign they met more often and for longer sessions and sent more papers to Philip, while committees, known as *juntas*, were added to the system.

In addition, the king employed private secretaries, at least four of whom, Francisco de Eraso, Mateo Vázquez, Gonzalo Pérez and Gonzalo's son Antonio, exercised a considerable amount of power.[70] Vázquez, for instance, was a kind of personal assistant to the king and sat next to him (on a stool, for hierarchical reasons), summarizing documents and writing some of the replies. He also mediated between the king and the *juntas*. This gave him, like Antonio Pérez, some scope for initiatives of his own. Spain, like England and Sweden, was experiencing the rule of the secretaries, even though Philip, mindful of his father Charles's instruction, 'depend on no one but yourself', insisted on taking the final decisions.[71]

Philip's government made an enormous collective effort to acquire information, but much less effort to communicate it to the right people when and where it was needed. A major disadvantage of the system was fragmentation: by region, by the ever-present hierarchy and by domains such as war, finance and religion. The problems of the government were exacerbated by difficulties of communication that have become increasingly hard to imagine ever since the invention of the telegraph and the telephone.

The system suffered from what has been called 'the tyranny of distance', famously analysed by the French historian Fernand Braudel, who called distance 'public enemy number one'.[72] In the age of Charles V, news of the Ottoman victory at the battle of Mohács in Hungary had taken fifty-one days to reach the emperor in Spain.[73] In the age of Philip, 'It took a minimum of two weeks for a letter from Madrid to reach Brussels or Milan; it took a minimum of two months for a letter from Madrid to reach Mexico; and it took a minimum of a year for a letter from Madrid to reach Manila.' There would be more delays as information flowed from the king to the Council of the Indies, or the other way round. As Gonzalo Pérez complained, 'decisions are taken so slowly that even a cripple could keep up with them'.[74]

Since rapid decisions are often necessary in politics, the consequences of what might be called this 'temporary ignorance' were far-reaching on both sides of the ocean. The ruler of a land empire might suffer from similar problems, as in the case of Catherine the Great of Russia. In her time it might take eighteen months for an imperial order sent from St Petersburg to reach Kamchatka in Siberia, and another eighteen months for the reply to be received in the capital.[75]

Another early modern monarch, Louis XIV, boasted in his – ghostwritten – memoirs, written for the instruction of his son, that he was 'informed of everything'. He was not. He knew less about his kingdom than some ministers, notably Jean Baptiste Colbert, recently described as 'the information master'. Even Colbert knew much less than everything. Marshal Vauban, famous for his designs of fortresses, was also interested in statistics and suggested that Louis order an annual census of France in order to know 'the number of his subjects, in total and by region, with all the resources, wealth and poverty in each place'. No action was taken, so the government remained ignorant of all these matters.[76]

## THE SECOND REVOLUTION IN GOVERNMENT

The second 'revolution in government' took place in the nineteenth century.[77] As in the first case, it was the culmination of longer trends, including the university courses in administration (*Staatswissenschaft*) offered in the later eighteenth century to future German-speaking civil servants. Knowledge about the state was described in German as *Statistik*, a term from which the English word 'statistics' is derived. This shift in meaning symbolizes the increasing interest taken by governments in surveys of factories and schools, poverty and hygiene, producing a wealth of information that could be presented in columns of figures or in the graphs or pie-charts that were originally devised in the early nineteenth century.

One might describe these surveys as a triumph of knowledge over ignorance, but as so often happens in triumphs, it involved losses as well as gains. There was simply too much information to digest. The rise of democracy solved some problems but also created new ones, since regimes that changed following elections every few years were necessarily regimes in which the leaders did not have time to inform themselves properly on the issues with which they were supposed to deal. In any case, their training, whether in the study of law or the classics, did not prepare them adequately for their new responsibilities.

Newly appointed ministers of agriculture or transport, education or health were not likely to know very much about these domains. They might make an effort to learn, but before very long in the post they might be transferred to another department in a cabinet reshuffle or ejected altogether following the fall of the government. There was more continuity in the civil service, but civil servants were supposed to advise ministers, not to take decisions themselves. In any case, relations between minister and ministry have often been difficult. As in the case of earlier periods, we are entitled to suspect that the flow of information upwards has often been filtered at different points on its journey.

Even the surveying and mapping of states, an obvious addition to knowledge, may also encourage ignorance, especially what James Scott has called 'thin simplifications', taking maps and statistical tables for reality, sometimes with disastrous consequences. Maps and statistics encourage an Olympian or 'imperial' overview that neglects the more varied and messier reality that is visible at ground level.[78] Such a neglect, which might be described as 'Olympian ignorance' (the converse of local knowledge), has led to failures of central planning, like the British government's 'Groundnut Scheme' (discussed earlier in chapter ten) and sometimes to even greater disasters, as in the case of Mao Zedong's 'Great Leap Forward' (to be discussed in chapter twelve).

Extreme cases make general problems more visible. The history of colonialism highlights organizational ignorance, since colonizers and colonized came from different cultures, spoke different languages and had different loyalties. In French West Africa, for instance, a French official, uncomfortably aware of being misinformed by the local interpreter and the local chief but unable to discover the true state of affairs, complained to his own superiors that he was unable to escape from what he called a 'circle of iron'. More generally, the 'mutual ignorance of French officials and local populations' was a major obstacle to the smooth running of the system.[79] Other blind spots in the 'imperial vision' become clear in the case of the British Empire in India.

## BRITISH RULE IN INDIA

The British Empire faced similar problems. Sir John Bowring, the Governor of Hong Kong from 1854 to 1859, had a poor opinion of both rulers and ruled in the colony, writing that 'We rule them in ignorance and they submit in blindness'.[80] India was effectively ruled from 1757 to 1858 by a corporation, the East India Company, which had already been trading there since its foundation in the year 1600.[81] Their administration, driven by the desire for profit, culminated in the disaster that used to be known as the 'Indian Mutiny' of 1857, a rebellion that Indians call the 'First War of Independence'. In that war, ignorance played an important role, as we shall see.

Ignorance had already played a role in the story of the British in India. Although Warren Hastings, appointed the first governor-general in 1772, knew Bengali, Urdu and Persian (which was the traditional language of administration), he complained that his officials were ignorant of local languages and customs. Officials of the Company in London knew even less. Statements made at the trial of Hastings for corruption in London in 1785 revealed 'the sheer ignorance of the British about the sub-continent'.[82]

There followed an 'information revolution' in the early nineteenth century, in which the Company drew on the Mughal information system. Nevertheless, as Christopher Bayly noted, there remained a 'zone of ignorance' where new institutions of government 'failed to mesh' with local knowledges.[83] Ignorance was amplified by the fact that for the five hottest months every year, the governor-general appointed by the Company left Calcutta together with his staff for the Himalayan village of Simla, 'connected to the outside world by a road little better than a goat path'.[84] There the government was isolated, like Philip II in El Escorial. The Company's problems of communication were also similar to Philip's. The ships taking people and letters from Britain to India (via the Cape) took about three months to arrive. As for communication within India, the construction of a railway system had hardly begun in 1857, while the first telegraph line, for the use of the Company, had been opened as recently as 1851.

Even more important than these institutional and technical problems was British ignorance of and lack of sympathy with Indian cultures. There was much that their new rulers did not know about India. 'Unlike earlier foreign conquerors, the British denied themselves access to the knowledge, information and gossip circulating in the women's quarters. Thus half of the Indian population remained virtually unknown to them.'[85] This ignorance produced serious misunderstandings, notably in three cases: that of the *zamindars*, that of caste and that of the events leading up to the notorious 'Mutiny' of 1857.

In Mughal India, *zamindars* were vassals, not owners of the land from which they drew their income. However, they were perceived by the British as independent landowners, on the model of the aristocrats and gentry at home. The Company's power enabled them to turn their misunderstandings into reality. Under the Permanent Settlement of 1793, the *zamindars* became landowners, and some of them were given the title of raja – raised to the peerage, one might say. It might be said that the British changed the structure of Indian society in a fit of absence of mind.[86]

Misunderstanding also played a role in the history of social stratification in India, a system now known as that of 'castes' (a term first used by the Portuguese, who had reached India before the British). As the historian Nicholas Dirks puts it, 'caste, as we know it today, is not in fact some unchanged survival of ancient India', but 'the product of an historical encounter between India and Western colonial rule'.[87] It was redefined by the British in their attempts to understand the system. Once again, new rulers had the power to convert their misunderstandings into a new reality.

The Rebellion of 1857 illustrates the tragic consequences of both ignorance and misunderstanding. It was in part the result of a failure in 'intelligence', an inability to read the signs of revolt and so prepare for what was coming. One reason for this failure was that 1857 was a time of transition between the traditional system of gathering information from native 'informers' and its recent replacement by a new system on the European model, including social surveys with results expressed in statistical form.[88]

The Rebellion may also be viewed as the result of a failure to understand the culture, or more exactly the different cultures of the Indians. 'Young and ignorant military officers' found it increasingly difficult to communicate with their Indian NCOs.[89] Once again, lack of information encouraged rumour. The Rebellion began with a mutiny of the 'sepoys' (Indian soldiers in Company service), triggered by rumours that a new issue of cartridges would contain grease derived from both beef and pork, thus offending Hindus and Muslims alike. In similar fashion, in the age of Covid, some vaccines have been falsely described to Muslims as based on gelatine from pigs.

The authorities eventually responded to these rumours, but by this time it was too late.[90] Once a local mutiny had taken place, it was followed by others, while the rebellion was joined by both soldiers and civilians who had other grievances against the regime.

No regime can be held responsible for the rumours that circulate about it, but before protests began a British officer had already warned the authorities of the need to prove that 'the grease employed in these cartridges is not of a nature to offend or interfere with the prejudices of caste', while the inspector-general of ordnance admitted that 'No extraordinary precaution appears to have been taken to insure the absence of any objectionable fat.'[91] Official carelessness is not the same as plain ignorance, but it does suggest a lack of interest, as if British officers did not respect the culture of the Indian soldiers. Their attitude to 'the prejudices of caste' revealed their own prejudices, if not a form of what is now known as 'institutional racism'.

As for the British at home, John Stuart Mill, who had worked for the East India Company in London, reflecting on the rebellion of 1857, noted the common ignorance of India and recommended a 'much more profound study of Indian experience, and of the conditions of Indian government, than either English politicians, or those who supply the English public with opinions, have hitherto shown any willingness to undertake'.[92]

The Rebellion led to the end of Company rule, replaced by administration by the British government, via a secretary of state for India and an India Office in London and a British viceroy in India itself. Communications became more rapid, thanks to the telegraph, the steamship and the railway.[93] However, this was not the end of official ignorance in British India. The chain of command was still long and complex. In India, the chain began with the viceroy and descended through provincial governors and their secretaries, commissioners, deputy commissioners, assistant commissioners and district magistrates, all of them British, known as 'Civilians' because they belonged to the Indian Civil Service. 'Each Civilian had on average 300,000 subjects', so that even the most conscientious and long-serving district magistrate could not know very much about the district he was expected to govern.[94]

As in the Company's time, the administration was composed of two layers, a higher layer of British and a lower layer of Indians (although a few of them were allowed to rise and, by 1905, 5 per cent of the higher layer was composed of Bengalis). Information from the grass-roots was doubtless lost or at least filtered on its long journey to the top of the tree.

This system endured until 1947, coming to a bloody end when the country was partitioned between an officially Hindu India and an officially Muslim Pakistan, which had been demanded by the Muslim leader

Muhammad Ali Jinnah. Two Indian states were themselves divided, the Punjab and Bengal. Jinnah, who came from Karachi and 'knew no more of the Punjab than Neville Chamberlain did of Czechoslovakia', resisted a possible 'Sikh-Muslim compromise regarding the sharing of power' there. As the senior superintendent of police in Delhi commented before the partition, 'Once a line of division is drawn in the Punjab all Sikhs to the West of it and all Muslims to the east of it will have their --- chopped off.'[95] From ten to twelve million of those who found themselves on the wrong side of the border chose to move, and many (at least several hundred thousand and possibly one or two million) were killed on the way. It is difficult to resist the conclusion that many of the casualties of Partition could have been avoided, had the risks been assessed in advance, preparations been less hurried and the movement of people supervised more carefully by the British troops stationed in India.

The hurry was the responsibility of the last viceroy, Lord Louis Mountbatten, 'an inexperienced and over-confident commander, with a known propensity for taking risks'. He had no experience of local conditions and chose not to follow local advice. For example, the governor of Bengal advised Prime Minister Clement Attlee that announcing a precise date for the withdrawal of the British would provoke 'massacres on a shocking scale'. Attlee therefore chose a vague date, in 1948, but was persuaded by Mountbatten to accept 15 August 1947, ten months earlier than the original plan. The new viceroy arrived in March 1947 and by May he was writing that 'all this partition business is sheer madness'. All the same, he continued to pursue the hurried plan, despite advice from Jawaharlal Nehru (soon to become the first prime minister of India) that he was moving too fast. The feared massacres duly took place.[96]

As for the new borders between India and Pakistan, they were drawn by the lawyer Cyril Radcliffe, who had never been to the subcontinent. 'Perhaps blessedly, he enjoyed a complete ignorance of Indian politics, and had never previously been east of Gibraltar.'[97] Partition was a final tragic illustration of British ignorance of conditions in India, or worse still, of knowingly ignoring them. Generalizing from some of the examples discussed earlier in the chapter, it may be suggested that 'imperial' or 'colonial' ignorance is an important variety of nescience. When the rulers come from one culture and the ruled from another, mistakes that are due to ignorance are simply waiting to happen.

After colonialism was replaced by neo-colonialism, this kind of mistake continued, as in the recent case of the American invasion of Iraq in 2003. When the invasion began, the Americans did not know whether Saddam had 'weapons of mass destruction' or not, but they went ahead anyway. They rapidly won the war against Saddam Hussein but they might be said to have lost the 'peace' that followed it, leaving chaos and violence behind them instead of the freedom that they had promised the Iraqi people. In any case, the notorious weapons could not be found by the inspectors. As even a supporter of the war admits, 'It seems perhaps that all along Baghdad could have been telling the truth when it claimed that Saddam's weapons of mass destruction had been destroyed in the aftermath of the First Gulf War in 1991.'[98]

Tony Blair continued to insist that he had been right to support the invasion, but some regrets were expressed on the American side. Colin Powell, for instance, the secretary of state at the time, later declared that 'he did not know if he would have supported the war if he had known there were no stockpiles'. David Kay, head of the Iraq Survey Group, put it more bluntly: 'We were all wrong.' The Israeli military historian Martin van Creveld has described the invasion of Iraq as 'the most foolish war since the Emperor Augustus sent his legions into Germany in 9 BC and lost them'.[99]

An American classic, *The Education of Henry Adams*, the memoirs of a former diplomat, aimed a number of its arrows at ignorant politicians. The author remarked, for instance, that 'The Southern secessionists' were 'stupendously ignorant of the world'; that around 1870, the American government 'prided itself on ignorance'; and that in the year 1903, shortly before the Russians were unexpectedly defeated by the Japanese, Adams himself 'felt as ignorant as the best-informed statesman'.[100] He died in 1918. If he could have returned to the United States a century later, what might Adams have said about President Trump?

# 12

# SURPRISES AND CATASTROPHES

The best laid schemes o' Mice an' Men
Gang aft agley [go oft astray]

Robert Burns

We all know that some surprises are good and others bad. Surprise plays a role in scientific discoveries, as we have seen, but many disasters have also surprised their victims. What can be done to reduce the possibility of bad surprises? Earlier chapters have discussed how decision-makers in war, politics and business have responded over the centuries to conditions of uncertainty, especially to 'known unknowns'. This chapter, on the other hand, is mainly concerned with the 'unknown unknowns', the ignorance of the future that disrupts what Burns called 'the best laid schemes o' Mice an' Men' – not to mention the many plans that have not been well laid.

In practice, the binary opposition between known and unknown unknowns is too sharp. It is more productive to think in terms of what is more or less unknown. We know, for instance, that fires, floods, earthquakes, famines and epidemics are all bound to happen in the future, but none of us knows when they will take place. Californians have been waiting for the next 'Big One' ever since San Francisco was struck by an earthquake in 1906.

There is less ignorance of the geography of disaster than of its timing. It has long been known that certain places are more vulnerable than others, whether they are liable to flood, like parts of Bangladesh, or situated near the fault-lines that make earthquakes happen, as in California or Japan. For this reason, it is possible to prepare to respond to some disasters – constructing dykes and granaries, organizing fire brigades and so on. It is even possible to make some preparations for the most uncertain and deadly risks of all, the 'existential risks' that threaten the extinction of humanity itself or at least the drastic reduction of its potential. Nevertheless, preparation has often been too little and too late – a problem that recurs so often that it deserves its own acronym: TLTL.

One reason for this is the pressure to pay attention to or spend money on something else, but another is ignorance or at any rate a low awareness of what was happening at ground level. As a recent study of 'existential risk' warns its readers, 'Ours is a world of flawed decision-makers, working with strikingly incomplete information, directing technologies which threaten the entire future of the species.'[1]

What follows here is the story not of our inevitable ignorance of the future (discussed in chapter fourteen) but of culpable ignorance and lack of preparation. When Hitler gave the order to invade the USSR in 1941, for instance, the German army had no time to prepare for the invasion, so that the troops had to face the rigours of a Russian winter without proper clothing. The Russians were also taken by surprise. When Valery Legasov, head of the commission of investigation into the nuclear explosion at Chernobyl in 1986, noted the 'lack of preparation at the plant', he compared it to the lack of preparation for the German invasion: 'Nineteen forty-one, but in an even worse version.'[2]

## FIRES, FLOODS, HURRICANES AND EARTHQUAKES

There are all too many cases in history of natural disasters striking after dangers had been ignored. In early modern Europe, in which many houses were constructed from wood, arrangements made to fight fires were generally insufficient and the burning of whole towns or a major part of them was a regular occurrence. In Scandinavia, for instance, Stockholm was burned down in 1625 and 1759, Copenhagen in 1728 and 1795, Christiania (now Oslo) in 1624, and both Bergen and Uppsala in 1702.

A still larger conflagration was the Great Fire of London in 1666, beginning by accident in a bakery around midnight and spreading rapidly among the largely wooden houses as a result of strong winds. Some Londoners claimed that the Catholics, at that time a persecuted minority of the population, had set the fire deliberately. They exemplify not only the role of rumour when information is scarce but also what might be described as 'Scapegoat Syndrome', a kind of collective paranoia, illustrating the need to make concrete individuals or groups responsible for a disaster that no one had planned or even expected.

Learning from experience, Londoners rebuilt their city in brick, while an insurance office opened in the city in 1681, soon to be followed by others.[3] It cannot be said that the earlier inhabitants of these cities were ignorant of the danger of fires, but awareness of the danger became sharper at this time, together with measures to limit the damage and to reduce the impact of this kind of catastrophe.

In the case of floods, some notorious disasters reveal a culpable lack of preparation, the result once again of ignoring danger. Simple ignorance it could hardly have been in these cases, given that methods of what is now called 'flood management' have long been known – the identification of vulnerable areas, drainage, dykes, levees and so on. Take the case of the Great Mississippi Flood of 1927, which affected ten states of the Union, and in which some 600,000 people lost their homes. The record rainfall could not have been predicted, but more efficient long-term preparations could and should have been made, as the passing of the Mississippi Flood Control Act in 1928 implicitly admitted.[4]

The impact of the Mississippi Flood was greatest on the poor, mainly African Americans. The same is true of another great flood in American history, the New Orleans flood of 2005, following Hurricane Katrina. As had been the case in 1927, the disaster revealed flaws in the engineering of the flood-protection system as well as what has been described as 'the unintended organization of ignorance'. The phrase, 'the Katrina Effect', has entered the language.[5]

Studies of that disaster emphasize the 'utter failure of government relief efforts', especially the work of the Federal Emergency Management

Agency (FEMA).[6] For those who lost their houses, the Agency provided temporary shelter in caravans and tents, but it was reluctant to place evacuees in hotels. The health care system was unprepared for the disaster. Since hurricanes hit New Orleans every year, lack of preparation was culpable. The poor, mainly African Americans, suffered most because they possessed fewer resources and lived in the low-lying areas more liable to flooding. The police prevented some people from leaving while many of those who remained did not receive aid. For those who were displaced, sometimes to distant cities, returning became as difficult as leaving had been. The authorities have been accused not only of indifference to suffering but also of institutional racism. As for the president, George W. Bush was on vacation when the disaster happened, failed to make an early visit to the scene and praised the inefficient director of FEMA (who resigned soon afterwards) for doing 'one heck of a job', when what he offered was yet another example of 'Too Little, Too Late'.

Hurricane Katrina revealed what might be called the 'social distribution' of ignorance. The poor, who lived in vulnerable zones of the city, were well aware of the dangers of floods. The officials, who lived in safer and more expensive districts, were not. They ignored local knowledge not at their peril but at the peril of others.[7] This theme is a recurrent one in the history of disasters, if not in history in general: those who know the local situation do not have the power to act, while those with the power do not have the necessary knowledge.

Earthquakes are the most dramatic natural disasters, given both the speed with which they happen and the unpredictability of their timing. In Europe, the Lisbon earthquake of 1755, which destroyed the city and killed from ten thousand to thirty thousand people, remains the most notorious, although its effects appear small by comparison to the earthquakes that devastated Sichuan in 2008 (with around ninety thousand deaths), destroyed Tokyo in 1923 (with 140,000 deaths) and destroyed Aleppo in 1138 (with more than 200,000 deaths, if modern calculations are correct).

It was the Lisbon earthquake that, thanks to the circulation of information in newly founded journals, provoked debate about the causes of such 'catastrophes' – a new word in the mid-eighteenth century, or more exactly, a new meaning for an old word, that shifted from a technical term in the discussion of drama to a synonym for 'disaster'. One response to the Lisbon disaster, Immanuel Kant's essay on the causes of earthquakes (1756), emphasized human ignorance of the depths of the earth.

Some scholars refer to what they call 'the invention of catastrophe' in the eighteenth century.[8] This vivid phrase does less than justice to the traditional notions of the Four Horsemen of the Apocalypse and the imminent end of the world.[9] However, an important shift took place from the idea of disaster as inevitable to the belief of one that it can, given the combination of knowledge with the will to act, be avoided.

## FAMINES

Famines are natural disasters in the sense that the size of the harvest depends on the weather, but man-made disasters in the sense that they generally result from failures by the authorities: failures to manage risks to the food supply by constructing public storehouses and failures to respond rapidly enough to crisis by importing food from other places. More than two million people died as a result of the Bengal Famine of 1770, around three million in the Bengal Famine of 1943–4. The Irish Famine of 1845–6 led to the death of a million people and the emigration of a million more. In the famine in Ethiopia in 1983, more than a million people died. More than three million people died in the famine in the Ukraine in 1932–3, although this was not the result of official ignorance but of Stalin's orders to confiscate the harvest.

Bengal and Ireland offer further examples of the colonial ignorance discussed earlier in chapter eleven. In 1770, Bengal was administered by the British East India Company. When famine broke out, some Company officials tried to prevent the hoarding or export of rice and distributed food to the starving. Nonetheless, measures for famine relief were inadequate, as the new governor-general, Warren Hastings, recognized when he ordered the building of public granaries.[10]

A second famine occurred in Bengal in 1943, when Bengal was part of the British Empire. This time, the official response was worse than inadequate, since the government of the province denied that a famine was taking place. The distribution of food, mainly in Calcutta, was too little and once again came too late. In Bengal itself there was 'administrative chaos'. As for Britain, Lord Wavell, who arrived as viceroy during the famine, wrote to Winston Churchill complaining that 'the vital problems of India are being treated by His Majesty's Government with neglect, even sometimes with hostility and contempt'.[11] Jawaharlal Nehru agreed, describing the British response (or lack of it) as an example of 'indifference, incompetence and complacency'.[12]

The journalist Kali Charan Ghosh, who experienced the famine and wrote about it at the time, noted that 'the measures that were able to avert great calamities . . . were either overlooked or completely ignored' and that highly placed officials tried 'to shake off responsibility under cover of feigned ignorance'.[13] The verdict of the economist Amartya Sen, who witnessed the famine as a child, is that the disaster revealed 'the conspicuous failure of the Government to anticipate the famine and to recognize its emergence'. In short, the British had ignored the possibility of famine and when it arrived, they did not want to know about it.[14]

The Great Irish Famine of 1845, another example of imperial ignorance, was the result of the failure of the potato crop, on which most of the population depended, aggravated by the lack of response from the British government. Once again, the measures taken were too little and too late. Charles Trevelyan, a civil servant who had worked in Bengal, was in charge of famine relief in Ireland. He believed in official inaction (*laissez-faire*) and indeed described the famine in an article on 'The Irish Crisis' in the *Edinburgh Review* (1848) as 'a direct stroke of an all-wise and all-merciful Providence', a means of ridding Ireland of an idle peasantry by death or emigration.[15] The Conservative prime minister Robert Peel organized shipments of maize to Ireland, but they took too long to arrive, while further delays ensued because Irish mills were not equipped for grinding the corn. Peel also tried to repeal the tariffs that kept the price of grain high (the 'Corn Laws') but was unable to do so as a result of the opposition of his own party, the party of the landowners.[16]

Further colonial examples come from British Africa, where 'It is striking how frequently colonial officials were either ignorant of, or insensitive to, the conditions of the people over whom they ruled . . . At times colonial neglect simply reflected the ill-informed nature of the administration.' In the case of famine in Northern Nigeria in 1908, the administration in Lagos 'apparently knew nothing of the famine until it read about it in an annual report'.[17]

The Great Famine in China in 1959–62 makes all the others seem small. Reliable figures are lacking and estimates vary widely, but around thirty million people are likely to have died. As in Stalin's USSR, the famine was the direct result of the policies of the leader, a mixture in this case of ignorance and arrogance by an individual 'sure of his own genius and infallibility'.[18] In his full account of the famine, the Dutch historian Frank Dikötter rarely if ever uses the word 'ignorance', but he does describe a number of situations during the rule of Mao Zedong where that term seems particularly appropriate.

In 1956, Mao 'called for unrealistic increases in the production of grain, cotton, coal and steel'. In 1957, an ambitious irrigation programme included a dam on the Yellow River, constructed in a hurry by forced labour, ignoring expert advice and, as a result, not fit for purpose.[19]

Mao also initiated what was officially known as the 'Great Leap Forward', an attempt to catch up with the West by rapid industrialization, carried out – as in the Maoist theory of revolution – not by the proletariat but by peasants, making steel in small furnaces in their backyards. They had not been trained to do this and were ignorant of the procedure. The result was that most of the iron ingots they produced were useless.[20]

Still worse was the effect on farming of the withdrawal of a large number of workers from sowing and harvesting in order to participate in the Leap. Over sixteen million peasants were transferred to the industrial sector and relocated in cities. At the same time, the government ordered the replacement of small individual farms with large collective ones. This policy led to severe food shortages and later to the famine.

Mao ordered an increase in the production of grain and visited the countryside to monitor progress, but his visits were stage-managed. In a notorious case of the 'Potemkin Effect', rice was transplanted along the route of his visits to give a good impression. 'All of China was a stage, all the people performers in an extravaganza for Mao.'[21] Warning signs of disaster were already visible by 1958, but the regime ignored them. Once again, those in power lacked knowledge (or did not want to know), while those with knowledge lacked power. Mistakes and thefts were covered up. As so often in authoritarian regimes, production statistics were faked to show that targets had been met or even exceeded.[22] In short, the Chinese famine was the unintended but direct result of central planning in the service of an unrealistic aim, a rapid increase of industrial production in what was still a fundamentally agrarian society.

## EPIDEMICS

Many vivid examples of the consequences of ignorance come from the history of disease. In the last half-century, humanity has suffered the attacks of four major new diseases: Ebola from 1976, AIDS from 1981, SARS from 2002 and the Coronavirus from 2020. As the present changes, the past is viewed from new angles. No wonder, then, that historians are returning to the study of major outbreaks of disease in the past. Such major outbreaks or pandemics include bubonic plague in Asia and Europe in 1348–9; smallpox in Central and South America in the 1520s; a return of bubonic plague in the seventeenth century (in north Italy in 1630, in London in 1665); cholera in nineteenth-century Europe (from London in 1854 to Hamburg in 1892); and Spanish flu, spreading around the globe in 1918. All these pandemics caught both sufferers and doctors by surprise. They were equally ignorant of the origin of the diseases, the manner in which they spread and the ways in which that spread might be limited or the sufferers cured.

## THE PLAGUE

In 1348–9, the rapid spread of bubonic plague from its origin on the Tibetan-Qinghai plateau, together with the huge number of deaths (around fifty million in Europe alone) was a traumatic event.[23] People were desperate for an explanation for its arrival as well as for a cure or at least a preventative for this killer, all the more fearsome because its transmission was invisible. One major 'theory' was that the plague was the work of God, punishing communities for their sins. Another common belief was that the Jews were responsible for the plague by poisoning the wells, a dramatic example of 'Scapegoat Syndrome'. Many doctors believed that the plague was transmitted by miasma or 'corrupted air' – an explanation long rejected by historians as an example of ignorance, but invoked once again by today's epidemiologists in the case of the Coronavirus.

It was also believed that plague entered the body via the sense of smell, which encouraged doctors to wear masks and those who could afford it to defend themselves with a 'pomander' (an orange filled with spices held to the nose). Only later was it discovered that fleas and their hosts, black rats, were responsible for the spread of the disease.

The beliefs of contemporaries shaped their responses to the epidemic. To placate the anger of God, people went in procession, sometimes whipping themselves in order to demonstrate their repentance (processions, like crowded churches, actually increased the probability of the spread of disease via physical contact). A second response was to attack the Jews. There were pogroms in Toulon in 1348, for instance, and in Barcelona, Erfurt and Basel in 1349.[24]

Europeans took a long time to forget the plague of 1348, known as 'the Black Death'. Memories were regularly revived, since plague frequently recurred, though on a smaller scale than before. In Milan, in 1630, about sixty thousand people died, half the population of the city. Londoners remembered the great 'plague year' of 1665–6, when deaths numbered over seventy thousand. The last major outbreak occurred in Marseilles in the year 1720, when fifty thousand people died.[25]

By the seventeenth century, European cities had been organized to fight the plague, especially in Italy. The practice of quarantine – the first form of 'lockdown' – goes back at least as far as the fourteenth century, when passengers in ships arriving in Venice from ports in infected regions were not allowed to disembark for forty days. By the seventeenth century, a cluster of measures was in place. Following news that the plague was spreading, frontiers would be closed, health boards established, health passes issued and infected clothes and furniture burned. Some physicians warned the public of the danger to participants in processions and public meetings. A professor at the University of Pisa, Stefano di Castro, claimed that the poor were wilfully ignorant, refusing to distance themselves from anyone infected.[26]

Rumours continued to flourish, as indeed they still do in similar situations. In Milan in 1630, it was claimed that the plague was deliberately spread by people known as *untori*, painting the walls of the city with a poisonous substance. Some individuals were arrested and put on trial for this offence. In Florence, a diarist wrote, 'The plague in Milan was caused by wicked men with poisons . . . who poison the holy water in the holy water stoups in the churches.'[27] Preachers in Florence and elsewhere continued to present the plague as a punishment for the sins of the community, and processions continued to take place.[28]

The Florentines were not the last people to think and behave in this way. During the epidemic of yellow fever in Rio de Janeiro in 1849, it was described in newspapers as an example of 'God's justice', while processions of religious confraternities were organized in order to appeal for help to the traditional protectors against the plague, St Roche and St Sebastian.[29]

## SMALLPOX

Smallpox, endemic in Europe, turned into an epidemic in the New World. From the 1520s onwards, shortly after the arrival of the Spanish conquerors, smallpox, together with typhus and measles, killed the majority of the population in Mexico and Peru. The population of Mexico in 1518 is now estimated at a figure between 9 and 25 million, reduced to one million by 1603. The population of Peru was between 5 and 9 million when Francisco Pizarro and his men arrived in 1528, down to 600,000 a century later. The Spaniards, who must have carried the disease with them from the Old World, were spared. The arrival of the disease, together with its rapid and fatal spread, was a shock to both conquerors and conquered, a totally unexpected event.[30]

Historians now explain the variation in vulnerability between the Spanish minority and the indigenous majority by the fact that the latter had not developed immunity as the Spaniards had done. In the sixteenth century, however, the concept of 'immunity' was lacking, and so the reason for the uneven spread of the disease was unknown.[31]

Later in the history of the New World, more was known about smallpox, at least by the conquerors. It was even possible to imagine using the disease as a weapon of mass destruction. In 1763, Lord Jeffery Amherst, an officer of the British army, attempted to suppress Pontiac's Rebellion (named after its leader, an Ottawa chief) by having blankets infected with smallpox sent to the rebels. 'Could it not be contrived,' Amherst wrote to one of his subordinates, 'to send the Small Pox among those disaffected tribes of Indians?' He later approved the stratagem of the blankets in order 'to Extirpate this Execrable Race'. Today, 'Lord Jeff' has the poisonous reputation of a pioneer in biological warfare.[32]

As for preventive measures, inoculation against smallpox, a practice long known in China and the Middle East, became the subject of vigorous debate before it was adopted in eighteenth-century Europe. One of its leading advocates was the English noblewoman Lady Mary Wortley Montagu, the wife of the British ambassador to the Ottoman sultan. Lady Mary had already recovered from smallpox herself but learned about the local practice while she was living in Istanbul and campaigned for its adoption in Britain on her return. Her campaign faced strong opposition from those who did not want to know about inoculation.[33]

The safer technique of vaccination, using a virus from cows, spread rapidly worldwide in the nineteenth century, despite facing a movement of resistance in some places. A dramatic case of this resistance occurred in Rio de Janeiro in 1904.[34] Smallpox was rife and the prefect ordered the demolition of slums, the *cortiços*, as part of a hygiene campaign which was also intended to eliminate bubonic plague and yellow fever. Many poor people resented displacement from their homes and the invasion of privacy by health inspectors. Still more people from different social groups objected to the new law making vaccination compulsory. Rio became the scene of battles between crowds throwing stones and bottles and the mounted police charging them and firing their revolvers.

To view what is known as the 'Vaccine Revolt' as simply driven by ignorance of medicine would be itself simplistic. It was also an angry response to what was seen as interference in people's lives by the authorities in a city with a history of riots, the 'smash-smash' (*quebra-quebra*) that continues to occur to this day. In a phrase which may remind today's readers of the Black Lives Matter campaign of 2020, one Black citizen, asked by a reporter about the reason for the revolt, replied, 'To show the government that it cannot put its foot on the people's neck' (*mostrar al governo che ele não põe o pé no pescoço do povo*).[35]

All the same, the vaccine was more than a pretext for revolt. To complicate the situation, Rio was the scene of a clash between two cultures, the culture of modern scientific medicine and the traditional African culture of the ex-slaves, each culture with its own diagnoses and cures.[36] Ignorance about the vaccine played its part, as it did in the case of the Covid virus in 2020. Many of the poor were illiterate and acquired their information from rumours, some of which claimed that the vaccine was an illness or a poison. One observer, Dr Romualdo Teixeira, emphasized the ignorance of the resisters, while another, the poet and journalist Olavo Bilac, described the revolt as the exploitation of the ignorant by the cunning.[37]

## CHOLERA

The nineteenth century witnessed another major debate among European doctors, this time about contagion. An outbreak of yellow fever in Barcelona in 1822 was used as a test case by the French physician Nicholas Chervin to show the disease had not spread by human contact, as had been generally assumed.[38] It was the turn of cholera to highlight ignorance when it spread from India, where it was endemic, to the Middle East, China, Japan and Europe. In some places, such as Prussia in 1830 and Russia in 1848, it reached the proportions of an epidemic. The crisis provoked debate about the transmission of cholera and the best way to combat the disease.

In Britain, for instance, a major outbreak of cholera occurred in 1832. The view that God sent the epidemic as punishment for the sins of the community was still current at the time and encouraged Methodist revivals. Debates continued to take place between supporters of contagion and of miasma, and opinions remained divided about the best means to fight the epidemic, whether by quarantine (resisted by business, as in 2020) or by burning clothing and furniture. The government, 'faced with two unpopular policies, and no pressing scientific justification for either, chose, like many governments in the same position, to do a little bit of both and did neither very well'.[39]

Different groups responded to the epidemic in different ways. The middle class blamed the working class, stereotyped as filthy, poor and drunken. The working class, or some of it, denied that there was an epidemic, calling the claim 'humbug'.[40] There were riots in Manchester against the regulations imposed by Boards of Health. Ignorance played its part: there were 'failures of authority, failures of information and failures of knowledge'. 'Any effective enquiry into the nature and causes of cholera was hampered by the absence of any research community in medicine' as well as by the lack of high-power microscopes.[41]

Florence Nightingale, who made her reputation nursing victims of cholera in the British army during the Crimean War (1853–6), was a firm believer in hand-washing. In this respect she was a pioneer, like Edwin Chadwick, a reformer whose report on insanitary conditions led to the passing of the Public Health Act in 1848. These examples remind us of the general ignorance of hygiene at this time. As awareness of its importance spread among the middle classes, ignorance of hygiene became associated with the working classes. In the United States, the middle class associated this form of ignorance with immigrants from southern and eastern Europe, and teaching hygiene became part of campaigns of 'Americanization'.[42]

In another respect, Nightingale followed tradition: she was a firm believer in the traditional 'miasma' theory of the transmission of disease.[43] It was only in the course of an outbreak of cholera in London in 1854 that the surgeon John Snow, acting like a detective, following clues and tracing the local diffusion of the disease to a pump near Liverpool Street station, offered circumstantial evidence for his theory that it spread via water that had been contaminated by human waste (a conclusion he had reached when he noted that the illness began in the stomach). He suggested cleansing the water with chlorine.[44]

In France, Louis Pasteur, using a new generation of microscopes, argued that some diseases were transmitted by micro-organisms, otherwise known as 'bacteria', 'microbes' or 'germs'. In Germany, Dr Robert Koch, who had been sent to Egypt in 1883 to investigate an epidemic of cholera there, supported Pasteur's germ theory. When a major outbreak of cholera took place in Hamburg in 1892, Koch went there to halt it. The fact that Hamburg, where the water supply came straight from the river, suffered, while its neighbour Altona, where the water was filtered, was spared, demonstrated on a large scale what Snow had noticed at the micro-level of the parish pump and led to the acceptance of the germ theory, thus saving many lives.[45]

## THE TWENTIETH AND TWENTY-FIRST CENTURIES

Medical knowledge marches in step with science, but as the Coronavirus made the public aware, when a new disease strikes, everyone is ignorant. Although influenza is not a new phenomenon, new strains of the virus were active in the epidemic of 1918–19. This epidemic was unprecedented in the scale on which it spread, in the wake of the First World War and as a result of the war. The new variants were created when American and North African forces met European ones in northern France, while malnutrition in the war years had made many people more vulnerable to the disease than they would have been in normal times.[46]

In our time, a century later, the chances of an epidemic spreading rapidly worldwide have greatly increased, thanks to globalization and the rise of intercontinental travel. It is surely no accident that the four new diseases mentioned earlier made their appearance in the last half-century, challenging doctors and epidemiologists to turn their initial ignorance into knowledge and their new knowledge into life-saving practices.

The first of these diseases was Ebola, identified in 1976 following outbreaks in two parts of Africa, South Sudan and Zaire (now the Democratic Republic of the Congo). The search for a vaccine came to a successful conclusion only in 2019. The second epidemic, HIV or AIDS, also originated in Africa, leaping from chimpanzees to humans and spreading outwards from Kinshasa to Haiti and then to the United States. The virus was identified by different groups of researchers in the early 1980s. Responses still include cases of Scapegoat Syndrome. In the USSR, it was claimed that the government of the USA had created the virus as a bio-weapon. Chinese sources made similar claims in the case of Covid-19.

The third epidemic was SARS, spreading outwards from South China to Hong Kong, Toronto and elsewhere. Ignorance helped the spread: in Hong Kong, some citizens criticized the government for failing to provide information about the disease quickly enough. The Coronavirus is – at least from the point of view of the bacteria – a more successful strain of SARS. Once again the disease began in China and once again the government has been blamed for not informing the public quickly enough about the danger. Conspiracy theories flourish once again. The American Republican senator Rick Scott has claimed that the Chinese government 'intentionally' allowed the virus to spread and attempted to 'sabotage' the search for a vaccine. Another Republican senator, Tom Cotton, has called the virus a Chinese 'bio-weapon'. In China, on the other hand, the media have placed the blame for the virus on the armed forces of the United States.[47] As in Rio de Janeiro in 1904, an anti-vaccine movement has arisen in the United States and elsewhere.

Ignorance has often been supported by prejudice. It took a long time for physicians to recognize the role of insects, birds and animals – not to mention bacteria – in the transmission of epidemics. They ignored the importance of fleas and rats in the case of bubonic plague, flies and lice in that of typhus, birds in the influenza of 1918, monkeys in HIV and bats in SARS. In a hierarchical society it was particularly difficult to imagine that mere insects such as fleas and lice, viewed as inferior to animals as well as humans, could kill millions of people. In that case, human hubris certainly produced its nemesis.

# 13

## SECRETS AND LIES

Secrecy, being an instrument of conspiracy, ought never to
be the system of a regular government

Jeremy Bentham

The main task of the social history of ignorance was described in the
introduction in a formula adapted from the American political scientist
Harold Lasswell. It is to discover 'Who is ignorant of What, When,
Where and with What Consequences'. This chapter goes beyond the
formula because, like other recent studies of ignorance, it is concerned
with the ways in which individuals and groups with certain kinds of
knowledge attempt to keep this knowledge from other groups, whether
they are enemies, competitors or the general public.[1] They allow, maintain, encourage, exploit or even require ignorance on the part of their
targets. Hence we need to ask: Who wants Whom not to know What
and for What Reasons? Who has the power (the opportunities and the
resources) to do this and what are the consequences of their actions?

As for the methods employed, they may be summed up (borrowing
the title from Mike Leigh's film of that name) as 'secrets and lies'. These
terms may be expanded to include denial, disinformation, 'fake news'
and 'cover-ups' (or to change the metaphor, 'hush-ups'). The practices to
which these terms refer are much older than the terms themselves, indeed
much older than is generally thought, as this chapter will attempt to
demonstrate. What we now call 'fake news' was known in the nineteenth

century as 'false reports', often taking the form of rumours. What, following Mikhail Gorbachev's glasnost, has become known in English as 'transparency' was described in the nineteenth century as 'publicity'. The term occurs in Jeremy Bentham's writings on political and legal theory, in which he called for 'the doors of all public establishments . . . to be thrown wide open to the body of the curious at large'. As for the Russian term *dezinformatsya*, in English, 'disinformation', it is effectively a euphemism for the traditional term 'lies'.

The story told in this chapter is essentially an account of the recurrent conflict between transparency and opacity, closure and disclosure, 'leaks' and 'plumbers', including substantial grey areas between these extremes. Neither absolute transparency nor absolute opacity is possible or, surely, even desirable. Governments, churches, corporations and other institutions naturally try to keep their secrets safe. They employ a number of means to this end, including censorship, ciphers and official denial.

Conversely, governments and corporations also wish to discover the secrets of others and for this purpose they employ spies, codebreakers and, more recently, hackers. Investigative journalists, helped by whistleblowers, specialize in bringing secrets to light, uncovering what had been covered up. Sometimes the attackers win this game of 'Veil and Reveal', and sometimes the defenders, but as long as some secrets are kept, it will always be impossible to say which side wins most often.

What follows will attempt to distinguish between what might be called 'ordinary' secrecy, especially on the part of governments and corporations, and 'extraordinary' attempts to cover up news about particular events that embarrass people in high places.

## SECRETS OF STATE

Governments have long been conscious of the importance of 'secrets of state' (in the phrase of the Roman historian Tacitus, *arcana imperii*). In early modern Europe, deceit was often discussed in commentaries on Tacitus (especially his remarks about the emperor Tiberius), and in treatises on 'reason of state'. Machiavelli offered a famous account of deceit in chapter fifteen of *The Prince*, remarking that a ruler needs not to be, but to appear to be 'merciful, trustworthy, humane, upright and devout'. For their part, courtiers were well advised to conceal their thoughts and feelings in the presence of the prince. Speaking truth to power was dangerous, while concealment of one's opinions was associated with prudence.

Deceit was recommended to private individuals in three discussions that became classics: Francis Bacon's essay 'Of Simulation and Dissimulation' (1597); the essay on 'Honourable Dissimulation' (*Della dissimulazione onesta*, 1641) by the Neapolitan secretary Torquato Accetto, who claimed that it was an essential part of polite behaviour; and the Spanish Jesuit Baltasar Gracián's handbook on the art of prudence (*Oráculo manual*, 1647).

Bacon distinguished three degrees of concealment: secrecy; 'Dissimulation, in the Negative; when a man lets fall Signs, and Arguments, that he is not, that he is'; and 'Simulation, in the Affirmative; when a Man industriously and expressly, feigns, and pretends to be, that he is not'. The writer offers what might be described today as a cost-benefit analysis of the advantages and disadvantages of all three, concluding that the best choice is 'Openness in Fame and Opinion; Secrecy in Habit; Dissimulation in seasonable use; and a power to feign, if there be no remedy'.[2]

As for Gracián, his book describes life as a perpetual struggle between dissimulation and its detection. The prudent individual dissimulates, since 'the player who shows his cards runs the risk of losing the game'. On the other hand, a close observer is able to 'decipher' the signs and discover what is really going on. For a social historian, something can be learned from the fact that although the author presented his handbook as a guide to life in general, it circulated in translation as a guide to life at court.[3]

During the Enlightenment, dissimulation became a matter of debate. The young Frederick the Great, for example, published a critique of Machiavelli (*L'Anti-Machiavel*, 1740), in which he rejected the idea that a ruler might have recourse to deception. Later in life he changed his mind, describing the people as 'this stupid mass, made to be led by those who take the trouble to deceive it' (*Le peuple . . . cette masse imbécile, et faite pour être menée par ceux qui se donnent la peine de la tromper*).[4]

Four decades after *L'Anti-Machiavel*, the philosophe Jean d'Alembert suggested to Frederick that for its essay prize, the Berlin Academy should choose the question 'Whether it might be useful to deceive the people' (*S'il peut être utile de tromper le peuple*). This was done in 1780, with the inclusion of a phrase that extended the topic beyond 'leading them into errors', to include 'maintaining them' in error, what is now known as the 'production' of ignorance. Forty-two essays were submitted.[5] Today, essays written for a similar competition would probably focus on the actions of governments and large companies. In contrast, in 1780, the competitors emphasized 'impostors' in religion.

## CENSORSHIP

When secrets were committed to writing, the message might be encoded. Codes and ciphers have a long history but were becoming increasingly sophisticated in the sixteenth century, with the help of mathematicians such as François Viète, who worked for kings Henri III and Henri IV of France.[6]

Another important way for governments to protect their secrets was censorship, denying permission to publish texts believed to be seditious or to reveal information useful to enemies, and removing sensitive passages from books and newspapers. In early modern Europe, publications were generally subjected to a double censorship, both religious and political. Catholic censorship took the form of the Index of Prohibited Books (a printed catalogue of books of which the faithful ought to be ignorant). This is at once the best-known case, the most widespread and the longest-lasting (from the early sixteenth to the mid-twentieth centuries). Protestant censorship was equally severe but less effective because it was decentralized and divided by denomination.

Secular censorship developed later than the religious variety and each nation had its own rules, more or less strict. According to the English Licensing Act of 1662, for example, law books had to be inspected by the lord chancellor and history books, which were considered particularly dangerous, by a secretary of state.[7] The French system – as well as its evasion – is best known, especially during the Enlightenment, when at least a thousand books were banned in the first half of the century, while forbidden books were smuggled into France from neighbouring Switzerland or from the Dutch Republic, where censorship was less strict than elsewhere.[8]

Ecclesiastical censorship continued into the nineteenth and even the twentieth century. The last edition of the Index of Prohibited Books was published as late as 1948 and continued to condemn Voltaire, as a teacher in my Jesuit school once pointed out to us, making it clear that he thought this prohibition to be quite anachronistic. However, secular censorship was dominant by the nineteenth century and the attention of censors shifted from books to newspapers, political caricatures and the theatre. In France in the age of Napoleon III, the famous caricaturist Honoré Daumier had regular problems with the censors.[9] In Russia in the last years of the tsars, Anton Chekhov experienced similar problems in the case of both his stories and his plays.

One of the strictest systems was the Press Law of 1819 that formed part of the 'Carlsbad Decrees' and applied to Austria and ten German states, including Prussia. The works of the poet and journalist Heinrich Heine were banned in the 1830s, while Karl Marx was forced to flee to Paris in 1843 after the journal for which he wrote was suppressed.[10]

The Austrian regime in Lombardy banned works by Machiavelli as well as Voltaire and Rousseau. Censorship in the Habsburg Empire became milder after 1848, but writers learned to police themselves in order to avoid problems. It was perhaps his experience of this regime, at least as a reader of newspapers, that led Freud to put forward his idea of an internal, unconscious censor. Another strict system was the Russian one, especially under Tsar Nicholas I, 1825–55. The journalist Alexander Herzen left Russia in 1847 to escape from surveillance by the police. In London he founded the Free Russian Press and a journal called 'The Bell' (*Kolokol*) in which opinions could be expressed without concern for censors.

Writers who remained in autocratic regimes but wished to criticize the political system resorted to what was known as 'the method of Aesop', in other words, allegory of the kind employed in Aesop's *Fables*, in which animals stand for humans. A remote place or period has often served to disguise one nearer to home. In the mid-nineteenth century, the Czech journalist Karel Havliček wrote about the British denial of independence to Ireland as a way of criticizing the Austrian denial of independence to the Czechs.[11] In China during the Cultural Revolution, a major stir was caused by Wu Han's historical opera, *Hai Rui Dismissed from Office*, about a virtuous official of the Ming dynasty who was dismissed by a tyrannical emperor.[12] In the 1970s and 1980s, the books by Ryszard Kapuściński about the fall of the emperor of Ethiopia and the shah of Iran were read by his fellow citizens as critiques of the authoritarian regime of Communist Poland.

## PUBLIC KNOWLEDGE AND PUBLIC IGNORANCE

Although it is obviously impossible to measure the ignorance of the actions of their governments on the part of ordinary citizens in what might be described as 'regimes of secrecy', something may still be said about it. In the USSR from Stalin to Gorbachev (1922–91), for instance, the attempt to keep the public ignorant of what was happening behind the scenes was supported by the official newspapers, *Pravda* ('Truth') and *Izvestia* ('News'). Political humour, transmitted by word of mouth between friends, is one way to criticize authoritarian regimes, and according to one Russian joke from Stalin's time, 'there is no news in *Pravda* and no truth in *Izvestia*'.

In most countries, rumour and other forms of oral communication are considered, rightly, to be less reliable than newspapers, but in the USSR it was for a long time the other way round.[13] Maps of the USSR were also unreliable, as they omitted whatever the government would have preferred not to exist (including churches), or wished to hide from the public (including gulags). Also off the map were the *naukograds*, new 'cities of science', in which research was concentrated, some of them located in Siberia and built by prisoners in labour camps.[14] As Andrei Sakharov, the nuclear physicist and dissident, wrote (from inside the USSR) in 1968, this was 'a closed society that does not inform its citizens of anything substantial, closed to the outside world, without freedom of travel or the exchange of information'.[15] The response of dissidents such as Sakharov was either to publish abroad, or to circulate information by *samizdat*, 'do-it-yourself' publications that were made and distributed secretly by hand.

Keeping secrets from the public is not a monopoly of the state. In early modern Europe, as in the Middle Ages, each craft had its secrets, the 'mystery' of the trade. Indeed, the word 'mystery' is related to the French word *métier*, meaning 'craft' or 'profession'.[16] Apprentices in a particular craft guild were initiated into trade secrets as if into a secret society. Indeed, the Freemasons were (and are) a secret society that emerged from the craft guild of masons. In the seventeenth century, when the Royal Society of London planned an investigation of the practical knowledges of artisans, they found them reluctant to divulge their trade secrets to outsiders.[17] In the eighteenth century, Denis Diderot, himself the son of an artisan who made cutlery, encountered opposition from the guilds, again for obvious economic reasons, when he published information about the crafts in his famous *Encyclopédie*. As chapter ten suggested, secrecy in business has a long history.

Secrets and lies can be found in the world of science and scholarship as well as in politics and industry. Many early modern scholars were interested in what we still call 'occult' (in other words, 'hidden') knowledges, especially alchemy, magic and the secret Jewish tradition of the Kabbalah. What they discovered they kept to themselves or passed on only to a select few. Natural philosophers investigated what were known as the secrets of nature, and some of them published what they knew in 'books of secrets', first in manuscript, for the few, and later in print, for a wider public.[18]

Plagiarism from academic colleagues may not be common practice, but this sin is not so rare either. In the controversies over priority in scientific discoveries from the seventeenth century onwards, the discoverers sometimes established their claim in coded form in order to prevent the secret being stolen by their rivals. In 1655, for instance, when the Dutch natural philosopher Christiaan Huygens discovered the rings of Saturn, he announced the discovery in the form of an anagram.[19]

As we saw earlier, failure to acknowledge assistance, especially by male scholars assisted by female ones, is a recurrent theme in the history of science, as the now notorious example of Rosalind Franklin reminds us.

## COVER-UPS

It has long been important to governments not only to prevent the exposure of secret knowledge but also to encourage disbelief in what has been exposed. Cover-ups are an old practice. In 1541, for instance, two French diplomats were assassinated on the orders of the governor of Lombardy, the Marchese del Vasto. If Vasto's responsibility had become public, there would have been a risk of war between France and the Holy Roman Empire, which included Lombardy at this time. The emperor, Charles V, was advised that to avoid a war, 'Your Majesty cannot approve what has been done.' Vasto 'should be praised, although to avoid any risks, this must be done in the utmost secrecy'. Charles agreed to hush things up.[20]

Awareness of cover-ups also goes back a long way. As we have seen, the South Sea scandal was covered up by Robert Walpole, and his action was described as a 'screen' by the journalist Richard Steele.[21] Another notorious example of both covering and uncovering concerns Louis XIV's second marriage, in 1683, to Madame de Maintenon, the former governess to the children of the king's mistress. Knowledge of the king's marriage to a social inferior would have damaged his reputation both at home and abroad, so an attempt was made to keep not only the French people but also foreign courts in ignorance of what had taken place.

Nevertheless, before the king's death, details of his private life had become public knowledge. That his secret marriage was well known to the king's enemies, such as the British, as well as at home, is clear from the publication of *The French King's Wedding*, a text of the early eighteenth century which claims to describe 'the Comical Courtship, Catterwauling and Surprizing Marriage Ceremonies of Lewis the XIVth with Madam Maintenon his late Hackney of State'. It would be fascinating to discover who was responsible for the leak.[22]

Some of the most dramatic examples of governments keeping the public in ignorance are cover-ups of major disasters. During the Bengal

Famine of 1943, for instance, the government forbade the use of the term 'famine', while the artist Chittaprosad Bhattacharya's book *Hungry Bengal* (1943) was banned and the copies destroyed.[23] Another notorious case is that of the Holodomor – the Great Famine in the Ukraine in 1932–3. The position taken by the Soviet government, both at the time and later, was to deny that a famine had occurred.[24]

Denial was also the reaction of the Soviet government to the Chernobyl disaster, ironically enough, in the age of Mikhail Gorbachev's policy of official 'transparency' (*glasnost*). The director of the plant, Anatoly Dyatlov, initially denied that the reactor core had exploded. The first news about the accident came from Sweden, where scientists in a nuclear power plant noticed that radiation levels were rising at an alarming rate. The Soviet government began by denying that anything untoward had happened, and then claimed that the accident was a minor one.

Later, a commission of investigation was appointed, but the head of the commission, Valery Legasov, committed suicide on the day before he was due to announce the results of the investigation, leaving tapes that criticized the cover-up of earlier accidents. It remains difficult to know how much Gorbachev knew about the disaster or when he knew it. He later claimed that Chernobyl may have been 'the real cause of the collapse of the Soviet Union'. It was only after that collapse that secret KGB reports about negligence during the construction of the plant and about earlier emergencies came to light.[25]

## THE MASSACRE IN KATYN FOREST

Telling one lie often requires other lies to support it, a point that may be illustrated by a notorious cover-up in Communist Poland. Early in the Second World War, in April and May 1940, more than twenty thousand Polish officers were shot by the Russian secret police and buried in the forest of Katyn in the Soviet Union.

Discussion of this topic was taboo in Communist Poland, where the massacre was officially attributed to the Germans. In order to make this attribution plausible, the date of the killings had to be changed to 1941, following the German invasion of Russia in June of that year. In 1946, a memorial was erected at Katyn claiming that the Germans were responsible. The Poles, especially the families who lost relatives in the massacre, were not deceived. They were well aware of the date after which letters home written by the victims stopped arriving.

Nevertheless, the charade continued. In 1981, for instance, an unofficial monument was erected in a Warsaw cemetery with an inscription including both the word 'Katyn' and the date of 1940. The monument was immediately removed by the secret police.[26] In 1985, an official monument was erected in Warsaw, still dating the massacre to 1941 and making the Germans responsible.

It was only after 1989 that the story finally changed. Poles and Russians agreed on a new inscription for the monument at Katyn without reference to the Germans. In 1993, Boris Yeltsin knelt before the monument in Warsaw, and said, 'Forgive us if you can.' The story of both the massacre and the attempts at cover-up was told in a moving film by the Polish director Andrzej Wajda, *Katyń*, released in 2007. The main facts of the case have now been established on the basis of statements from survivors and local witnesses as well as from the dates of letters found in the pockets of corpses exhumed from the mass graves.[27]

## THE GREAT WALL OF SILENCE

Since the installation of the Communist regime in China in 1949, a number of embarrassing episodes have been covered up in what might be called the construction of a Great Wall of Silence. As in the USSR, disasters have been kept out of the national news. A recent example is the outbreak of the Covid virus in Wuhan. A Chinese epidemiologist, Professor Kwok-Yung Yuen, interviewed on the BBC's *Panorama* programme, declared his suspicion 'that they have been doing some cover-up locally at Wuhan': 'The local officials who are supposed to be immediately relaying the information [have] not allowed this to be done as rapidly as it should.'[28]

Earlier examples of cover-ups include the Great Famine of 1958–62, discussed in chapter twelve; the Cultural Revolution of 1966–76; and the student protests on Tiananmen Square on 4 June 1989 and their violent suppression, in the course of which about 2,600 people were killed. All three events have become unmentionable and they are indeed omitted from history textbooks used in schools. References to what is officially known by the euphemism 'the June 4 incident' of 1989 are discouraged by the regime. On the anniversary of 4 June, sensitive words are banned from the Internet, including 'today' or 'that year'. When the mother of a boy killed on 4 June gave an interview about it to a Hong Kong newspaper in 1991, she was warned that if she persisted, her musician husband might be forbidden to travel abroad. In Hong Kong, a June 4 Memorial Museum opened in 2012, but it was shut down four years later.[29]

The most memorable comment on the government's attitude is not verbal but pictorial. The Chinese cartoonist Badiucao, who now lives in Australia, illustrated the cover-up in a drawing entitled 'A Piece of Red Cloth' in 2014. Under the red cloth we see the shape of a tank, the equivalent of the elephant in the room.[30] It is of course impossible for the generations that experienced these three events to forget them, but later generations have been brought up in ignorance of what happened. The elephant is becoming smaller. For example, the photograph of a young man confronting a tank on the square is well known in the West but not in China. In 2016, a journalist showed the image of 'Tank Man' to students in four Chinese universities where students had taken a prominent part in the protest, and found that only fifteen out of a hundred students were able to identify the picture correctly.[31]

As for their elders, who were adults and often witnesses of the events of 1989, they generally collude with the regime in its pretence of ignorance, whatever their personal views about the events of 4 June. They know what not to know, or at least try to obliterate their knowledge.[32] In Freudian terms, official suppression is aided by unofficial repression of the truth. In 2013, the novelist Yan Lianke commented in the *New York Times* on the situation of Chinese intellectuals: 'You will be awarded power, fame and money as long as you are willing to see what is allowed to be seen, and look away from what is not allowed to be looked at . . . our amnesia is a state-sponsored sport.'[33] When the journalist Louisa Lim asked ordinary Chinese people about the 'incident', she received replies such as the following: 'This problem is quite sensitive. Let's not talk about it now. Let's live in today's world and not dwell on the past', or 'I have no thoughts about it . . . I just want to live a good life and earn some money. If you're always looking back, what's the point of that?'[34]

## SPYING

Attempts to discover or uncover secrets must be as old as secrets themselves, but these attempts have gone through several different phases between the sixteenth century and the early twenty-first. At the same time as keeping their own secrets, governments have done their best to crack the secrets of their enemies, their rivals, their allies and even their citizens, only to bury this information once again in secret reports. Early modern European governments already employed informers and spies, although spying was not so much a profession in that period as something that a merchant or diplomat might be asked to do in his spare time. His principal occupation provided a cover story.[35]

From the early nineteenth century onwards, we see both the professionalization and the specialization of spying together with the rise of the secret police and of secret services (both military and civilian, and concerned with both domestic and foreign affairs). In Russia, for instance, the notorious 'Third Section' was founded in 1826 in response to the unsuccessful revolt of the army officers known as the 'Decembrists'. Ten years later, it was keeping over 1,600 people under surveillance, as well as censoring plays. The Third Section was followed by the Department of State Police or Okhrana (1881), a response to the assassination of Tsar Alexander II. After the Bolshevik Revolution came the Cheka, founded in 1917 to investigate counter-revolution and sabotage; then the GPU/OGPU (1922), the NKVD (1934), the KGB (1954) and the FSB (1995).

It may seem odd to call these police forces 'secret', since they wore special uniforms and everyone knew of their existence. However, many of their operations were and are secret – arrests on the basis of secret reports from anonymous informers, secret trials and secret executions, sometimes on a massive scale, as in the case of the Katyn Forest massacre. When they thought that no one was listening, ordinary Russians sometimes referred to Stalin's NKVD as the 'Oprichnina', the private army in the service of the sixteenth-century tsar Ivan 'The Terrible' (*Ivan Grozny*), which killed people without trial or indeed without giving any reason. Sergei Eisenstein's film *Ivan the Terrible, Part 1* (1944) also implied a comparison with Stalin, and so the second part of the film was not released until 1958, as part of the campaign of 'destalinization'.[36]

Professionalization and specialization accelerated during and immediately after the First World War. Lenin's Cheka and the British MI5 date from that time, while in the USA the Espionage Act was passed in 1917.[37] The trends continued during the Second World War and the Cold War, with the growth of the CIA (founded 1947) and the KGB (1954). They went further still, at least in the USA, after 9/11.[38] It is above all the change in the scale of operations, including the increasing amount of information that is kept from the public, that makes the recent history of political secrets and lies different from earlier periods.[39] A worker in the Internet Research Agency in St Petersburg in 2014–15 later described it as 'a kind of factory', 'that turned lying . . . into an industrial assembly line'.[40]

The secret services – and their budgets – grow larger and larger. At its peak, the KGB had nearly half a million employees. The intelligence community in the USA (the CIA and fifteen other agencies) employs about 100,000 people today (2021), with an annual budget of about $50 billion (the share of the CIA is about $15 billion).[41]

The methods of these agencies for penetrating the secrets of others, while disguising their own operations, have become increasingly sophisticated. The traditional methods of obtaining secret information – infiltrating institutions, deciphering messages and bugging rooms – are now supplemented if not replaced by flying drones and hacking computers. The technology is constantly changing, as each new means of attack is countered by a new means of defence.

A traditional means of defence was the maintenance of secrecy about secrecy, for example the long-standing anonymity of the director-general of MI5. The policy was mocked by the Scottish writer Compton Mackenzie (a former MI6 officer whose memoirs had been suppressed under the Official Secrets Act) in a farce in which the director defends this anonymity on the grounds that 'if the head of the Secret Service is known, what chance do we stand against the enemy?'[42]

## UNCOVERING SECRETS

Attempts to uncover secrets of state have long been the concern of private individuals and dissident groups as well as of rival governments, but if publications on the subject are a reliable indicator, concern with what happens behind the scenes was growing in the later sixteenth century. The period 1550–1650 is known as an age of religious wars between Catholics, Lutherans and Calvinists, first in France and the Netherlands (including what is now Belgium) and later in Central Europe, the theatre of the Thirty Years War (1618–48). These wars were generally presented to the public as fought for religious reasons, but it was clear enough to some observers that religion was only a pretext, or in the more concrete language of the time, a 'mask' or 'cloak' to hide political aims such as the attempt of the King of Spain, Philip II, to dominate France.

In the seventeenth century, poets, dramatists, historians and philosophers all showed unusual concern with the gap between appearance and reality (*être/paraître, ser/parecer, Sein/Schein* and so on) and with the 'disillusionment' (*desengaño*) of those who perceived it. Books and pamphlets claimed to 'unmask', or 'unveil', secrets, to 'discover' (in the sense of 'uncover') them, or to open the box or 'cabinet' in which they were hidden. Among the secrets revealed in this way were those of the Jesuits, the Masons and of courts (Spain in the seventeenth century and France in the eighteenth).[43]

One of the masterpieces of historical writing in the early modern period was the *History of the Council of Trent* published in 1619 by the Venetian friar Paolo Sarpi. The Council, composed of bishops and theologians, was called to discuss the reform of the Catholic Church, including a reduction in the power of the popes. However, successive popes were able to manipulate the debates by the appointment of a chairman who would obey instructions regularly sent to him from Rome. Sarpi exposed what had been happening behind the scenes, making him a pioneer of what Italians now call *dietrologia*, the study of what lies behind appearances. It was for this reason that the poet John Milton called him 'the Great Unmasker of the Trentine Council', while a portrait of Sarpi now in the Bodleian Library Oxford describes him as 'Disemboweller of the Council of Trent' (*Concilii Tridentini Eviscerator*).[44] Sarpi believed in a conspiracy between the pope, the king of Spain and the Jesuits, threatening the independence of Venice. We know now that he exaggerated the cohesion of these three forces, but his vision of the gap between the public world of appearances and pretexts and the secret world of plots is a powerful and penetrating one. Like later whistleblowers, Sarpi tried to cover his traces, smuggling out his manuscript for publication in Protestant London in 1619 under a pseudonym, 'Pietro Soave Polano'. His secret history had its own secret history.[45]

Another masterpiece of historical writing was produced by Edward Hyde, Lord Clarendon, a former adviser to Charles I. The message of this account of the British Civil War, or as Clarendon called it, the 'Rebellion', may be summed up in a phrase from his autobiography: 'religion was made a cloak to cover the most impious designs' on the part of Parliament.[46] In similar fashion, the famous memoir of the court of Louis XIV by the Duc de Saint-Simon sometimes uses the language of the theatre, notably *scène* and *les derrières*.[47]

By the time that Clarendon's *History of the Rebellion* was published (posthumously, in 1702–4), the term 'secret history' had become a common one in several European languages. It was coined to describe a new genre of historical writing, claiming to describe what was really happening behind the public facade. Scores of these texts were published, anonymously or pseudonymously, between the late seventeenth and the early eighteenth centuries. The authors, who revelled in scandal, claimed to be insiders, eyewitnesses of intrigues at court, for instance, or in the conclaves in which popes were elected. There was a *Secret History of the Freemasons* and a *Secret History of the South Sea Scheme* (in other words, the Bubble). Sometimes the protagonists were given pseudonyms, leaving readers to guess their true identities. In the case of Mary Manley's *Secret History of Queen Zarah* (1705) it was easy enough to guess the identity of Queen Anne's favourite, Sarah, Duchess of Marlborough, whose shrewd analysis of the South Sea Bubble was quoted in chapter ten.

The secret historians worked to undermine the official version of events at a time when many governments employed official historians. Their authors were usually malicious, told some lies and passed on a good deal of unreliable information. However, these texts also made public a number of unofficial and uncomfortable truths. Hence it may be argued that these 'private eyes' made a serious contribution to the rise of the 'public sphere'.[48]

## FROM MUCKRAKERS TO WHISTLEBLOWERS

The mantle of the secret historians is now worn by investigative journalists, who have been active from the later nineteenth century onwards. In Britain, for instance, W. T. Stead exposed the practice of child prostitution in 1885 in a series of articles in the *Pall Mall Gazette* under the general title, 'The Maiden Tribute of Modern Babylon'.[49] He was, predictably, denounced as a 'muckraker'. Stead's equivalent in the USA was Lincoln Steffens, who was denounced in the same terms when he investigated municipal corruption in articles in a magazine that he edited, *McClure's*, in articles such as 'Shame of Minneapolis', 'Shamelessness of St Louis' and 'Philadelphia: Corrupt and Contented', bringing the muck to the public eye, or rather the public nose.[50] A third muckraker was Ida Tarbell, who also wrote for *McClure's*. Her articles exposing the ruthless methods of John D. Rockefeller were collected in her *History of the Standard Oil Company* (1904).[51]

Newspapers have remained important in bringing secret material to public notice, whether journalists discover it themselves or receive it from others, from officials to hackers. They are prominent among the individuals blowing whistles to warn the public than something suspicious is going on.

In 1969, as we saw in chapter nine, Seymour Hersh wrote an account of the massacre of Vietnamese civilians by American soldiers near My Lai. In 1971, the *New York Times* published the *Pentagon Papers*, secret documents on the role of the American government in Indo-China from 1945 to 1968 that had been leaked by Daniel Ellsberg, who was working for the RAND corporation. In 1972, Bob Woodward and Carl Bernstein, both of them reporters at the *Washington Post*, helped uncover the Watergate scandal, in other words the attempt to cover up the US government's involvement in the break-in to the headquarters of the Democratic National Committee, as well as the use of 'fake press leaks, fake letters'. The exposure of the cover-up forced the resignation of President Richard Nixon.[52]

In the twenty-first century, the rise of the Internet has meant that both the volume of leaks and the speed of their spread have increased to a degree scarcely imaginable before. Ellsberg, for instance, had to photocopy every page of the seven thousand pages of the documents he released, while in what has become known as 'Cablegate', the Australian activist and hacker Julian Assange simply downloaded 250,000 documents.[53]

In 2010, revelations about the war in Afghanistan and Iraq (as well as selections from confidential American diplomatic cables) were published in five newspapers: the *New York Times*, the *Guardian*, *Der Spiegel*, *El País* and *Le Monde*. The cables offered particularly rich evidence for links between the government and organized crime in Putin's Russia. This treasure trove of confidential information was provided by WikiLeaks, a website founded by Assange in 2006 and based in Iceland. The revelations simultaneously made Assange famous and put him in danger, flitting from place to place and on occasion disguising himself as a woman.[54]

Assange, who has made a career out of mediating between the world of secrecy and the world of journalism, did not stop in 2010. A year later, he published 779 secret documents about the prisoners held in Guantánamo Bay. In 2012, he was granted political asylum in the

Ecuadorian embassy in London to protect him from possible extradition to the United States on a charge of spying. Spying for whom? The obvious answer is an unusual one: 'spying for the public', supporting transparency and undermining trust in governments only insofar as this public trust had been based on ignorance. Assange remained in asylum, continuing to publish secret documents (some of them from the files of the CIA) until 2019, when the embassy allowed British police to arrest him. However, WikiLeaks continues to function.

The British historian Timothy Garton Ash, who described the cables published in 2010 as 'a banquet of secrets', 'the historian's dream' and 'the diplomat's nightmare', has offered a balanced commentary on the general issues raised by these leaks. On one side, 'There is a public interest in understanding how the world works and what is done in our name.' On the other, 'There is a public interest in the confidential conduct of foreign policy', since it is impossible to negotiate and make compromises with the media looking over one's shoulder. 'The two public interests conflict.' Garton Ash also pointed out that 'The *Guardian*, like the *New York Times* and other responsible news media, has tried to ensure that nothing we publish puts anyone at risk. We should all demand of WikiLeaks that it does the same.'[55]

In 2013, the government of the USA was embarrassed by still more revelations. Articles written by the American journalist Glenn Greenwald and published in both the *Washington Post* and the *Guardian* discussed the secret programmes of global surveillance by the National Security Agency. In 2020, Greenwald, who lives in Rio de Janeiro, was charged with 'cybercrimes' after publishing articles questioning the impartiality of Sérgio Moro, the chief prosecutor in an investigation of corruption in Brazil that was nicknamed 'Car Wash' (*Lava Jato*). In 2022, the Supreme Federal Court of Brazil confirmed the suggestion that Moro had been biased.

The long struggle between covering and uncovering has taken new forms in the twenty-first century. Fake news has gone online, and investigative journalism has followed it, as in the career of Eliot Higgins, who founded the website Bellingcat in 2014. Higgins and his team do their research online as well as communicating the results in this way. They became famous following their discoveries of what lay behind the Malayan Airlines plane crash in 2014 and the poisoning of Sergei Skripal in 2018 and Alexei Navalny in 2020.[56] Their methods offer an alternative to the two main ways in which secrets come to light today: leaking and hacking.

## LEAKS AND MOLES

From a retrospective point of view, leaks reveal the previous ignorance of the public, lifting the veil of secrecy about secrecy, including its scale.[57] A social history of leaks needs to ask, Who leaked What to Whom, through which Media, for What Purposes and with What Consequences?

Although leaks receive more publicity than they used to, the practice of divulging secret information is not new. In seventeenth-century Venice, for instance, where politics was supposed to be a monopoly of the patricians, copies of sensitive documents such as the reports of ambassadors might be offered for sale, finding their way into libraries in different parts of Europe, from Oxford to Vienna. Ironically enough, the government sometimes practised leaking. 'What was initially kept secret in order not to upset the public, was made public in order to influence the conduct of negotiators who were supposed to work in secret.'[58]

Leakers act for a variety of reasons: economic, moral and political. As he admitted, the desire for money drove Charles Marvin, a clerk in the British Foreign Office who doubled as a journalist, to sell the draft of a secret treaty with Russia to a newspaper, *The Globe*, in 1878.[59] On the other hand, in the last half century, individuals in government service, especially in Britain and the USA, have risked dismissal and prison by divulging official secrets, because they were shocked by what their employers were doing – attacking innocent civilians in Afghanistan and Iraq, torturing prisoners, tapping the phones of allies, and so on. They believed that the public should not be kept in ignorance of what had happened.

One of these whistleblowers did not contact the press. Clive Ponting, a British civil servant in the Ministry of Defence, was asked to write a secret report on the sinking of the Argentinian cruiser the *General Belgrano* during the Falklands War (the 'Malvinas War' for the Argentinians). He discovered that the cruiser had been attacked while it was outside the 'exclusion zone' set up by the British, since it was steaming away from the islands at the time. It followed that both the minister of defence and the prime minister (Margaret Thatcher) had lied to Parliament about this, since they had claimed that the *Belgrano* was approaching the zone when it was attacked. Ponting was so shocked by this discovery that in 1984 he sent the evidence for his discovery to a Member of Parliament, Tam Dalyell, whose investigations into what happened had been blocked by the government. After his resignation from the Civil Service in 1985 and his acquittal in a trial in which he was charged with a criminal offence under the Official Secrets Act, Ponting published a book about the affair.[60]

Another British civil servant, Sarah Tisdall, was not so lucky: she was sent to prison in 1983 for leaking to the *Guardian* documents about the arrival of American cruise missiles. Other whistleblowers who went to the press between 1971 and 2013 include Daniel Ellsberg, who leaked what became known as the 'Pentagon Papers' to the *New York Times*; Mark Felt, a senior official in the FBI, who used the pseudonym 'Deep Throat' to pass information about Watergate to the journalist Bob Woodward; Katharine Gun, a translator in GCHQ (Government Communications Headquarters) in Cheltenham, responsible for a leak to the *Observer* in 2003; Bradley Manning (now Chelsea Manning), a private in the US Army working as an intelligence analyst in Iraq, who furnished the material for Julian Assange to leak in 2010; and Edward Snowden.

Snowden is a former employee of the CIA and the National Security Agency, where his job was to monitor messages on the Internet. He became increasingly uncomfortable with the 'secret regime of mass surveillance', including what he was asked to do, which was contrary to the American Constitution, a copy of which he kept next to his computer, to the surprise of his colleagues. Snowden leaked material on the NSA's surveillance programmes to the journalist Glenn Greenwald. Accused of violating the US Espionage Act, Snowden sought political asylum, but his passport was cancelled by the US government while he was in mid-air. His career is the subject of a documentary film, *Citizenfour*, released in 2014, while he published his autobiography in 2019, explaining how he learned to hack, why he chose to blow the whistle and how he ended up in 'exile in a country that wasn't my choice' (Putin's Russia).[61]

## HACKERS

The rise of the Internet opened a new phase in the history of spies, moles and whistleblowers, since it was no longer necessary to break into an office in order to steal or to photograph documents that had been written, typed or printed on paper. All that was needed now was to hack into the secret files at home and send them out online.

Governments have made full use of the new facility. The CIA, for instance, has developed a series of hacking tools such as 'Weeping Angel', installed on TVs, and 'Pandemic', installed on computers. Whistleblowers have done the same. Manning, for instance, who has described himself (now herself) as a 'hacktivist', took advantage of the lax security in his unit in Iraq to copy secret material, placing it on the CD of music by Lady Gaga to which he had been listening in the office.

## DENIAL

Denial is a defence mechanism for both individuals and institutions confronted with 'information that is too disturbing, threatening or anomalous to be fully absorbed or openly acknowledged'.[62] Public denial is a form of disinformation, while private denial, or silent refusal to acknowledge, is a form of wilful ignorance, 'knowing what not to know'.

At government level, public denials have a long history. To return to the sixteenth century, the emperor Charles V lied when he denied that he had approved an attack on Rome in 1527 that had led to the imprisonment of the pope and the sack of the city, and he lied again when he denied that he had lied the first time.[63]

Denial became more frequent, or at least better known, in the twentieth century. Atrocities in warfare, such as those committed by the

Germans during the First World War, have often been denied by the perpetrators, and only revealed to the public much later.[64] The killing of more than a million Armenians by the Ottoman government in 1915, now known as the Armenian 'genocide', is still officially denied in Turkey. The government attempts to prevent the word 'genocide' being used in public in this context.[65]

In the United States, inconvenient information has often been officially denied, from the president downwards.[66] Again, as we saw in chapter seven, a small group of leading American scientists combined to cast doubt on a number of facts that were inconvenient for industry and the government from the 1950s to the 1980s. The facts included the existence of acid rain, the hole in the ozone layer and, above all, global warming.[67]

Formal denial of this kind is part of a larger phenomenon of not wanting to know, or wanting not to know, something that would threaten or embarrass the knower. It involves a conspiracy of silence, the collective ignoring of 'the elephant in the room'.[68]

In Germany during the Second World War, the civilians living near extermination camps such as Mauthausen did not want to know that the camps were there, since talk about them might lead to a visit from the Gestapo. Indeed, the SS explicitly warned civilians to look away from the prisoners and the trains that delivered them. Most of them 'learned to walk a narrow line between unavoidable awareness and prudent disregard', though the camp commandant complained about 'curious onlookers', and one lady complained to the police about the shooting of prisoners who were working in the quarries.[69]

The research of the historian Walter Laqueur has made it 'impossible to believe that no resident of Gleiwitz, Beuthen or Katowitz had any idea of what went on within a distance of a few miles from their homes', since the flames from the furnaces were visible miles away, not to mention the stench of burning corpses. As a resident of a village near the camp, interviewed in the 1970s, put it, 'We all knew about it.' More generally, too many people – camp guards, railway workers, civil servants and so on – were involved in the 'final solution' for the information to be kept secret.[70]

Laqueur concludes that 'The German experience shows that secrets cannot, in fact, be kept even in a totalitarian regime once they have percolated beyond a certain small group.' 'By the end of 1942, millions in Germany knew that . . . most or all of those who had been deported were no longer alive.' The task of maintaining ignorance was simply too great, even among a population with no wish to know. In other words, the death camps had become an open secret, or as some scholars now say, a 'public secret', a useful oxymoron to describe an ambiguous situation.[71] Despite so many attempts to combat it, Holocaust denial is still with us.

## THE BUSINESS OF DENIAL

Denial, like evasion, is all too common in business. It is obvious enough that the leaders of the oil industry, for instance, do not want to know about climate change. Exxon (later Exxon Mobil) supported research on the subject until 1978, when one of their scientists, James Black, reported the inconvenient conclusion that the use of fossil fuels was a major factor in global warming. The company cast doubt on his research, but this response has come to appear less and less plausible over the years. One might say that the climate of opinion has also changed in the last few decades, although Rupert Murdoch claims that the recent rise of bush fires in Australia was the work of arsonists. His newspaper *The Australian* still supports the denial of global warming, like his TV channels Sky News and Fox News.[72]

Industrial pollution and its deadly consequences have often been denied and covered up by the corporate perpetrators.[73] An example made famous by the film *Erin Brockovich* (2000) concerns the American law clerk of that name who brought a case against Pacific Gas & Electric for polluting drinking water in southern California and so causing cancer.

A particularly well-documented case of big companies refusing to accept the conclusions of scientists is of course the tobacco industry, which was confronted as early as 1950 with evidence for the link between smoking and lung cancer.[74] One of the reactions of the tobacco companies was outright denial, employing a public relations firm to commission an article in *True* magazine in 1968 entitled 'Cigaret [*sic*] Cancer Link is Bunk'.[75] Other responses were more subtle. One was sowing doubt, claiming for instance that the research was not 'conclusive'. A notorious speech from a vice-president of marketing tobacco in 1969 admitted that 'Doubt is our product.'[76]

Another method employed by the companies was to distract public attention from the link between smoking and cancer. For example, a Tobacco Industry Research Council was founded in order to conduct research on the causes of disease in general. This 'red herring research' was supposed to distract attention from the smoking–cancer link. The industry also continued to employ the traditional method of censorship, the 'suppression of research', especially 'when the investigator seemed to be getting too close to inconvenient truths'.[77]

These methods have sometimes been described as the 'manufacture' of ignorance. The study of letters from consumers to tobacco companies shows that 'many people have been profoundly ignorant about cigarettes'. One individual wrote that 'This idea of smoking being bad for one's health to me is a lot of malarky.'[78] However, the goal of the industry was 'not an absence of knowledge but rather the insinuation of a specific body of knowledge, or belief and feeling', that would support the sale of cigarettes.[79] It might therefore be more accurate in this case to speak of the maintenance of ignorance. Alternatively, one might refer to the production of 'misinformation', or (since the process was deliberate), of what the Russians were the first to call 'disinformation'.[80]

## DISINFORMATION

Ladislav Bittman, who defected from the Czech Secret Service after the Russian invasion of 1968, once defined disinformation as 'an elegant expression for activities called in plain English "dirty tricks"'.[81] Elsewhere he described it as 'the deception game' and defined it more formally as disseminating 'half-true, misleading or wholly false information to deceive the enemy'.[82] These practices are also known as 'political warfare', 'psychological warfare' or 'active measures', a euphemism invented in the USSR and itself a form of disinformation along with other euphemisms such as 'special projects' (including the assassination of critics of the regime). Putin's description of the invasion of Ukraine as a 'special operation' follows the KGB tradition. Disinformation both maintains ignorance and depends on ignorance for its success.

At this point a social historian needs to ask, Who exactly is being misled or disinformed? Foreign spies? Foreign governments? Or the general public, both abroad and at home? During the Cold War, for instance, disinformation, combined with secrecy, helped to keep ordinary citizens in the dark about what was happening on both sides of the Iron Curtain. The aims of disinformation included damaging the reputation of the enemy, as in the case of anti-Semitic incidents in West Germany that were later traced back to the East German intelligence service, the Stasi. Bittman himself confessed to participating in 'Operation Neptune', a spectacular attempt to plant secret Nazi documents (which had been sent to Czechoslovakia from a Soviet archive) in a lake in Bohemia and then to 'discover them' in 1965. The point of the operation was to discredit West Germany by reminding the world of Nazi war crimes twenty years after the war had ended.[83] Another major aim of the Communist intelligence services during the Cold War was to divide the enemy, including the different nations participating in NATO and the two conservative parties in West Germany, the CDU and the CSU.

The general aim of disinformers is to sow doubt and confusion among the enemy. On occasion, disinformation was also used as a substitute for kidnapping, as in the case of the secret agent Sidney Reilly (originally Rosenblum) who was born in Odessa and worked for the Russians before turning to the British. Reilly, who is said to have helped inspire Ian Fleming's James Bond, was invited back to Russia after 1917. Believing that his contact was anti-Bolshevik, he accepted the invitation. After his arrival, he was arrested and later executed.[84]

The Bolsheviks were not the first to use this trick, which goes back at least as far as the seventeenth century. Ferrante Pallavicino was a writer who became notorious for his satires on the Papacy. He was lured from his safe haven in Venice by a fake invitation to work for Cardinal Richelieu in Paris. He set off for France in 1642 but when passing through Avignon (an enclave of the Papal State at this time) he was arrested and executed.[85]

The methods of disinformers, like their aims, have been diverse. One traditional method is to spread false rumours. In 1979, for instance, when the Grand Mosque in Mecca was seized by radical Muslims, the KGB spread the news that the US government was secretly involved in the seizure, as well as a second story that the Pakistan government was behind the attacks on the US Embassy in Islamabad.[86] Another method is to produce printed propaganda, operating behind 'front' organizations such as the World Peace Council (1950), founded by the Comintern. Its opposite number, the Congress for Cultural Freedom, was founded in the same year and funded by the CIA, supporting the British monthly *Encounter* and many other journals.[87]

A third method was to interfere in elections in a hostile country, an all-too-topical subject since 2016. As far back as 1952, the CIA interfered in elections in the German Democratic Republic.[88] In 1980, the East German secret service, the Stasi, interfered in the West German elections, encouraging the split between the Christian Democrats and the Christian Social Union. All that was new in the Russian interference in the Hillary Clinton campaign in 2016 was the technology, including hacking into the email of the campaign chairman.[89]

## FORGERY

One of the most important methods of disinformation was and is forgery. A notorious example of the use of forgery in the service of disinformation is the so-called 'Zinoviev Letter' – which also offers an early instance of interference in elections. Grigory Zinoviev was head of the Communist International, the Comintern. A letter in his name addressed to the British Communist Party was published by a British conservative newspaper, the *Daily Mail*, four days before the General Election of 1924. The Labour prime minister Ramsay MacDonald suspected that the letter was not genuine, while Trotsky called it 'a document that cries aloud that it is a forgery'. All the same, the letter probably made a contribution to the defeat of the Labour government in the election. The identity of the disinformers is not known, but they are unlikely to have been Bolsheviks. The chief suspect, Ivan Pokrovsky, was an anti-Bolshevik, while the dissemination of the letter was apparently the work of individuals in the British Secret Services.[90]

Forgeries were used by both sides during the Cold War. The CIA, for instance, set up a front organization in the German Democratic Republic that produced forged issues of a variety of East German publications, including an astrological magazine. The CIA also commissioned the *Penkovsky Papers*, published in 1966 and apparently written by Oleg Penkovsky, a colonel in Soviet intelligence who passed secret material to the West. In fact this text was a semi-forgery, ghostwritten in English, although it did make use of taped conversations with the 'author'.[91]

On the other side, in 1957, *Neues Deutschland* (the official East German newspaper), published a letter claiming to be from Nelson Rockefeller to President Eisenhower, presenting a plan for the USA to dominate the world. The news was spread all over the world by Radio Moscow. After 1963, when the double agent Kim Philby was exposed and defected to the USSR, he was employed to make sure that forgeries of British documents were written in idiomatic English. Around 1970, the KGB published a forged supplement to the *US Army Field Manual* in order to embarrass the Americans. It revealed the names of CIA agents abroad and recommended the organization of 'special action', such as terrorist attacks, to convince the USA's allies that they were in danger. In 1985, the KGB launched a campaign to spread the theory that the USA had manufactured AIDS as part of a Pentagon experiment with biological weapons.[92]

Forged documents require a good deal of knowledge, not only of techniques but also of the events and people mentioned in them. Even minor mistakes undermine the authenticity of the document. Always ready to tell a story against himself and his former organization, Ladislav Bittman described a forgery by the Czechoslovak intelligence service of a letter from the US ambassador in Leopoldville addressed to Moïse Tshombe, aimed at demonstrating the existence of an American plot to return Tshombe to the Congo in July 1964. It was already too late when Bittman noticed 'two major errors' in the document, one in Tshombe's title (calling him 'President' instead of 'Prime Minister') and the other in the date of the letter, which was several days before Tshombe took office.[93] Ignorance of apparently minor details can have major consequences.

## POST-TRUTH

In the last few years, the idea has spread that we are living in a 'post-truth era' in which the public are maintained in ignorance not by silence but by a surfeit of lies, 'disinformation' that circulates in newspapers, on TV shows and, increasingly, online. The journalist Peter Oborne, citing examples from Tony Blair and Peter Mandelson, among others, has claimed that 'truth has become indistinguishable from falsehood' in British politics. A book with the title 'Post Truth' was published by another British journalist, Matthew d'Ancona.[94] Another phrase that has recently become popular is that of 'Fake News', popularized by the tweets of President Trump. Trump has claimed both that he invented the phrase and that the accusation that he won the election with Russian support is an example of the phenomenon.[95]

A similar claim, not quite so radical, is that we live in an age in which politicians and their advisers manipulate the facts rather than inventing them *ex nihilo*. A French TV series, *Les Hommes de l'ombre*, shown in 2012, centred on two rival figures of this kind. When the series was shown on British television in 2016, the title was translated as 'Spin' (another euphemism, since 'spinning' the news sounds better than an older term, 'twisting' it).[96]

The claim that we live in a new era is an arresting one, and the examples offered are certainly worrying. The problem with the claim is that the journalists who advance it assume that politicians used to tell the truth, without bothering to examine the England of Robert Walpole as well as that of Tony Blair, or the Russia of Stalin as well as of Putin. After all, it is over five hundred years since Machiavelli wrote his treatise on the prince, advising rulers to deceive both their enemies and their subjects. Machiavelli acquired a bad reputation with posterity for his advice, but he was only putting into words what the princes of his day, Charles V for instance, put into action.

Ideas and even the words that express them are often older than people think. A book on 'The Post-Truth Era' was published in 2004, while the phrase appears to have been coined twelve years earlier, in 1992. The phrase 'spin doctors', was employed in the *New York Times* in the 1940s.[97] In French, the phrase *fausses nouvelles*, not far from 'fake news', is a traditional one, like the English 'false reports'. Another traditional term is *canard*, discussed in Balzac's vivid description of the world of journalism in the Paris of his time. 'We call a *canard*,' a seasoned journalist explains to a neophyte, 'a fact that has the air of truth but is invented to sell the *Faits-Paris* [a newspaper] when the facts are insipid' (*Nous appelons un canard un fait qui a l'air d'être vrai, mais qu'on invente pour relever les Faits-Paris quand ils sont pâles*).[98]

An even older concept is that of 'lies'. The British journalist Jeremy Paxman, who has interviewed many politicians, has said that on each occasion he used to ask himself, 'Why is this lying bastard lying to me?' This phrase has also been attributed to an earlier journalist, the American Louis Heren.[99]

A more moderate claim than that of a 'post-truth' era comes from a study by two philosophers of science that was published in 2019. The authors remark that 'lying is hardly new, but the deliberate propagation of false or misleading information has exploded in the past century, driven both by new technologies for disseminating information – radio, television, the internet – and by the increased sophistication of those who would mislead us'.[100] The media spread not only 'disinformation' but also 'misinformation', the result of ignorance or carelessness rather than deliberate deception.

## THE PRESIDENT'S LIES

In a study published in 2004, it was claimed that 'In American politics today, the ability to lie convincingly has come to be considered an almost *prima facie* qualification for holding high office.' If this claim sounds exaggerated, it is worth remembering that in 1962, the assistant secretary of defense went so far as to claim that the government had a 'right' to 'lie to save itself', while in the age of George W. Bush, the Department of Justice argued for the right 'to give out false information'.[101]

Since 1945, most American presidents have lied to the people about matters of major importance. Franklin D. Roosevelt lied about concessions to Stalin made at Yalta concerning Poland and the Far East, while Harry Truman kept Roosevelt's secret. John F. Kennedy lied about the concessions made to Nikita Khrushchev at the time of the Cuban missile crisis – the removal of American missiles from Turkey as the price of the removal of Soviet missiles from Cuba. Lyndon Johnson lied about the beginning of the war in Vietnam, with reports 'intended to portray the Vietnamese as more aggressive than they had so far proven to be' and 'the United States as more pacific'. George W. Bush lied about Saddam Hussein's possession of weapons of mass destruction.[102] The lies told by Trump while in office are too many to enumerate here.

These lies have often had unexpected negative consequences. For example, 'McCarthyism drew considerable power from the Democrats' dishonesty about Yalta', which made it look as if Stalin had broken the agreement when he had not. Again, the denial by John and Robert Kennedy of the concessions made to Khrushchev was a lie that led to more lies, a decrease in official transparency and a consequent increase in distrust of the actions of the American government. This distrust, and Johnson's reluctance to allow an open debate about the Vietnam war, was bad for the reputation of the USA both at home and abroad.[103]

The current proliferation of 'fake news' is an alarming one, but the prospects for truth are not completely black. Just as cover-ups are followed by uncovering, so the lies current in the media are regularly exposed by fact-checking agencies on their websites.

A number of these agencies are active in the USA and the UK: Snopes.com, founded in 1994; FactCheck.org, founded in 2003 and owned by an American academic institution, the Annenberg School for Communication in Philadelphia; PolitiFact, founded in 2007, owned by the Poynter Institute for Media Studies in Florida and famous for its annual exposure of the 'Lie of the Year'; Full Fact, founded in the UK in 2009 by the businessman Michael Samuel; Bellingcat, founded by Eliot Higgins in 2014; and Media Bias/Fact Check, founded in 2015 by the journalist Dave Van Zandt.

Beyond the Anglophone world, these agencies include the German Faktenfinder (2017), the Italian Pagella Politica (2013), the Brazilian Aos Fatos (2015) and the Bolsonômetro, a kind of thermometer that measures the proportion of cold facts to hot air (not to mention lies) in the news bulletins of the president of Brazil.[104]

# 14

## UNCERTAIN FUTURES

Living means navigating in a sea of uncertainty

Edgar Morin

Uncertainty may be described as a kind of ignorance, ignorance of the future. As we have seen in the cases of business, politics and war, many important decisions have depended on what was expected to happen in the future. The trouble is that what actually happens is often very different from what was expected. Indeed, on occasion those consequences may be 'perverse', the exact opposite of what was intended.[1]

The side effects of medicines offer dramatic examples of perverse consequences. In politics, there are classic cases of reforms that led to the destruction rather than the preservation of the regime that passed them, making the people aware that change is possible and so whetting their appetite for more. One famous example comes from France in the years immediately before 1789, leading the political theorist Alexis de Tocqueville to conclude that 'experience teaches that the most dangerous time for a bad government is usually when it begins to reform'.[2]

Another famous example comes from Russia after 1905. Under a new prime minister, Pyotr Stolypin, peasants were given loans to buy land and trade unions were legalized. These reforms were followed by the Revolution of 1917. Closer to our own time, the reforms of Gorbachev, designed to maintain the system, led to the end of Communism and the dissolution of the Soviet Union in 1991.

There have been many attempts over the millennia to read the future – via oracle bones, for instance, the entrails of birds or the position of the planets.[3] In Renaissance Italy, for instance, astrology was taken seriously by many people, though rejected by some. The future was often viewed as the realm of fortune, whether imagined as a wheel on which individuals inevitably rose and fell or personified in the form of a goddess whose flowing hair represented an opportunity that might be grasped.

Alternatively, fortune was imagined as a wind, to which skilled sailors were able to adapt themselves by raising or lowering their sails. For this reason, the Rucellai, a merchant family of Florence, adopted the sail as their badge. Machiavelli agreed with this compromise between freedom and determinism, writing in the twenty-fifth chapter of *The Prince* that while fortune controls half our actions, the other half is free.[4]

These images became obsolete – 'Fortuna actually died' – in the seventeenth century, thanks to the 'taming of chance' by the mathematicians, whose calculations of probabilities, as we shall see in a moment, transformed the practice of insurance.[5] However, the goddess appears to have returned in our own age of the 'risk society' and 'radical uncertainty'.[6]

Analysts of risk study known unknowns in business, international relations or technology. Risk is supposed to be measurable in degrees of probability, like the weather forecast of 80 per cent chance of rain tomorrow. Risk management has become a profession, with its own periodicals like the *Journal of Risk Research*. 'The essence of risk management lies in maximizing the areas where we have some control.'[7] Investors, for example, diversify their portfolios, while many of us insure our houses and our lives.

The insurance industry has a long history. It began with insurance against shipwreck, followed by insurance against fire and then by insurance against an early death. Maritime insurance goes back to the Mediterranean world of the late Middle Ages, when the loss of cargoes by shipwreck was a common hazard. In the early modern Dutch Republic, France and England, maritime insurance included the lives of slaves on board ship, since they were treated as property in the laws of the time.[8] In Britain, 'marine underwriters' founded the Society of Lloyd's in 1771.

Memories of the Great Fire of London of 1666 were still vivid when the Fire Office was founded in 1680 by Nicholas Barbon, a physician turned speculative builder, in order to offer insurance for property. He was probably inspired by the example of the Hamburger *Feuerkasse*, founded in 1676 and said to be the first insurance company in the world. By the middle of the nineteenth century, British fire insurance was dominated by three large companies: Sun, Royal Exchange and Phoenix.[9]

Life insurance for individuals (apart from slaves) depended on the development of the mathematics of probability. In the Dutch Republic, two leading members of the ruling class, Jan de Witt and Johannes Hudde, applied this form of mathematics to schemes for selling life annuities by constructing tables of mortality.[10] Both the Dutch and the British governments raised money in this way, although 'no British government before 1789 appears to have made the cost of an annuity a function of the age of the purchaser'. Eighteenth-century insurance companies were 'ignorant of statistical methods . . . Experience counted; counting didn't.' Insurance therefore remained something of a gamble, 'betting on lives'.[11] The lack of knowledge of probable outcomes was shared by many purchasers of annuities in both the Dutch Republic and Britain. This case of 'investor ignorance' resembles that of the South Sea Bubble, discussed earlier, though on a smaller scale.

Whether or not a given individual will still be alive in thirty years is anyone's guess, but if the same question is asked about a large enough group of people, it is possible to work out the percentage of survivors and so set a price that allows a profit. This process has been described as the 'taming of chance'.[12] Thanks to mathematicians such as Jacques Bernoulli, whose book *The Art of Conjecturing* was published posthumously in 1713, life insurance became a successful industry in Britain in the eighteenth century and in the USA in the nineteenth. Where astrologers had drawn up horoscopes for individuals, actuaries now analysed more reliable general trends.[13]

Increasing doubt has been expressed about attempts to measure risk, which are 'fundamentally limited by ignorance'.[14] An age of confidence in measures of risk is being replaced by an age of uncertainty. Analysts of uncertainty, especially of what has become known as 'radical uncertainty', are concerned with incalculable unknowns. A well-known book by Nassim Taleb, whose job description is 'Professor of the Sciences of Uncertainty', argues that 'our world is dominated by the extreme, the unknown, and the very improbable'. A similar case has been argued by the economists John Kay and Mervyn King, whose ideas are discussed in this chapter.[15]

Another well-known book, by the German sociologist Ulrich Beck, is entitled 'Risk Society' (*Risikogesellschaft*, 1986), a concept that was launched by this lucid and provocative essay. Beck claimed to have discovered a new kind of modernity and a new kind of society, visible from the later twentieth century onwards. In the age of the first modernity, he argued, industrialization solved problems, but in the age of the second modernity, it turned into the problem.

Threats to the environment, for instance, are by-products or side effects of industrialization, 'hazards and insecurities induced and introduced by modernization itself' (it seems appropriate that Beck's book should have appeared in the same year as the Chernobyl disaster).[16] The author concluded that 'the calculation of risk as it has been established so far by science and legal institutions *collapses*'. For this reason, it has been suggested that a more exact title for his book would have been 'Danger Society'.[17]

A study of risk from an anthropological point of view, published four years before Beck, offered a different perspective, suggesting that 'The perception of risk is a social process' and that each 'type of society . . . focusses concern on particular dangers', selected 'to conform with a specific way of life'.[18]

In similar fashion, from a historian's point of view, all societies appear to be 'risk societies', though each period has its own package of risks. In preindustrial times, which Beck did not discuss, the package included major plagues, famines and wars, as well as the everyday risks of being stabbed in the street or tavern or becoming a victim of witchcraft. Some of these risks were unavoidable uncertainties, but others were the result of individual or collective decisions. Travellers were advised to make their wills before deciding to make a voyage by sea, while municipal governments needed to decide how much grain to store against the possibility of famine.[19] In the Middle Ages, some of these risks were already global. The Mongols ravaged both Europe and Asia in the thirteenth century and so did the plague known as the 'Black Death' a century later.

Despite these qualifications, Beck's point about the shift from measurable risks to incalculable uncertainties, like the points made by Taleb and others, provokes further reflection. In 'World at Risk' (*Weltrisikogesellschaft*, 1997) and especially in its later editions, Beck revised and developed his ideas. In the light of 9/11, he now described terrorism and finance as major threats and placed more emphasis on the globalization of major risks, which do not respect national frontiers.

In a challenge to the insurance industry, Beck emphasized the incalculability of the new threats to society. 'The absence of adequate *private* insurance protection is *the* institutional indicator of the transition to the uncontrollable risk society of the second modernity.'[20] Beck admitted that it was possible to take precautionary measures against catastrophe, but he claimed that 'The preventive measures against catastrophic risks themselves trigger catastrophic risks, which may in the end be even greater than the catastrophes to be prevented' (he was writing before the American invasion of Iraq in 2003, but that event offers a vivid illustration of his point). Beck's conclusion was that 'Non-knowledge rules in a world risk society'.[21]

At this point it may be illuminating to distinguish between risk, which is the realm of forecasting, and uncertainty, which is the domain of futurology. These two approaches to the future will be discussed in order.

## FORECASTING

Forecasting harvests, the weather and economic trends became everyday activities in the USA from the 1860s onwards, a 'culture of prediction' encouraged by the financial panic of 1907. The meteorologist Henry

H. Clayton offered regular forecasts of business cycles as well as the weather. In France, the astronomer Urbain Le Verrier, best known for his discovery of the planet Neptune, was also a pioneer in the organization of weather forecasts.[22]

Planning for the future by governments (especially socialist ones) became increasingly common in the nineteenth and twentieth centuries. It included economic planning, town planning and planning for defence.[23] In the USSR, five-year plans for the economy were regularly launched from the late 1920s until the regime came to an end. In 1946, the French government, advised by the many-sided Jean Monnet, established a planning commission (Commissariat Général du Plan) for the reconstruction of postwar France. Ministries of planning can be found in countries such as India, Pakistan, Myanmar and Cambodia.

As for defence, the Norwegian government includes a Department of Defence Policy and Long-Term Planning. In the USA, forecasting has been funded by RAND (a think tank founded in 1948 for research on behalf of the armed forces) and IARPA, an organization within the American intelligence community. As the intelligence analyst Thomas Fingar suggests, although uncertainty cannot be avoided, it can be reduced by spending money on research 'to anticipate problems, identify opportunities and avoid mistakes'.[24]

It is of course possible to extrapolate from past trends to possible future ones, extrapolation being a systematic form (if not a fancy name) for what we do all the time, making plans that assume that the sun will rise tomorrow or that the London Underground will be crowded at 'rush hour'. Demographers, economists and civil servants have done this for centuries, analysing trends in their own countries or looking in the direction of a nation such as the United States where, as a German analyst argued in 1952, the future 'is already here'.[25]

However, we learn from history that trends do not always continue. Every so often there arrives what Nassim Taleb has christened a 'Black Swan', a highly improbable event with an extreme impact – a Big Surprise such as the Great Crash or the fall of the Berlin Wall.[26] As

Stuart Firestein remarked, 'one of the most predictable things about predictions is how often they're wrong'.[27] Indeed, all that we can be sure of is that we cannot be sure, so we have to learn to expect the unexpected. As the French sociologist Edgar Morin said in an interview in 2020, 'Living means navigating in a sea of uncertainty.'[28]

It might be said that the study of the future is both necessary, in order to plan, and impossible, because what is to come remains uncertain. Making a plan for the future and sticking to it, come what may, is both arrogant and dangerous, though it is equally arrogant and dangerous not to prepare for possible catastrophes, including what the philosopher Nick Bostrom calls 'existential catastrophes', the 'Big Ones' that would affect not only the present but the future as well, destroying 'humanity's long-term potential'.[29] Fortunately, it is possible to distinguish different degrees of uncertainty. Decision-makers who concern themselves with the near future are more likely to make correct predictions than futurologists concerned with events that are further away. Forecasting has been particularly common – and controversial – in two domains, politics and economics.

## POLITICAL RISKS

In the study of politics, a major debate continues. On one side there are scholars who believe that politics is a science in which situations recur and predictions are possible, and on the other, those who claim that every event is unique and unpredictable.[30] Two important studies, both of them published in the 1960s but still worth reading today, occupy the middle ground. The first, by Thomas Schelling, a professor of international relations, drew on game theory to discover the best strategies to pursue in conflicts. Schelling argued that conflicts are analogous to games in which information about the other players is 'imperfect', in other words a situation of partial ignorance.[31]

The second study, by the historian Saul Friedländer, pointed out that 'forecasting is an essential prerequisite of action' and argued that it is both difficult and possible. It is difficult because decision-makers in one country are ignorant of the aims of their opposite numbers in another country. It is possible because the freedom of each decision-maker (whether an individual or a small group) is reduced by the aims that are chosen. This freedom 'shrinks' with each step taken.[32] Friedländer also noted the importance of imagining scenarios. 'In most cases the observer can list the different possibilities open to the actor he is observing.' Describing the attempts of Kennedy and Khrushchev to read each other's intentions during the Cuban missile crisis, the author stresses the need to 'see the situation through the eyes of the actor under observation' and to be aware of the personal 'style' of decision-makers, their particular patterns of behaviour. It has been argued that failure to do this was one of the basic flaws in the American intelligence estimate of the probability of the existence of weapons of mass destruction in Saddam Hussein's Iraq.[33]

To achieve a sense of this personal style requires what Friedländer calls 'intuition'.[34] Intuition is also emphasized in a book by the psychologist Philip Tetlock, published half a century after Friedländer's essay.[35] Tetlock led the Good Judgment Project, launched in order to identify successful forecasters and to analyse their methods. He asked for volunteers and organized tournaments in which each of these volunteers, more than twenty thousand altogether, made hundreds of forecasts of future events – whether a foreign military would carry out operations within Syria before 1 December 2014, for instance, or whether there would be less ice in the Arctic sea on 15 September 2014 than on the same date a year earlier. The 'future', in the case of this project, was more limited than Friedländer's, since it extended no further than five years and was generally restricted to a year or so ahead.

Thanks to these tournaments, Tetlock was able to identify a small group of what he calls 'superforecasters', amateurs who consistently made more accurate predictions than the professionals. These amateurs spent much time investigating the questions they were asked to answer and regularly updated their estimates until the deadline. They excelled in 'probabilistic thinking' and also in intuition, in the sense of 'pattern recognition' based on knowledge that is apparently forgotten yet remains ready for use when needed.

## ECONOMICS

In economics as in politics there has been a long debate about the possibility and the limits of predictability. A recent study by two senior economists, John Kay and Mervyn King, confessed that in their youth, they learned to approach problems via mathematical models. By this means, 'behaviour could be predicted by evaluating the "optimal" solution to those problems'. However, their practical experience led the authors to question this approach because businesses, governments and households all confront 'an uncertain future', knowing that they do not know what is going to happen.[36] Hence Kay and King advocate the replacement of mathematical models by a focus on uncertainty in economic life.

In similar fashion, a century earlier, the American economist Frank Knight had distinguished risks, which could be measured, from uncertainty, which could not. Knight criticized the assumption of the 'practical omniscience' of economic actors and emphasized the element of surprise.[37] A few years after Knight, John Maynard Keynes made the same point in a characteristically memorable way, writing that 'The prospect of a European war is uncertain, or the price of copper and the rate of interest twenty years hence, or the obsolescence of a new invention . . . About these matters, there is no scientific basis on which to form any calculable probability whatever. We simply do not know!'[38]

Keynes also wrote about the need 'to defeat the dark forces of time and ignorance which envelop our future'. A similar emphasis on time and ignorance, as well as unintended consequences, can be found in the writings of some Austrian economists, from Joseph Schumpeter to Friedrich von Hayek. They criticized neo-classical economists both for ignoring change and for assuming that economic agents act with perfect knowledge, an assumption that is as unrealistic as that of perfect competition.[39]

Yet another contribution to the study of uncertainty came from the British economist George Shackle. Shackle has been described by the risk analyst Nassim Taleb as a 'great underestimated thinker', adding that 'It is unusual to see Shackle's work mentioned at all, and I had to buy his books from second-hand dealers in London.'[40] These books emphasized what the author called 'unknowledge' and discussed how to deal with it.

## FUTUROLOGY

While forecasters generally study the next year or two (or even five), the futurologists or futurists are concerned with the longer term, twenty or thirty years or more. Futurology requires – among other qualities – a strong imagination, so it is no surprise to find novelists engaging in this enterprise, among them Jules Verne in France and in Britain H. G. Wells, whose novel *The Shape of Things to Come* (1933) described events up to the year 2106.[41]

A few writers of fiction have made successful predictions. Verne imagined a moon landing and a submarine, while Wells, who had been trained in biology, imagined genetic engineering. A few years before the First World War, Wells predicted the use of tanks (which he called 'Land Ironclads') as well as 'war in the air'. More recently, Arthur C. Clarke, best known for his collaboration with Stanley Kubrick in *2001: A Space Odyssey* (1968), predicted both online banking and online shopping.

Wells also wrote non-fiction, including a series of articles in the *Fortnightly Review* in 1901, published in book form as *Anticipations of the Reaction of Mechanical and Scientific Progress upon Human Life and Thought*. His book was an early contribution to futurology, a term that was actually coined (in German, *Futurologie*) by the lawyer Ossip Flechtheim in 1943. Another contribution came from the American sociologist William Ogburn, a member of the research committee on recent social trends set up by President Hoover. Asked by the *New York Times* in 1931 to offer predictions for the year 2011, Ogburn suggested that government would have more impact on people's lives and that the lives of women would be closer to those of men.

Long-term predictions became more common from the late 1950s onwards. Like science fiction, they helped the public to imagine alternative future scenarios.[42] Three Frenchmen made important contributions to this growing field. Gaston Berger, whose interests included both philosophy and management, coined the term 'prospective' (the complementary opposite of 'retrospective'). He founded a centre for its study in 1957. Bertrand de Jouvenel, a political philosopher, edited a collection of essays entitled *Futuribles* (neatly combining the idea of possible futures into a single word). A third Frenchman, the economist Jean Fourastié, based his estimates of future trends on the study of past centuries rather than the last few decades.[43]

By the 1960s, futurology had become an international enterprise. In 1967, Herman Kahn, who worked for the American Research and Development Corporation (known as RAND), published a book on *The Year 2000*, subtitled 'a framework for speculation on the next thirty-three years'.[44] This was also the time of the launch of the journal *Futures* (1968) and the foundation of the World Future Society (1966), the Club of Rome (1968) and the Copenhagen Institute for Futures Studies (1969).

From this point onwards it may be useful to distinguish between four main groups involved in the study of the future. One group has been associated with government, especially but not exclusively the intelligence community. In the early 1970s, for instance, the Swedish government funded a Secretariat for Futures Studies. In the 1990s, the American intelligence community began producing studies of global trends twenty years ahead. Research for the volume on the year 2025 began in 2004, and the book was published in 2008.[45]

A second group has been especially concerned with the technology of the future and social consequences of its use. The group included the sociologist Daniel Bell, who predicted the rise of 'post-industrial society' and the impact of computers on everyday life.[46] It also included a number of inventors, who like both to imagine and to shape the future. The engineer Dennis Gabor, for instance, claimed that although 'the future cannot be predicted', 'futures can be invented'. In this second group, the most remarkable figure was surely the polymath Buckminster Fuller, (known as 'Bucky'). Among many other things, Fuller was the designer of a mass-produced house; of an automobile that was supposed to travel with equal ease on land, sea and air; and of 'geodesic domes' that could be erected over spaces of different sizes, from a greenhouse to a city.[47] These domes, light but strong, are attracting renewed attention today as a possible means for the inhabitants of cities to cope with climate change.

A third group of futurologists comes from business, is concerned with corporate strategy and has included the management consultant Peter Drucker – who once remarked that 'the best way to predict the future is to create it' – Peter Schwartz, founder of Global Business Network; and Peter Fisk, founder of GeniusWorks. A fourth group, less optimistic than the second and third, has been concerned with the limits to economic growth and the future of the environment. It includes members of the Club of Rome such as Donella and Dennis Meadows and Jørgen Randers. It was in 2013 that Randers, a Norwegian systems analyst, published his 'global forecast' for the year 2052.

The most recent recruits to futures studies come from philosophy and include Nick Bostrom and Toby Ord. They work at the Future of Humanity Institute at Oxford, founded in 2005 and concerned with 'existential risk', in other words the risk of human extinction or at least of a drastic reduction in the potential of humanity. Bostrom and Ord are among the analysts who try to turn speculative futurology into careful forecasting. The gap between short-term forecasting and long-term futurology appears to be diminishing, as students of the future focus on the medium term – in other words, the next few decades, or at most the next hundred years.

Ord, for instance, discusses 'natural' risks such as a meteorite striking earth or a ' "super-volcanic" eruption', but focuses on five major threats: nuclear weapons, climate change, environmental damage, pandemics (whether natural or 'engineered') and what the author describes as 'unaligned artificial intelligence', in the event that AI, still a servant of humanity, will one day become its master. Shane Legg, the founder of DeepMind, a company that builds AI systems, has called this 'my number one risk for this century'.[48]

The methods employed in these 'futures studies' are as various as the groups involved in them.[49] Bertrand de Jouvenel wrote about 'the art of conjecture', while Herman Kahn described his account of the year 2000 as 'speculation'. The base for the edifice of conjecture used to be the analysis of statistics, extrapolating from trends in the recent past to trends in the future. Since the 1970s, however, increasing use has been made of computer simulation. The Club of Rome, for instance, employed computer models of what they called 'World 3', updating the 'World 2' model of the computer engineer Jay Forrester in order to calculate the effects of future interactions between population, industry and environment and so estimate the limits to economic growth. Humanity is still navigating in a sea of uncertainty, but at least, so far as our environment is concerned, it now possesses the equivalent of an astrolabe.

If threats to the environment can be estimated with some degree of probability, threats that result from human action cannot. Unlike Andrei Amalrik, a Russian dissident writing twenty years earlier, scholars studying the Soviet Union generally failed to predict its break-up in 1990. Amalrik had predicted a crisis in the Soviet system, extrapolating from the rise of the 'Cultural Opposition', 'passive discontent' and the 'nationalistic tendencies of the non-Russian peoples of the Soviet Union'. He suggested alternative scenarios (including war with China) and cited parallels to the conditions that led to the revolutions of 1905 and 1917.[50]

The futurologist Herman Kahn, writing in 1970, put his money on the rise of the Japanese economy, claiming that by the year 2000 it would equal or surpass that of the USA. He did not imagine the possible rise of China.[51] Economists generally failed to predict the Great Crash of 1929. They also failed to foresee the 'awful' banking crisis of 2008 – as the queen remarked at the time.

The problem with extrapolating from current trends is that they sometimes go into sudden reverse, like the prices of shares in the stock market or, to take Nassim Taleb's memorable example, the expectation of future meals on the part of turkeys who are fed well just before Thanksgiving.[52] If we read the predictions of futurologists decades after they have been made, the failures spring to our eyes. Writing about risks is itself a risky business. That these risks can be reduced, to a certain extent, by the study of the past is the central argument of the following chapter.

# 15

## IGNORING THE PAST

Fools say that they learn from experience. I prefer to profit by
others' experience

attributed to Bismarck

This chapter will explore ignorance of the past on the part of three
different groups. In the first place are historians, who never know as
much about the past as they would like, and often less than they think
they do. In the second place, the general public, whose ignorance, like
the ignorance of voters, has been the object of some recent surveys. In
the third place, the most important, the ignorance of decision-makers,
who often fail to learn from their predecessors. Ignoring the past, they
make the same mistakes all over again.

### HISTORICAL SCEPTICISM

Ernst Gombrich, who had a gift, like a number of Viennese intellectuals, for a sharp and witty phrase, used to tell his students that 'history
is like a Swiss cheese, full of holes'.[1] On the map of the past, there are
many blank spaces. For the history of many parts of the world in many
periods, the sources are sparse, if not almost entirely lacking. Awareness
of this problem, together with the rediscovery of the ancient philosopher Sextus Empiricus (discussed in chapter two), underlay the movement of historical scepticism or 'pyrrhonism' in Europe from the

sixteenth to the eighteenth centuries, a campaign to reveal ignorance of the past in general and the history of the ancient world in particular.

In 1528, the famous Spanish preacher and moralist Antonio de Guevara published a semi-fictional biography of the emperor Marcus Aurelius. When he was criticized for inventing historical details, Guevara defended himself by claiming that so far as secular and pagan histories are concerned 'we have no certainty that some [historians] tell the truth more than others'.[2] Later in the century, Sir Philip Sidney defended poetry against its critics by launching an attack on history, mocking the historian 'loden with old mouse-eaten records', but 'for the most part authorizing himself on the notable foundations of hearsay'.[3]

The mid-seventeenth century was a moment when the possibility, the limits and the foundations of historical knowledge became a matter of particularly vigorous debate, especially though not exclusively in France. In his *Discourse on Method* (1637), René Descartes argued that the works of historians were useless or even dangerous. He compared them to the fashionable romances of chivalry, since they omitted apparently trivial circumstances (*les plus basses et moins illustres circonstances*) and so encouraged readers 'to fall into the extravagances of the paladins of our romances', making plans that it was beyond their power to execute.[4]

The problem of 'the uncertainty of history' was discussed in more detail by the philosopher François La Mothe Le Vayer in a controversial study, *Du peu de certitude qu'il y a dans l'histoire* (1668). The debate on the subject was even more vigorous a generation later in the age of the sceptic Pierre Bayle, although it rumbled on well into the eighteenth century, when Voltaire published an essay on *Le Pyrrhonisme de l'Histoire* (1768).[5] The 'pyrrhonists', as they were known at the time, offered two main arguments. The first was the argument from bias and the second, the argument from lack of evidence.

What historians still call 'bias' (a metaphor from the game of bowls) takes us back to the problem of standpoints, discussed, as we have seen, by the sociologist Karl Mannheim in the 1920s and by feminists in the 1980s but going back at least as far as the seventeenth century. What would our image of the Punic Wars be today, asked La Mothe Le Vayer, if we only had access to an account from the Carthaginian point of view? How would Caesar's Gallic Wars appear to us if Vercingetorix and not Caesar had been the one to write his memoirs?[6]

As for Bayle, he compared the work of historians to that of cooks. 'History is treated something like the food in a kitchen . . . every nation, every religion, every sect takes the same raw facts . . . and seasons them according to its taste' (*l'on accommode l'Histoire à peu près comme les viands dans une Cuisine . . . chaque nation, chaque Religion, chaque Secte prend les mêmes faits tout cruds . . . et les assaisonne selon son goût*). Hence (so Bayle claimed) he hardly ever read historians to learn what happened in the past, but only to discover 'what is said in each nation and in each party'. What interested him in a particular historian was precisely the prejudice.[7]

Voltaire was not saying anything new but summing up more than a century of debate when he discussed the problem of bias in his essay on *Historical Pyrrhonism* (1769). He even used La Mothe's example of the influence of Caesar's memoirs on posterity's view of the Punic Wars. 'In order to judge fairly,' he wrote, 'it would be necessary to have access to the archives of Hannibal's family.' Since he was Voltaire, he could not resist wishing that he could also see the memoirs of Caiaphas and Pontius Pilate.[8]

The second major argument employed by the sceptics was the argument from the lack of evidence for many events in the past, together with the claim that some sources that had previously been regarded as reliable were not to be trusted and may even have been forged. A French Jesuit named Jean Hardouin went so far as to claim that the majority of classical texts were forgeries. Hardouin would be diagnosed as paranoid today, since he believed in a conspiracy to forge texts. He may have been a suitable case for treatment, but he was only an extreme example of a general trend, combining the doubts already expressed about many of these documents with a few of his own.[9]

The case of Hardouin shows vividly how these specific challenges might have a cumulative effect. It is no wonder that the adjective 'critical' became a fashionable one in book titles in the later seventeenth century. An increasing amount of what had been generally accepted as true history – the foundation of ancient Rome by Romulus, for example, the lives of certain saints, or the foundation of the French monarchy by Pharamond, was now dismissed as invention, as myth.

An important example of the new historical criticism was the work of the Huguenot scholar Louis de Beaufort, *Dissertation sur l'incertitude des cinq prèmiers siècles de l'histoire romaine* (1738). We have returned to the problem of the Swiss cheese, combined with that of the unreliability of surviving sources for the history of the remote past, in this case the historian Livy, writing at the time of the birth of Christ about events that took place, if they took place at all, some seven hundred years earlier.[10] Historians had to admit that they knew less about earlier centuries than they had claimed, that their sources were less reliable than they had assumed and that, even at best, their statements lacked the certainty to be found in mathematics.[11]

Ignorance of the past was emphasized once again in the 'post-modern' age, when historiography (if not history) appeared to be repeating itself. A second crisis of historical consciousness became visible, in which, curiously enough, three French philosophers once again played a leading role.

The trio of Descartes, La Mothe and Bayle was replaced by that of Michel Foucault, Jacques Derrida and Jean-François Lyotard. Doubts about the existence of Caesar, for instance, were replaced by doubts about the reality of the Holocaust and the whole past was sometimes viewed as a cultural 'construction'. In apparent ignorance of the parallel, partici-pants in the debate in the 1990s echoed their predecessors in the 1690s.[12]

## SELECTIVE IGNORANCE

More important in the long run than radical doubt was the discovery of the 'selective ignorance' mentioned in chapter one, notably the realization that history has been written for the most part by elites, about elites and for elites. Roman history was written by senators for senators, Chinese history by mandarins for mandarins, and medieval European history (for a time) by monks for monks. The history of other kinds of people has often been rejected as not worth knowing – usually implicitly but occasionally in so many words – as an affront to the 'dignity of history' (a classical phrase that was still in use in the early twentieth century).

In the 1820s, when the great Russian writer Alexander Pushkin was studying the history of the peasant revolt led by Yemelyan Pugachev, the tsar, Nicholas I, told him, 'such a man has no history'. In the 1950s, when a British historian wrote his dissertation on a popular movement that formed part of the French Revolution, his examiner – Lewis Namier, no less – asked him, 'Why do you bother with these bandits?'[13]

Historical research in the twentieth century offers a number of cases of selection. Early in the century, it focused on political events, viewed from above, from the perspective of the leaders. This kind of history was rejected as superficial by economic historians who focused on structures and trends rather than events or individuals. In a later generation, social historians rejected economic history as reductionist. In the 1960s, history from below, as written by Edward Thompson and Eric Hobsbawm – who quite literally bothered with bandits – focused on ordinary people, the ruled rather than the rulers, including their point of view as well as their lives and sufferings. If history from below began with working-class men, it soon came to include women's history as well.[14]

As we have seen in earlier chapters, new knowledge has led to increasing awareness of past ignorance – ignorance of the history of the working class, of the peasants, of women and still more recently, of the environment.

## THE IGNORANCE OF THE PUBLIC

Like the ignorance of politics, ignorance of history has been the object of surveys. In 2015, for instance, a survey of a sample of the British public showed that 'three out of four Britons have little or no knowledge of the battle of Waterloo. Young people think Waterloo is an Abba song; older people know it as a railway station . . . many name Francis Drake or Winston Churchill, rather than the Duke of Wellington, as the architect of victory, and quite a few think that the French won.'[15]

In the USA, Gallup Youth Surveys conducted in 1977 and 2000 showed that 'knowledge of world history has slipped', with fewer respondents able to associate Hitler with Germany, Napoleon with France or Churchill with England. Another survey of the year 2000, concerned this time with American history, found that only 42 per cent of respondents knew that 1492 was the year that Columbus discovered America, while 56 per cent did not know the date of American independence.[16]

The situation may be getting worse, but the problem is not a new one. A Gallup poll of 1996 showed that less than 25 per cent of British sixteen- to twenty-four-year olds knew that it was Christopher Wren who designed St Paul's Cathedral, and only 10 per cent knew which English king signed Magna Carta. A book entitled *1066 and All That*, first published in 1930 and now a classic, is among other things a hilarious account of 'all the history you can remember', in other words mistakes about the past based on the experience of one of the authors, Walter Sellar, who taught history in English schools for most of his career.

If the pupils are often ignorant of the past, this is not always because they were absent or asleep during lessons. Their textbooks may be at fault. A study of twelve textbooks of American history intended for use in schools might be described as '1492 and All That', although it actually bears the even more catchy title, *Lies My Teacher Told Me*. In fact, the sins committed by the authors of these texts are not so much lies as inaccuracies and, above all, sins of omission, such as failing to mention that Columbus was not the first to explore the New World, since 'People from other continents had reached the Americas many times before 1492'. Again, 'while textbooks now show the horror of slavery and its impact on black America, they remain largely silent regarding the impact of slavery on white America, North or South'.[17]

Ignorance of history on the part of voters, a kind of collective amnesia, sometimes has important consequences. Take the case of Spain at the time of writing (2021). The return to democracy after the death of Franco was assisted by memories of the Civil War, when the Left was defeated largely because it was divided. Memories of that defeat encouraged different parties to work together in the 1970s. Now that virtually no one alive remembers the Civil War, Spanish democracy appears to be becoming more fragile.

## THE IGNORANCE OF DECISION-MAKERS

Historians are often asked by their friends, relatives and students, What is the use of history? The question becomes easier to answer if it is reversed, translated into What are the dangers of ignorance of history? Investors with a knowledge of history have a better chance of avoiding losses in the stock market. Economic booms and crashes recur, often for the same reasons, among them the reckless offer of credit and the promises of unscrupulous manipulators of the market. Investors in the dot.com share market in the 1990s would have been well advised to read about earlier bubbles, including two that were analysed in chapter ten, the South Sea Bubble in Britain in 1720 and the bubble that preceded the 'Great Crash' of the New York stock market in 1929. The celebrated American economist John Kenneth Galbraith studied the Great Crash on the grounds that, 'As a protection against financial illusion or insanity, memory is far better than law.' His phrase about an 'immunizing memory' is itself a memorable one. Galbraith also suggested that after everyone who experienced a disaster is dead, history is able to do the work of memory.[18]

History does not repeat itself, but some types of situation recur, making certain future scenarios more probable than others. On various occasions decisions taken by statesmen and generals in ignorance of past experiences have had unfortunate if not disastrous consequences. Take the case of the Bengal Famines of 1770 and 1943. The journalist Kali Charan Ghosh, writing about official responses to both disasters, noted that 'all the sins of omission and commission . . . were repeated in every detail'.[19]

As we saw in chapter nine, the consequences of ignorance are most immediately obvious in the history of war. Commanders are often criticized for attempting to fight the last war over again and taking too little account of the differences between past and present. However, some of them make mistakes for the opposite reason, ignoring the lessons of the past.

Take the case of two major invasions of Russia, the first by Napoleon and his army in 1812 and the second at the orders of Hitler in 1941. There are of course major differences between the two invasions. Napoleon led his army in person, while Hitler led from a position well to the rear. Napoleon's army marched on foot or rode on horseback and was followed by a long train of camp followers and baggage, while some of the German invaders moved rapidly in their tanks (though horses remained indispensable).

Some of the participants in the second invasion were all too well aware of the similarities between the problems they experienced and those of the French in 1812. Hitler would not allow his generals to advance on Moscow in what was 'partly a superstitious avoidance of Napoleon's foot-steps'. Some of the officers in the invading army, including the commander of Army Group Centre, Field-Marshal Günther von Kluge, read the memoirs of General Armand de Caulaincourt, who had accompanied Napoleon in 1812. The Panzer General Erich Hoepner was not the only one to see that 'our situation has despairing similarities with Napoleon in 1812'.[20]

In both cases, the destruction of the invaders owed less to the defending armies than to geographical and meteorological constants, two in particular. One was the vast size of the country in which the invaders were inevitably dispersed as if they had been swallowed up. One German officer who had read Caulaincourt's memoirs recorded his 'bad feelings about the enormous space of Russia'. Another officer declared that 'the vastness of Russia devours us'. A third called the Russian steppe 'an ocean that might drown the invader'.[21] As Carl von Clausewitz wrote at the time, 'The Russian campaign of 1812 demonstrated . . . that a country of such size could not be conquered.'[22]

The second constant was the weather. The greatest threat to both the French and the German armies was what the Russians called 'General Winter'. It is true that Napoleon had lost more than half his troops before his retreat, but the weather certainly added to his difficulties.[23] The French army had nearly 700,000 men when it invaded Russia. At this point it was summer, and the army suffered from the heat. However, by the time that Napoleon finally ordered a retreat from Moscow, it was 20 October. The emperor knew that it did not normally become seriously cold until December, so he thought that he had plenty of time. 'What he did not realize, in common with many who do not know those climates, was just how sudden and savage changes of temperature can be, and how temperature is only one factor, which along with wind, water and terrain can turn nature into a viciously powerful opponent.'[24] Incidentally, Caulaincourt, who was already familiar with Russia from his days as a diplomat, had tried to dissuade Napoleon from the invasion and had warned him of the danger of passing the winter there.

This is not a simple case of 'pure' ignorance. Napoleon knew that the Russian winter was cold and that warm clothing would be needed. It is a case of what might be called 'applied' ignorance, in other words failure to apply this knowledge to this particular case by giving the appropriate orders. This failure to mobilize knowledge in the service of decision-making was encouraged by arrogance, notably the over-optimistic assumption that the French victory would be so rapid that the invaders would be safely out of Russia by the autumn.

Caulaincourt's warning turned out to be justified. By 6 November 1812, the temperature had dropped and thick snow had fallen. The army, which had been reduced by this time to only 100,000 men, was short of supplies. The army was unable to take with them from Moscow enough food for themselves or fodder for the horses. The army also lacked winter clothing. 'There was no such thing as a winter uniform, since in those days armies did not fight in winter.'[25] As in the case of the British retreat from Kabul twenty-eight years later, frostbite in their hands made it impossible for the soldiers to shoot, and frostbite in their feet made it impossible for them to march. By late November the French army had been reduced from 700,000 to 25,000 men – the rest were either dead, wounded or prisoners.[26]

In 1941, history began to repeat itself. Hitler ordered the invasion of Russia in June, this time with about three million soldiers. In 'total ignorance of the Arkhangelsk campaign' in the First World War, the German commanders were surprised by the problems of waging war in low temperatures in the snow.[27] Hitler was not ignorant of what had happened to Napoleon's army but he certainly ignored it. He was confident that with more troops, not to mention tanks and aeroplanes, he would succeed where Napoleon had failed. He did not.

The Russians fought back and finally defeated the German armies. Their defence was assisted by the Russian winter – once again, the invading forces lacked proper winter clothing, including gloves and socks. Like Napoleon, Hitler had expected the defeat of the Russians before the weather turned cold. As a result of the lack of preparation, many German soldiers froze to death, while others suffered from frostbite or survived only by stuffing newspapers under their shirts and wearing civilian clothes beneath their uniforms.[28] The invading armies also lacked sufficient vehicles, spare parts and petrol, owing to the neglect of logistics by the planners. As Goebbels admitted, 'The supply problem is without question the decisive one in the east. We did not recognize this before the outbreak of the eastern campaign.'[29]

The Russians too suffered from both ignorance and the weather. For example, the German invasion took them by surprise, unprepared for resistance. However, as in the case of the Franco-Prussian war, relative ignorance can be decisive. In this case, the Russians, who were fighting on home ground, were less ignorant than the Germans. They had learned the lessons of their defeat by the Finns not long before, following their invasion of Finland in 1939, when 'Stalin ignored his military advisers and rushed into the invasion without adequate preparation'.[30] In the 'Winter War' that followed, a small force of Finns had virtually destroyed a Soviet division because, unlike the Russians, they had been trained to fight in the snow, sometimes attacking on skis. The Russians learned the lesson, and Soviet units on skis played an important role in the encirclement of the German 6th Army in 1942.

## INVADING AFGHANISTAN

What makes it particularly difficult to understand the American decision to go to war in Vietnam, discussed earlier, and to conduct it in the way that they did, is the apparent unawareness, on the part of both military and civilian decision-makers, of the lessons of the war that had just ended when their own involvement in the region began. In the Indo-China War of 1946–54, the colonial power, the French, was defeated by the forces of the Viet Minh. In this case too, a regular army from outside the region was opposed by guerrilla forces from within, using 'hit and run' tactics against the French supply lines, until they were strong enough for a decisive battle. At Dien Bien Phu, in northwest Vietnam, the Viet Minh were able to surround the French and to bombard them into surrender.[31]

The Americans failed to learn from the French experience. 'How could Dien Bien Phu be so ignored?'[32] One answer to this question is that the Americans 'did not learn from the French because they thought that the French simply did not have enough tools of war; the United States had many more'.[33] In similar fashion, ordering the invasion of Russia, Hitler believed that an army with tanks would succeed where an army with horses had failed. Refusal to learn from the past led to a re-enactment of defeat.

Another dramatic example of ignoring the lessons of the past is the invasion of Afghanistan, more exactly three invasions: by the British in 1839, by the Russians in 1979 and by the Americans in 2001. Some of the same mistakes were made on each occasion.[34]

In the British case, as we saw earlier, General Winter rode again. In the case of the Russians, 'Their decisions were bedevilled by ignorance.' A Russian general had already noted in 1921 that Afghanistan was 'difficult to conquer and even more difficult to hold', thanks to 'its mountainous nature and the proud and freedom-loving nature of its people'.[35] In 1980, the British Foreign Office presented a visiting Russian minister with a history of the British wars in Afghanistan. His response was that 'This time it will be different.'[36] It was not.

The guerrillas, the Mujahideen, ambushed the Russians and took their weapons. They also received arms from abroad, especially from the USA and Egypt. As for their tactics, they 'would man the heights overlooking the route of the slow-moving Soviet columns . . . They would knock out the first and last vehicles with a mine or a rocket, and then systematically destroy the remainder.' It took time and heavy losses for the Russians to learn (as the British had done) to occupy the heights themselves, or to make use of new technology and protect their forces with helicopters. In short, 'the Soviet commanders had not worked out in advance how to deal with small, lightly equipped and highly mobile groups of strongly motivated men moving across difficult terrain with which they were intimately acquainted'.[37]

In 2001, it was the turn of the Americans to make mistakes. Eleven years later, the Scottish historian William Dalrymple published a history of the British Afghan War in which he drew parallels between the British invasion of 1839 and the American invasion of 2001. Soon after his book was published, Dalrymple was invited to brief 'National Security, CIA and Defense' on the history of Afghanistan.[38] It seemed that the Americans had finally learned their lesson, although their hurried and disastrous withdrawal from Afghanistan in 2021 suggests otherwise.

There are, of course, dangers in pressing analogies between past and present too far, or simply choosing the wrong analogy. In the 1950s, for instance, analogies from the 1930s shaped the policies of both the USA and Britain. President Truman reacted aggressively to the invasion of South Korea by North Korea in 1950 because 'Communism was acting in Korea just as Hitler, Mussolini and the Japanese had acted'.[39] In 1956, when Prime Minister Gamal Abdel Nasser ordered the closing of the Suez Canal, the British prime minister Anthony Eden viewed Nasser as a new Hitler. He chose to respond with force because he identified nego-tiation with the British failure to resist Hitler's occupation of Czechoslovakia in 1938. The result was the unsuccessful British invasion of the Canal zone, an aborted campaign now known as the Suez fiasco.

In similar fashion, President Johnson and his adviser Henry Cabot Lodge, ambassador to South Vietnam, viewed the crisis in Vietnam in 1965 as a kind of replay of the Munich crisis of 1938 and they were determined, like Eden, to avoid the mistake of 'appeasing' the aggressor. At a meeting with the president, Lodge exploded: 'Can't we see the simi-larity to our own indolence at Munich?'[40] Johnson himself explained that 'Everything I knew about history told me that if I got out of Vietnam . . . then I'd be doing what Chamberlain did in World War II.'[41]

Analogies can be dangerous, since they 'obscure aspects of the present case that are different from the past one'.[42] To avoid the dangers, a careful examination of what might be called 'dis-analogies' may be recommended. However, the refusal to draw analogies is also dangerous. The philosopher George Santayana's well-known epigram makes this point well: 'Those who cannot remember the past are condemned to repeat it.'

# CONCLUSION
## NEW KNOWLEDGE AND
## NEW IGNORANCE

Perhaps every new learning makes room for itself by creating
a new ignorance

C. S. Lewis

As we have seen, the triumphalist or 'Whig' interpretation of history in
terms of inevitable progress, dominant in the eighteenth and nineteenth
centuries and even later, presented a simple story of the defeat of ignorance by knowledge. In contrast, this book has argued that the rise of
new knowledge(s) over the centuries has necessarily involved the rise of
new ignorance(s). Collectively, humanity knows more than ever before,
but individually, we do not know more than our predecessors.

Old knowledges have been abandoned in order to make room for new.
In the days when encyclopaedias were consulted in the form of heavy
printed volumes rather than online, updating them involved discarding
some old information in order to make space in their pages for new
discoveries. Knowledge of the fine points of cars, for instance, has replaced
knowledge of the fine points of horses. Knowledge of heraldry, once
considered essential for a gentleman, is now virtually confined to a small
group of enthusiasts such as the members of the British Heraldry Society.

In Europe, from the Renaissance to the early twentieth century,
males of the upper and middle classes were expected to be familiar with
the history, philosophy, language and literature of ancient Greece and
Rome. British Members of Parliament and other gentlemen were

expected to recognize classical allusions in speeches in the House of Commons or in the pages of *The Times*. This expectation was a reasonable one at a time when the classics formed a large part of education in both schools and universities and higher education was virtually restricted to male elites.

Today, when academic curricula offer no more than a small niche for classics, Boris Johnson's use of Latin has become an eccentricity (loveable or irritating, according to taste) as well as a sign that he was educated at a traditional elite school. If names such as Aristotle and Plato, Homer and Virgil, Caesar and Cicero remain familiar, it can no longer be assumed that many people have read some of their works, even in translation.

Knowledge of the classics in vernacular languages was also widespread in the past. In Italy, from the sixteenth century onwards, familiarity with the poems of Dante and Ariosto was far from confined to the upper classes. In France, Racine and Balzac became classics of this kind. In Spain, Cervantes. In Germany, Goethe. In Britain, Shakespeare, Milton, Scott and Dickens.

Today, these texts have to compete for the attention of readers with works from other cultures – Borges and García Márquez from Latin America, for instance, *The Dream of the Red Chamber* from China, *The Tale of Genji* from Japan, and so on. As in the case of cuisine, acquaintance with global varieties has increased while familiarity with local products has diminished. For languages, the story is a similar one. Knowledge of French and German has declined in much of Europe, while knowledge of American English, Chinese and Spanish has increased in many parts of the world.

In Europe in the age of the Reformation, debates on theology were widespread, not only among the clergy (Catholic, Lutheran or Calvinist) but among ordinary men and women as well. Thanks to the practice of learning the catechism by heart at an early age, it could be taken for granted, at least by preachers in towns, that references to theological concepts such as the 'sacraments' or even 'transubstantiation' would be widely understood, like references to the Bible, the Old Testament as well as the New. Knowledge of this kind can no longer be taken for granted, as it could, for instance, in the late nineteenth-century novels of Thomas Hardy, which are filled with biblical references. On the evidence of recent surveys, Christians in the USA, Britain and elsewhere know less theology than earlier generations did. Instead they know more about Hinduism and Buddhism than their ancestors because they have travelled to Asia or learned something about these religions in school.

In the case of geography, knowledge that was commonplace in Britain, the USA and elsewhere among the generation that went to school in the 1960s such as the position of major countries on the map and the names of their capitals, can no longer be counted on, owing to changes in the curriculum that 'made geography more relevant and rigorous, but at the price of narrowing its former range'. A geography teacher of the later 1980s and early 1990s remembers how 'the book cupboards of my geography department were purged of old textbooks'.[1]

In natural history, the evidence is less direct, but an enterprising journalist has noted that a new edition of the *Oxford Junior Dictionary* has dropped words such as 'buttercup', 'catkin' and 'conker', while adding 'broadband', 'chatroom' and 'celebrity' to accommodate changes of interest in the younger generation.[2]

In the case of science, the golden age for the popularization of scientific knowledge was surely the nineteenth century, when experiments in physics and chemistry were performed to crowded audiences, the theory of evolution was debated, and amateur geologists and botanists, women as well as men, abounded. However, as the British chemist-turned-novelist C. P. Snow pointed out in a famous lecture given in Cambridge in 1959, the natural sciences and the humanities had become 'two cultures', increasingly remote from each other, so that an individual well educated in the humanities would probably be ignorant of the second law of thermodynamics.[3] Today, at a time of ever-increasing specialization, the idea of only 'two' cultures has surely become an understatement.

In the case of history, knowledge of ancient Greece and Rome was replaced by knowledge of the national past, which is undergoing replacement in its turn, this time by global history – once again, a widening of horizons, together with a decline of the knowledge of what is close at hand. The shift from the history viewed from above, the history of leaders, to history viewed from below, the history of ordinary people, has hugely increased our knowledge and understanding of the past, but it too has come at a price. A younger generation of history students knows little about past decision-makers. As a leading older historian, John Elliott, has remarked, 'Something is amiss when the name of Martin Guerre threatens to become better known than that of Martin Luther.'[4] That knowledge of Martin Luther's career had been declining for some time is suggested by comparing his entry in the famous 1911 edition of the *Encyclopaedia Britannica* with the entry in the *New Encyclopaedia Britannica* sixty-three years later. Luther was allocated fourteen columns of text in 1911, but only one in 1974.

Given the brevity of human life, the need for sleep, and the competition for attention by new forms of art or sport, it should be obvious enough that each generation in each culture is scarcely able to know more than its predecessors. It simply knows about the poems of Tu Fu rather than Tennyson, for instance, or about the history of Africa rather than that of the Tudors. We also face the paradox, noted by the economist Friedrich von Hayek, that the greater the increase of collective knowledge, thanks to the researches of scientists and scholars, 'the smaller the share of all that knowledge . . . that any one mind can absorb'.[5]

At a more practical level, we have seen how advances in the knowledge of the people by the government, a knowledge acquired by surveys and represented by maps and statistical tables, has sometimes led to blindness, a lack of awareness of the difference between these representations and local realities in all their messiness.

In short, as this book has argued, we need to think of knowledges and ignorances in the plural rather than the singular, noting that what is common knowledge or conventional wisdom varies both from place to place and from one period to another. 'New knowledge makes new kinds of ignorance possible.'[6] To return to C. S. Lewis, 'Perhaps every new learning makes room for itself by creating a new ignorance.'[7] We should always think twice before describing any individual, culture or period as ignorant, since there is simply too much to know – an old complaint but one that has become more and more justified in our time.[8] To return to Mark Twain, 'We are all ignorant, just about different things.' The trouble is that those with power often lack the knowledges they need, while those who possess those knowledges lack power.

# GLOSSARY

The following list concentrates on terms that recur in this book and is not intended to be complete.

| | |
|---|---|
| **active ignorance** | not wanting to know |
| **agnoiology** | the study of ignorance |
| **agnotology** | the study of the production of ignorance |
| **asymmetrical ignorance** | occurs when group A knows less about group B than vice versa |
| **blameless ignorance** | cf. invincible or unavoidable ignorance |
| **blameworthy ignorance** | cf. culpable ignorance |
| **conscious ignorance** | knowing that one does not know |
| **creative ignorance** | ignorance of the past that helps innovation |
| **culpable ignorance** | cf. blameworthy ignorance |
| **deep ignorance** | concerning a question without plausible answers |
| **deliberate ignorance** | cf. voluntary or wilful ignorance |
| *docta ignorantia* | an ignorance acquired via study or meditation |
| **genuine ignorance** | absence of knowledge, cf. plain and simple ignorance |
| **group ignorance** | cf. organizational ignorance |

| | |
|---|---|
| **ignoring** | a conscious or unconscious form of resistance to knowledge, cf. voluntary or wilful ignorance |
| **illiteracy** | a kind of ignorance imputed by specialists to a part of the laity |
| **imputed ignorance** | the ignorance of others |
| **inadvertent ignorance** | cf. unconscious ignorance |
| **inscrutable ignorance** | cf. unknown unknowns |
| **insightful ignorance** | awareness of a gap in knowledge |
| **interested ignorance** | a form of not wanting to know |
| **invincible ignorance** | cf. blameless or involuntary ignorance |
| **known unknowns** | what someone knows that they do not know |
| **learned ignorance** | cf. *docta ignorantia* |
| **local ignorance** | the complementary opposite of local knowledge |
| **macro-ignorance** | collective ignorance |
| **manufacture of ignorance** | keeping others ignorant, cf. production of ignorance |
| **meta-ignorance** | not knowing that one does not know |
| **moral ignorance** | 'incorrect judgements' about rights and wrongs |
| **nescience, non-knowledge** | ambiguous concepts referring either to what is not known yet or to the complete absence of knowledge |
| **opaque ignorance** | unknown unknowns |
| **organizational ignorance** | the effect of the uneven distribution of knowledge within an organization |
| **plain ignorance** | absence of knowledge, cf. genuine or simple ignorance |
| **practical ignorance** | not knowing how to do something |
| **primary ignorance** | ignorance of ignorance, cf. meta-ignorance |

| | |
|---|---|
| **production of ignorance** | keeping others ignorant, cf. manufacture of ignorance |
| **rational ignorance** | refraining from learning when the cost outweighs the benefit |
| **relative ignorance** | relative to rivals or enemies |
| **resolute ignorance** | wanting not to know |
| **sanctioned ignorance** | the collective dismissal of some information as unimportant |
| **selective ignorance** | choosing to ignore |
| **simple ignorance** | absence of knowledge, cf. genuine or plain ignorance |
| **specified ignorance** | ignoring what is considered irrelevant |
| **strategic ignorance** | deliberately keeping others ignorant |
| **symmetrical ignorance** | where two parties are equally ignorant |
| **unanticipated ignorance** | surprise |
| **unavoidable ignorance** | cf. blameless or invincible ignorance |
| **uncertainty** | a hesitation between knowledge and ignorance |
| **unconscious ignorance** | not knowing that one does not know |
| **unknowability** | the impossibility of knowing something |
| **unknown knowns** | unconscious knowledge |
| **unknown unknowns** | what someone does not know they do not know |
| **useful ignorance** | ignorance with a positive function, cf. virtuous ignorance |
| **vincible ignorance** | cf. blameworthy or culpable ignorance |
| **virtuous ignorance** | ignorance that is useful |
| **voluntary ignorance** | cf. deliberate or wilful ignorance |
| **white ignorance** | ignorance or false beliefs about Black people |
| **wilful ignorance** | cf. deliberate or voluntary ignorance |

# NOTES

## PREFACE AND ACKNOWLEDGEMENTS

1. As I write, the *Guardian* reports that David Puttnam, resigning from the House of Lords, has accused MPs of 'pig-ignorance' of the problems of the Irish border during the Brexit negotiations, 16 October 2021, www.theguardian com.politics.
2. Françoise Waquet, *Parler comme un livre: L'oralité et le savoir (XVIe–XXe siècle)* (Paris, 2003); *Les enfants de Socrate: Filiation intellectuelle et transmission du savoir, XVIIe–XXIe siècle* (Paris, 2008); *L'ordre materiel du savoir: Comment les savants travaillent, XVIe–XXIe siècle* (Paris, 2015); *Une histoire émotionelle du savoir, XVIIe–XXIe siècle* (Paris, 2019).

## 1 WHAT IS IGNORANCE?

1. Gustave Flaubert to Louise Colet, 16 January 1852, in his *Correspondance*, ed. Bernard Masson (Paris, 1975), 156.
2. Lord Clarendon, *A Compleat Collection of Tracts* (London, 1747), 237.
3. George Washington, *Circular to the States*, June 1783. On the history of the phrase, Lucie Varga, *Das Schlagwort der 'Finsteren Mittelalter'* (Baden, 1932); Theodore Mommsen, 'Petrarch's conception of the "Dark Ages"', *Speculum* 17 (1942), 226–42.
4. William E. Shepard, 'The Age of Ignorance', in *Encyclopaedia of the Qur'an*, vol. 1 (Leiden, 2001), 37–40.
5. William Beveridge, *Social Insurance and Allied Services* (London, 1942), http://www.bl.uk/onlinegallery/takingliberties/staritems/712beveridgereportpic.html.
6. Charles Simic, 'Age of Ignorance', *New York Review of Books* (20 March 2012), https://www.nybooks.com/daily/2012/03/20/age-of-ignorance; 'Robert Proctor', in Janet Kourany and Martin Carrier (eds), *Science and the Production of Ignorance* (Cambridge MA, 2020), 53.
7. Martin Mulsow, *Prekäres Wissen: Eine andere Ideengeschichte der Frühen Neuzeit* (Berlin, 2012). Cf. Renate Dürr (ed.), *Threatened Knowledge: Practices of Knowing and Ignoring from the Middle Ages to the Twentieth Century* (London, 2021).
8. Rhodri Marsden, 'Filter Failure: Too Much Information?', *Independent*, 31 May 2011. The term 'filter failure' was coined by Clay Shirky, a professor of media studies at New York University. Cf. Shaheed Nick Mohammed, *The (Dis)Information Age: The Persistence of Ignorance* (New York, 2012), 2.
9. Hans Blumenberg, 'Curiosity is Enrolled in the Catalogue of Vices', in *The Legitimacy of the Modern Age* (1966: English trans. Cambridge MA, 1983), 309–23; Neil Kenny, *The Uses of Curiosity in Early Modern France and Germany* (Oxford, 2004), 99, and (criticizing Blumenberg), 165–7.

10. Eliza Butler, *The Fortunes of Faust* (Cambridge, 1952).
11. Franco Venturi, 'Was ist Aufklärung? Sapere Aude!', *Rivista storica italiana* 71 (1959), 119–28.
12. Henry Thoreau, 'Walking' (1851), faculty.washington.edu/timbillo/Readings and documents/Wilderness, visited 27 October 2020.
13. Alain Corbin, *Terra Incognita: A History of Ignorance in the Eighteenth and Nineteenth Centuries* (2020: English trans. Cambridge, 2021), 4.
14. Quoted in Sandrine Bergès, 'Olympe de Gouges versus Rousseau', *Journal of the American Philosophical Association* (2018), 433–51, at 444.
15. José González García, *The Eyes of Justice: Blindness and Farsightedness, Vision and Blindness in the Aesthetics of the Law* (Frankfurt, 2016).
16. John Rawls, *A Theory of Justice* (Cambridge MA, 1971).
17. Wilbert Moore and Melvin Tumin, 'Some Social Functions of Ignorance', *American Sociological Review* 14 (1949), 787–96; Heinrich Popitz, *Über die Präventivwirkung des Nichtwissens* (Tübingen, 1968); Roy Dilley, 'Reflections on Knowledge Practices and the Problem of Ignorance', *Journal of the Royal Anthropological Institute* 16 (2010), 176–92; Peter Wehling (ed.), *Vom Nutzen des Nichtwissens* (Bielefeld, 2011); Nick Bostrom, 'Information Hazards: A Typology of Potential Harms from Knowledge', *Review of Contemporary Philosophy* 10 (2011), 44–79.
18. Susan Matt and Luke Fernandez (2021), 'Ignorance is Power, as well as Joy', in Dürr (ed.), *Threatened Knowledge*, 212–31, at 212.
19. Anthony Tjan, 'The Power of Ignorance', *Harvard Business Review*, 9 August 2010, hbr.org/2010/08/the-power-of-ignorance.html. Cf. Ursula Schneider, *Das Management der Ignoranz: Nichtwissen als Erfolgsfaktor* (Wiesbaden, 2006), and Piero Formica, *The Role of Creative Ignorance* (New York, 2014).
20. *New Yorker*, 10 February 1945. Ford quoted in Formica, *Creative Ignorance*, 10.
21. James Ferrier, *Institutes of Metaphysic* (Edinburgh, 1854), 405.
22. Halcyon Backhouse, (ed.), *The Cloud of Unknowing* (London, 2009).
23. Matthias Gross, '"Objective Culture" and the Development of Nonknowledge: Georg Simmel and the Reverse Side of Knowing', *Cultural Sociology* 6 (2012), 422–37, at 433.
24. Michael J. Smithson, 'Social Theories of Ignorance', in Robert N. Proctor and Londa Schiebinger (eds), *Agnotology: The Making and Unmaking of Ignorance* (Stanford CA, 2008), 209–29, at 209–12.
25. News briefing, US Department of Defense, 12 February 2002, replying to a question about the lack of evidence for weapons of mass destruction in Iraq, https://en.wikipedia.org/wiki/There_are_known_knowns.
26. Slavoj Žižek, 'What Rumsfeld Doesn't Know That He Knows About Abu Ghraib', *In These Times*, 21 May 2004. My thanks to Lukas Verburgt for this reference.
27. Sigmund Freud, *Introductory Lectures on Psychoanalysis* (1916–17: English trans. London, 1922), 100.
28. Jacques Lacan, *My Teaching* (London, 2008).
29. Charles Mills, 'White Ignorance', in Shannon Sullivan and Nancy Tuana (eds), *Race and Epistemologies of Ignorance* (Albany NY, 2007), 13–28, at 33.
30. 'Traces of Terrorism', *New York Times*, 17 May 2002, www.nytimes.com, 17 May 2002, visited 26 July 2021.
31. Andrew Abbott, 'Varieties of Ignorance', *American Sociologist* 41 (2010), 174–89; Nikolaj Nottelmann, 'The Varieties of Ignorance', in Rik Peels and Martijn Blaauw (eds), *The Epistemic Dimensions of Ignorance* (Cambridge, 2016), 33–56.
32. Gilbert Ryle, 'Knowing How and Knowing That', *Proceedings of the Aristotelian Society* 46, 1–16.
33. Linsey McGoey, *The Unknowers: How Strategic Ignorance Rules the World* (London, 2019), 326.
34. Gayatri Chakravorty Spivak, *Critique of Postcolonial Reason* (Cambridge MA, 1999).
35. Jane Austen, *Northanger Abbey* (London, 1817), chap. 2.

36. Paul Hoyningen-Huene, 'Strong Incommensurability and Deeply Opaque Ignorance', in Kourany and Carrier (eds), *Science*, 219–41, at 222.
37. Lucien Febvre, *Le problème de l'incroyance au XVIe siècle* (Paris, 1942), 385–8.
38. Thomas Kuhn, *The Structure of Scientific Revolutions* (Chicago IL, 1962); Menachem Fisch and Yitzhak Benbaji, *The View from Within: Normativity and the Limits of Self-Criticism* (Notre Dame IN, 2011).
39. The classic discussion of this topic is in Robin Horton, 'African Traditional Thought and Western Science', *Africa* 37 (1967), 50–71.
40. Peter Burke, 'Alternative Modes of Thought', *Common Knowledge* (2022), 41–60.
41. William Beer, 'Resolute Ignorance: Social Science and Affirmative Action', *Society* 24 (1987), 63–9.
42. Michel-Rolph Trouillot, *Silencing the Past: Power and the Production of History* (Boston MA, 1995).
43. Letter to Étienne Falconet in 1768, quoted in Peter Gay, *The Enlightenment: An Interpretation*, vol. 2, *The Science of Freedom* (New York, 1969), 520.
44. Lytton Strachey, *Eminent Victorians* (London, 1918), preface.
45. Roxanne L. Euben, *Journeys to the Other Shore* (Princeton NJ, 2006), 136.
46. Mary Louise Pratt, *Imperial Eyes: Travel Writing and Transculturation* (London, 1992), 159–60; Indira Ghose, *Women Travellers in Colonial India: The Power of the Female Gaze* (Delhi, 1998).
47. Robert Halsband (ed.), *The Complete Letters of Lady Mary Wortley Montagu*, 3 vols (Oxford, 1965–7), vol. 1, 315.
48. Grace Browne, 'Doctors Were Sure They Had Covid 19. The Reality Was Worse', *Wired*, 23 April 2021, www.wired.co.uk.
49. Robert K. Merton, 'Three Fragments from a Sociologist's Notebooks: Establishing the Phenomenon, Specified Ignorance, and Strategic Research Materials', *Annual Review of Sociology* 13 (1987), 1–28. Cf. Peter Burke, 'Paradigms Lost: from Göttingen to Berlin', *Common Knowledge* 14 (2008), 244–57.
50. Karl Popper, *Logik der Forschung* (1934: English adaptation, *The Logic of Scientific Discovery* (London, 1959)).
51. David Gilmour, *Curzon* (London, 1994), 481.
52. Matt Seybold, 'The Apocryphal Twain', https://marktwainstudies.com/category/the-apocryphal-twain. Accessed 12 May 2022.
53. Proctor and Schiebinger, *Agnotology*.
54. William Scott, 'Ignorance and Revolution', in Joan H. Pittock and Andrew Wear (eds), *Interpretation and Cultural History* (London, 1991), 235–68, at 241.
55. On stupidity, Carlo Cipolla, *The Laws of Stupidity* (1976: English trans. London, 2019); Barbara Tuchman, *The March of Folly: From Troy to Vietnam* (London, 1984).
56. On conceptual history, Melvin Richter, *The History of Political and Social Concepts* (Oxford, 1995), 27–51.
57. Gaston Bachelard, *The Formation of the Scientific Mind: A Contribution to a Psychoanalysis of Objective Knowledge* (1938: English trans. Manchester 2002). Cf. Burke, 'Paradigms Lost'.
58. John Barnes, 'Structural Amnesia' (1947: repr. in *Models and Interpretations*, Cambridge 1990, 226–8); Jack Goody and Ian Watt, 'The Consequences of Literacy' (1963: repr. in Goody (ed.), *Literacy in Traditional Societies*, Cambridge, 1968), 27–68 at 32–3; David W. DeLong, *Lost Knowledge: Confronting the Threat of an Aging Workforce* (Oxford, 2004).
59. Robert Merton, *The Sociology of Science* (Chicago IL, 1973), 402–3, cited by Malhar Kumar, 'A Review of the Types of Scientific Misconduct in Biomedical Research', *Journal of Academic Ethics* 6 (2008), 211–28, at 214.
60. Stanley Cohen, *States of Denial: Knowing About Atrocities and Suffering* (Cambridge, 2001).
61. Exceptions to this neglect include Erik Zürcher, *Dialoog der misverstanden* (Leiden, 1962); Wenchao Li, *Die christliche China-Mission im 17. Jht: Verständnis, Unverständnis, Misverständnis* (Stuttgart, 2000); Martin Espenhorst (ed.), *Unwissen und Misverständnisse im vormodernen Friedensprozess* (Göttingen, 2013).

62. Marshall Sahlins, *Islands of History* (Chicago IL, 1985). This interpretation was challenged by another anthropologist, Gananath Obeyesekere in *The Apotheosis of Captain Cook* (Princeton NJ, 1992).

## 2 PHILOSOPHERS ON IGNORANCE

1. *The Sayings of Confucius* (English trans. James R. Ware, New York, 1955), Book 2, chap. 17. Today, scholars believe that this collection of sayings is a collective rather than an individual production that was gradually enlarged over the centuries: Michael Nylan, *The Five 'Confucian' Classics* (New Haven CT, 2001).
2. Laozi, *Daodejing*, chap. 71, trans. Ernest R. Hughes. My thanks to Cao Yiqiang for clarifying this passage. On 'empty words', Geoffrey Lloyd and Nathan Sivin, *The Way and the Word: Science and Medicine in Early China and Greece* (New Haven CT, 2002), 204, 209. See also Alan Chan, 'Laozi', *Stanford Encyclopedia of Philosophy* (Stanford CA, 2018), https://plato.stanford.edu/archives/win2018/entries/laozi.
3. Chuang Tzu, *Basic Writings*, trans. Burton Watson (New York, 1964), 40.
4. Socrates is quoted in Plato, *Apology*, 21d, 23a.
5. Diogenes Laertius, *Lives of Eminent Philosophers* (English trans., 2 vols, Cambridge MA, 1925), vol.1, 163. Cf. W. K. C. Guthrie, 'The Ignorance of Socrates', *History of Greek Philosophy* (Cambridge, 1969), vol. 3, 442–9; Gregory Vlastos, 'Socrates' Disavowal of Knowledge', *Philosophical Quarterly* 35 (1985), 1–31; Gareth Matthews, *Socratic Perplexity and the Nature of Philosophy* (Oxford, 1999); and Hugh Benson, *Socratic Wisdom* (New York, 2000).
6. Jacques Brunschwig, 'Pyrrhon' and 'Scepticisme', in Brunschwig and Geoffrey Lloyd (eds), *Le savoir grec* (Paris, 1996), 801–6, 1001–20; Brunschwig, 'The Beginnings of Hellenistic Epistemology', in Keimpe Algra et al. (eds), *The Cambridge History of Hellenistic Philosophy* (Cambridge, 1999), 229–59, at 229, 241, 246; Luca Castagnoli, 'Early Pyrrhonism', in James Warren and Frisbee Sheffield (eds), *The Routledge Companion to Ancient Philosophy* (London, 2014), 496–510.
7. Sextus Empiricus, *Outlines of Pyrrhonism* (English trans. New York, 1933), 27–9.
8. Michael Frede, 'The Skeptic's Beliefs' (1979), repr. in his *Essays in Ancient Philosophy* (Oxford, 1987), 179–200, at 186; Katja Vogt, 'Ancient Skepticism', in Edward N. Zalta (ed.), *Stanford Encyclopedia of Philosophy* (Stanford CA, 2018), plato.stanford.edu/entries/skepticism-ancient.
9. Nicolette Zeeman, Kantik Ghosh and Dallas Denery II, 'The Varieties of Uncertainty', in Denery, Ghosh and Zeeman (eds), *Uncertain Knowledge: Scepticism, Relativism and Doubt in the Middle Ages* (Turnhout, 2014), 1–12, at 9.
10. Richard Popkin, *The History of Scepticism: From Savonarola to Bayle* (1964: 3rd edn, New York, 2003), 1–16, 50. On the contrast between ancient and early modern scepticism, Myles Burnyeat in Richard Popkin and Charles Schmitt (eds), *Skepticism from the Renaissance to the Enlightenment* (Wiesbaden, 1987), 13–14.
11. Popkin, *History of Scepticism*, 44–57 (Montaigne) and 57–61 (Charron).
12. Michael Moriarty, 'Montaigne and Descartes', in Philippe Desan (ed.), *The Oxford Handbook of Montaigne* (Oxford, 2016). I owe the phrase 'methodological ignorance' to Lukas Verburgt.
13. Elisabeth Labrousse, *Pierre Bayle*, 2 vols (The Hague, 1963–4).
14. Peter Burke, 'The Age of the Baroque' (1998: English original in Burke, *Identity, Culture and Communications in the Early Modern World* (Brighton, 2018)), 119–48, at 120.
15. Ferrier, *Institutes of Metaphysic*; Jenny Keefe, 'James Ferrier and the Theory of Ignorance', *The Monist* 90 (2007), 297–309.
16. Thomas Carlyle, *Sartor Resartus* (1831). Cf. Ruth apRoberts, 'Carlyle and the History of Ignorance', *Carlyle Studies Annual* 18, 73–81.
17. On Marx and Freud, Sandra Harding, 'Two Influential Theories of Ignorance and Philosophy's Interests in Ignoring Them', *Hypatia* 21 (2006), 20–36.

18. Steve Fuller, *Social Epistemology* (Bloomington IN, 1988, 2nd edn 2002), xxix. Cf. Miranda Fricker and Jennifer Hornsby (eds), *The Routledge Handbook of Social Epistemology* (London, 2000).
19. Shannon Sullivan and Nancy Tuana, 'Introduction', in Sullivan and Tuana, *Race and Epistemologies of Ignorance*, 1.

## 3 COLLECTIVE IGNORANCE

1. Joanne Roberts, 'Organizational Ignorance', in Matthias Gross and Linsey McGoey (eds), *Routledge International Handbook of Ignorance Studies* (London, 2015), 361–9; Tore Bakken and Erik-Lawrence Wiik, 'Ignorance and Organization Studies', *Organization Studies* 39 (2018), 1109–20. Cf. 'Systemic ignorance', in Moore and Tumin, 'Social Functions', 789.
2. DeLong, *Lost Knowledge*.
3. Michel Crozier, *The Bureaucratic Phenomenon* (1963: English trans. London, 1964), 190, 42, 51.
4. Serhii Plokhy, *Chernobyl: History of a Tragedy* (London, 2018), 20, 34, 43, 54.
5. Silvio Funtowicz and Jerome Ravetz, *Uncertainty and Quality in Science for Policy* (Dordrecht, 1990), 1.
6. James C. Scott, *Seeing Like a State: How Certain Schemes to Improve the Human Condition Have Failed* (New Haven CT, 1998). Cf. Roy Dilley and Thomas G. Kirsch (eds), *Regimes of Ignorance: Anthropological Perspectives on the Production and Reproduction of Non-Knowledge* (Oxford, 2015).
7. Sei Shōnagon, *Pillow Book* (English trans. London, 1960), 66; Ivan Morris, *The World of the Shining Prince: Court Life in Ancient Japan* (Oxford, 1964), 85; Mark Bailey, 'The Peasants and the Great Revolt', in Sian Echard and Stephen Rigby (eds), *Historians on John Gower* (Cambridge, 2019), chap. 4; on La Bruyère, Carlo Ginzburg, *Occhiacci di Legno: Nove Riflessioni sulla Distanza* (Milan, 1998), 26.
8. Andrew McKinnon, 'Reading "Opium of the People"', *Critical Sociology* 31 (2005), 15–38, at 17. The text by Marx is *Zur Kritik der Hegelschen Rechtsphilosophie* (1844).
9. Antonio Gramsci, *Selections from the Prison Notebooks*, ed. Quintin Hoare and Geoffrey Nowell Smith (London, 1971), 58.
10. Michel Foucault, *Power/Knowledge: Selected Interviews and Other Writings* (Brighton, 1980), 8.
11. Shirley Ardener, 'Introduction' to Ardener (ed.), *Perceiving Women* (London, 1975), vii–xxiii, at 12. Cf. Shirley Ardener, 'Ardener's Muted Groups: The Genesis of an Idea and its Praxis', *Women and Language* 28 (2005), 50–54, and Gayatri Spivak, *Can the Subaltern Speak?* (Basingstoke, 1988).
12. Charles W. Mills, *The Racial Contract* (Ithaca NY, 1997), 97; Mills, 'White Ignorance', 11–38, at 17; Eric Malewski and Nathalia Jaramillo (eds), *Epistemologies of Ignorance in Education* (Charlotte NC, 2011).
13. On female credibility, Lorraine Code, *What Can She Know? Feminist Theory and the Construction of Knowledge* (Ithaca NY, 1991), 222–64.
14. Jean Donnison, *Midwives and Medical Men: A History of Inter-Professional Rivalries and Women's Rights* (London, 1977), 21–41; Londa Schiebinger, *The Mind Has No Sex? Women in the Origins of Modern Science* (Cambridge MA, 1989), 108. Cf. Ruth Ginzberg, 'Uncovering Gynocentric Science', *Hypatia* 2 (1987), 89–105, at 95, 102.
15. François Fénelon, *L'éducation des filles* (1687: new edn, Paris 1885), chaps 1–2.
16. On the deletion, Andrew Bennett, *Ignorance: Literature and Agnoiology* (Manchester, 2009), 203, note 14.
17. Virginia Woolf, *Three Guineas* (1938), quoted in William Whyte, 'The Intellectual Aristocracy Revisited', *Journal of Victorian Culture* 10 (2005), 15–45, at 20.
18. Christine de Pizan, *The Book of the City of Ladies* (1405: English trans. New York, 1998), 70–83.
19. Anna Maria van Schurman, *De ingenii muliebris ad doctrinam et meliores litteras aptitudine* (1638), English trans. *The Learned Maid* (London, 1659).

20. François Poullain de la Barre, *L'égalité des deux sexes* (1671: bilingual edn, *The Equality of the Two Sexes*, Lampeter, 1989), 6–7, 29–30, 84.
21. Gabrielle Suchon, *Traité de la Morale* (Paris, 1693), vol. 3, 11–12; selections ed. and trans. Domna Stanton and Rebecca Wilkins as *A Woman Who Defends All the Persons of Her Sex* (Chicago IL, 2010), 73, 133. Cf. Michèle Le Dœuff, *The Sex of Knowing* (1998: English trans. New York, 2003), 36, 40.
22. Cavendish is quoted in Schiebinger, *The Mind Has No Sex?*, 48; Mary Astell, 'A serious proposal to the ladies' (1694–7: new edn, London 1997), 1, 25–6; Astell, *Reflections Upon Marriage* (1700: repr. in her *Political Writings*, ed. Patricia Springborg, Cambridge 1996), 28.
23. Maria Lúcia Pallares-Burke, 'Globalizing the Enlightenment in Brazil', *Cultural History* 9 (2020), 195–216.
24. 'Sophia', *Woman Not Inferior to Man* (London, 1739), 45; Mary Wollstonecraft, *A Vindication of the Rights of Woman* (London, 1792), chaps 4 and 13, section six.
25. Le Doeuf, *Sex of Knowing*, 104.
26. Quoted in Joan Kelly, 'Early Feminist Theory and the "Querelle des Femmes"', *Signs* 8 (1982), 4–28, at 18, 20, 25.
27. This problem is the focus of a number of recent studies such as Jill Tietjen, *Engineering Women: Re-visioning Women's Scientific Achievement and Impact* (Cham, 2017) and other contributions to the Springer series, 'Women in Engineering and Science'.
28. For a general discussion, see Evelyn Fox-Keller, *Reflections on Gender and Science* (New Haven CT, 1985); Schiebinger, *The Mind Has No Sex?*
29. Ruth Sime, *Lise Meitner: A Life in Physics* (Berkeley CA, 1996); Hugh Torrens, 'Anning, Mary', *Oxford Dictionary of National Biography* 2 (Oxford, 2004), 240–41.
30. James Watson, *The Double Helix: A Personal Account of the Discovery of DNA* (1968: 2nd edn, London 1997). Cf. Howard Markel, *The Secret of Life: Rosalind Franklin, James Watson, Francis Crick and the Discovery of DNA's Double Helix* (New York, 2021), 313, 315, 333, 387, and on 'conspiracy', 200, 335, 360, 385.
31. Contrast John Chadwick, *The Decipherment of Linear B* (Cambridge, 1958) with Margalit Fox, *The Riddle of the Labyrinth: The Quest to Crack an Ancient Code* (London, 2013).
32. Ruth Hagengruber and Sarah Hutton (eds), *Women Philosophers from the Renaissance to the Enlightenment* (London, 2021).
33. Linda Nochlin, 'Why Have There Been No Great Women Artists?', *ArtNews*, January 1971, 22–39, 67–71; Rozsika Parker and Griselda Pollock, *Old Mistresses: Women, Art and Ideology* (London, 1981).
34. Ann Oakley, *The Sociology of Housework* (1974: new edn Bristol, 2018), 1–26; Renate Bridenthal and Claudia Koonz (eds), *Becoming Visible: Women in European History* (Boston MA, 1977).
35. Donna Haraway, 'Situated Knowledges: The Science Question in Feminism', *Feminist Studies* 14 (1988), 575–99. In the 1920s, Karl Mannheim had discussed the relativity of standpoints without reference to gender: *Essays on the Sociology of Knowledge* (English trans. London, 1952), 103–4 and passim.
36. Alison Jagger, 'Love and Knowledge: Emotion in Feminist Epistemology', in Ann Garry and Marilyn Pearsall (eds), *Women, Knowledge and Reality* (New York, 1996), 166–90, at 175–7, 185; Mary Belenky et al., *Women's Ways of Knowing* (1986: 2nd edn New York, 1997), 11, 95, 6. For a critique, see Code, *What Can She Know?* 251–62.
37. Lorraine Code, 'Taking Subjectivity into Account', in Linda Alcoff and Elizabeth Potter (eds), *Feminist Epistemologies* (London, 1993), 15–48, at 32.
38. Evelyn Fox-Keller, 'Gender and Science' (1978: repr. in Fox-Keller, *Reflections on Gender and Science*), 75–94. Cf. Alison Wylie, 'Feminism in Philosophy of Science', in Miranda Fricker and Jennifer Hornsby (eds), *The Cambridge Companion to Feminism in Philosophy* (Cambridge, 2000), 166–84.

## 4 STUDYING IGNORANCE

1. Fox-Keller, *Reflections on Gender and Science*.
2. Nancy Levit and Robert Verchick, *Feminist Legal Theory* (2006: 2nd edn New York, 2016); Ann Scales, *Legal Feminism* (New York, 2006).
3. Carole Pateman, *Participation and Democratic Theory* (Cambridge, 1970); Pateman, *The Disorder of Women* (Cambridge, 1989), 1, 121 and passim.
4. Gillian Rose, *Feminism and Geography* (Minneapolis MI, 1993); Joni Seager and Lise Nelson (eds), *Companion to Feminist Geography* (Oxford, 2004).
5. Esther Boserup, *Woman's Role in Economic Development* (London, 1970), 5.
6. Oakley, *Sociology of Housework*; Dorothy Smith, 'Women's Perspective as a Radical Critique of Sociology', *Sociological Inquiry* 44 (1974), 7–13.
7. Margaret Mead, *Coming of Age in Samoa: A Psychological Study of Primitive Youth for Western Civilisation* (New York, 1928); Ruth Landes, *City of Women* (New York, 1947). Mead was strongly criticized in Derek Freeman, *Margaret Mead and Samoa: The Making and Unmaking of an Anthropological Myth* (Cambridge MA, 1983). The controversy still continues.
8. Richard Fardon, *Mary Douglas: An Intellectual Biography* (London, 1999), 243.
9. Marilyn Strathern, 'Culture in a Netbag: The Manufacture of a Subdiscipline in Anthropology', *Man* 16 (1981), 665–88; Henrietta Moore, *Feminism and Anthropology* (Cambridge, 1988).
10. Joan Gero and Margaret Conkey (eds), *Engendering Archaeology: Women and Prehistory* (Oxford, 1991).
11. Marija Gimbutas, *The Civilization of the Goddess* (San Francisco CA, 1991), 222, 324.
12. Leszek Gardeła, *Women and Weapons in the Viking World: Amazons of the North* (Oxford, 2021).
13. Gero and Conkey (eds), *Engendering Archaeology*, 163–223.
14. Bennett, *Ignorance*, 2.
15. Paulo Freire, *Pedagogy of the Oppressed* (1968: English trans. Harmondsworth, 1970), 45–6; José de Souza Martins, 'Paulo Freire, Educador', *Eu & Fim de Semana* 22, no. 1084, 1 October 2021.
16. Peter K. Austin and Julia Sallabank (eds), *The Cambridge Handbook of Endangered Languages* (Cambridge, 2011).
17. Mark Plotkin, 'How We Know What We Do Not Know', in Kurt Almqvist and Matthias Hessérus (eds), *Knowledge and Information* (Stockholm, 2021), 25–31, at 25.
18. Heinz Post, 'Correspondence, Invariance and Heuristics', *Studies in History and Philosophy of Science* 2 (1971), 213–55, at 229. The reference is to Kuhn, *Structure*.
19. Peter Galison, 'Removing Knowledge', *Critical Inquiry* 31 (2004), 229–43.
20. Julius Lukasiewicz, *The Ignorance Explosion* (Ottawa, 1994), the amplification of an article of the same title in *Leonardo* 7 (1974), 159–63.
21. Quoted in Erwin Panofsky, 'The First Page of Vasari's Libro' (1930: English trans. in *Meaning in the Visual Arts* (Garden City NY, 1955)), 169–235.
22. Joseph Addison, *The Spectator*, no. 1 (London, 1711); Ziauddin Sardar, 'The Smog of Ignorance', *Futures* 120 (2020), www.sciencedirect.com, visited 26 July 2021.
23. Quoted in Varga, *Schlagwort*, 125.
24. Astell, 'A serious proposal', 21.
25. Report of the Trustees, quoted in G. Ward Hubbs, ' "Dissipating the Clouds of Ignorance": The First University of Alabama Library, 1831–1865', *Libraries & Culture* 27 (1992), 20–35, at 24.
26. Edward Gibbon, *Decline and Fall of the Roman Empire* (1776–89), vol. 6, chap. 66.
27. Quoted in Varga, *Schlagwort*, 119.
28. George Eliot, *The Mill on the Floss* (1860: Harmondsworth, 1979), 427, 185.
29. George Eliot, *Daniel Deronda* (London, 1876), chap. 21. Cf. Linda K. Robertson, 'Ignorance and Power: George Eliot's Attack on Professional Incompetence', *The George Eliot Review* 16 (1985), https://digitalcommons.unl.edu/ger/24.

30. Bennett, *Ignorance*, 106.
31. Cf. J. Hillis Miller, 'Conscious Perjury: Declarations of Ignorance in the *Golden Bowl*', in *Literature as Conduct: Speech Acts in Henry James* (New York, 2005), 228–90.
32. Michael Smithson, 'Ignorance and Science', *Knowledge: Creation, Diffusion, Utilization* 15 (1993), 133–56, at 133. He had already published a book on the subject: *Ignorance and Uncertainty: Emerging Paradigms* (New York, 1989).
33. Théodore Ivainer and Roger Lenglet, *Les ignorances des savants* (Paris, 1996), 6.
34. Gross, 'Objective Culture'. Cf. Moore and Tumin, 'Social Functions', 789–95.
35. Friedrich von Hayek, 'Coping with Ignorance', *Imprimis* 7 (1978), https://imprimis. hillsdale.edu/coping-with-ignorance-july-1978.
36. Andrew Martin, *The Knowledge of Ignorance from Genesis to Jules Verne* (Cambridge, 1985); Philip Weinstein, *Unknowing: The Work of Modernist Fiction* (Ithaca NY, 2005); Bennett, *Ignorance*, especially chap. 6 on 'Joseph Conrad's Blindness'.
37. C. S. Lewis, 'New Learning and New Ignorance', *English Literature in the Sixteenth Century, Excluding Drama* (Oxford, 1954), 1–65; Bennett, *Ignorance*, 1; Steven Connor, *The Madness of Knowledge: On Wisdom, Ignorance and Fantasies of Knowing* (London, 2019).
38. Ivainer and Lenglet, *Ignorances*, 5; Mills, *Racial Contract*, 97.
39. Murray Last, 'The Importance of Knowing About Not-Knowing' (1981: repr. in S. Feierman and J. Janzen (eds), *The Social Basis of Health and Healing in Africa* (Berkeley CA, 1992)), 393–406; Ronald Duncan and Miranda Weston-Smith, *The Encyclopaedia of Medical Ignorance* (Oxford, 1984); Lewis Thomas, 'Medicine as a Very Old Profession', in James B. Wyngaarden and L. H. Smith (eds), *Cecil Textbook of Medicine* (Philadelphia PA, 1985), 9–11.
40. Marlys Witte, Ann Kerwin et al., 'A Curriculum on Medical Ignorance', *Medical Education* 23 (1989), 24–9.
41. Roberta Bivins, *Alternative Medicine? A History* (Oxford, 2007), 52, 56, 75, 78, 135.
42. In a special issue of the journal *Knowledge*, vol. 15, with contributions from Ann Kerwin, Jerome R. Ravetz, Michael J. Smithson and S. Holly Stocking.
43. Matthias Gross, *Ignorance and Surprise: Science, Society and Ecological Design* (Cambridge MA, 2010); Gross, *Experimentelles Nichtwissen: Umweltinnovationen und die Grenzen sozial-ökologischer Resilienz* (Bielfeld, 2014); Ana Regina Rêgo and Marialva Barbosa, *A Construção Intencional da Ignorância: O Mercado das Informações Falsas* (Rio, 2020); José de Souza Martins, *Sociologia do desconhecimento: ensaios sobre a incerteza do instante* (São Paulo, 2021).
44. Gross and McGoey, *Routledge Handbook of Ignorance Studies*.
45. 'Vaguen' (Chris Gibbs and T. J. Dawe), *The Power of Ignorance: 14 Steps to Using Your Ignorance* (London, 2006); David H. Swendsen, *The Power of Ignorance: The Ignorance Trap* (self-published, 2019); Dave Trott, *The Power of Ignorance: How Creative Solutions Emerge When We Admit What We Don't Know* (London, 2021).

## 5 HISTORIES OF IGNORANCE

1. Antoine Thomas, *Essay on the Characters, Manners and Genius of Women in Different Ages. Enlarged from the French of M. Thomas by Mr Russell* (London, 1773); Christoph Meiners, *History of the Female Sex: Comprising a View of the Habits, Manners and Influence of Women Among All Nations from the Earliest Ages to the Present Time* (London, 1808).
2. Daniel Woolf, 'A Feminine Past? Gender, Genre and Historical Knowledge in England, 1500–1800', *American Historical Review* 102 (1997), 645–79; Natalie Z. Davis, 'Gender and Genre: Women as Historical Writers 1400–1820', in Patricia Labalme (ed.), *Beyond Their Sex: Learned Women of the European Past* (New York, 1980), 153–75; Bonnie Smith, *The Gender of History: Men, Women and Historical Practice* (Cambridge, 1998).
3. Mary R. Beard, *Woman as Force in History: A Study in Traditions and Realities* (New York, 1946), 1, 273.
4. Smith, *Gender of History*, 207.

5. Natalie Z. Davis, 'Women's History in Transition', *Feminist Studies* 3 (1975), 83–103; Davis, 'City Women and Religious Change', in *Society and Culture in Early Modern France* (London, 1975), 65–95. Cf. Joan Scott, 'Women's History', in Peter Burke (ed.), *New Perspectives on Historical Writing* (Cambridge, 1991), 42–66.
6. Natalie Z. Davis, *The Return of Martin Guerre* (Cambridge MA, 1983).
7. General studies include Heide Wunder, *He is the Sun, She is the Moon: Women in Early Modern Germany* (1992: English trans. Cambridge MA, 1998); Merry Wiesner-Hanks, *Women and Gender in Early Modern Europe* (1993: 4th edn Cambridge, 2019); Olwen Hufton, *The Prospect Before Her: A History of Women in Western Europe, 1500–1800* (London, 1995).
8. Marshall Sahlins, *Historical Metaphors and Mythical Realities* (Ann Arbor MI, 1981).
9. Davis, 'Women's History', 90.
10. Peter Galison and Robert Proctor, 'Agnotology in Action', in Kourany and Carrier (eds), *Science*, 27–54, at 27–8; Proctor and Schiebinger, *Agnotology*. More recent work is discussed in Lukas Verburgt, 'The History of Knowledge and the Future History of Ignorance', *Know* 4 (2020), 1–24.
11. Among plain historians, an early exception is Scott, 'Ignorance and Perceptions of Social Reality in Revolutionary Marseilles', in Pittock and Andrew (eds), *Interpretation and Cultural History*, 235–68.
12. Robert DeMaria Jr, *Johnson's Dictionary* (Oxford, 1986), 77.
13. François La Mothe Le Vayer, *Du peu de certitude qu'il y a dans l'histoire* (Paris, 1668).
14. Varga, *Schlagwort*, 119, 123.
15. Bernard de Fontenelle, *De l'origine des fables* (1724: ed. Jean-Raoul Carré, Paris, 1932), 11–12, 37.
16. Nicolas de Condorcet, *Esquisse d'un tableau historique des progrès de l'esprit humain* (1794–5: ed. Oliver H. Prior, Paris 1933).
17. The phrase was coined and the interpretation criticized in Herbert Butterfield, *The Whig Interpretation of History* (London, 1931).
18. Martin Kintzinger, '*Ignorantia diplomatica*. Konstrukiv Nichtwissen in der Zeit des Hundertjähriges Krieges', in Espenhorst, *Unwissen und Missverständnisse*, 13–40; Cornel Zwierlein, *Imperial Unknowns: The French and the British in the Mediterranean, 1650–1750* (Cambridge, 2016), and Zwierlein (ed.), *The Dark Side of Knowledge: Histories of Ignorance, 1400 to 1800* (Leiden, 2016); Corbin, *Terra Incognita*.
19. Elliot W. Eisner, *The Educational Imagination* (New York, 1979), 83–92, at 83.
20. Samples of what might be done can be found in Peter Burke, *A Social History of Knowledge*, vol. 2: *From the Encyclopédie to Wikipedia* (Cambridge, 2012), 149–50.
21. Scott Frickel, 'Absences: Methodological Note about Nothing, in Particular', *Social Epistemology* 28 (2014), 86–95; Jenny Croissant, 'Agnotology: Ignorance and Absence or Towards a History of Things that Aren't There', ibid., 4–25.
22. Francesco Petrarca, 'De sui ipsius et multorum ignorantia' (1368: in *Opera*, Basel, 1554), 1123–68, English trans. 'On His Own Ignorance and That of Many Others', in Ernst Cassirer, Paul O. Kristeller and John H. Randall Jr (eds), *The Renaissance Philosophy of Man* (Chicago IL, 1948), 47–133.
23. Gómara's *Historia General de las Indias y Nuevo Mundo*, quoted in José Antonio Maravall, *Antiguos y modernos* (Madrid, 1966), 446.
24. Marc Bloch, *Caractères originaux de l'histoire rurale française* (Oslo, 1931).
25. Febvre, *Problème de l'incroyance*, part 2, book 2, chap. 2.
26. Arthur Conan Doyle, 'The Silver Blaze', in *Memoirs of Sherlock Holmes* (London, 1892); Werner Sombart, *Warum gibt es in den Vereinigten Staaten keine Sozialismus?* (Tübingen, 1906).
27. Zwierlein, *Imperial Unknowns*, 189–91.
28. Edward Janak, 'What Do You Mean It's Not There? Doing Null History', *American Archivist* 83 (2020), 57–76.
29. Burke, *Knowledge*, vol. 2, 139–59.

30. C. S. Lewis, *English Literature in the Sixteenth Century, excluding Drama* (Oxford, 1954), 31.
31. Harold Lasswell, 'The Structure and Function of Communication in Society', in Lyman Bryson (ed.), *The Communication of Ideas* (New York, 1948), 37–51.
32. Zwierlein, *Imperial Unknowns*, 2, 118, etc.
33. Quoted in David Vincent, *The Culture of Secrecy: Britain, 1832–1998* (Oxford, 1998), 160–61.
34. Michel Foucault, *The History of Sexuality*, vol. 1 (1976: English trans. London, 1978), 3, 123, 127. In contrast, Peter Gay, in *The Education of the Senses* (New York, 1984), 468, dismissed Foucault's argument as 'almost wholly unencumbered by facts'.
35. Madeleine Alcover, 'The Indecency of Knowledge', *Rice University Studies* 64 (1978), 25–40; Bathsua Makyn, *An Essay to Revive the Antient Education of Gentlewomen* (London, 1673); Jerome Nadelhaft, 'The Englishwoman's Sexual Civil War', *Journal of the History of Ideas* 43 (1982), 555–79. Cf. Le Doeuf, *Sex of Knowing*.
36. Peter Burke, 'Cultural History as Polyphonic History', *Arbor* 186 (2010), DOI: 10.3989/arbor.2010.743n1212.

# 6 IGNORANCE OF RELIGION

1. Justin McBrayer, 'Ignorance and the Religious Life', in Peels and Blaauw, *Epistemic Dimensions*, 144–59, at 149.
2. Silvia Berti, 'Scepticism and the *Traité des trois imposteurs*', in Richard Popkin and Arjo Vanderjagt (eds), *Scepticism and Irreligion in the Seventeenth and Eighteenth Centuries* (Leiden, 1993), 216–29.
3. Denys Hay, *The Church in Italy in the Fifteenth Century* (Cambridge, 1977), 49.
4. Eamon Duffy, *The Stripping of the Altars: Traditional Religion in England, 1400–1580* (New Haven CT, 1992), 53.
5. Quoted in Jean Delumeau, *Le Catholicisme entre Luther et Voltaire* (Paris, 1971), 270.
6. Christopher Hill, 'Puritans and the "Dark Corners of the Land"', *Transactions of the Royal Historical Society* 13 (1963), 77–102, at 80.
7. On ignorant priests, Hay, *The Church*, 49–57; on pastors, Gerald Strauss, 'Success and Failure in the German Reformation', *Past & Present* 67 (1975), 30–63, at 51, 55.
8. Bernard Heyberger, *Les chrétiens du proche-orient au temps de la réforme catholique* (Rome, 1994), 140.
9. Quoted in Larry Wolff, *Inventing Eastern Europe: The Map of Civilization on the Mind of the Enlightenment* (Stanford CA, 1994), 175, 177.
10. Quoted in Keith Thomas, *Religion and the Decline of Magic* (London, 1971), 164.
11. Hill, 'Puritans', 82.
12. Strauss, 'Success and Failure', 43.
13. Hilding Pleijel, *Husandakt, husaga, husförhör* (Stockholm, 1965). My thanks to Dr Kajsa Weber for this reference.
14. Gigliola Fragnito, *Proibito capire: la Chiesa e il volgare nella prima età moderna* (Bologna, 2005).
15. Peter Burke, 'The Bishop's Questions and the People's Religion' (1979: repr. in *Historical Anthropology of Early Modern Italy* (Cambridge, 1987)), 40–47.
16. Leonard P. Harvey, *Muslims in Spain, 1500 to 1614* (Chicago IL, 2005), 25.
17. David M. Gitlitz, *Secrecy and Deceit: The Religion of the Crypto-Jews* (1996: 2nd edn Albuquerque NM, 2002), 135.
18. Gitlitz, *Secrecy*, 87–8, 100, 117.
19. Quoted in Thomas, *Religion and the Decline of Magic*, 164–6.
20. Rudyerd quoted in Hill, 'Puritans', 96.
21. Adriano Prosperi, 'Otras Indias', in Paola Zambelli (ed.), *Scienze, credenze occulte, livelli di cultura* (Florence, 1982), 205–34, at 208.
22. Will Sweetman, 'Heathenism, Idolatry and Rational Monotheism among the Hindus', in Andreas Gross et al. (eds), *Halle and the Beginning of Protestant Christianity in India* (Halle, 2006), 1249–72.

23. Heyberger, *Les chrétiens du proche-orient*, 140.
24. Hildegarde Fast, '"In at One Ear and Out at the Other": African Response to the Wesleyan Message in Xhosaland, 1825–1835', *Journal of Religion in Africa* 23 (1993), 147–74, at 150.
25. Scipione Paolucci, *Missioni de'Padri della Compagnia de Giesù nel Regno di Napoli* (Naples, 1651), 29; Antoine Boschet, *Le Parfait Missionaire, ou la vie du r. p. Julien Maunoir* (Paris, 1697), 96; Louis Abelly, *La vie de St Vincent de Paul*, vol. 2 (Paris, 1664), 76.
26. Fast, 'In at One Ear'.
27. Adrian Hastings, *The Church in Africa, 1450–1950* (Oxford, 1994), 258.
28. Luke A. Veronis, 'The Danger of Arrogance and Ignorance in Missions: A Case Study from Albania', https://missions.hchc.edu/articles/articles/the-danger-of-arrogance-and-ignorance-in-missions-a-case-study-from-albania. Accessed 28 June 2022.
29. Quoted in David Maxwell, *Religious Entanglement and the Making of the Luba Katanga in Belgian Congo* (forthcoming, 2022).
30. James Clifford, *Person and Myth: Maurice Leenhardt in the Melanesian World* (Berkeley CA, 1982).
31. https://www.reuters.com/article/us-britain-bible-idINTRE56A30S20090711. Accessed 28 June 2022.
32. https://www.pewforum.org/2010/09/28/u-s-religious-knowledge-survey-who. Accessed 13 May 2022.
33. Zwierlein, *Imperial Unknowns*, 118–24, 134.
34. Nicholas Rescher, *Ignorance: On the Wider Implications of Deficient Knowledge* (Pittsburgh PA, 2009), 14.
35. Tamotsu Shibutani, *Improvised News: A Sociological Study of Rumour* (Indianapolis IN, 1966). Cf. Gordon Allport and Leo Postman, *The Psychology of Rumor* (New York, 1947).
36. Andrew McGowan, 'Eating People: Accusations of Cannibalism against Christians in the Second Century', *Journal of Early Christian Studies* 2 (1994), 413–42.
37. Norman Daniel, *Islam and the West: The Making of an Image* (Edinburgh, 1958), 217; Michael Camille, *The Gothic Idol: Ideology and Image-Making in Medieval Art* (Cambridge, 1989), 165–75.
38. James Parkes, *The Conflict of the Church and the Synagogue* (London, 1934); Joshua Trachtenberg, *The Devil and the Jews: The Medieval Conception of the Jew and its Relation to Modern Antisemitism* (New Haven CT, 1943), 97–155; Miri Rubin, *Gentile Tales: The Narrative Assault on Late Medieval Jews* (New Haven CT, 1999); Ronald P. Hsia, *The Myth of Ritual Murder: Jews and Magic in Reformation Germany* (New Haven CT, 1988).
39. Trachtenberg, *The Devil and the Jews*, 174.
40. Nicholas of Cusa, *On Learned Ignorance* (1440: English trans. Minneapolis MN, 1981), book 1, chap. 25.
41. Heiko Oberman, *The Roots of Anti-Semitism in the Age of Renaissance and Reformation* (1981: English trans. Philadelphia PA, 1984), 25, 30, 40.
42. Christopher Probst, *Demonizing the Jews: Luther and the Protestant Church in Nazi Germany* (Bloomington IN, 2012), 39–45.
43. Pierre de l'Ancre, *L'incredulité et mescréance du sortilege* (Paris, 1622), quoted in Hugh Trevor-Roper, *The European Witch-Craze of the Sixteenth and Seventeenth Centuries* (Harmondsworth, 1969), 36.
44. Norman Cohn, *Warrant for Genocide: The Myth of the Jewish World Conspiracy and the Protocols of the Elders of Zion* (London, 1967).
45. Richard M. Hunt, 'Myths, Guilt, and Shame in Pre-Nazi Germany', *Virginia Quarterly Review* 34 (1958), 355–371
46. Probst, *Demonizing the Jews*, 137.
47. Daniel, *Islam and the West*, 309–13; Richard W. Southern, *Western Views of Islam in the Middle Ages* (Cambridge MA, 1962), 14, 25, 28, 32; Camille, *The Gothic Idol*, 129–64, at 129, 142.
48. Pim Valkenberg, 'Learned Ignorance and Faithful Interpretation of the Qur'an in Nicholas of Cusa', in James L. Heft, Reuven Firestone and Omid Safi (eds), *Learned Ignorance: Intellectual Humility among Jews, Christians and Muslims* (Oxford, 2011), 34–52, at 39, 45.

49. Marco Polo, *The Travels*, ed. Robin Latham (Harmondsworth, 1958), 57, 134.
50. Robert Irwin, *For Lust of Knowing: The Orientalists and Their Enemies* (London, 2006), 82–108.
51. Glenn J. Ames (ed.), *Em Nome de Deus: The Journal of the First Voyage of Vasco da Gama to India, 1497–1499* (Boston, 2009), 66n, 72, 75–6. Cf. Sanjay Subrahmanyam, *The Career and Legend of Vasco da Gama* (Cambridge, 1997), 132–3.
52. Donald Lach, *Asia in the Making of Europe*, 2 vols (Chicago IL, 1965), 439, 449.
53. Partha Mitter, *Much Maligned Monsters: A History of European Reactions to Indian Art* (1977: 3rd edn Oxford, 2013), 15, 17, 22, 25; Inga Clendinnen, *Ambivalent Conquests: Maya and Spaniard in Yucatan, 1517–1570* (1987: 2nd edn Cambridge, 2003), 45–56; Diego de Landa, *Relación de las Cosas de Yucatan* (Paris, 1928), chap. 18.
54. Peter Marshall (ed.), *The British Discovery of Hinduism in the Eighteenth Century* (Cambridge, 1970), 48, 50, 107, 145.
55. Lynn Hunt, Margaret Jacob and Wijnand Mijnhardt, *The Book that Changed Europe: Picart and Bernard's Religious Ceremonies of the World* (Cambridge MA, 2010); Hunt, Jacob and Mijnhardt (eds), *Bernard Picart and the First Global Vision of Religion* (Los Angeles CA, 2010).
56. Robert Pomplun, Joan-Pau Rubiès and Ines G. Županov, 'Early Catholic Orientalism and the Missionary Discovery of Asian Religions', *Journal of Early Modern History* 24 (2020), 463–70.
57. Luciano Petech (ed.), *I missionari italiani nel Tibet e nel Nepal*, part 6 (Rome: Istituto Poligrafico dello Stato, 1955), 115ff; Philip C. Almond, *The British Discovery of Buddhism* (Cambridge, 1988), 7.
58. Melville J. Herskovits, 'African Gods and Catholic Saints in New World Negro Belief', *American Anthropologist* 39 (1937), 635–43; Paul C. Johnson, *Secrets, Gossip and Gods: The Transformation of Brazilian Candomblé* (Oxford, 2002), 71.
59. Harvey, *Muslims*, 61–2. Cf. Antonio Domínguez Ortiz, *Historia de los Moriscos: Vida y Tragedia de una Minoría* (Madrid, 1978).
60. Brian Pullan, 'The Marranos of Iberia and the Converts of Italy', in *The Jews of Europe and the Inquisition of Venice, 1550–1670* (Oxford, 1983), 201–312, at 223. Cf. Perez Zagorin, 'The Marranos and Crypto-Judaism', in *Ways of Lying: Dissimulation, Persecution and Conformity in Early Modern Europe* (Cambridge MA, 1990), 38–62; Gilitz, *Secrecy*.
61. Delio Cantimori, *Eretici italiani del Cinquecento* (Florence, 1939); Carlo Ginzburg, *Il Nicodemismo: simulazione e dissimulazione religiosa nell' Europa del '500* (Turin, 1970); Zagorin, *Ways of Lying*, 83–152.
62. Mauro Bonazzi, *The Sophists* (Cambridge, 2020), 113.
63. Sextus Empiricus, *Outlines of Pyrrhonism*, 329.
64. Friedrich Nietzsche, *Genealogie der Moral* (1887), section 25; Marcel Proust, *Le Côté de Guermantes* (Paris, 1920).
65. T. H. Huxley, 'Agnosticism and Christianity' (1899).
66. Bernard Lightman, *The Origins of Agnosticism: Victorian Unbelief and the Limits of Knowledge* (Baltimore MD, 1987).
67. Denys Turner, *The Darkness of God: Negativity in Christian Mysticism* (Cambridge, 1995); William Franke, 'Learned Ignorance', in Gross and McGoey (eds), *Routledge Handbook of Ignorance Studies*, 26–35; Jonathan Jacobs, 'The Ineffable, Inconceivable and Incomprehensible God', in Jonathan Kvanvig (ed.), *Oxford Studies in Philosophy of Religion* 6 (Oxford, 2015), 158–76.
68. Moses Maimonides, *Guide for the Perplexed* (English trans. New York, 1956), 81.
69. Nicholas of Cusa, *On Learned Ignorance*, book 1, chap. 26; Peter Casarella (ed.), *Cusanus: The Legacy of Learned Ignorance* (Washington DC, 2006); Blaise Pascal, *Pensées* (1670: English trans. London, 1958), numbers 194, 242; Lucien Goldmann, *The Hidden God: A Study of Tragic Vision in Pascal's Pensées and the Tragedies of Racine* (1959: English trans. London, 1964); Volker Leppin, '*Deus Absconditus* und *Deus Revelatus*', *Berliner Theologischer Zeitschrift* 22 (2005), 55–69.

70. Peter Gay, *Deism: An Anthology* (Princeton NJ, 1968).
71. Alexander Pope, *Essay on Man* (1732–4), Epistle II, lines 1–2.
72. https://www.rt.com/uk/231811-uk-atheism-report-decline and https://www.cnn.com/2019 /04/13/us/no-religion-largest-group-first-time-usa-trnd, both visited 18 November 2020.
73. 'Evangelical Ignorance', 15 March 2018, brucegerencser.net.
74. Peter Stanford, 'Christianity, Arrogance and Ignorance', *Guardian*, 3 July 2010, https:// www.theguardian.com.
75. 'What Americans Know About Religion', www.pewforum.org/2019. Accessed 13 May 2022.
76. 'A Review of Survey Research on Muslims in Britain', https://www.ipsos.com/en-uk/ review-survey-research-muslims-britain-0. Accessed 13 May 2022.
77. Reported in *The Economist*, 3–9 July 2021, 54.

## 7 IGNORANCE OF SCIENCE

1. Peter Wehling, 'Why Science Does Not Know: A Brief History of (the Notion of) Scientific Ignorance in the 20th and Early 21st Century', *Journal of the History of Knowledge* 2 (2021), https://doi.org/10.5334/jhk.40; Proctor and Schiebinger, *Agnotology*.
2. Jerome R. Ravetz, 'The Sin of Science: Ignorance of Ignorance', *Knowledge* 15 (1993), 157–65.
3. The indirect evidence for this remark is discussed in https://todayinsci.com/N/Newton_ Isaac/NewtonIsaac-PlayingOnTheSeashore.htm. Accessed 13 May 2022.
4. Isaac Newton, *Four Letters to Dr Bentley* (London, 1756), 20 (Newton's second letter to Bentley, written in 1693).
5. Quoted in Leonard Huxley, *Life and Letters of Thomas Huxley* (London, 1900), 261.
6. Quoted in Stuart Firestein, *Ignorance: How it Drives Science* (New York, 2012).
7. Ferdinand Vidoni, *Ignorabimus! Emil Du Bois-Reymond und die Debatte über die Grenzen wissenschaftlicher Erkenntnis im 19 Jahrhundert* (Frankfurt, 1991).
8. www.nobelprize.org/prizes/physics/2004/gross/speech. Accessed 13 May 2022.
9. Firestein, *Ignorance*, 5, 44.
10. Voltaire, *Lettres philosophiques* (Paris, 1734), chap. 12.
11. James Ussher, *Annals of the World* (London, 1658), 1.
12. Brent Dalrymple, *The Age of the Earth* (Stanford CA, 1994); James Powell, *Mysteries of Terra Firma: The Age and Evolution of the World* (New York, 2001).
13. Yuval Noah Harari, *Sapiens: A Brief History of Humankind* (2011: English trans. London, 2014), 275–306, at 279.
14. Herbert Spencer, *First Principles of a New System of Philosophy* (London, 1862), 17. Blaise Pascal had employed this metaphor two hundred years earlier.
15. Quoted in Firestein, *Ignorance*, 7, 4.
16. Firestein, *Ignorance*, 44.
17. Quoted in Steven Shapin, *The Scientific Life: A Moral History of a Late Modern Vocation* (Chicago IL, 2008), 135, 142. Cf. Firestein, *Ignorance*; Verburgt, 'History of Knowledge', 1–24; Wehling, 'Why Science Does Not Know'.
18. Francis Crick, *What Mad Pursuit: A Personal View of Scientific Discovery* (1988: new edn London, 1989), 35, 141–2.
19. Quoted in Firestein, *Ignorance*, 136, 44.
20. Janet Kourany and Martin Carrier, 'Introducing the Issues', in Kourany and Carrier (eds), *Science*, 3–25, at 14.
21. Quoted in Formica, *Creative Ignorance*, 13.
22. Hans-Jörg Rheinberger, *Toward a History of Epistemic Things* (Stanford CA, 1997); Hans-Jörg Rheinberger, 'Man weiss nicht genau, was man nicht weiss. Über die Kunst, das Unbekannte zu erforschen', *Neue Zürcher Zeitung*, 5 May 2007. https://www.nzz.ch/arti-cleELG88-ld.409885.
23. Gross, *Ignorance and Surprise*, 1.

24. Ian Taylor, 'A bluffer's guide to the new fundamental law of nature', *Science Focus*, 8 April 2021, www.sciencefocus.com/news/a-bluffers-guide; 'Mapping the Local Cosmic Web: Dark matter map reveals hidden bridges between galaxies', 25 May 2021, phys.org.

25. Richard Southern, *The Making of the Middle Ages* (London, 1953), 210.

26. Dimitri Gutas, *Greek Thought, Arabic Culture: The Graeco-Arabic translation movement in Baghdad and early Abbasid Society* (London, 1998); Charles Burnett, *Arabic into Latin in the Middle Ages: The Translators and Their Intellectual and Social Context* (London, 2009).

27. Mulsow, *Prekäres Wissen*.

28. Guy Deutscher, *Through the Language Glass: Why the World Looks Different in Other Languages* (London, 2010), 79, 83, 85.

29. William Bateson, *Mendel's Principles of Heredity* (Cambridge, 1913).

30. Bernard Barber, 'Resistance by Scientists to Scientific Discovery', *Science* 134 (1961), 596–602, at 598.

31. On 'anomalies', Kuhn, *Structure*, 52–65.

32. Max Planck, *Scientific Autobiography* (1945: English trans. London, 1948), 33–4.

33. Andrew D. White, *A History of the Warfare of Science with Theology in Christendom* (New York, 1896).

34. Edward Grant, 'In Defense of the Earth's Centrality and Immobility: Scholastic Reaction to Copernicanism in the Seventeenth Century', *Transactions of the American Philosophical Society* 74 (1984), 1–69, at 4; Christopher Graney, *Setting Aside All Authority: Giovanni Battista Riccioli and the Science Against Copernicus in the Age of Galileo* (Notre Dame IN, 2015), 63.

35. Rivka Feldhay, *Galileo and the Church: Political Inquisition or Critical Dialogue?* (Cambridge, 1995).

36. Ludovico Geymonat, *Galileo* (Turin, 1957), chap. 4. Cf. Ernan McMullin, 'Galileo's Theological Venture', in McMullin (ed.), *The Church and Galileo* (Notre Dame IN, 2005), 88–116.

37. Quoted in Edward Lurie, *Louis Agassiz: A Life in Science* (Chicago IL, 1960), 151.

38. Peter Bowler, *The Eclipse of Darwinism: Anti-Darwinian Evolution Theories in the Decades around 1900* (Baltimore MD, 1983); James R. Moore, *The Post-Darwinian Controversies* (Cambridge, 1979).

39. Freeman Henry, 'Anti-Darwinism in France: Science and the Myth of Nation', *Nineteenth-Century French Studies* 27 (1999), 290–304.

40. Quoted in Moore, *Post-Darwinian Controversies*, 1.

41. Naomi Oreskes, *The Rejection of Continental Drift: Theory and Method in American Earth Science* (New York, 1999), 316. Cf. John Stewart, *Drifting Continents and Colliding Paradigms: Perspectives on the Geoscience Revolution* (Bloomington IN, 1990), 17–19, 22–44.

42. Quoted in Powell, *Mysteries of Terra Firma*, 77.

43. Quoted in Oreskes, *Rejection of Continental Drift*, 277.

44. Naomi Oreskes and Erik M. Conway, *Merchants of Doubt: How a Handful of Scientists Obscured the Truth on Issues from Tobacco Smoke to Global Warming* (New York, 2010).

45. Scott Frickel et al., 'Undone Science', *Science, Technology and Human Values* 35 (2010), 444–73; David Hess, *Undone Science: Social Movements, Mobilized Publics, and Industrial Transitions* (Cambridge MA, 2016).

46. Roy Porter, *Quacks: Fakers and Charlatans in English Medicine* (Stroud, 2000); David Wootton, *Bad Medicine: Doctors Doing Harm Since Hippocrates* (Oxford, 2006).

47. Ben Goldacre, *Bad Pharma: How Drug Companies Mislead Doctors and Harm Patients* (London, 2012), 311, 242.

48. William Eamon, *Science and the Secrets of Nature: Books of Secrets in Medieval and Early Modern Culture* (Princeton NJ, 1994).

49. Charles Webster, *Paracelsus: Medicine, Magic and Mission at the End of Time* (New Haven CT, 2008).

50. Quoted in F. N. L. Poynter, 'Nicholas Culpeper and His Books', *Journal of the History of Medicine and Allied Sciences* 17 (1962), 152–67, at 157.

51. Culpeper quoted in Benjamin Woolley, *The Herbalist: Nicholas Culpeper and the Fight for Medical Freedom* (London, 2004), 297. On him, Patrick Curry, 'Culpeper, Nicholas', *Oxford Dictionary of National Biography* 14, 602–5.

52. Lisbet Koerner, in Nicholas Jardine, James Secord and Emma Spary (eds), *Cultures of Natural History* (Cambridge, 1996), 145.

53. Simon Schaffer, 'Natural Philosophy and Public Spectacle in the Eighteenth Century', *History of Science* 21 (1983), 1–43.

54. Aileen Fyfe and Bernard Lightman (eds), *Science in the Marketplace: 19th-century Sites and Experiences* (Chicago IL, 2007).

55. Edward Larson, *Summer for the Gods: The Scopes Trial and America's Continuing Debate over Science and Religion* (New York, 1997).

56. Larson, *Summer*, 281; cf. Larson, *The Creation-Evolution Debate* (Athens GA, 2007), 23–6.

57. Glenn Branch, 'Understanding Gallup's Latest Poll on Evolution', *Skeptical Inquirer* 41 (2017), 5–6.

58. C. P. Snow, *The Two Cultures* (Cambridge, 1959).

59. 'Survey Reveals Public Ignorance of Science', 14 July 1989, https://www.newscientist.com.

60. Melissa Leach, Ian Scoones and Brian Wynne (eds), *Science and Citizens: Globalization and the Challenge of Engagement* (London, 2005).

61. Alan Irwin, *Citizen Science* (London, 1995).

62. Firestein, *Ignorance*, 171.

## 8 IGNORANCE OF GEOGRAPHY

1. John Morgan, 'The Making of Geographical Ignorance?' *Geography* 102.1 (2017), 18–25, at 18–20.

2. John R. Short, *Cartographic Encounters: Indigenous Peoples and the Exploration of the New World* (London, 2009).

3. The text is reproduced at 'Governor Bourke's Proclamation, 26 August 1835 – Wikisource, the free online library'.

4. Corbin, *Terra Incognita*.

5. On Ptolemy, Pierre-Ange Salvadori, *Le Nord de la Renaissance: La carte, l'humanisme suédois et la genèse de l'Arctique* (Paris, 2021), 29.

6. Danilo Dolci, *Inchiesta a Palermo* (1956: new edn Palermo, 2013).

7. Wolff, *Inventing Eastern Europe*, 174.

8. Janet Abu-Lughod, *Before European Hegemony: The World System, ad 1250–1350* (New York, 1989).

9. W. G. L. Randles, 'Classical Models of World Geography and Their Transformation Following the Discovery of America', and James Romm, 'New World and "Novos Orbes": Seneca in the Renaissance Debate over Ancient Knowledge of the Americas', in Wolfgang Haase and Meyer Reinhold (eds), *The Classical Tradition and the Americas*, vol. 1 (Berlin, 1994), 6–76 and 77–116.

10. Edmundo O'Gorman, *The Invention of America* (1958: English trans. Bloomington IN, 1961); Eviatar Zerubavel, *Terra Cognita: The Mental Discovery of America* (New Brunswick NJ, 1992).

11. Paolo Chiesa, 'Marckalada: The First Mention of America in the Mediterranean Area (c.1340)', *Terrae Incognitae* 53.2 (2021), 88–106.

12. Jean-Jacques Rousseau, *Discours sur Inégalité* (1755: Paris 2004 edn, 110 (my translation)).

13. Shibutani, *Improvised News*.

14. John B. Friedman, *The Monstrous Races in Medieval Art and Thought* (Cambridge MA, 1981).

15. Robert Silverberg, *The Realm of Prester John* (1996: 2nd edn London, 2001), 26, 38.

16. Silverberg, *Prester John*, 40–73.

17. Silverberg, *Prester John*, 163–92.

18. Ames, *Em Nome de Deus*, 51.

19. Kathleen March and Kristina Passman, 'The Amazon Myth and Latin America', in Haase and Reinhold, *Classical Tradition*, 286–338, at 300–307.

20. Dora Polk, *The Island of California: A History of the Myth* (Spokane WA, 1991), 105–20, 301. The romance was 'The Exploits of Esplandián' (*Las Sergas de Esplandián*), by Garci Rodríguez de Montalvo.

21. Robert Silverberg, *The Golden Dream: Seekers of El Dorado* (Athens OH, 1985), 4–5; cf. Jean-Pierre Sánchez, 'El Dorado and the Myth of the Golden Fleece', in Haase and Reinhold, *Classical Tradition*, 339–78; John Hemming, *The Search for El Dorado* (London, 2001).

22. Lach, *Asia in the Making of Europe*.

23. Andrea Tilatti, 'Odorico da Pordenone', *DBI* 79.

24. Marco Polo, *Il Milione*, ed. Luigi Benedetto (Milan, 1932: English trans., *Travels*).

25. John Larner, *Marco Polo and the Discovery of the World* (New Haven CT, 1999), 131.

26. Marco Polo, *Travels*, 218.

27. Timothy Brook, *Great State: China and the World* (2019: new edn London, 2021), 46–7.

28. Larner, *Marco Polo*, 97, 108.

29. Stephen Greenblatt, *Marvelous Possessions: The Wonder of the New World* (Oxford, 1991), 26–51; Iain M. Higgins, *Writing East: The 'Travels' of Sir John Mandeville* (Philadelphia PA, 1997), 6, 156–78; Carlo Ginzburg, *The Cheese and the Worms: The Cosmos of a Sixteenth-Century Miller* (1976: English trans. London, 1980), section 12.

30. Larner, *Marco Polo*, 151–70, at 155.

31. Brook, *Great State*, 148.

32. Lach, *Asia in the Making of Europe*, 731–821.

33. Nicholas Trigault (ed.), *De christiana expeditione apud Sinas* (Augsburg, 1615).

34. Kenneth Ch'en, 'Matteo Ricci's Contribution to, and Influence on Geographical Knowledge in China', *Journal of the American Oriental Society* 59 (1939), 325–59; Cordell Yee, 'The Introduction of European Cartography', in J. Brian Harley and David Woodward (eds), *The History of Cartography*, vol. 2, book 2, *Cartography in the Traditional East and Southeast Asian Societies* (Chicago IL, 1994), 170–202, at 176.

35. Edwin Van Kley, 'Europe's Discovery of China and the Writing of World History', *American Historical Review* 76 (1971), 358–85.

36. Philippe Couplet et al., *Confucius Sinarum Philosophus* (Paris, 1687).

37. Virgile Pinot, *La Chine et la formation de l'esprit philosophique en France* (Paris, 1932).

38. Hugh Honour, *Chinoiserie* (London, 1961).

39. Felix Greene, *A Curtain of Ignorance* (London, 1965), xiii. Cf. Greene, *Awakened China: The Country Americans Don't Know* (New York, 1961). His sympathy for the Communist regime compensated for the hostile reports in the American press at the time.

40. Brook, *Great State*, 226. Cf. Brook, 'Europaeology? On the Difficulty of Assembling a Knowledge of Europe in China', in Antoni Ücerler (ed.), *Christianity and Cultures: Japan and China in Comparison, 1543–1644* (Rome, 2009), 269–93.

41. John Henderson, 'Chinese Cosmographical Thought', in Harley and Woodward (eds), *History of Cartography*, 203–27. On Europe, Grant, 'In Defense of the Earth's Centrality and Immobility', 1–69, at 22.

42. Ch'en, 'Matteo Ricci's Contribution', 325–59, at 326, 329–32, 341.

43. James Cahill, *The Compelling Image: Nature and Style in Seventeenth-Century Chinese Painting* (Cambridge MA, 1982). Cf. Michael Sullivan, *The Meeting of Eastern and Western Art* (Berkeley CA, 1989).

44. Eugenio Menegon, *Un Solo Cielo: Giulio Aleni SJ (1582–1649): Geografia, arte, scienza, religion dall'Europa alla Cina* (Brescia, 1994), 38–9, 42–3.

45. Nathan Sivin, 'Copernicus in China', *Studia Copernicana* 6 (1973), 63–122; Roman Malek, *Western Learning and Christianity in China: The Contribution and Impact of Johann Adam Schall von Bell SJ (1592–1666)* (Sankt Agustin, 1998); Florence Hsia, *Sojourners in a Strange Land: Jesuits and Their Scientific Missions in Late Imperial China* (Chicago IL, 2009).

46. Marta Hanson, 'Jesuits and Medicine in the Kangxi Court', *Pacific Rim Report* 43 (2007), 1–10, at 5, 7.
47. Mario Cams, 'Not Just a Jesuit Atlas of China: Qing Imperial Cartography and its European Connections', *Imago Mundi* 69 (2017), 188–201.
48. My thanks to Joseph McDermott for this suggestion.
49. *Lettres edifiantes* vol. 24, 334, 375, quoted in Jürgen Osterhammel, *Unfabling the East: The Enlightenment's Encounter with Asia* (1998: English trans. Princeton NJ, 2018), 85.
50. Ricci, quoted in Ch'en, 'Matteo Ricci's Contribution', 343.
51. Brook, 'Europaeology?', 285; Roger Hart, *Imagined Civilizations: China, the West and Their First Encounter* (Baltimore MD, 2013), 19, 188–91.
52. Ren Dayuan, 'Wang Zheng', in Malek, *Western Learning*, vol. 1, 359–68; on Mei Wending, Benjamin Elman, *On Their Own Terms: Science in China, 1550–1900* (Cambridge MA, 2005), 154–5.
53. Brook, 'Europaeology?', 270.
54. Ch'en, 'Matteo Ricci's Contribution', 348. Cf. George Wong, 'China's Opposition to Western Science during Late Ming and Early Ch'ing', *Isis* 54 (1963), 29–49.
55. Brook, 'Europaeology?', 291; Brook, *Great State*, 263.
56. Discussed in Shang Wei, 'The Literati Era and its Demise (1723–1840)', in Kang-I Sun Chang and Stephen Owen (eds), *The Cambridge History of Chinese Literature*, vol. 2 (Cambridge, 2010), 245–342, at 292, 294. Thanks to Joe McDermott for this reference.
57. Henderson, 'Chinese Cosmographical Thought', 209, 223, 225.
58. John Frodsham (ed.), *The First Chinese Embassy to the West* (Oxford, 1974), xvii, xxii, 148.
59. James Polachek, *The Inner Opium War* (Cambridge MA, 1992).
60. Jane Leonard, *Wei Yuan and China's Discovery of the Maritime World* (Cambridge MA, 1984), 101.
61. Frodsham, *First Chinese Embassy*, 97.
62. Elman, *On Their Own Terms*, xxvii, 320.
63. Adrian Bennett, *John Fryer: The Introduction of Western Science and Technology into Nineteenth-Century China* (Cambridge MA, 1967).
64. Benjamin Schwartz, *In Search of Wealth and Power: Yen Fu and the West* (Cambridge MA, 1964); Douglas Howland, *Translating the West* (Honolulu, 2001).
65. Michael Cooper (ed.), *The Southern Barbarians: The First Europeans in Japan* (Tokyo, 1971); Derek Massarella, *A World Elsewhere: Europe's Encounter with Japan in the Sixteenth and Seventeenth Centuries* (New Haven CT, 1990).
66. Charles Boxer, *Jan Compagnie in Japan* (The Hague, 1936); Grant K. Goodman, *Japan and the Dutch, 1600–1853* (1967: revised edn Richmond, 2000); Beatrice Bodart-Bailey and Derek Massarella (eds), *The Furthest Goal: Engelbert Kaempfer's Encounter with Tokugawa Japan* (Folkestone, 1996).
67. Donald Keene, *The Japanese Discovery of Europe 1720–1830* (1952: revised edn Stanford CA, 1969).
68. William G. Beasley, *Japan Encounters the Barbarian: Japanese Travellers in America and Europe* (New Haven CT, 1995).
69. The description originated in William Griffis, *Corea: The Hermit Nation* (New York, 1882).
70. Hendrick Hamel, *Journaal* (1668: ed. Henny Savenije, Rotterdam, 2003).
71. Rodney Needham, 'Psalmanazar, Confidence-Man', in *Exemplars* (Berkeley CA, 1985), 75–116; Richard M. Swiderski, *The False Formosan* (San Francisco CA, 1991); Michael Keevak, *The Pretended Asian* (Detroit MI, 2004). On his confession, Percy Adams, *Travelers and Travel Liars, 1660–1800* (Berkeley CA, 1962), 93.
72. Richard Burton, *Personal Narrative of a Pilgrimage to al-Madinah and Mecca* (London, 1856); Christiaan Snouck Hurgronje, *Het Mekkaansche Feest* (Leiden, 1880).
73. Petech, *I missionari*, 115ff.
74. Peter Hopkirk, *Trespassers on the Roof of the World* (London, 1983), 23; *Oxford Dictionary of National Biography*, 'Montgomerie, Thomas'.
75. Frank Kryza, *The Race for Timbuktu* (New York, 2007).

76. Peter Hopkirk, *Foreign Devils on the Silk Road: The Search for the Lost Cities and Treasures of Chinese Central Asia* (London, 1980), 32–43.
77. Wilfrid Thesiger, *Arabian Sands* (London, 1959).
78. Vicente de Salvador, *Historia do Brasil* (1627: new edn São Paulo, 1918).
79. Leo Africanus, *Descrizione dell'Africa* (Venice, 1550); Oumelbanine Zhiri, *L'Afrique au miroir de l'Europe, Fortunes de Jean Léon l'Africain à la Renaissance* (Geneva, 1991); Natalie Davis, *Trickster Travels: A Sixteenth-Century Muslim Between Worlds* (New York, 2007).
80. Miles Bredin, *The Pale Abyssinian: A Life of James Bruce, African Explorer and Adventurer* (London, 2000), 72. Cf. *Oxford Dictionary of National Biography*, 'Bruce, James, of Kinnaird'.
81. James Bruce, *Travels to Discover the Source of the Nile*, 5 vols (Edinburgh, 1790).
82. Bredin, *The Pale Abyssinian*, 163.
83. Bredin, *The Pale Abyssinian*, 25.
84. Bredin, *The Pale Abyssinian*, 161.
85. The editor of *Proceedings of the Association for Promoting the Discovery of the Interior Parts of Africa*, quoted in Roxanne Wheeler, 'Limited Visions of Africa', in James Duncan and Derek Gregory (eds), *Writes of Passage: Reading Travel Writing* (London, 1999), 14–48, at 16.
86. Henry Stanley, *Through the Dark Continent* (London, 1878), 2.
87. Kryza, *Race for Timbuktu*.
88. Kenneth Lupton, *Mungo Park: The African Traveller* (Oxford, 1979); Christopher Fyfe, 'Park, Mungo', *Oxford Dictionary of National Biography*.
89. Stanley, *Dark Continent*, preface.
90. Quoted in Joe Anene, *The International Boundaries of Nigeria, 1885–1960* (London, 1970), 3.
91. J. Brian Harley, 'Silences and Secrecy' (1988: repr. *The New Nature of Maps: Essays in the History of Cartography*, Baltimore MD, 2001), 84–107.
92. Bailie W. Diffie, 'Foreigners in Portugal and the "Policy of Silence"', *Terrae Incognitae* 1 (1969), 23–34; David Buisseret (ed.), *Monarchs, Ministers and Maps: Emergence of Cartography as a Tool of Government in Early Modern Europe* (Chicago IL, 1992), 106.
93. 'André João Antonil' (Giovanni Antonio Andreoni), *Cultura e opulência do Brasil* (1711: ed. Andrée Mansuy, Paris, 2019).
94. Rachel Zimmerman, 'The 'Cantino Planisphere', https://smarthistory.org/cantino-planisphere. Accessed 13 May 2022.
95. Alison Sandman, 'Controlling Knowledge: Navigation, Cartography and Secrecy in the Early Modern Spanish Atlantic', in James Delbourgo and Nicholas Dew (eds), *Science and Empire in the Atlantic World* (London, 2008), 31–52, at 35; Maria L. Portuondo, *Secret Science: Spanish Cosmography and the New World* (Chicago IL, 2009).
96. Harley, 'Silences and Secrecy', 90.
97. Craig Clunas, *Fruitful Sites: Garden Culture in Ming Dynasty China* (London, 1996), 191.
98. Patrick van Mil (ed.), *De VOC in de kaart gekeken* (The Hague, 1988), 22.
99. Woodruff D. Smith, 'Amsterdam as an Information Exchange in the 17th Century', *Journal of Economic History* 44 (1984), 985–1005, at 994. Cf. Karel Davids, 'Public Knowledge and Common Secrets: Secrecy and its Limits in the Early-Modern Netherlands', *Early Science and Medicine* 10 (2005), 411–27, at 415.
100. Elspeth Jajdelska, 'Unknown Unknowns: Ignorance of the Indies among Late Seventeenth-century Scots', in Siegfried Huigen, Jan L. de Jong and Elmer Kolfin (eds), *The Dutch Trading Companies as Knowledge Networks* (Leiden, 2010), 393–413.
101. Matthew H. Edney, *Mapping an Empire: The Geographical Construction of British India, 1765–1843* (Chicago IL, 1997), 143.
102. Marie-Noelle Bourguet et al. (eds), *L'invention scientifique de la Méditerranée* (Paris, 1998), 108.
103. G. Lappo and Pavel Polian, 'Naoukograds, les villes interdites', in Christian Jacob (ed.), *Lieux de Savoir* (Paris, 2007), 1226–49; Sean Keach, 'Revealed: 11 Secret Google Maps locations you're not allowed to see', *The Sun*, 17 February 2021.

104. Adams, *Travelers and Travel Liars*.
105. Higgins, *Writing East*, 49, 161.
106. Marco Polo, *Travels*, 272–7.
107. Marco Polo, *Travels*, 244.
108. Eileen Power, *Medieval People* (1924: new edn 1937), 55, 65; Larner, *Marco Polo*, 59–60.
109. John W. Haeger, 'Marco Polo in China? Problems with Internal Evidence', *Bulletin of Sung and Yuan Studies* 14 (1978), 26, 28.
110. Luigi Benedetto (ed.), *Il Milione* (Florence, 1928), xx, xxii, xxv.
111. Adams, *Travelers and Travel Liars*.
112. Frances Wood, *Did Marco Polo Go to China?* (London, 2018), 148–50. Contrast Larner, *Marco Polo*, 58–62.
113. Haeger, 'Marco Polo', 22–9.
114. Quoted in Rebecca D. Catz, 'Introduction' to Fernão Mendes Pinto, *Travels* (Chicago IL, 1989), xv–xlvi, at xxvii.
115. Jonathan Spence, 'The Peregrination of Mendes Pinto', *Chinese Roundabout* (New Haven CT, 1990), 25–36, at 30.
116. Bredin, *The Pale Abyssinian*.
117. Cyril Kemp, *Notes on Van der Post's Venture to the Interior and The Lost World of the Kalahari* (London, 1980), 176, 443; Simon Cooke, *Travellers' Tales of Wonder: Chatwin, Naipaul, Sebald* (Edinburgh, 2013).
118. Toby Ord, *The Precipice: Existential Risk and the Future of Humanity* (London, 2021), 62, 92.
119. Jonathan Schell, *The Fate of the Earth* (London, 1982).
120. Rachel Carson, *Silent Spring* (1962: new edn London, 2000), 24, 29, 51, 64, 82. For the situation today, see Julian Cribb, *Earth Detox: How and Why We Must Clean Up Our Planet* (Cambridge, 2021).
121. Bill McKibben, *The End of Nature* (1989: 2nd edn New York, 2006), 60.
122. Keith Thomas, *Man and the Natural World* (London, 1983), 15.
123. 'Plastic in the Ocean', https://www.worldwildlife.org/magazine/issues/fall-2019/articles/plastic-in-the-ocean. Accessed 13 May 2022.
124. Elizabeth Kolbert, *The Sixth Extinction: An Unnatural History* (London, 2014).

## PART II: CONSEQUENCES OF IGNORANCE

1. https://www.diariocentrodeundocom.br.

## 9 IGNORANCE IN WAR

1. Sun Tzu, *The Art of War* (English trans. London, 2002), 21–3.
2. John Presland, *Vae Victis: The Life of Ludwig von Benedek* (London, 1934), 232, 275; Oskar Regele, *Feldzeugmeister Benedek: Der Weg zu Königgratz* (Vienna, 1960).
3. Owen Connelly, *Blundering to Glory: Napoleon's Military Campaigns* (Lanham MD, 2006), 100, 107, 113.
4. Huw Davies, *Wellington's War* (New Haven CT, 2012).
5. Marc Bloch, 'Réflexions d'un historien sur les fausses nouvelles de la guerre', *Revue de Synthèse Historique* 33 (1921), 13–35.
6. Tolstoy, *War and Peace* (*Voina i Mir*, 1869), book 3, part 2, chap. 33.
7. Peter Snow, *To War with Wellington: From the Peninsula to Waterloo* (London, 2010), 59–60, 109, 161; Rory Muir, *Wellington* (New Haven CT, 2013), 46, 589.
8. Henri Troyat, *Tolstoy* (1965: English trans. London 1968), 105–26.
9. Lonsdale Hale, *The Fog of War* (London, 1896).
10. Erik A. Lund, *War for the Every Day: Generals, Knowledge and Warfare in Early Modern Europe, 1680–1740* (Westport CT, 1999), 15.

11. David Chandler, *The Campaigns of Napoleon* (1966: London, 1993), 411; Robert Goetz, *1805, Austerlitz: Napoleon and the Destruction of the Third Coalition* (2005: 2nd edn Barnsley, 2017), 283–4, 291.

12. Davies, *Wellington's War*, 231–4.

13. Cecil Woodham-Smith, *The Reason Why: Story of the Fatal Charge of the Light Brigade* (London, 1953); George R. Stewart, *Pickett's Charge* (Boston MA, 1959); Earl J. Hess, *Pickett's Charge* (Chapel Hill NC, 2001).

14. Gregory Daly, *Cannae* (London, 2002).

15. Basil Liddell Hart, *Scipio Africanus: Greater than Napoleon* (London, 1926); Howard Scullard, *Scipio Africanus* (London, 1970).

16. Maximilien Foy, quoted in Snow, *To War with Wellington*, 167; Torres Vedras, ibid., 79, 96.

17. Brian Lavery, *Nelson and the Nile* (1998: 2nd edn London, 2003), 170, 178.

18. For a detailed account, Thaddeus Holt, *The Deceivers: Allied Military Deception in the Second World War* (New York, 2004).

19. Antony Beevor, *Stalingrad* (London, 2018), 239–330, especially 226–7, 246.

20. Zola, *La Débâcle* (1892: Paris, 1967), 364.

21. Adam Roberts, in Howard's obituary, *Guardian*, 1 December 2019.

22. Michael Howard, *The Franco-Prussian War* (London, 1961), 70, 147, 206, 209.

23. Howard, *Franco-Prussian War*, 191, 198.

24. James M. Perry, *Arrogant Armies: Great Military Disasters and the Generals Behind Them* (New York, 1996).

25. On *jezails*, T. R. Moreman, *The Army in India and the Development of Frontier Warfare, 1849–1947* (Basingstoke, 1998), 13, 37.

26. John Kaye, *History of the First Afghan War* (London, 1860); Perry, *Arrogant Armies*, 109–40; John Waller, *Beyond the Khyber Pass: The Road to British Disaster in the First Afghan War* (New York, 1990); William Dalrymple, *Return of a King: The Battle for Afghanistan* (London, 2012).

27. Richard Burton, translator, *The Arabian Nights* (London, 1885), introduction.

28. Alfred Martin, *Mountain and Savage Warfare* (Allahabad, 1898); George Younghusband, *Indian Frontier Warfare* (London, 1898). Cf. Moreman, *Army in India*, 46–7, 75.

29. Euclides da Cunha, *Os Sertões* (1902: new edn, 2 vols, Porto, 1980); Robert M. Levine, *Vale of Tears: Revisiting the Canudos Massacre* (Berkeley CA, 1992); Adriana Michéle Campos Johnson, *Sentencing Canudos: Subalternity in the Backlands of Brazil* (Pittsburgh PA, 2010).

30. Da Cunha, *Os Sertões*, 57.

31. James Gibson, *The Perfect War: Technowar in Vietnam* (Boston MA, 1986), 12.

32. Harrison Salisbury (ed.), *Vietnam Reconsidered: Lessons from a War* (New York, 1984).

33. Gibson, *Perfect War*, 17.

34. Salisbury, *Vietnam Reconsidered*, 39.

35. Tuchman, *March of Folly*, 376.

36. Josiah Heyman, 'State Escalation of Force', in Heyman (ed.), *States and Illegal Practices* (Oxford, 1999), 285–314, at 288.

37. Salisbury, *Vietnam Reconsidered*, 55, 64.

38. Ronald H. Spector, *After Tet* (New York, 1993), 314.

39. Eric Alterman, *When Presidents Lie: A History of Official Deception and Its Consequences* (New York, 2004), 178; Gibson, *Perfect War*, 124–5, 462.

40. Robert McNamara and Brian VanDeMark, *In Retrospect: The Tragedy and Lessons of Vietnam* (New York, 1995), 322.

41. Quoted in James Blight and Janet Lang, *The Fog of War: Lessons from the Life of Robert McNamara* (Lanham MD, 2005).

42. Leonard Bushkoff, 'Tragic Ignorance in Vietnam', *Christian Science Monitor*, 30 November 1992; M. S. Shivakumar, 'Ignorance, Arrogance and Vietnam', *Economic and Political Weekly*, 16 December 1995. Cf. H. R. McMaster, *Dereliction of Duty: Lyndon Johnson, Robert McNamara, the Joint Chiefs of Staff and the Lies that Led to Vietnam* (New York, 1997).

43. Salisbury, *Vietnam Reconsidered*, 117, 149.
44. Salisbury, *Vietnam Reconsidered*, 161.
45. Kendrick Oliver, *The My Lai Massacre in American History and Memory* (2nd edn, Manchester, 2006), 4 (quoted from the ex-soldier Ronald Ridenhour), 41. Seymour Hersh, *My Lai: A Report on the Massacre and its Aftermath* (New York, 1970).
46. Oliver, *The My Lai Massacre*, 19, 49.
47. Salisbury, *Vietnam Reconsidered*, 43.
48. Carl von Clausewitz, *On War* (1832: English trans. Princeton NJ, 1976), book 2, chap. 2.
49. Vasily Grossman, *Stalingrad* (1952: English trans. London, 2019), 121; Grossman, *Life and Fate* (written 1959, published 1980: English trans. London, 2006), 49.
50. Beevor, *Stalingrad*, 345.
51. David Stahel, *Retreat From Moscow: A New History of Germany's Winter Campaign, 1941–1942* (New York, 2019), 294 and indeed passim. Cf. Jonathan Dimbleby, *Barbarossa: How Hitler Lost the War* (London, 2021).

## 10 IGNORANCE IN BUSINESS

1. William Cronon, *Changes in the Land: Indians, Colonists and the Ecology of New England* (New York, 1983), 36.
2. Thomas R. Dunlap, *Nature and the English Diaspora* (Cambridge, 1999), 46.
3. Dunlap, *Nature*, 80–88, at 81.
4. Pietro Lanza, Principe di Trabia, *Memoria sulla decadenza dell'agricultura nella Sicilia: ed il modo di rimediarvi* (Naples, 1786).
5. R. J. Shafer, *The Economic Societies in the Spanish World, 1763–1821* (Syracuse NY, 1958).
6. Scott, *Seeing Like a State*.
7. J. S. Hogendorn and K. M. Scott, 'The East African Groundnut Scheme', *African Economic History* 10 (1981), 81–115; Richard Cavendish, 'Britain Abandons the Groundnut Scheme', *History Today* 51 (2001).
8. Wei Li and Dennis Tao Yang, 'The Great Leap Forward: Anatomy of a Central Planning Disaster', *Journal of Political Economy* 113 (2005), 840–77; Frank Dikötter, *Mao's Great Famine: The History of China's Most Devastating Catastrophe, 1958–62* (2010: 2nd edn London, 2017).
9. Donald Worster, 'Grassland Follies: Agricultural Capitalism on the Plains', in Worster, *Under Western Skies* (New York, 1992), 93–105.
10. Warren Dean, *With Broadax and Firebrand: The Destruction of the Brazilian Atlantic Forest* (Berkeley CA, 1995).
11. Bengt Holmström et al., 'Opacity and the Optimality of Debt for Liquidity Provision', https://www.researchgate.net/publication/268323724_Opacity_and_the_Optimality_of_Debt_for_Liquidity_Provision. Accessed 13 May 2022.
12. George A. Akerlof, 'The Market for "Lemons": Quality Uncertainty and the Market Mechanism', *Quarterly Journal of Economics* 84 (1970), 488–500.
13. John von Neumann and Oskar Morgenstern, *Theory of Games and Economic Behavior* (1944: new edn Princeton NJ, 2004).
14. Eric Maskin and Amartya Sen, *The Arrow Impossibility Theorem* (New York, 2014).
15. Cornel Zwierlein, 'Coexistence and Ignorance: what Europeans in the Levant did not Read (ca.1620–1750)', in Zwierlein, *The Dark Side*, 225–65; Julian Hoppit, *Risk and Failure in English Business 1700–1800* (Cambridge, 1987), 69.
16. Hoppit, *Risk and Failure*, 139, 177, 114–15.
17. Joel Mokyr, *The Gifts of Athena: Historical Origins of the Knowledge Economy* (Princeton NJ, 2003), 37n. Cf. David Hey, 'Huntsman, Benjamin', *Oxford Dictionary of National Biography*.
18. Svante Lindqvist, *Technology on Trial: The Introduction of Steam Power Technology into Sweden, 1715–36* (Uppsala, 1984); John R. Harris, *Industrial Espionage and Technology Transfer: Britain and France in the Eighteenth Century* (Aldershot, 1998).

19. Hedieh Nasheri, *Economic Espionage and Industrial Spying* (Cambridge, 2005).
20. Malcolm Balen, *A Very English Deceit* (London, 2002), 41.
21. Smith, 'Amsterdam as an Information Exchange', 1001–3.
22. Vance Packard, *The Hidden Persuaders* (London, 1957); Stefan Schwarzkopf and Rainer Gries (eds), *Ernest Dichter and Motivational Research* (New York, 2010).
23. John K. Galbraith, *The Great Crash* (1954: new edn London, 2009), 70.
24. Elizabeth W. Morrison and Frances J. Milliken, 'Organizational Silence', *The Academy of Management Review* 25 (2000), 706–25.
25. Gabriel Szulanski, *Sticky Knowledge: Barriers to Knowing in the Firm* (Thousand Oaks CA, 2003).
26. Morrison and Milliken, 'Organizational Silence', 708.
27. Miklós Haraszti, *A Worker in a Worker's State* (1975: English trans. Harmondsworth, 1977); Dikötter, *Mao's Great Famine*.
28. Clinton Jones, 'Data Quality and the Management Iceberg of Ignorance' (2017), www.jonesassociates.com/?p=808. The chairman is quoted in John S. Brown and Paul Duguid, 'Organizational Learning and Communities of Practice', in E. L. Lesser, M. A. Fontaine and J. A. Slusher (eds), *Knowledge and Communities* (Oxford, 1991), 123.
29. DeLong, *Lost Knowledge*, 13, 101–18. Cf. Arnold Kransdorff, *Corporate Amnesia: Keeping Know-how in the Company* (Oxford, 1998), especially 21–8.
30. On France in the late 1950s, Crozier, *Bureaucratic Phenomenon*, discussed briefly in chapter one above. On the response to the problem, Ikujiro Nonaka and Hirotaka Takeuchi, *The Knowledge Creating Company: How Japanese Companies Create the Dynamics of Innovation* (New York, 1995); Nancy M. Dixon, *Common Knowledge: How Companies Thrive by Sharing What They Know* (Boston MA, 2000).
31. Már Jónsson, 'The Expulsion of the Moriscos from Spain', *Journal of Global History* 2 (2007), 195–212; Warren C. Scoville, *The Persecution of Huguenots and French Economic Development, 1680–1720* (Berkeley CA, 1960).
32. Dorothy Davis, *A History of Shopping* (London, 1966); Sheila Robertson, *Shopping in History* (Hove, 1984); Evelyn Welch, *Shopping in the Renaissance* (New Haven CT, 2009).
33. Ernest S. Turner, *The Shocking History of Advertising* (London, 1952); Packard, *Hidden Persuaders*.
34. George A. Akerlof and Robert Shiller, *Phishing for Phools: The Economics of Manipulation and Deception* (Princeton NJ, 2015).
35. Goldacre, *Bad Pharma*, 278–82, 292–8.
36. www.accountingliteracy.org/about-us.html. Accessed 13 May 2022.
37. Annamaria Lusardi and Olivia S. Mitchell, 'Financial Literacy Around the World', *Journal of Pension Economics and Finance* 10 (2011), 497–508.
38. Jacob Soll, *The Reckoning: Financial Accountability and the Making and Breaking of Nations* (London, 2014).
39. Daniela Pianezzi and Muhammad Junaid Ashraf, 'Accounting for Ignorance', *Critical Perspectives on Accounting* (2020), repository.essex.ac.uk/26810.
40. Nils Steensgaard, 'The Dutch East India Company as an Institutional Innovation', in Maurice Aymard (ed.), *Dutch Capitalism and World Capitalism* (Cambridge, 1982), 447–50; Lodowijk Petram, *The World's First Stock Exchange* (New York, 2014).
41. Steve Fraser, *Every Man a Speculator: A History of Wall Street in American Life* (New York, 2005).
42. William Quinn and John D. Turner, *Boom and Bust: A Global History of Financial Bubbles* (Cambridge, 2020), index.
43. Robert J. Shiller, *Irrational Exuberance* (2000: 3rd edn Princeton NJ, 2015), 190, 195–6, 200–203.
44. Quinn and Turner, *Boom and Bust*, 8.
45. On Ponzi, Shiller, *Irrational Exuberance*, 117–18. The maxim was used by the Better Business Bureau to warn the public about scams: 'If something sounds too good to be true, it probably is' (5 June 2009), www.barrypopik.com.

46. Shiller, *Irrational Exuberance*, 127, 148, 204–5.
47. Jonathan Israel, 'The Amsterdam Stock Exchange and the English Revolution of 1688', *Tijdschrift voor Geschiedenis* 103 (1990), 412–40; Richard Dale, *Napoleon is Dead: Lord Cochrane and the Great Stock Exchange Scandal* (Stroud, 2006).
48. Charles P. Kindleberger and R. Z. Aliber, *Manias, Panics and Crashes* (Basingstoke, 2005).
49. Thomas Lux, 'Herd Behaviour, Bubbles and Crashes', *Economic Journal* 105 (1995), 881–96. Cf. Shiller, *Irrational Exuberance*, 200–203.
50. Shiller, *Irrational Exuberance*, 112–14.
51. Quoted in Julian Hoppit, 'Attitudes to Credit in Britain, 1680–1780', *Historical Journal* 33 (1990), 305–22, at 309.
52. John Carswell, *The South Sea Bubble* (1960: revised edn London, 1993); Balen, *Very English Deceit*; Julian Hoppit, 'The Myths of the South Sea Bubble', *Transactions of the Royal Historical Society* 12 (2002), 141–65; Richard Dale, *The First Crash* (Princeton NJ, 2004); Helen Paul, *The South Sea Bubble* (Abingdon, 2011); William Quinn and John D. Turner, '1720 and the Invention of the Bubble', in Quinn and Turner, *Boom and Bust*, 16–38; Stefano Condorelli and Daniel Menning (eds), *Boom, Bust and Beyond: New Perspectives on the 1720 Stock Market Bubble* (Berlin, 2019); Daniel Menning, *Politik, Ökonomie und Aktienspekulation: 'South Sea' und Co. 1720* (Berlin, 2020).
53. Carswell, *Bubble*, 89.
54. Dale, *First Crash*, 2, 82, 120.
55. Carswell, *Bubble*, 57n., 119.
56. Carswell, *Bubble*, 132; Balen, *Very English Deceit*, 119.
57. Dale, *First Crash*, 17, 93.
58. The term 'screened' was first used by Richard Steele, the former editor (with Joseph Addison) of *The Spectator*: Carswell, *Bubble*, 175.
59. Archibald Hutchison in 1720, quoted in Dale, *First Crash*, 85, 98.
60. Balen, *Very English Deceit*, 97, 105, 116.
61. Adam Smith, *Wealth of Nations* (1776), ed. Roy Campbell and Andrew Skinner (2 vols, Oxford, 1976), vol.2, 745–6.
62. Quoted in Dale, *First Crash*, 101, from *The Secret History of the South Sea Scheme* (attributed to John Toland, London, 1726).
63. Galbraith, *Crash*; Maury Klein, *Rainbow's End* (New York, 2001); William Quinn and John D. Turner, 'The Roaring Twenties and the Wall Street Crash', in Quinn and Turner, *Boom and Bust*, 115–33.
64. Galbraith, *Crash*, 9.
65. Galbraith, *Crash*, 28, 32, 187.
66. Galbraith, *Crash*, 75–80, 100. In contrast, the journalist Eunice Barnard, writing at this time, described a group of female speculators watching the ticker tape and discussing the information as it came in: Eunice Barnard, 'Ladies of the Ticker', *North American Review* 227 (1929), 405–10, cited in Daniel Menning, 'Doubt All Before You Believe Anything: Stock Market Speculation in the Early Twentieth-Century United States', in Dürr, *Threatened Knowledge*, 74–93, at 74–5.
67. Galbraith, *Crash*, 121–2, 133–5, 148–9.
68. Galbraith, *Crash*, 51, 125.
69. Menning, 'Doubt All', 90.
70. Heyman, *States and Illegal Practices*.
71. Daniel Okrent, *Last Call: The Rise and Fall of Prohibition* (New York, 2010), 150–53, 165, 207–11, 215, 272–4.
72. Dikötter, *Mao's Great Famine*, 197–207.
73. Friedrich Schneider and Dominik H. Enste, *The Shadow Economy* (2nd edn Cambridge, 2013).
74. Misha Glenny, *McMafia* (London, 2008), 251, 385.
75. Paul Gootenberg, 'Talking Like a State: Drugs, Borders and the Language of Control', in Willem van Schendel and Itty Abraham (eds), *Illicit Flows and Criminal Things* (Bloomington IN, 2005),

101–27, at 109; Gootenberg (ed.), *Cocaine: Global Histories* (London, 1999); Gootenberg, *Andean Cocaine: The Making of a Global Drug* (Chapel Hill NC, 2008); Mark Bowden, *Killing Pablo: The Hunt for the Richest, Most Powerful Criminal in History* (London, 2007).

76. Peter Reuter and Edwin M. Truman, *Chasing Dirty Money: The Fight Against Money Laundering* (Washington DC, 2004); Douglas Farah, 'Fixers, Super Fixers and Shadow Facilitators: How Networks Connect', in Michael Miklaucic and Jacqueline Brewer (eds), *Convergence: Illicit Networks and National Security in the Age of Globalization* (Washington DC, 2013), 75–95, the quotation at 77.

77. Ian Smillie, 'Criminality and the Global Diamond Trade', in Van Schendel and Abraham, *Illicit Flows*, 177–200, at 181.

78. Jason C. Sharman, *Havens in a Storm: The Struggle for Global Tax Regulation* (Ithaca NY, 2006); Nicholas Shaxson, *Treasure Islands: Uncovering the Damage of Offshore Banking and Tax Havens* (London, 2011).

79. Shaxson, *Treasure Islands*, 54; Sébastien Guex, 'The Origins of the Swiss Banking Secrecy Law', *Business History Review* 74 (2000), 237–66, at 241.

80. R. T. Naylor, *Hot Money* (London, 1987), 234–9.

81. Pino Arlacchi, *Mafia Business* (1983: English trans. Oxford, 1988); Diego Gambetta, *The Sicilian Mafia: The Business of Private Protection* (Cambridge MA, 1993); Yiu-kong Chu, *The Triads as Business* (London, 2000); Vadim Volkov, *Violent Entrepreneurs: The Use of Force in the Making of Russian Capitalism* (Ithaca NY, 2002), 43. Cf. Federico Varese, *The Russian Mafia: Private Protection in a New Market Economy* (Oxford, 2001).

82. Varese, *Russian Mafia*, 22–9, 55–9.

83. Alan Knight, *The Mexican Revolution*, 2 vols (Cambridge, 1986).

84. Peter Andreas, 'The Clandestine Political Economy of War and Peace in Bosnia', *International Studies Quarterly* 48 (2004), 29–51, at 31.

85. Douglas Farah and Stephen Braun, *Merchant of Death* (Hoboken NJ, 2007).

86. Kenneth I. Simalla and Maurice Amutari, 'Small Arms, Cattle Raiding and Borderlands', in Van Schendel and Abraham, *Illicit Flows*, 201–25, at 217.

87. Paul Grendler, *The Roman Inquisition and the Venetian Press, 1540–1605* (Princeton NJ, 1977).

88. Robert Darnton, *The Forbidden Best-Sellers of Pre-Revolutionary France* (New York, 1996), 3, 7, 18–20.

89. Frances Yates, 'Paolo Sarpi's *History of the Council of Trent*', *Journal of the Warburg and Courtauld Institutes* 7 (1944), 123–44.

90. Adrian Johns, *Piracy: The Intellectual Property Wars from Gutenberg to Gates* (Chicago IL, 2009); Paul Kruse, 'Piracy and the *Britannica*', *Library Quarterly* 33 (1963), 318–38.

91. Glenny, *McMafia*, 382.

92. Roberto Saviano, *Gomorrah* (2006: English trans. New York, 2007).

93. Saviano, *Gomorrah*, 25–33. Some of these workers appear in the film made from the book, *Gomorrah* (2008).

94. Saviano, *Gomorrah*, 7.

95. On La Salada, Matías Dewey, *Making It at Any Cost: Aspirations and Politics in a Counterfeit Clothing Marketplace* (Austin TX, 2020).

96. Dewey, *Making It*, 6.

97. Jane Schneider and Peter Schneider, 'Is Transparency Possible? The Political-Economic and Epistemological Implications of Cold War Conspiracies and Subterfuge in Italy', in Heyman (ed.), *States and Illegal Practices*, 169–98, at 169.

98. Pino Arlacchi, *Addio Cosa Nostra* (Milan, 1994), 159, quoted in Varese, *Russian Mafia*, 234–5.

99. Diego Gambetta, 'The Price of Distrust', in Gambetta (ed.), *Trust* (Oxford, 1988), 158–75.

## 11 IGNORANCE IN POLITICS

1. Foucault, *Power/Knowledge*; Lorraine Code, 'The Power of Ignorance', in Sullivan and Tuana (eds), *Race and Epistemologies*, 213–30.

2. Hubert Dreyfus and Paul Rabinow (eds), *Michel Foucault: Beyond Structuralism and Hermeneutics* (Brighton, 1982), 187, from a personal communication to the authors.

3. Richelieu, *Testament Politique*, ed. Françoise Hildesheimer (Paris, 1995), 137; Daniel Roche, *France in the Enlightenment* (1993: English trans. Cambridge MA, 1998), 346.

4. Frederick the Great quoted in Gay, *Science of Freedom*, 521–2; Frederick VI quoted in Robert J. Goldstein (ed.), *The War for the Public Mind: Political Censorship in Nineteenth-Century Europe* (Westport CT, 2000), 3.

5. Oldenburg to Samuel Hartlib (1659), in A. Rupert Hall and Marie Boas Hall (eds), *The Correspondence of Henry Oldenburg*, 13 vols (Madison WI, 1965–86).

6. Ryszard Kapuściński, *Shah of Shahs* (1982: English trans. London, 1986), 150.

7. Shibutani, *Improvised News.*

8. Quoted in Janam Mukherjee, *Hungry Bengal* (New York, 2016), 83.

9. Raymond A. Bauer and David B. Gleicher, 'Word-of-Mouth Communication in the Soviet Union', *Public Opinion Quarterly* 17 (1953), 297–310.

10. Stanley Cohen, *Folk Devils and Moral Panics: The Creation of Mods and Rockers* (London, 1972).

11. John Kenyon, *The Popish Plot* (London, 1972).

12. W. C. Abbott, 'The Origins of Titus Oates's Story', *English Historical Review* 25 (1910), 126–9, at 129; Allport and Postman, *Psychology of Rumour*; Shibutani, *Improvised News.*

13. https://journals.plos.org/plosone/article?id=10.1371/journal.pone.0233879, accessed 28 June 2022; https://www.bbc.co.uk/bitesize/articles/zgfgf82, accessed 28 June 2022.

14. On Venice, Paolo Preto, *I servizi segreti di Venezia* (Milan, 1994).

15. On the first meaning, Alison Bailey, 'Strategic Ignorance', in Sullivan and Tuana, *Race and Epistemologies*, 77–94. Cf. James C. Scott, *Domination and the Arts of Resistance* (New Haven CT, 2008). On the second, McGoey, *Unknowers.*

16. Jefferson to Charles Yancey (1816); Madison to William Barry (1822).

17. John Foster, *An Essay on the Evils of Popular Ignorance* (London, 1824), 214.

18. *Hansard*, July 1833, 143–6, 'National Education' (30 July 1833), http://hansard.millbank-systems.com. Cf. S. A. Beaver, 'Roebuck, John Arthur', *Oxford Dictionary of National Biography.*

19. Michael Cullen, 'The Chartists and Education', *New Zealand Journal of History* 10 (1976), 162–77, at 163, 170.

20. John Stuart Mill, *Representative Government* (1867: repr. *On Liberty, Utilitarianism and Other Essays*, Oxford, 2015), 239; Walter Bagehot, *The English Constitution* (1867: ed. Paul Smith, Cambridge 2001), 327.

21. To be exact, he had declared in a speech in Parliament that it was necessary for 'our future masters to learn their letters': Jonathan Parry, 'Lowe, Robert', *Oxford Dictionary of National Biography.* In the cultural memory, the epigram became more forceful.

22. Oscar Wilde, *The Importance of Being Earnest* (1895), Act One. My thanks to Ghil'ad Zuckermann for reminding me of this passage.

23. Dolci, *Inchiesta a Palermo*, 76.

24. 'What Americans Know, 1989–2007', news release, Pew Research Center, 15 April 2007, https://www.pewresearch.org/wp-content/uploads/sites/4/legacy-pdf/319.pdf. Accessed 28 June 2022. On surveys at the time of the 2008 election, Ilya Somin, *Democracy and Political Ignorance* (2013: revised edn Stanford CA, 2016), 34–5. Somin (162), notes the problem of making comparisons between the present state of ignorance and its state in the nineteenth and early twentieth centuries, given the absence of surveys – absence of evidence about the absence of knowledge.

25. Anthony Downs, *An Economic Theory of Democracy* (New York, 1957).

26. Linda Martín Alcoff on the Epistemology of Ignorance and the 2016 Presidential Election (24 February 2017), https://philosophy.commons.gc.cuny.edu/linda-martin-alcoff.

27. Philip Kitcher, *Science in a Democratic Society* (Amherst NY, 2011).

28. Simon Kaye, 'On the Complex Relationship between Political Ignorance and Democracy' (5 April 2017), http://eprints.lse.ac.uk/72489.

29. Sophia Kaitatzi-Whitlock, 'The Political Economy of Political Ignorance', in Janet Wasko, Graham Murdock and Helena Sousa (eds), *The Handbook of Political Economy of Communications* (Oxford, 2011), 458–81.
30. Mario Sabino, 'FHC, Suplicy, O Preço do Paõzinho, o General Medici e Eu', *Crusoé*, 17 August 2018, https://crusoe.com.br.
31. Adam Nicolson, *When God Spoke English: The Making of the King James Bible* (London, 2011), 7.
32. Geoffrey Parker, *Emperor: A New Life of Charles V* (New Haven CT, 2019).
33. Parker, *Emperor*, 35, 136, 208, 265, 317.
34. Parker, *Emperor*, 58, 86, 195–6, 290.
35. Geoffrey Parker, *Philip II* (1978: 4th edn Chicago IL, 2002), especially 24–37.
36. Paul Dover, 'Philip II, Information Overload and the Early Modern Moment', in Tonio Andrade and William Reger (eds), *The Limits of Empire: European Imperial Formations in Early Modern World History* (Farnham, 2012).
37. Quoted in Albert W. Lovett, *Philip II and Mateo Vázquez de Leca* (Geneva, 1977), 66; Stafford Poole, *Juan de Ovando* (Norman OK, 2004), 162.
38. Soll, *The Reckoning*, ix, 87.
39. Isabel de Madariaga, *Russia in the Age of Catherine the Great* (London, 1981), 371; Simon Montefiore, *Prince of Princes: The Life of Potemkin* (London, 2001), 380–33.
40. Quoted in Ladislav Bittman, *The Deception Game* (Syracuse NY, 1972), 58.
41. Richard Cobb, 'The Informer and his Trade', in Cobb, *The Police and the People* (Oxford, 1970), 5–8.
42. Scott, *Seeing Like a State*, 2.
43. Sheldon Ungar, 'Ignorance as an Under-Identified Social Problem', *British Journal of Sociology* 59 (2008), 301–26, at 306.
44. Adam Tooze, *Statistics and the German State, 1900–1945: The Making of Modern Economic Knowledge* (Cambridge, 2001), 84.
45. Frank Cowell, *Cheating the Government: The Economics of Evasion* (Cambridge MA, 1990), 38.
46. Sir William Hayter (British ambassador to Moscow, 1953–7), quoted in Anna Aslanyan, *Dancing on Ropes: Translators and the Balance of History* (London, 2021), 13.
47. Lothar Gall, *Bismarck: The White Revolutionary*, vol. 1 (1851–71: English trans. London, 1986), 180.
48. Christopher Clark, *The Sleepwalkers: How Europe Went to War in 1914* (London, 2013), 200–1.
49. Margaret MacMillan, *Peacemakers: The Paris Conference of 1919 and its Attempt to End War* (London, 2001), 43, 48–9.
50. Bartlomiej Rusin, 'Lewis Namier, the Curzon Line and the Shaping of Poland's Eastern Frontier', *Studia z Dziejów Rosji i Europy Środkowy-Wschodniej* 48 (2013), 5–26, at 6, n. 3. Since Lloyd George opposed Polish claims, the 'legend' may be a Polish one.
51. Russell H. Fifield, *Woodrow Wilson and the Far East: The Diplomacy of the Shantung Question* (New York, 1952), 240–41.
52. James Headlam-Morley, quoted in D. W. Hayton, *Conservative Revolutionary: The Lives of Lewis Namier* (London, 2019), 108.
53. John W. Wheeler-Bennett, *Munich: Prologue to Tragedy* (London, 1948), 264, 157.
54. Constantin Dumba, quoted in Larry Wolff, *Woodrow Wilson and the Reimagining of Eastern Europe* (Stanford CA, 2020), 5.
55. John M. Cooper, *Woodrow Wilson* (New York, 2009), 182.
56. Quoted in MacMillan, *Peacemakers*, 41.
57. Wolff, *Woodrow Wilson*, 228, 231.
58. Cooper, *Woodrow Wilson*, 490. Cf. Harold Nicolson, *Peacemaking 1919* (London, 1933); David Fromkin, *A Peace to End All Peace* (1989).
59. The letter is quoted in Hugh and Christopher Seton-Watson, *The Making of a New Europe* (London, 1981), 343. The seminar was attended by the young Zara Steiner, quoted in

David Reynolds, 'Zara Steiner', *Biographical Memoirs of Fellows of the British Academy* XIX (London, 2021), 467–81, at 470. Cf. Nicolson, *Peacemaking*, 200, 203.

60. R. W. Seton-Watson, *Masaryk in England* (Cambridge, 1943), 67.

61. 'Resign! Alexander Lukashenko heckled by factory workers in Minsk', *Guardian*, 17 August 2020.

62. 'Trump touts hydrochloroquine as a cure for Covid-19', *Guardian*, 6 April 2020; 'Coronavirus: Trump says he's been taking hydrochloroquine for "a few weeks"', *The Independent*, 19 May 2020; 'Bolsanaro bets "miraculous cure" for COVID-19 can save Brazil – and his life', *Reuters Health News*, 8 July 2020.

63. Oreskes and Conway, *Merchants of Doubt*.

64. Joanne Roberts, 'Organizational Ignorance', in Gross and McGoey (eds), *Routledge Handbook of Ignorance Studies*, 361–9; Bakken and Wiik, 'Ignorance and Organization Studies', 1109–20.

65. Michael Zack, 'Managing Organizational Ignorance', *Knowledge Directions* 1 (1999), http://web.cba.neu.edu/~mzack/articles/orgig/orgig.htm. Accessed 28 June 2022.

66. Continuity with the Middle Ages is emphasized in G. L. Harriss, 'A Revolution in Tudor History?', *Past & Present* 25 (1963), 8–39.

67. Geoffrey Elton, *The Tudor Revolution in Government* (Cambridge, 1953); Max Weber, *Soziologie*, ed. Johannes Winckelmann (Stuttgart, 1956), 151–4.

68. On Persson, Michael Roberts, *The Early Vasas: A History of Sweden, 1523–1611* (Cambridge, 1968), 224–5, 237–9, and Marko Hakanen and Ulla Koskinen, 'Secretaries as Agents in the Middle of Power Structures (1560–1680)', and 'The Gentle Art of Counselling Monarchs', in Petri Karonen and Marko Hakanen (eds), *Personal Agency at the Swedish Age of Greatness* (Helsinki, 2017), 5–94. On Cromwell, Diarmaid MacCulloch, *Thomas Cromwell* (London, 2018); on Richelieu, Orest Ranum, *Richelieu and the Councillors of State* (Oxford, 1968), especially 45–76.

69. Ranum, *Richelieu*, 63.

70. On Eraso, Carlos Javier de Carlos Morales, 'El Poder de los Secretarios Reales: Francisco de Eraso', in José Martínez Millán (ed.), *La corte de Felipe II* (Madrid, 1994), 107–48.

71. Gregorio Marañón, *Antonio Pérez* (Madrid, 1947); Lovett, *Philip II*.

72. Fernand Braudel, *The Mediterranean and the Mediterranean World in the Age of Philip II* (1949: English trans. 2 vols, London, 1972–3), part 2, chap. 1, section 1. Cf. Geoffrey Blainey, *The Tyranny of Distance: How Distance Shaped Australia's History* (Melbourne, 1966), and Parker, *Emperor*, 382, 653.

73. Parker, *Emperor*, 385.

74. Parker, *Philip II*, 25, 28. On Philip and his empire, Arndt Brendecke, *The Empirical Empire: Spanish Colonial Rule and the Politics of Knowledge* (2009: English trans. Berlin, 2016), especially chap. 1 on 'the blindness of the king', and Brendecke, 'Knowledge, Oblivion and Concealment in Early Modern Spain: The Ambiguous Agenda of the Archive of Simancas', in Liesbeth Corens, Kate Peters and Alexandra Walsham (eds), *Archives and Information in the Early Modern World* (Oxford, 2018), 131–49.

75. Simon Franklin and Katherine Bowers (eds), *Information and Empire: Mechanisms of Communication in Russia, 1600–1850* (Cambridge, 2017).

76. Scott, *Seeing Like a State*, 11; cf. Jacob Soll, *The Information Master: Jean-Baptiste Colbert's Secret State Intelligence System* (Ann Arbor MI, 2009); Michèle Virol, *Vauban* (Seyssel, 2003).

77. Oliver MacDonagh, 'The Nineteenth-Century Revolution in Government', *Historical Journal* 1 (1958), 52–67.

78. Scott, *Seeing Like a State*, 33, 77.

79. Emily Osborn, 'Circle of Iron: African Colonial Employees and the Interpretation of Colonial Rule in French West Africa', *Journal of African History* 44 (2003), 29–50.

80. Philip Bowring, *Free Trade's First Missionary: Sir John Bowring in Europe and Asia* (Hong Kong, 2014), 170,

81. William Dalrymple, *The Anarchy: The Relentless Rise of the East India Company* (London, 2019).

82. Dalrymple, *Anarchy*, 237, 313.
83. Christopher A. Bayly, *Empire and Information: Intelligence Gathering and Social Communication in India, 1780–1870* (Cambridge, 1996), 14.
84. Dalrymple, *Return of a King*, 130.
85. Bayly, *Empire and Information*, 178.
86. Ranajit Guha, *A Rule of Property for Bengal* (Paris, 1963).
87. Nicholas B. Dirks, *Castes of Mind: Colonialism and the Making of Modern India* (Princeton NJ, 2001).
88. Bayly, *Empire and Information*, 102, 212, 245–6.
89. Bayly, *Empire and Information*, 315–37, at 315–16.
90. Kim Wagner, *The Great Fear of 1857* (Oxford, 2010).
91. Wagner, *Great Fear*, 28, 30.
92. John Stuart Mill, *Representative Government*, conclusion, quoted in McGoey, *Unknowers*, 161.
93. Bayly, *Empire and Information*, 338.
94. Clive Dewey, *Anglo-Indian Attitudes: The Mind of the Indian Civil Service* (London, 1993), 3.
95. Penderel Moon, *Divide and Quit: An Eyewitness Account of the Partition of India* (1961: 2nd edn Delhi, 1998), 37, 88.
96. Alex von Tunzelmann, *Indian Summer: The Secret History of the End of an Empire* (New York, 2007), 3, 154, 185, 190, 199, 201.
97. Tunzelmann, *Indian Summer*, 232.
98. Anthony Tucker-Jones, *The Iraq War: Operation Iraqi Freedom, 2003–2011* (Barnsley, 2014), 137.
99. Quoted in Brian Whitaker, 'Nowhere to Run', *Guardian*, 29 November 2005. The correct date is 9 CE.
100. Henry Adams, *The Education of Henry Adams* (1907: new edn Cambridge MA, 1918), 100, 296, 462.

## 12 SURPRISES AND CATASTROPHES

1. Ord, *The Precipice*. Cf. Nick Bostrom 'Existential Risks', *Journal of Evolution and Technology* 9 (2002), https://nickbostrom.com/existential/risks.html; Bostrom, 'Existential Risk Prevention as Global Priority', *Global Policy* 4 (2013), 15–31.
2. Quoted in Plokhy, *Chernobyl*, 269.
3. Neil Hanson, *The Dreadful Judgement: The True Story of the Great Fire of London* (New York, 2001).
4. John M. Barry, *Rising Tide: The Great Mississippi Flood of 1927 and How It Changed Americans* (New York, 1997).
5. William M. Taylor (ed.), *The 'Katrina Effect': On the Nature of Catastrophe* (London, 2015).
6. Chester Hartman and Gregory Squires (eds), *There Is No Such Thing as a Natural Disaster: Race, Class, and Hurricane Katrina* (London, 2006), vii, 121–9, 194. Cf. Douglas Brinkley, *The Great Deluge: Hurricane Katrina, New Orleans and the Mississippi Gulf Coast* (New York, 2006).
7. Scott Frickel and M. Bess Vincent, 'Hurricane Katrina, Contamination, and the Unintended Organization of Ignorance', *Technology in Society* 29 (2007), 181–8.
8. Gregory Quenet, *Les tremblements de terre aux XVII et XVIIIe siècles: La naissance d'un risque* (Champvallon, 2005), 305–56; Michael O'Dea, 'Le mot "catastrophe"' and Anne Saada, 'Le désir d'informer: le tremblement de terre de Lisbonne', in Anne-Marie Mercier-Faivre and Chantal Thomas (eds), *L'invention de la catastrophe au XVIIIe siècle: Du châtiment divin au désastre naturel* (Geneva, 2008), 35–48 and 209–30.
9. Cf. John Leslie, *The End of the World: The Science and Ethics of Human Extinction* (London, 1996).
10. David Arnold, *Famine: Social Crisis and Historical Change* (Oxford, 1988); Dalrymple, *Anarchy*, 219–26.

11. Quoted in Amartya Sen, *Poverty and Famines* (Oxford, 1981), 76.
12. Quoted in Arnold, *Famine*, 117.
13. Kali Charan Ghosh, *Famines in Bengal, 1770–1943* (1944: 2nd edn Calcutta, 1987), preface, 122.
14. Sen, *Poverty and Famines*, 79. Paul Greenough, *Prosperity and Misery in Modern Bengal: The Bengal Famine of 1943–44* (New York, 1982); Mukherjee, *Hungry Bengal*.
15. Quoted in Robin Haines, *Charles Trevelyan and the Great Irish Famine* (Dublin, 2004), 401, which defends Trevelyan from the charge of 'a malignant relief policy' (xiii).
16. Cecil Woodham-Smith, *The Great Hunger: Ireland 1845–1849* (London, 1962); Mary Daly, *The Famine in Ireland* (Dundalk, 1986); Christine Kineally, *This Great Calamity: The Irish Famine, 1845–52* (Dublin, 1995); James S. Donnelly, *The Great Irish Potato Famine* (Stroud, 2002); Cormac Ó Gráda (ed.), *Ireland's Great Famine: Interdisciplinary Perspectives* (Dublin, 2006).
17. Arnold, *Famine*. Cf. Polly Hill, *Population, Prosperity and Poverty: Rural Kano in 1900 and 1970* (Cambridge, 1977).
18. Jasper Becker, *Hungry Ghosts: Mao's Secret Famine* (New York, 1996); Dikötter, *Mao's Great Famine*, 6. For criticisms of the latter book, together with a reply by the author, see Felix Wemheuer, 'Sites of Horror: *Mao's Great Famine*', *The China Journal* 66 (2011), 155–64.
19. Dikötter, *Mao's Great Famine*, 8, 25–6.
20. Dikötter, *Mao's Great Famine*, 56–63.
21. Quotation from Mao's doctor, Li Zhisui, who accompanied him. Dikötter, *Mao's Great Famine*, 41, 67–72.
22. Dikötter, *Mao's Great Famine*, 29, 37, 62, 69, 130.
23. Monica Green, 'Taking "Pandemic" Seriously: Making the Black Death Global', in Green (ed.), *Pandemic Disease* (Kalamazoo MI, 2015), 27–61, at 37. Cf. Timothy Brook, 'The Plague', in Brook, *Great State*, 53–75.
24. Philip Ziegler, *The Black Death* (London, 1969); William H. McNeill, *Plagues and Peoples* (Garden City NY, 1976); Samuel K. Cohn Jr, 'The Black Death and the Burning of Jews', *Past & Present* 196 (2007), 3–36.
25. Carlo Cipolla, *Cristofano and the Plague* (London, 1973); Cipolla, *Faith, Reason and the Plague in Seventeenth-Century Tuscany* (New York, 1981); A. Lloyd Moote and Dorothy C. Moote, *The Great Plague: The Story of London's Most Deadly Year* (Baltimore MD, 2004); John Henderson, *Florence under Siege: Surviving Plague in an Early Modern City* (New Haven CT, 2019).
26. Carlo Cipolla, *Fighting the Plague in Seventeenth-Century Italy* (Madison WI, 1981); Stefano di Castro, cited by Henderson, *Florence under Siege*, 55.
27. Giuseppe Farinelli and Ermanno Paccagnini (eds), *Processo agli untori* (Milan, 1988); Giovanni Baldinucci, quoted in Henderson, *Florence under Siege*, 43.
28. Henderson, *Florence under Siege*, 149–82.
29. Sidney Chaloub, *Cidade Febril: Cortiços e Epidemias na Cidade Imperial* (São Paulo, 1996), 62–3.
30. Woodrow Borah and Sherburne Cook, *The Aboriginal Population of Central Mexico in 1548* (Berkeley CA, 1960); Rudolph Zambardino, 'Mexico's Population in the Sixteenth Century', *Journal of Interdisciplinary History* 11 (1980), 1–27; Noble David Cook, *Born to Die: Disease and New World Conquest, 1492–1650* (Cambridge, 1998).
31. Jonathan B. Tucker, *Scourge: The Once and Future Threat of Smallpox* (New York, 2001).
32. https://people.umass.edu/derrico/amherst/lord_jeff.html. Accessed 28 June 2022.
33. Jo Willett, 'Lady Mary Wortley Montagu and her Campaign against Smallpox', https://www.historic-uk.com/HistoryUK/HistoryofBritain/Lady-Mary-Wortley-Montagu-Campaign-Against-Smallpox/. Accessed 13 May 2022.
34. Nicolau Sevcenko, *A Revolta da Vacina* (São Paulo, 1983); José Murilo de Carvalho, 'Cidadãos ativos: a Revolta da Vacina', in Murilo de Carvalho, *Os Bestializados* (São Paulo, 1987), 91–130; Chaloub, *Cidade Febril*; Teresa Meade, *'Civilizing' Rio: Reform and Resistance in a Brazilian City, 1889–1930* (Philadelphia PA, 1997); Jane Santucci, *Cidade Rebelde: As Revoltas Populares no Rio de Janeiro no Início do Século XX* (Rio, 2008).

35. Chaloub, *Cidade Febril*, 139.
36. Chaloub, *Cidade Febril*, 125.
37. Chaloub, *Cidade Febril*, 123–6.
38. Manfred Waserman and Virginia Mayfield, 'Nicholas Chervin's Yellow Fever Survey', *Journal of the History of Medicine and Allied Sciences* 26 (1971), 40–51.
39. Robert J. Morris, *1832 Cholera: The Social Response to an Epidemic* (London, 1976), 30, 35.
40. Morris, *1832 Cholera*, 85, 96–100.
41. Morris, *1832 Cholera*, 74, 161, 192.
42. Suellen Hoy, *Chasing Dirt: The American Pursuit of Cleanliness* (New York, 1995), especially 88–9, 124–7.
43. Mark Bostridge, *Florence Nightingale* (London, 2008).
44. Morris, *1832 Cholera*; Stephanie J. Snow, 'Snow, Dr John', *Oxford Dictionary of National Biography*.
45. Richard Evans, *Death in Hamburg* (Oxford, 1987); Thomas Brock, *Robert Koch: A Life in Medicine and Bacteriology* (Washington, D.C., 1999). Cf. Frank M. Snowden, *Naples in the Time of Cholera, 1884–1911* (Cambridge, 1995).
46. Laura Spinney, *Pale Rider: The Spanish Flu of 1918 and How It Changed the World* (London, 2017).
47. 'US Senator says China trying to sabotage vaccine development', *Reuters*, 7 June 2020, www.reuters.com; Alexandra Sternlicht, 'Senator Tom Cotton Ramps Up Anti-China Rhetoric', *Forbes*, 26 April 2020.

## 13  SECRETS AND LIES

1. A pioneering essay of this kind is Georg Simmel, 'The Sociology of Secrecy and of Secret Societies', *American Journal of Sociology* 11 (1906), 441–98.
2. Francis Bacon, *Essays* (1597: Cambridge, 1906).
3. Baltasar Gracián, *Oráculo Manual y Arte de Prudencia* (1647: bilingual edn, London, 1962), numbers 13, 49, 98–100. General discussions in Rosario Villari, *Elogio della Dissimulazione. La lotta politica nel Seicento* (Rome, 1987); Jean-Pierre Cavaillé, *Dis/simulations* (Paris, 2002); Jon R. Snyder, *Dissimulation and the Culture of Secrecy in Early Modern Europe* (Berkeley CA, 2009).
4. Quoted in Ulrich Ricken, 'Oppositions et polarités d'un champ notionnel: Les philosophes et l'absolutisme éclairé', *Annales historiques de la Révolution française* 51 (1979), 547–57, at 547.
5. Werner Krauss (ed.), *Est-il utile de tromper le peuple?* (Berlin, 1966). Readers will appreciate the irony of publishing these essays in East Germany in the 1960s.
6. David Kahn, *The Codebreakers: The Story of Secret Writing* (New York, 1967).
7. A. C. Duke and C. A. Tamse (eds), *Too Mighty to be Free: Censorship and the Press in Britain and the Netherlands* (Zutphen, 1987); Gigliola Fragnito (ed.), *Church, Censorship and Culture in Early Modern Italy* (English trans. Cambridge, 2001).
8. Daniel Roche, 'Censorship and the Publishing Industry', in Robert Darnton and Daniel Roche (eds), *Revolution in Print* (Berkeley CA, 1989), 3–26; Robert Darnton, *The Forbidden Best-Sellers of Pre-Revolutionary France* (New York, 1996).
9. Judith Wechsler, 'Daumier and Censorship, 1866–1872', *Yale French Studies* 122 (2012), 53–78.
10. Goldstein, *War*, 22, 41, 45, 88.
11. Goldstein, *War*, 25.
12. Clive Ansley, *The Heresy of Wu Han: His Play 'Hai Jui's Dismissal' and its Role in China's Cultural Revolution* (Toronto, 1971); Mary G. Mazur, *Wu Han, Historian: Son of China's Times* (Lanham MD, 2009).
13. Bauer and Gleicher, 'Word-of-Mouth Communication', 297–310.
14. F. J. Ormeling, '50 Years of Soviet Cartography', *American Cartographer* 1 (1974), 48–9; Lappo and Polian, 'Naoukograds', 1226–49.

15. Andrei Sakharov, *Thoughts on Progress, Peaceful Coexistence, and Intellectual Freedom* (Petersham, 1968). Cf. Masha Gessen, 'Fifty Years Later', *New Yorker*, 25 July 2018.

16. Pamela O. Long, *Openness, Secrecy, Authorship: Technical Arts and the Culture of Knowledge from Antiquity to the Renaissance* (Baltimore MD, 2001); Karel Davids, 'Craft Secrecy in Europe in the Early Modern Period: A Comparative View', *Early Science and Medicine* 10 (2005), 340–48.

17. Eamon, *Science and the Secrets of Nature*, 130–33.

18. Eamon, *Science and the Secrets of Nature*.

19. Nicole Howard, 'Rings and Anagrams: Huygens's System of Saturn', *Papers of the Bibliographical Society of America* 98 (2004), 477–510.

20. Parker, *Emperor*, xvi.

21. Carswell, *Bubble*, 175.

22. Anon., *The French King's Wedding* (London, 1708); Peter Burke, *The Fabrication of Louis XIV* (New Haven CT, 1992), 136–7.

23. Mukherjee, *Hungry Bengal*, 125.

24. Anne Applebaum, *Red Famine: Stalin's War on Ukraine* (London, 2017).

25. William Taubman, *Gorbachev* (London, 2017); Plokhy, *Chernobyl*; Adam Higginbotham, *Midnight in Chernobyl: The Untold Story of the World's Greatest Nuclear Disaster* (London, 2019).

26. Louis FitzGibbon, *The Katyn Cover-Up* (London, 1972); Alexander Etkind et al., *Remembering Katyn* (Cambridge, 2012), 13–34.

27. Etkind, *Remembering Katyn*, 35–53; Jane Rogoyska, *Surviving Katyń: Stalin's Polish Massacre and the Search for Truth* (London, 2021). On local witnesses, Rogoyska, 206–7, 227; on evidence for the date, 229, 236, 240.

28. Reported in *The Independent*, 27 July 2020: for the video, see https://www.independent.co.uk/news/world/asia/wuhan-officials-coronavirus-cases-spread-cover-up-leading-scientist-a9639806.html.

29. Louisa Lim, *The People's Republic of Amnesia* (New York, 2014), 99, 115; Margaret Hillenbrand, *Negative Exposures: Knowing What not to Know in Contemporary China* (Durham NC, 2020), 181, 196.

30. Hillenbrand, *Negative Exposures*, 177.

31. Lim, *People's Republic*, 85–6.

32. Lim, *People's Republic*, 214. This is the central theme of Hillenbrand, *Negative Exposures*.

33. Lim, *People's Republic*, 49–50.

34. Lim, *People's Republic*, 3, 140.

35. On early modern spying, Miguel Angel Echevarria Bacigalupe, *La diplomacia secreta en Flandres, 1598–1643* (Vizcaya, 1984); Lucien Bély, *Espions et ambassadeurs* (Paris, 1990); Preto, *I servizi secreti*.

36. Sidney Monas, *The Third Section: Police and Society Under Nicholas I* (Cambridge MA, 1961); Ronald Hingley, *The Russian Secret Police: Muscovite, Imperial Russian and Soviet Political Security Operations, 1565–1970* (London, 1970); Christopher Andrew and Oleg Gordievsky, *KGB: The Inside Story of its Foreign Operations from Lenin to Gorbachev* (London, 1990).

37. George Leggett, *The Cheka: Lenin's Political Police* (Oxford, 1986).

38. Andrew and Gordievsky, *KGB*; Rhodri Jeffreys-Jones and Christopher Andrew (eds), *Eternal Vigilance? 50 Years of the CIA* (London, 1997).

39. Galison, 'Removing Knowledge'; Galison, 'Secrecy in Three Acts', *Social Research* 77 (2010), 941–74.

40. Quoted in Thomas Rid, *Active Measures: The Secret History of Disinformation and Political Warfare* (London, 2020), 401. A former Czechoslovak intelligence officer had already referred to 'the mass production of disinformation operations' in a 'disinformation factory': Bittman, *Deception Game*, 89, 126.

41. Jeffreys-Jones and Andrew, *Eternal Vigilance?*; Andrew and Gordievsky, *KGB*.

42. Compton Mackenzie, *Water on the Brain* (London, 1933), quoted in Vincent, *Culture of Secrecy*, 182–3. Only in 1993 was the new Director-General's name revealed (the first woman, Stella Rimington).

43. Burke, 'Baroque'; Burke, 'Publicizing the Private: The Rise of "Secret History" ', in Christian J. Emden and David Midgley (eds), *Changing Perceptions of the Public Sphere* (New York, 2012), 57–72.

44. Peter Burke, 'The Great Unmasker', *History Today* (1965), 426–32; Burke (ed.), *Sarpi* (New York, 1967), i–xli.

45. 'Pietro Soave Polano' is an anagram of 'Paolo Sarpi Veneto'.

46. Edward Hyde, *The Life of Edward, Earl of Clarendon* (Oxford, 1760), vol. 2, 512.

47. Peter Burke, 'On the Margins of the Public and the Private: Louis XIV at Versailles', *International Political Anthropology* 2 (2009), 29–36.

48. Burke, 'Publicizing the Private'.

49. R. L. Schults, *Crusader in Babylon: W. T. Stead and the Pall Mall Gazette* (Lincoln NE, 1972); Grace Eckley, *Maiden Tribute: A Life of W. T. Stead* (Philadelphia PA, 2007).

50. Justin Kaplan, *Lincoln Steffens* (New York, 1974); Peter Hartshorn, *I Have Seen the Future: A Life of Lincoln Steffens* (Berkeley CA, 2011), 102, 104, 108.

51. Kathleen Brady, *Ida Tarbell: Portrait of a Muckraker* (Pittsburgh PA, 1989); Steve Weinberg, *Taking on the Trust: The Epic Battle of Ida Tarbell and John D. Rockefeller* (New York, 2008).

52. Carl Bernstein and Bob Woodward, *All the President's Men* (London, 1974), 14, 135; Lamar Waldron, *Watergate: The Hidden History* (Berkeley CA, 2012). The name 'Watergate' was derived from an office building in Washington.

53. Patrick McCurdy, 'From the Pentagon Papers to Cablegate: How the Network Society Has Changed Leaking', in Bendetta Brevini, Arne Hintz and Patrick McCurdy (eds), *Beyond WikiLeaks: Implications for the Future of Communications, Journalism and Society* (Basingstoke, 2013), 123–45.

54. David Leigh and Luke Harding, *WikiLeaks: Inside Julian Assange's War on Secrecy* (London, 2013), 22.

55. Timothy Garton Ash, 'US Embassy Cables: A Banquet of Secrets', *Guardian*, 28 November 2010, www.theguardian.com.

56. Eliot Higgins, *We are Bellingcat: An Intelligence Agency for the People* (London, 2021).

57. On the proliferation of secret information, Galison, 'Removing Knowledge'.

58. Filippo de Vivo, *Information and Communication in Venice: Rethinking Early Modern Politics* (Oxford, 2007), 57–8, 181.

59. Vincent, *Culture of Secrecy*, 78–81.

60. Clive Ponting, *The Right to Know: The Inside Story of the Belgrano Affair* (London, 1985).

61. Edward Snowden, *Permanent Record* (Basingstoke, 2019).

62. Cohen, *States of Denial*, 1.

63. Parker, *Emperor*, 279.

64. John Horne and Alan Kramer, *German Atrocities, 1914: A History of Denial* (2001).

65. Fatma Müge Göçek, *Denial of Violence: Ottoman Past, Turkish Present and Collective Violence Against the Armenians, 1789–2009* (Oxford, 2015); Maria Karlsson, *Cultures of Denial: Comparing Holocaust and Armenian Genocide Denial* (Lund, 2015).

66. Alterman, *When Presidents Lie*.

67. Oreskes and Conway, *Merchants of Doubt*.

68. Cohen, *States of Denial*; Eviatar Zerubavel, *The Elephant in the Room: Silence and Denial in Everyday Life* (New York, 2006).

69. Gordon J. Horwitz, *In the Shadow of Death: Living Outside the Gates of Mauthausen* (New York, 1990), 27–36. Cf. Elmer Luchterhand, 'Knowing and Not Knowing: Involvement in Nazi Genocide', in Paul Thompson (ed.), *Our Common History* (Atlantic Highlands NJ, 1982), 251–72.

70. Walter Laqueur, 'Germany: A Wall of Silence?', in Laqueur, *The Terrible Secret: Suppression of the Truth about Hitler's Final Solution* (Boston MA, 1980), 17–40, especially 18, 22–3; Luchterhand, 'Knowing', 255.

71. Robert Eaglestone, 'The Public Secret', in Eaglestone, *The Broken Voice: Reading Post-Holocaust Literature* (Oxford, 2017), chap. 1. General discussions in Michael Taussig, *Defacement: Public Secrets and the Labor of the Negative* (Stanford CA, 1999) and Hillenbrand, *Negative Exposures.*

72. Michael E. Mann, *The Hockey Stick and the Climate Wars* (New York, 2012); Mann, 'When it Comes to the Australian Bush Fires, Rupert Murdoch is an Arsonist', *Newsweek*, 14 January 2020.

73. Gerald Markowitz and David Rosner, *Deceit and Denial: The Deadly Politics of Industrial Pollution* (Berkeley CA, 2002).

74. Ernest L. Wynder and Everts Graham, 'Tobacco Smoking as a Possible Etiologic Factor in Bronchiogenic Carcinoma', *Journal of the American Medical Association* 143 (1950), 329–46.

75. Samuel Epstein, *The Politics of Cancer* (San Francisco CA, 1978), which deals with environmental causes in general; Robert Proctor, *Golden Holocaust* (Berkeley CA, 2011).

76. Proctor, *Golden Holocaust*, 290–92, listing 14 'strategies for creating doubt'.

77. Proctor, *Golden Holocaust*, 260, 263–7.

78. Quoted in Proctor, *Golden Holocaust*, 317.

79. Proctor, *Golden Holocaust*, 301.

80. Richard S. Schultz and Roy Godson, *Dezinformatsia* (New York, 1984); Rid, *Active Measures.*

81. Quoted in Rid, *Active Measures*, 147.

82. Bittman, *Deception Game*, ix.

83. Bittman, *Deception Game*, 39–59. Cf. Rid, *Active Measures*, 157–66.

84. Rid, *Active Measures*, 27–8.

85. Mario Infelise, 'Pallavicino, Ferrante', *DBI.*

86. Rid, *Active Measures*, 249–50.

87. Frances S. Saunders, *Who Paid the Piper? The CIA and the Cultural Cold War* (1999).

88. Rid, *Active Measures*, 81.

89. Rid, *Active Measures*, 213, 377–86.

90. Gill Bennett, *The Zinoviev Letter: The Conspiracy that Never Dies* (Oxford, 2018).

91. Rid, *Active Measures*, 170–75.

92. Rid, *Active Measures*, 104–6, 231–42, 318–19.

93. Bittman, *Deception Game*, 84–6.

94. Peter Oborne, *The Rise of Political Lying* (London, 2005), 5; Matthew d'Ancona, *Post-Truth* (London, 2017). Cf. Ari Rabin-Havt and Media Matters, *Lies Incorporated: The World of Post-Truth Politics* (New York, 2016).

95. Andrew Buncombe, 'Donald Trump dismisses as "fake news" claims that Russia gathered compromising information about him', www.independent.co.uk, 11 January 2017, accessed 4 July 2022; Chris Cillizza, 'Donald Trump just claimed he invented "Fake News"', edition.cnn.com, 26 October 2017.

96. Andrew Marr, 'How Blair put the Media in a Spin', news.bbc.co.uk, 10 May 2007; Timothy Bewes 'The Spin Cycle: Truth and Appearance in Politics', http://signsofthe-times.org.uk/pamphlet1/The%20Spin%20Cycle.html, accessed 16 May 2022; David Greenberg, 'A Century of Political Spin', *Wall Street Journal*, http://www.wsj.com, 8 January 2016; David Greenberg, *Republic of Spin: An Inside History of the American Presidency* (New York, 2016). On Russia, Peter Pomerantsev, *Nothing is True and Everything is Possible* (2014: 2nd edn London, 2017), 54–8, 65, 77–90.

97. Ralph Keyes, *The Post-Truth Era* (New York, 2004); Greenberg, 'A Century of Political Spin'.

98. Honoré de Balzac, *Illusions Perdues* (1837–43: new edn, Paris 1961), 395.

99. 'Why is this Lying Bastard Lying to Me?', blogs.bl.uk, 2 July 2014; 'Louis Heren', https://en.wikipedia.org, accessed 30 October 2017.

100. Cailin O'Connor and James Owen Weatherall, *The Misinformation Age: How False Beliefs Spread* (New Haven CT, 2019), 9.

101. Alterman, *When Presidents Lie*, 1, 92, 296.
102. Alterman, *When Presidents Lie*, 38, 61–3, 102–4, 204, 297–300.
103. Alterman, *When Presidents Lie*, 76, 133–4, 183.
104. Rêgo and Barbosa, *Construção da Ignorância*, 154, 156.

## 14 UNCERTAIN FUTURES

1. Robert Merton, 'The Unanticipated Consequences of Purposive Social Action', *American Sociological Review* 1 (1936), 894–904; Raymond Boudon, *Effets pervers et ordre social* (Paris, 1977); Albert Hirschman, *The Rhetoric of Reaction: Perversity, Futility, Jeopardy* (Cambridge MA, 1991); Matthias Gross, 'Sociologists of the Unexpected: Edward A. Ross and Georg Simmel on the Unintended Consequences of Modernity', *American Sociologist* 34 (2003), 40–58.
2. Alexis de Tocqueville, *The Ancien Régime and the French Revolution* (1856: English trans. Cambridge, 2011), 157.
3. Georges Minois, *Histoire de l'Avenir* (Paris, 1996); Martin van Creveld, *Seeing into the Future: A Short History of Prediction* (London, 2020).
4. José M. González García, *La Diosa Fortuna: Metamorphosis de una metáfora política* (Madrid, 2006).
5. Arndt Brendecke and Peter Vogt (eds), *The End of Fortuna and the Rise of Modernity* (Berlin, 2017), 6; Ian Hacking, *The Taming of Chance* (Cambridge, 1990).
6. José M. González García, 'El regreso de la diosa de Fortuna en la "sociedad del riesgo", *Contrastes* 2 (1997), 129–43, a meditation on a theme of Ulrich Beck's.
7. Peter L. Bernstein, *Against the Gods: The Remarkable Story of Risk* (New York, 1998), 197. Cf. Ulrich Beck, *Risk Society: Towards a New Modernity* (1986: English trans. London, 1992); Stefan Böschen, Michael Schneider and Anton Lerf (eds), *Handeln trotz Nichtwissen: Vom Umgang mit Chaos und Risiko in Politik, Industrie und Wissenschaft* (Frankfurt, 2004); Bostrom, 'Existential Risks'.
8. Alberto and Branislava Tenenti, *Il prezzo del rischio: l'assicurazione mediterranea vista da Ragusa, 1563–1591* (Rome, 1985); Adrian Leonard (ed.), *Marine Insurance: Origins and Institutions, 1300–1850* (Basingstoke, 2016); Karin Lurvink, 'The Insurance of Mass Murder: The Development of Slave Life Insurance Policies of Dutch Private Slave Ships, 1720–1780' (2019), doi:10.1017/eso.2019.33.
9. Peter Koch, *Pioniere der Versicherungsgedanken, 1550–1850* (Wiesbaden, 1968); Robin Pearson, *Insuring the Industrial Revolution: Fire Insurance in Great Britain, 1700–1850* (Aldershot, 2004).
10. Ian Hacking, *The Emergence of Probability* (Cambridge, 1975), 114–21; Lorraine Daston, *Classical Probability in the Enlightenment* (Princeton NJ, 1988), 27.
11. Geoffrey Clark, *Betting on Lives: The Culture of Life Insurance in England, 1695–1775* (Manchester, 1999), 7, 49–53.
12. Hacking, *Emergence of Probability*; Hacking, *The Taming of Chance* (Cambridge, 1990); Daston, *Classical Probability*.
13. Clark, *Betting on Lives*; Timothy Alborn and Sharon Ann Murphy (eds), *Anglo-American Life Insurance, 1800–1914*, 3 vols (London, 2013).
14. Holger Hoffman-Riem and Brian Wynne, 'In Risk Assessment One Has to Admit Ignorance', *Nature* 416, 14 March 2002, 123.
15. Nassim N. Taleb, *The Black Swan: The Impact of the Highly Improbable* (2008: revised edn London 2010); John Kay and Mervyn King, *Radical Uncertainty: Decision-making for an Unknowable Future* (London, 2020). Kay and King were inspired by Frank Knight, whose book *Risk, Uncertainty and Profit* was published in 1921.
16. Beck, *Risk Society*, 21.
17. Beck, *Risk Society*, 22; González García, 'El regreso'.
18. Mary Douglas and Aaron Wildavsky, *Risk and Culture: An Essay on the Selection of Technical and Environmental Dangers* (Berkeley CA, 1982), 6–7, 9.

19. Julius Ruff, *Violence in Early Modern Europe* (Cambridge, 2001).
20. Ulrich Beck, *World at Risk* (1999: English trans. Cambridge, 2009), 132. Richard Ericson and Aaron Doyle noted the adaptability of the insurance industry to the new risks in 'Catastrophe Risk, Insurance and Terrorism', *Economy and Society* 33 (2004), 135–73.
21. Beck, *World at Risk*, 10–11, 115, 119. Cf. Böschen, Schneider and Lerf, *Handeln trotz Nichtwissen*.
22. Jamie Pietruska, *Looking Forward: Prediction and Uncertainty in Modern America* (Chicago IL, 2017); Fabien Locher, *Le savant et la tempête: étudier l'atmosphère et prévoir le temps au XIXe siècle* (Paris, 2008).
23. Rolf Schwendter, *Zur Geschichte der Zukunft: Zukunftsforschung und Sozialismus* (Frankfurt, 1982); Lucian Hölscher, *Die Entdeckung der Zukunft* (Frankfurt, 1999), 122–6; Hölscher (ed.), *Die Zukunft des 20. Jahrhunderts* (Frankfurt, 2017).
24. Thomas Fingar, *Reducing Uncertainty: Intelligence Analysis and National Security* (Stanford CA, 2011), 1.
25. Robert Jungk, *Tomorrow is Already Here* (1952: English trans. London, 1954). Jungk regretted the trends that he predicted.
26. Taleb, *The Black Swan*.
27. Firestein, *Ignorance*, 48.
28. Edgar Morin, 'Vivre, c'est naviguer dans un mer d'incertitude', *Le Monde*, 6 April 2020.
29. Ord, *The Precipice*, 37.
30. Philip E. Tetlock, *Expert Political Judgement: How Good is It?* (Princeton NJ, 2005).
31. Thomas C. Schelling, *The Strategy of Conflict* (Cambridge MA, 1960).
32. Saul Friedländer, 'Forecasting in International Relations', in Bertrand de Jouvenel (ed.), *Futuribles*, vol. 2 (Geneva, 1965), 1–111, at 2, 54. Cf. Robert Jervis, *Perception and Misperception in International Politics* (Princeton NJ, 1976), 205.
33. Fingar, *Reducing Uncertainty*, 95–106.
34. Friedländer, 'Forecasting', 10–11, 21–3, 28, 41, 101.
35. Philip E. Tetlock with Dan Gardner, *Super-forecasting: The Art and Science of Prediction* (New York, 2015).
36. Kay and King, *Radical Uncertainty*, xiv–xv.
37. Frank Knight, *Risk, Uncertainty and Profit* (New York, 1921). Cf. Kay and King, *Radical Uncertainty*, 15, 72–4.
38. John Maynard Keynes, 'The General Theory', *Quarterly Journal of Economics* 51 (1937), 209–33.
39. John Maynard Keynes, *The General Theory of Employment, Interest and Money* (London, 1936), quoted in Gerald P. O'Driscoll Jr and Mario J. Rizzo, *The Economics of Time and Ignorance* (1985: 2nd edn London, 1996), 1.
40. George Shackle, *Expectation in Economics* (Cambridge, 1949). Cf. J. L. Ford, 'Shackle's Theory of Decision-Making under Uncertainty', in Stephen Frowen (ed.), *Unknowledge and Choice in Economics* (Basingstoke, 1990), 20–45, and Taleb, *The Black Swan*. Cf. Jerome Ravetz, 'Economics as an Elite Folk Science: The Suppression of Uncertainty', *Journal of Post-Keynsian Economics* 17 (1994–5), 165–84, especially 172ff.
41. Sarah Cole, *Inventing Tomorrow: H. G. Wells and the Twentieth Century* (New York, 2019).
42. Brian J. Loasby, 'The Use of Scenarios in Business Planning', in Frowen, *Unknowledge*, 46–63.
43. Jouvenel, *Futuribles*; Jean Fourastié, *Prévision, futurologie, prospective* (Paris, 1974).
44. Elke Seefried, *Zukünfte: Aufstieg und Krise der Zukunftsforschung 1945–1980* (Berlin, 2015).
45. Björn Wittrock, 'Sweden's Secretariat', *Futures* 9 (1977), 351–7; Fingar, *Reducing Uncertainty*, 54–8.
46. Daniel Bell, *The Coming of Post-Industrial Society: A Venture in Social Forecasting* (New York, 1973).
47. Dennis Gabor, *Inventing the Future* (London, 1963); Jonathan Keats, *You Belong to the Universe: Buckminster Fuller and the Future* (New York, 2016). The term 'Dymaxion' combined 'dynamic' and 'maximum' with 'tension'.

48. Bostrom, 'Existential Risks'; Legg quoted in Ord, *The Precipice*, 367.
49. Brita Schwarz, Uno Svedin and Björn Wittrock, *Methods in Futures Studies* (Boulder CO, 1982).
50. Andrei Amalrik, *Will the Soviet Union Survive Until 1984?* (New York, 1970).
51. Herman Kahn, *The Emerging Japanese Superstate* (Englewood Cliffs NJ, 1970).
52. 'How to Learn from the Turkey', in Taleb, *The Black Swan*, 40–42.

## 15 IGNORING THE PAST

1. Peter Burke, interview with E. H. Gombrich, *The Listener* 90 (27 December 1973), 881–3, https://gombricharchive.files.wordpress.com/2011/04/showdoc19.pdf.
2. Eugenio de Ochoa (ed.), *Epistolario español* (Madrid, 1856), 237; William Nelson, *Fact or Fiction: The Dilemma of the Renaissance Storyteller* (Cambridge MA, 1973), 35–6; Augustin Redondo, *Antonio de Guevara et l'Espagne de son temps* (Geneva, 1976), 558.
3. Philip Sidney, *Defence of Poetry*, ed. Jan van Dorsten (Oxford, 1973), 83.
4. René Descartes, *Discours de la méthode*, in his *Oeuvres philosophiques*, ed. Ferdinand Alquié (Paris, 1963), 574.
5. Meta Scheele, *Wissen und Glaube in der Geschichtswissenschaft* (Heidelberg, 1930); Carlo Borghero, *La certezza e la storia: cartesianesimo, pirronismo e conoscenza storica* (Milan, 1983); Peter Burke, 'Two Crises of Historical Consciousness', *Storia della Storiografia* 33 (1998), 3–16.
6. La Mothe Le Vayer, *Du peu de certitude*; cf. Vittorio I. Comparato, 'La Mothe dalla critica storica al pirronismo', in *Ricerche sulla letteratura libertina*, ed. Tullio Gregory (Florence, 1981), 259–80.
7. Pierre Bayle, *Oeuvres Diverses* (Paris, 1737), 510; Bayle, *Critique générale de l'histoire du Calvinisme de M. de Maimbourg*, ('Villefranche', 1683), 13–18, 28–9.
8. Voltaire, *Le pyrrhonisme de l'histoire* (Paris, 1769), 54.
9. Jean Hardouin, *Prolegomena* (Amsterdam, 1729); cf. Jean Sgard, 'Et si les anciens étaient modernes . . . le système du P. Hardouin', in *D'un siècle à l'autre: anciens et modernes*, ed. L. Godard (Marseille, 1987), 209–20; Anthony Grafton, 'Jean Hardouin: The Antiquary as Pariah', *Journal of the Warburg and Courtauld Institutes* 62 (1999), 241–67.
10. Michele Sartori, 'L'incertitude dei primi seculi di Roma: il metodo storico nella prima metà del '700', *Clio* 18 (1982), 7–35.
11. Borghero, *La certezza*.
12. Burke, 'Two Crises', 3–16. This account has borrowed a few sentences from that article.
13. Cobb, *Police and People*, 81.
14. Jim Sharpe, 'History from Below', in Burke, *New Perspectives*, 24–41. Classics in the field include Eric Hobsbawm, *Primitive Rebels* (Manchester, 1959), Edward Thompson, *The Making of the English Working Class* (London, 1963) and Hufton, *Prospect Before Her*.
15. Stephen Moss, '1066 and All That: 20 Questions to Test Your History Knowledge', *Guardian*, 17 April 2015, www.theguardian.com.
16. Joseph Carroll, 'Teens' Knowledge of World History Slipping', news.gallup.com, 5 March 2002.
17. James W. Loewen, *Lies My Teacher Told Me: Everything Your American History Textbook Got Wrong* (New York, 1995), 30, 135. Cf. Frances Fitzgerald, *America Revised* (New York, 1979).
18. Galbraith, *Crash*, 10–11, 29.
19. Ghosh, *Famines in Bengal*, preface.
20. Beevor, *Stalingrad*, 13, 32; David Stahel, *Operation Barbarossa and Germany's Defeat in the East* (Cambridge, 2009), 449n; Hoepner to his wife, quoted in Stahel, *Retreat from Moscow*, 84.
21. Beevor, *Stalingrad*, 14, 31, 76.
22. Clausewitz, *On War*, 258.
23. Allen F. Chew, *Fighting the Russians in Winter* (Fort Leavenworth KS, 1981), vii.

24. Adam Zamoyski, *1812: Napoleon's Fatal March on Moscow* (London, 2004), 351–2.
25. Zamoyski, *1812*, 391.
26. Zamoyski, *1812*, 393, 447; Cf. Dominic Lieven, *Russia Against Napoleon* (2010).
27. Chew, *Fighting the Russians*, 38.
28. Beevor, *Stalingrad*, passim; Chew, *Fighting the Russians*, 31–41; Stahel, *Retreat from Moscow*, 315–17.
29. Quoted from Goebbels's diary by Stahel, *Retreat from Moscow*, 186.
30. Chew, *Fighting the Russians*, 17.
31. Martin Windrow, *The French IndoChina War 1946–54* (London, 1998).
32. Tuchman, *March of Folly*, 287.
33. Gibson, *Perfect War*, 18.
34. M. Hassan Kakar, *Afghanistan: The Soviet Invasion and the Afghan Response* (Berkeley CA, 1995); Rodric Braithwaite, *Afgantsy: The Russians in Afghanistan, 1979–1989* (London, 2011).
35. Andrei Snesarev, quoted in Braithwaite, *Afgantsy*, 7–9.
36. Braithwaite, *Afgantsy*, 109.
37. Braithwaite, *Afgantsy*, 127–9.
38. Dalrymple, *Return of a King*, 489–92.
39. Quoted in Jervis, *Perception and Misperception*, 218.
40. Yuen Foong Khong, *Analogies at War: Korea, Munich, Dien Bien Phu and the Vietnam Decisions of 1965* (Princeton NJ, 1992), 3, 5, 61–2.
41. Quoted in Alterman, *When Presidents Lie*, 174.
42. Jervis, *Perception and Misperception*, 218, 220.

## CONCLUSION: NEW KNOWLEDGE AND NEW IGNORANCE

1. Morgan, 'The Making of Geographical Ignorance?', 23.
2. Phoebe Weston in the *Observer*, 29 August 2021, 29.
3. Snow, *The Two Cultures*.
4. The sixteenth-century peasant and soldier Martin Guerre was the subject of a film first shown in 1982 and of a study by the American historian Natalie Davis, *The Return of Martin Guerre* (Cambridge MA, 1983).
5. Hayek, 'Coping with Ignorance'. Cf. Lukasiewicz, 'Ignorance Explosion', 159–63.
6. Miriam Solomon, 'Agnotology, Hermeneutical Injustice and Scientific Pluralism', in Kourany and Carrier, *Science*, 145–60, at 157.
7. Lewis, *English Literature*, 31.
8. Ann Blair, *Too Much to Know* (New Haven CT, 2010).

# FURTHER READING

This list is limited to books available in English. Articles and books in foreign languages can be found in the endnotes.

Peter Burke, *A Social History of Knowledge*, 2 vols, Polity Press 2000, 2012

Stanley Cohen, *States of Denial: Knowing About Atrocities and Suffering*, Polity Press 2001

Alain Corbin, *Terra Incognita: A History of Ignorance in the Eighteenth and Nineteenth Centuries*, Polity Press 2021

Roy Dilley and Thomas Kirsch (eds), *Regimes of Ignorance*, Berghahn 2015

Ronald Duncan and Miranda Weston-Smith (eds), *The Encyclopaedia of Ignorance*, Pergamon 1977

Renate Dürr (ed.), *Threatened Knowledge: Practices of Knowing and Ignoring from the Middle Ages to the Twentieth Century*, Routledge 2021

Stuart Firestein, *Ignorance: How It Drives Science*, Oxford University Press 2012

Matthias Gross and Linsey McGoey (eds), *Routledge International Handbook of Ignorance Studies*, Routledge 2015

John Kay and Mervyn King, *Radical Uncertainty*, Bridge Street Press 2020

Janet Kourany and Martin Carrier (eds), *Science and the Production of Ignorance: When the Quest for Knowledge is Thwarted*, MIT Press 2020

Linsey McGoey, *The Unknowers: How Strategic Ignorance Rules the World*, Zed Books 2019

Andrew Martin, *The Knowledge of Ignorance, from Genesis to Jules Verne*, Cambridge University Press 1985

Martin Mulsow, *Knowledge Lost: A New View of Early Modern Intellectual History*, Princeton University Press 2022

Toby Ord, *The Precipice: Existential Risk and the Future of Humanity*, Bloomsbury 2020

Naomi Oreskes and Erik M. Conway, *Merchants of Doubt: How a Handful of Scientists Obscured the Truth on Issues from Tobacco Smoke to Global Warming*, Bloomsbury 2010

Richard H. Popkin, *History of Scepticism: From Savonarola to Bayle*, revised edn, Oxford University Press 2005

Robert N. Proctor and Londa Schiebinger (eds), *Agnotology: The Making and Unmaking of Ignorance*, Stanford University Press 2008

Nicholas Rescher, *Ignorance: On the Wider Implications of Deficient Knowledge*, University of Pittsburgh Press 2009

Nassim Nicholas Taleb, *The Black Swan: The Impact of the Highly Improbable*, Penguin 2008

Eviatar Zerubavel, *The Elephant in the Room: Silence and Denial in Everyday Life*, Oxford University Press 2006

Cornel Zwierlein (ed.), *The Dark Side of Knowledge: Histories of Ignorance, 1400 to 1800*, Brill 2016

# INDEX